DISTRICT VOTING TRENDS IN INDIA

A Research Tool

Compiled by

Craig Baxter

Published by
Southern Asian Institute
School of International Affairs
Columbia University
New York, New York

Distributed by
Columbia University Press
New York and London

Printed in the United States of America

TABLE OF CONTENTS

Introduction   xv

Symbols and Abbreviations   xix

INDIA - SUMMARY TABLE   1

ANDHRA PRADESH   2

   Andhra   3

   Srikakulam   4

   Visakhapatnam   5

   East Godavari (Kakinada)   6

   West Godavari (Eluru)   7

   Krishna (Masulipatam)   8

   Guntur   9

   Nellore   10

   Chittoor   11

   Cuddapah   12

   Anantapur   13

   Kurnool   14

   Telengana   15

   Mahbubnagar   16

   Hyderabad   17

   Medak   18

   Nizamabad   19

   Adilabad   20

   Karimnagar   21

   Warangal   22

   Khammam   23

   Nalgonda   24

ASSAM   25

    Hill Areas   26

    Mizo Hills   27

    North Cachar Hills   28

    Mikir Hills   29

    United Khasi and Jaintia Hills   30

    Garo Hills   31

    Brahmaputra Valley and Cachar   32

    Cachar   33

    Goalpara   34

    Kamrup   35

    Darrang   36

    Nowgong   37

    Sibsagar   38

    Lakhimpur   39

BIHAR   40

    Patna Division   42

    Patna   43

    Gaya   44

    Shahabad   45

    Tirhut Division   46

    Muzaffarpur   47

    Saran   48

    Champaran   49

    Darbhanga   50

    Bhagalpur Division   51

    Bhagalpur   52

    Monghyr   53

Purnea   54

Santhal Parganas   55

Saharsa   56

Chota Nagpur Division   57

Ranchi   58

Hazaribagh   59

Palamau   60

Singhbhum   61

Dhanbad   62

GUJARAT   63

Saurashtra and Kutch   64

Kutch   65

Surendranagar   66

Rajkot   67

Jamnagar   68

Junagadh   69

Amreli   70

Bhavnagar   71

Former Bombay Areas   72

Ahmedabad   73

Mehsana   74

Banaskantha   75

Sabarkantha   76

Panch Mahals   77

Kaira   78

Baroda   79

Broach   80

Surat   81

iii

Bulsar and Dangs	82
HARYANA	83
Ambala	85
Karnal	86
Jind	87
Rohtak	88
Gurgaon	89
Mahendragarh	90
Hissar	91
JAMMU AND KASHMIR	92
Kashmir Province	93
Baramulla	94
Srinagar	95
Anantnag	96
Ladakh	97
Jammu Province	98
Doda	99
Udhampur	100
Kathua	101
Jammu	102
Poonch	103
KERALA (Also see Appendix)	104
Malabar	106
Cannanore	107
Kozhikode	108
Palghat	109
Travancore-Cochin	110
Trichur	111

Ernakulam   112

Kottayam   113

Alleppey   114

Quilon   115

Trivandrum   116

MADHYA PRADESH   117

Madhya Bharat and Bhopal   118

Morena   119

Bhind   120

Gwalior   121

Shivpuri   122

Guna   123

Vidisha   124

Rajgarh   125

Shajapur   126

Ujjain   127

Indore   128

Dewas   129

Nimar (Khargone)   130

Dhar   131

Jhabua   132

Ratlam   133

Mandsaur   134

Sehore   135

Raisen   136

Vindhya Pradesh   137

Datia   138

Tikamgarh   139

Chhatarpur   140

Panna   141

Satna   142

Rewa   143

Sidhi   144

Shahdol   145

Mahakoshal   146

Surguja   147

Raigarh   148

Bilaspur   149

Raipur   150

Bastar   151

Durg   152

Balaghat   153

Mandla   154

Jabalpur   155

Damoh   156

Sagar   157

Narsimhapur   158

Seoni   159

Chhindwara   160

Betul   161

Hoshangabad   162

Nimar (Khandwa)   163

MAHARASHTRA   164

Bombay Division   165

Ratnagiri   166

Kolaba   167

Bombay 168

Thana 169

Nasik 170

Dhulia (West Khandesh) 171

Jalgaon (East Khandesh) 172

Nagpur Division (Vidarbha) 173

Buldhana 174

Akola 175

Amravati 176

Wardha 177

Nagpur 178

Bhandara 179

Chanda and Rajura 180

Yeotmal 181

Aurangabad Division (Marathwada) 182

Nanded 183

Parbhani 184

Aurangabad 185

Bhir 186

Osmanabad 187

Poona Division 188

Sholapur 189

Ahmednagar 190

Poona 191

Satara (North Satara) 192

Sangli (South Satara) 193

Kolhapur 194

MYSORE 195

Bombay, Madras and Hyderabad Karnatak 196

Bidar 197

Gulbarga 198

Raichur 199

Bellary 200

South Kanara (Mangalore) 201

North Kanara (Karwar) 202

Dharwar 203

Belgaum 204

Bijapur 205

"Old Mysore" and Coorg 206

Chitradurga 207

Tumkur 208

Kolar 209

Bangalore Urban 210

Bangalore Rural 211

Mandya 212

Mysore 213

Coorg 214

Hassan 215

Chikmagalur 216

Shimoga 217

NAGALAND 218

ORISSA 219

Western Orissa 220

Phulbani (Baudh-Kondmals) 221

Kalahandi 222

Bolangir 223

Sambalpur 224

Sundargarh 225

Keonjhar 226

Dhenkanal 227

Mayurbhanj 228

Coastal Orissa 229

Koraput 230

Ganjam 231

Puri 232

Cuttack 233

Balasore 234

PUNJAB 235

Ferozepur 237

Amritsar 238

Gurdaspur 239

Hoshiarpur 240

Kapurthala 241

Jullundur 242

Ludhiana 243

Rupar 244

Patiala 245

Sangrur 246

Bhatinda 247

RAJASTHAN 248

Ganganagar 249

Bikaner 250

Churu 251

Jhunjhunu 252

Sikar   253

Jaipur   254

Alwar   255

Bharatpur   256

Sawai Madhopur   257

Tonk   258

Ajmer   259

Bundi   260

Kotah   261

Jhalawar   262

Chittorgarh   263

Banswara   264

Dungarpur   265

Udaipur   266

Bhilwara   267

Pali   268

Sirohi   269

Jalore   270

Barmer   271

Jaisalmer   272

Jodhpur   273

Nagaur   274

TAMIL NADU   275

Madras   276

Chingleput   277

North Arcot (Vellore)   278

South Arcot (Cuddalore)   279

Dharmapuri   280

Salem   281

Nilgiris   282

Coimbatore   283

Madurai   284

Tiruchirappalli   285

Thanjavur (Tanjore)   286

Ramanathapuram   287

Tirunelveli (Tinnevelli)   288

Kanyakumari (Cape Comorin)   289

UTTAR PRADESH   290

Uttarkhand and Kumaun Divisions   292

Uttar Kashi   293

Tehri Garhwal   294

Garhwal   295

Chamoli   296

Pithoragarh   297

Almora   298

Naini Tal   299

Rohilkhand Division   300

Bijnor   301

Moradabad   302

Rampur   303

Budaun   304

Bareilly   305

Pilibhit   306

Shahjahanpur   307

Lucknow Division   308

Kheri   309

Sitapur   310

Hardoi   311

Unnao   312

Lucknow   313

Rae Bareli   314

Faizabad Division   315

Pratapgarh   316

Sultanpur   317

Faizabad   318

Bara Banki   319

Bahraich   320

Gonda   321

Gorakhpur Division   322

Basti   323

Gorakhpur   324

Deoria   325

Azamgarh   326

Varanasi Division   327

Ballia   328

Ghazipur   329

Varanasi   330

Jaunpur   331

Mirzapur   332

Allahabad Division   333

Allahabad   334

Fatehpur   335

Kanpur   336

Etawah   337

Farrukhabad   338

Jhansi Division   339

Banda   340

Hamirpur   341

Jhansi   342

Jalaun   343

Agra Division   344

Mainpuri   345

Etah   346

Agra   347

Mathura   348

Aligarh   349

Meerut Division   350

Bulandshahr   351

Meerut   352

Muzaffarnagar   353

Saharanpur   354

Dehra Dun   355

WEST BENGAL   356

Cooch Behar   358

Jalpaiguri   359

Darjeeling   360

West Dinajpur   361

Malda   362

Murshidabad   363

Nadia   364

24 Parganas   365

Calcutta   366

Howrah   367

Hooghly   368

Midnapur   369

Purulia   370

Bankura   371

Burdwan   372

Birbhum   373

HIMACHAL PRADESH   374

"Old" Himachal Pradesh   375

Former Punjab Area   375

APPENDIX - KERALA   376

Malappuram   376

Kozhikode (Residual)   377

Palghat (Residual)   378

INTRODUCTION

This study of district election results in India is an outgrowth of my The Jana Sangh, A Biography of an Indian Political Party.[1] I found that the only meaningful way to compare the voting record of the Jana Sangh from election to election was to use the district as the unit for comparison. The state was too large while the constituency was too frequently changed.[2]

The district has been the standard unit of administration in India for more than a century and, by and large, has been a stable geographic expression. The principal exception to this stability was the changes consequent upon the reorganization of the states in the fifties. Otherwise there have been few changes; some districts have been divided to create smaller districts, other alterations have taken place in subsequent realignments of the states.

The district is also a standard reporting unit for many arms of the central and state governments including, most notably, the Census Commission.

The Election Commission, however, has reported elections on a constituency level and has accumulated the results by states and nationally, thereby overlooking the intermediate district level. It is this gap that this research tool is intended to fill. It also fills another gap, that resulting from the reorganization of the states. The 1951-52 data are here arranged according to the present

---

[1]Philadelphia, University of Pennsylvania Press, 1969.

[2]See, for example, W. H. Morris-Jones and B. Das Gupta, "India's Political Areas: Interim Report on an Ecological Electoral Investigation", Asian Survey, June 1969, pp. 399-424, in which the writers use district data. The Morris-Jones-Das Gupta study, however, excludes 1951-52 election data which is included in this compilation.

state and district alignment. Additionally, in some states, divisional
or other accumulations are given, e.g., the Madhya Bharat area of Madhya
Pradesh and the Malabar area of Kerala.

Constituencies are assigned to districts according to the present
district location of the place giving the constituency its name. It is
possible that in a few cases the bulk of the territory in a 1951-52 constituency may be in another district but these cases will be very small
in number and the territory of the vast majority of the constituencies
will fall in the same district as the place giving the constituency its
name. A problem was incurred with a few 1951-52 double-member constituencies which crossed district lines, e.g., one which straddles
Lucknow and Rae Bareli Districts in Uttar Pradesh. Arbitrarily these
constituencies have been assigned to the district containing the place
first given in the constituency name.

Census data concerning rural/urban distribution and religious
affiliation have been included for each district for which the information is available. The source of this material is Census Paper No. 1,
1963.

Religious data is given for all districts for Hindus, and for
Muslims and Christians as the most widely dispersed minority religions.
Data for Jains, Buddhists and Sikhs is given only when the number of
adherents seems to be significant. Whether or not the total percentage
adds to 100 it should be noted that in almost every district there are
some members of each religious group. The percentage for "Other" given
in some districts refers both to non-reported religious groups
(e.g., Parsis, Jews) and to tribal religious groups.

Sources. The official reports of the Election Commission are the
basic sources for each election except those held in 1961 in Orissa and

in 1968 and 1969 in Haryana, Punjab, Uttar Pradesh, Bihar, West Bengal and Nagaland. For these elections the reports and releases of the Press Information Bureau have been the primary source, supplemented by press reports.

The official reports contain many errors.[3] There are many mistakes in totals, accumulation and identification of candidates. These have been corrected, in some cases from personal knowledge and in other cases by checking press reports. In correcting many of the errors it was found that internal evidence in the reported result could determine the correct result, e.g., when the printer reversed two digits or when two candidates were identified as belonging to the same party.

The Tables. The use of the tables is explained in the symbols and abbreviations section following the introduction. The 1957 official report unfortunately does not identify the candidates of non-recognized parties. In some cases it has been possible from other sources to identify the winning candidates belonging to non-recognized parties and the information is given in the tables.

The tables are arranged geographically. The entries in the Table of Contents following an underlined divisional or area entry are included in that divisional or area entry. Thus Madhya Bharat includes all the districts through Raisen, as those districts are presently constituted. The Sironj constituency which was in Rajasthan in 1951-52 therefore is included in the tables with Madhya Bharat. The other divisional and area results are arranged similarly.

---

[3]Some of the deficiencies of the 1969 report are noted in R. Chandidas, "Quick, But Not Accurate Enough", Economic and Political Weekly, September 14, 1968.

Acknowledgements. My Foreign Service colleagues Herbert G. Hagerty in New Delhi and H. Donald Gelber in Calcutta were most helpful in providing material for the 1969 elections. Adi S. Iyengar of the American Embassy in New Delhi has been of great assistance in digging out missing returns. However, this study neither bears the imprimatur of the Foreign Service or the Department of State nor is it sponsored by either. Professor W. Howard Wriggins has made possible the publication by the Southern Asian Institute at Columbia University. My wife, Carol, has assisted very much, not only through encouragement but in proofreading and in helping prepare material for the typist, Ardith Humphrey, to whom special thanks are due.

Arlington, Virginia   Craig Baxter
June 30, 1969

Symbols Used in Tables

Cont   Candidates of a party contesting in the district. For independents (IND) figure in Cont column is number of seats contested while figure preceding in parentheses is total number of independent candidates. Thus: (8)5 indicates that independents contested five seats and there were eight individual candidates in the five seats. Similarly in the total line the figure in parentheses is the total candidates and the figure following is the total number of seats contested by the candidates.

Won   Seats won by the party's candidates.

LD   Number of the party's candidates who lost their security deposits, i.e., polled less than 1/6 of the votes in a single-member constituency, less than 1/12 in double-member, or less than 1/18 in three-member.

Pct.   Percentage of the total valid votes in the district polled by the party's candidates.

*   One or more candidates elected uncontested. See note below table.

Less than 0.05%.

@   Only winning candidates of the party can be identified. Cont, LD and Pct. data are included in the IND line.

Part   Valid votes expressed as a percentage of the electorate. Invalid votes are excluded.

Party Abbreviations

ACK	Achik Asongna Chilchakgipa Kotak
AD	Akali Dal
ADM	Akali Dal (Master Group)
ADR	Akali Dal (Raman Group)
ADS	Akali Dal (Sant Group)
APHLC	All Party Hill Leaders' Conference
BC	Bangla Congress
BCP	Backward Classes Party
BKD	Bharatiya Kranti Dal
BLC	Bharatiya Lok Congress
Bolsh	Bolshevik Party
BS	Brij Samaj
Cmwl	Commonweal Party
Cochin	Cochin Party
CONG	Congress Party (Indian National Congress)

```
CPI          Communist Party of India
CP(L)        Lal Communist Party
CPM          Communist Party-Marxist

DCA          Depressed Classes Association
DCL          Depressed Classes League
DMK          Dravida Munnetra Kazhagam
DNC          Democratic National Conference
DPN          Democratic Party of Nagaland

FB           Forward Bloc
FB(M)        Forward Bloc (Marxist)
FB(R)        Forward Bloc (Ruikar)

GL           Gorkha League
GP           Ganatantra Parishad
GNC          Garo National Council

HF           Haryana Front
HJ           HUL Jharkhand
HLS          Haryana Lok Samiti
HM           Harijan Mandal
HMS          Hindu Mahasabha

IND          Independent
INDC         Indian National Democratic Congress
INDF         Indian National Democratic Front

Janata       Janata Party
JC           Jana Congress
Jhkh         Jharkhand Party
JKD          Jana Kranti Dal
JS           Jana Sangh
Justice      Justice Party

KC           Kerala Congress
KJD          Khasi-Jaintia Durbar
KJSP         Kisan Janta Samyukta Party
KKP          Kamgar Kisan Paksha
KLP          Krishikar Lok Party
KMM          Kisan Mazdoor Mandal
KMP          Kisan Mazdoor Parishad
KMPP         Kisan Mazdoor Praja Party
KP           Krishikar Party
KS           Khedut Sangh (Gujarat)
KS           Kisan Sabha (Madhya Pradesh)
KSP          Kerala Socialist Party

LD           Lok Dal
LKS          Lok Kalyan Sangh
LSS          Lok Sevak Sangh
LTCD         Loktantric Congress Dal
```

MES	Maharashtra Ekikaran Samiti
ML	Muslim League
MP	Mazdoor Parishad
MU	Mizo Union
NC	National Conference
NMGJP	Nutan Mahagujarat Janata Parishad
NNO	Naga National Organization
NPB	National Party of Bengal
PBI	Proutist Bloc of India
PDF	People's Democratic Front
PML	Progressive Muslim League
PP	Praja Parishad (Jammu and Kashmir)
PP	Purusharthi Parishad (Rajasthan)
Praja	Praja Party
PSP	Praja Socialist Party
PWP	Peasants and Workers Party
RCPI	Revolutionary Communist Party of India
RCPI-T	RCPI (Tagore faction)
Repub	Republican Party
RPI	Republican Party of India
RPI-A	RPI (Ambedkarite)
RRP	Ram Rajya Parishad
RSP	Revolutionary Socialist Party
SBP	Sanjukta Bipladi Parishad
SC	Socialist Congress
SCF	Scheduled Caste Federation
SD	Soshit Dal
SKP	Shetkari Kamgar Paksha
SLP	Socialist Labour Party
SP	Socialist Party
SSP	Samyukta Socialist Party
SUC	Socialist Unity Centre
Swat	Swatantra Party
TC	Tamilnad Congress
TNP	Tamil National Party
TNTP	Tamilnad Toilers' Party
TPF	Tamilnad People's Front
TrL	Tribal League
TrS	Tribal Sangha
TTNC	Travancore Tamilnad Congress
TUP	Tribal Union Party
UKS	United Kisan Sabha
UMFO	United Mizo Front Organization
UNF	United Naga Front
UPPP	Uttar Pradesh Praja Party
UPRSP	Uttar Pradesh Revolutionary Socialist Party
USCF	United Scheduled Castes Federation

VHP	Vishal Haryana Party
WP	Workers' Party
WT	We Tamils
ZP	Zamindar Party

LEGISLATIVE ASSEMBLIES SUMMARY

The following are uncorrected all-India totals taken from the official
reports of the Election Commission. Major parties only are shown.

1952					1957				
Party	Cont	Won	LD	Pct.	Party	Cont	Won	LD	Pct.
CONG	3153	2207	85	42.2	CONG	2894	1893	50	45.5
SP	1799	122	1039	9.7	PSP	1136	195	398	10.1
KMPP	1005	77	653	5.1	CPI	654	161	179	7.7
CPI	465	106	197	4.3	JS	608	46	361	4.0
JS	717	34	485	2.8	Others &				
Others &					IND	(5519)	611	3186	32.7
IND	(8171)	737	5902	35.9		(10811)	2906	4174	
	(15310)	3283	8361						

1962					1967				
Party	Cont	Won	LD	Pct.	Party	Cont	Won	LD	Pct.
CONG	2852	1772	49	44.4	CONG	3443	1692	136	40.0
CPI	833	153	311	8.6	JS	1607	268	853	8.8
Swat	1038	166	546	7.4	Swat	978	257	468	6.7
PSP	1064	149	528	7.0	SSP	813	180	419	5.2
JS	1140	116	726	6.1	CPM	511	128	189	4.6
SP	607	59	435	2.7	CPI	625	121	312	4.1
RPI	301	11	211	1.6	PSP	768	106	512	3.4
Others &					RPI	378	23	285	1.5
IND	(4761)	419	3531	22.2	Others &				
	(12596)	2845	6337		IND	(6380)	709	4669	25.7
						(15503)	3484	7843	

ANDHRA PRADESH

STATE SUMMARY

Population: 35,983,447
Urban: 17.4 Rural: 82.6
Hindu: 88.4 Muslim: 7.4 Christian: 4.0

1952

Party	Cont	Won	LD	Pct.
CONG	233	82*	20	31.7
CPI+PDF	108	77	10	21.8
KMPP	78	20	36	9.9
SP	108	17	58	8.4
KLP	63	15*	26	5.8
SCF	26	4	15	2.9
USCF	4	0	3	0.3
Praja	6	0	5	0.2
Repub	4	0	3	0.1
RRP	7	0	6	0.1
DCA	3	0	3	0.1
HMS	4	0	4	0.1
ML	2	0	2	0.1
FB(M)	1	0	1	#
PWP	1	0	1	#
IND	(311)170	24	214	18.5
	(959)239	239	407	

Part: 54.3
*Uncontested: CONG (3), KLP (2)

1955 + 1957

Party	Cont	Won	LD	Pct.
CONG	246	187*	4	41.8
CPI+PDF	230	37	25	29.5
PSP	71	14	27	5.6
KLP	37	22	0	5.1
Praja	19	7	5	2.2
PWP	3	0	1	0.3
SCF	2	1	1	0.2
JS	8	0	8	0.1
IND	(259)172	32	150	15.2
	(875)300	300	221	

Part: n/a
*Uncontested: CONG (7)

1962

Party	Cont	Won	LD	Pct.
CONG	300	177*	1	47.3
CPI	136	51	6	19.5
Swat	140	19	69	10.4
JS	70	0	69	1.0
SP	15	2	12	0.6
RPI	18	0	17	0.4
PSP	6	0	4	0.3
IND	(303)189	51	175	20.5
	(988)300	300	353	

Part: 62.7
*Uncontested: CONG (6)

1967

Party	Cont	Won	LD	Pct.
CONG	286	165*	7	45.3
Swat	89	29	28	9.8
CPI	104	11	47	7.8
CPM	83	9	26	7.6
JS	81	3	70	2.1
SSP	8	1	5	0.4
RPI	11	1	10	0.3
PSP	3	0	2	0.2
IND	(402)226	68	241	26.5
	(1067)287	287	436	

Part: 66.2
*Uncontested: CONG (2)

ANDHRA

Districts formerly included in Madras Presidency
Population: 23,271,662
Urban: 16.4 Rural: 83.6
Hindu: 88.7 Muslim: 6.2 Christian: 5.0

1952

Party	Cont	Won	LD	Pct.
CONG	134	38	15	28.7
CPI	63	41	8	19.9
KMPP	77	20	35	14.2
KLP	63	15*	26	8.4
SP	50	6	33	6.0
SCF	13	1	10	2.1
HMS	4	0	4	0.1
ML	2	0	2	0.1
RRP	2	0	2	#
FB(M)	1	0	1	#
IND	(225)110	17	161	20.4
	(634)138	138	297	

Part: 58.9
*Uncontested: KLP (2)

1955

Party	Cont	Won	LD	Pct.
CONG	141	119*	4	39.4
CPI	166	15	22	31.0
KLP	37	22	0	7.3
PSP	44	13	16	5.6
Praja	12	6	0	2.8
JS	6	0	6	0.1
IND	(172)108	20	113	13.8
	(578)195	195	161	

Part: n/a
*Uncontested: CONG (3)

1962

Party	Cont	Won	LD	Pct.
CONG	194	113*	0	45.9
CPI	86	33	3	18.7
Swat	117	16	50	13.8
JS	53	0	52	1.1
RPI	12	0	12	0.3
PSP	3	0	1	0.3
SP	4	0	4	0.1
IND	(190)118	32	114	19.8
	(659)194	194	236	

Part: 65.8
*Uncontested: CONG (3)

1967

Party	Cont	Won	LD	Pct.
CONG	186	101	4	45.1
Swat	70	29	12	13.6
CPI	62	7	28	7.3
CPM	54	5	16	7.2
JS	35	2	31	1.4
PSP	3	0	2	0.3
RPI	6	0	6	0.2
SSP	2	0	2	0.1
IND	(249)142	42	156	24.8
	(667)186	186	257	

Part: 69.1

SRIKAKULAM DISTRICT

Population: 2,340,872
Urban: 8.7 Rural: 91.3
Hindu: 98.7 Christian: 1.0 Muslim: 0.3

1952

Party	Cont	Won	LD	Pct.
CONG	14	5	0	30.4
KLP	15	6	4	24.8
SP	7	1	3	9.7
CPI	3	0	2	4.9
KMPP	2	0	1	1.5
IND (23)	14	3	9	28.7
(64)	15	15	19	

Part: 44.2

1955

Party	Cont	Won	LD	Pct.
KLP	11	7	0	21.3
CONG	9	6	0	18.2
PSP	6	2	0	12.9
CPI	12	0	4	12.7
IND (45)	19	5	29	34.9
(83)	20	20	33	

Part: n/a

1962

Party	Cont	Won	LD	Pct.
CONG	20	13*	0	43.6
Swat	17	5	3	29.1
CPI	5	0	1	5.6
JS	2	0	1	1.6
PSP	1	0	0	1.2
IND (19)	11	2	12	18.9
(64)	20	20	17	

Part: 58.0
*Uncontested: CONG (1)

1967

Party	Cont	Won	LD	Pct.
CONG	19	4	0	35.4
Swat	15	10	1	32.3
CPM	3	0	1	3.2
CPI	2	0	2	1.2
JS	4	0	4	1.0
IND (25)	16	5	15	26.9
(68)	19	19	23	

Part: 64.0

VISAKHAPATNAM DISTRICT

Population: 2,290,759
Urban: 18.0 Rural: 82.0
Hindu: 98.0 Muslim: 1.2 Christian: 0.7

1952

Party	Cont	Won	LD	Pct.
SP	7	4	1	31.8
CONG	12	0	4	20.3
KLP	7	5*	1	15.8
KMPP	6	1	3	6.7
CPI	3	2	0	6.7
IND (23)	10	2	17	18.7
(58)	14	14	26	

Part: 46.5
*Uncontested: KLP (1)

1955

Party	Cont	Won	LD	Pct.
PSP	11	9	2	33.1
CPI	17	0	8	19.0
CONG	12	4	4	17.6
KLP	7	3	0	10.9
Praja	1	0	0	2.0
IND (20)	16	4	13	17.4
(68)	20	20	27	

Part: n/a

1962

Party	Cont	Won	LD	Pct.
CONG	20	12	0	46.1
Swat	14	2	3	20.1
CPI	8	3	1	13.2
JS	6	0	6	2.1
IND (14)	10	3	7	18.5
(62)	20	20	17	

Part: 55.7

1967

Party	Cont	Won	LD	Pct.
CONG	18	9	1	43.4
Swat	9	2	1	19.1
CPI	6	1	3	6.6
JS	4	1	3	4.7
CPM	3	1	1	2.8
RPI	1	0	1	0.4
PSP	1	0	1	0.1
IND (25)	14	4	16	22.9
(67)	18	18	27	

Part: 61.5

ANDHRA PRADESH

EAST GODAVARI DISTRICT

Population: 2,608,375
Urban: 18.5 Rural: 81.5
Hindu: 96.2 Christian: 2.4 Muslim: 1.4

1952				
Party	Cont	Won	LD	Pct.
CONG	16	4	0	28.4
KMPP	14	4	3	28.0
CPI	8	6	0	22.3
SCF	6	1	4	9.6
KLP	8	1	5	4.6
SP	7	0	6	3.7
IND (11)	8	0	10	3.4
(70)	16	16	28	
Part: 65.6				

1955				
Party	Cont	Won	LD	Pct.
CPI	22	6	1	37.8
Praja	8	5	0	16.7
CONG	8	8*	0	15.7
KLP	4	1	0	7.5
PSP	2	0	2	0.7
IND (22)	14	3	12	21.6
(66)	23	23	15	
Part: n/a				
*Uncontested: CONG (1)				

1962				
Party	Cont	Won	LD	Pct.
CONG	22	18	0	49.3
CPI	10	1	1	14.7
Swat	11	0	8	5.3
RPI	7	0	7	1.6
PSP	1	0	0	1.6
JS	9	0	9	1.1
IND (29)	18	3	17	26.4
(89)	22	22	42	
Part: 67.7				

1967				
Party	Cont	Won	LD	Pct.
CONG	21	11	0	44.0
CPI	8	3	1	11.6
CPM	5	0	2	3.4
PSP	1	0	0	2.2
RPI	3	0	3	0.8
Swat	3	0	2	0.5
JS	4	0	4	0.5
IND (41)	18	7	27	37.0
(86)	21	21	39	
Part: 68.6				

WEST GODAVARI DISTRICT

Population: 1,978,257
Urban: 15.9 Rural: 84.1
Hindu: 91.3 Christian: 6.6 Muslim: 2.1

1952

Party	Cont	Won	LD	Pct.
KMPP	12	5	1	31.2
CPI	8	5	1	28.7
CONG	12	2	0	25.5
SP	5	0	4	2.6
SCF	2	0	1	2.5
IND	(21) 10	0	19	9.5
	(60) 12	12	26	

Part: 76.9

1955

Party	Cont	Won	LD	Pct.
CONG	16	16	0	54.7
CPI	16	0	0	41.1
PSP	2	0	2	0.5
IND	(11) 9	0	10	3.7
	(45) 16	16	12	

Part: n/a

1962

Party	Cont	Won	LD	Pct.
CONG	16	10	0	49.1
CPI	9	5	0	25.3
Swat	9	0	8	3.5
RPI	3	0	3	0.4
JS	2	0	2	0.3
SP	2	0	2	0.2
IND	(15) 12	1	8	21.2
	(56) 16	16	23	

Part: 72.9

1967

Party	Cont	Won	LD	Pct.
CONG	16	10	0	46.9
CPM	9	2	3	13.6
CPI	8	0	4	9.4
Swat	3	0	3	0.6
RPI	2	0	2	0.4
JS	1	0	1	0.3
IND	(28) 15	4	19	28.8
	(67) 16	16	32	

Part: 75.9

ANDHRA PRADESH

KRISHNA DISTRICT

Population: 2,076,956
Urban: 23.5 Rural: 76.5
Hindu: 84.2 Christian: 10.2 Muslim: 5.5

1952

Party	Cont	Won	LD	Pct.
CPI	11	10	0	46.3
CONG	12	2	1	24.8
KLP	4	0	4	3.1
KMPP	4	0	3	2.9
SCF	3	0	3	2.0
SP	5	0	5	1.3
RRP	1	0	1	0.1
IND	(20) 10	0	15	19.5
	(60) 12	12	32	

Part: 75.0

1955

Party	Cont	Won	LD	Pct.
CONG	14	12	0	45.7
CPI	17	3	0	43.3
KLP	2	1	0	4.4
JS	3	0	3	0.3
PSP	3	0	3	0.3
IND	(6) 6	1	5	6.0
	(45) 17	17	11	

Part: n/a

1962

Party	Cont	Won	LD	Pct.
CONG	17	10	0	47.7
CPI	14	6	0	38.0
Swat	12	0	12	4.9
JS	11	0	11	1.7
RPI	1	0	1	0.1
IND	(10) 8	1	7	7.6
	(65) 17	17	31	

Part: 76.5

1967

Party	Cont	Won	LD	Pct.
CONG	17	13	0	48.5
CPI	10	0	3	13.9
CPM	7	0	1	12.5
JS	6	0	6	1.6
Swat	1	0	1	0.8
IND	(20) 13	4	12	22.7
	(61) 17	17	23	

Part: 76.1

GUNTUR DISTRICT

Population: 3,009,900
Urban: 20.8 Rural: 79.2
Hindu: 78.0 Christian: 13.4 Muslim: 8.6

1952

Party	Cont	Won	LD	Pct.
CPI	13	10	0	30.2
CONG	18	3	6	23.5
KLP	15	0	7	15.0
KMPP	14	3	10	12.0
SP	2	0	1	1.2
FB(M)	1	0	1	0.1
RRP	1	0	1	0.1
IND (40)	15	2	34	17.9
(104)	18	18	60	

Part: 67.1

1955

Party	Cont	Won	LD	Pct.
CPI	25	2	0	40.8
CONG	17	16	0	39.3
KLP	7	7	0	15.7
PSP	4	0	2	1.6
Praja	1	0	0	0.7
JS	1	0	1	0.2
IND (12)	8	0	12	1.7
(67)	25	25	15	

Part: n/a

1962

Party	Cont	Won	LD	Pct.
CONG	25	11	0	41.2
CPI	17	10	0	27.2
Swat	19	0	6	18.9
JS	11	0	11	1.2
SP	1	0	1	0.1
IND (15)	10	4	9	11.4
(88)	25	25	27	

Part: 67.6

1967

Party	Cont	Won	LD	Pct.
CONG	24	19	1	49.1
Swat	7	3	0	12.7
CPM	12	0	4	12.4
CPI	15	0	10	8.1
JS	9	0	8	2.0
SSP	1	0	1	0.2
IND (28)	14	2	19	15.5
(96)	24	24	43	

Part: 71.6

NELLORE DISTRICT

Population: 2,033,679
Urban: 11.0 Rural: 89.0
Hindu: 87.4 Muslim: 7.6 Christian: 5.0

1952

Party	Cont	Won	LD	Pct.
CONG	13	5	1	32.5
CPI	5	3	1	13.7
KMPP	6	2	3	12.6
KLP	2	0	0	4.0
SP	4	0	4	2.1
SCF	1	0	1	1.6
IND	(26) 11	3	18	33.5
	(57) 13	13	28	
Part: 51.9				

1955

Party	Cont	Won	LD	Pct.
CONG	14	11	0	51.6
CPI	17	4	1	37.1
KLP	2	0	0	3.1
Praja	1	1	0	2.3
PSP	3	0	3	1.0
JS	1	0	1	0.2
IND	(10) 6	1	7	4.7
	(48) 17	17	12	
Part: n/a				

1962

Party	Cont	Won	LD	Pct.
CONG	17	14	0	50.6
CPI	8	2	0	21.3
Swat	9	0	1	17.8
JS	6	0	6	2.4
RPI	1	0	1	1.0
SP	1	0	1	0.2
IND	(8) 6	1	6	6.7
	(50) 17	17	15	
Part: 67.9				

1967

Party	Cont	Won	LD	Pct.
CONG	16	6	1	42.3
Swat	6	4	1	17.3
CPI	4	1	0	9.2
CPM	4	0	0	7.9
JS	2	1	1	2.0
IND	(12) 10	4	6	21.3
	(44) 16	16	9	
Part: 69.6				

CHITTOOR DISTRICT

Population: 1,914,639
Urban: 11.5 Rural: 88.5
Hindu: 91.6 Muslim: 7.2 Christian: 1.2

1952

Party	Cont	Won	LD	Pct.
CONG	9	5	1	37.5
KLP	5	2*	1	16.2
KMPP	6	1	5	11.2
CPI	4	1	3	4.7
SP	3	0	3	1.8
HMS	1	0	1	0.3
IND	(13) 7	1	8	28.3
	(41) 10	10	22	

Part: 63.0
*Uncontested: KLP (1)

1955

Party	Cont	Won	LD	Pct.
CONG	13	12*	0	46.3
CPI	10	0	3	15.0
KLP	3	2	0	9.6
IND	(16) 10	2	9	29.1
	(42) 16	16	12	

Part: n/a
*Uncontested: CONG (1)

1962

Party	Cont	Won	LD	Pct.
CONG	16	7	0	40.8
Swat	10	3	2	23.2
CPI	5	3	0	13.9
JS	2	0	2	0.2
IND	(27) 12	3	20	21.9
	(60) 16	16	24	

Part: 62.8

1967

Party	Cont	Won	LD	Pct.
CONG	15	9	0	46.1
Swat	12	3	0	33.3
CPI	3	1	2	4.1
CPM	4	0	3	2.8
IND	(18) 10	2	14	13.7
	(52) 15	15	19	

Part: 68.5

CUDDAPAH DISTRICT

Population: 1,342,015
Urban: 13.2 Rural: 86.8
Hindu: 81.5 Muslim: 14.0 Christian: 4.5

1952

Party	Cont	Won	LD	Pct.
CONG	8	3	1	31.7
KMPP	4	2	1	18.8
CPI	4	2	0	16.7
SP	3	0	1	8.3
KLP	1	0	0	4.0
SCF	1	0	1	1.0
IND	(13) 7	1	11	19.5
	(34) 8	8	15	

Part: 56.2

1955

Party	Cont	Won	LD	Pct.
CONG	10	9	0	52.8
CPI	8	0	3	19.1
PSP	1	1	0	5.3
IND	(9) 6	1	3	22.8
	(28) 11	11	6	

Part: n/a

1962

Party	Cont	Won	LD	Pct.
CONG	11	2	0	43.1
Swat	5	5	0	19.6
CPI	3	0	0	7.3
IND	(13) 9	4	8	30.0
	(32) 11	11	8	

Part: 69.6

1967

Party	Cont	Won	LD	Pct.
CONG	11	7	0	53.4
Swat	3	1	1	8.6
CPM	1	0	0	1.7
IND	(16) 10	3	9	36.3
	(31) 11	11	10	

Part: 70.9

ANANTAPUR DISTRICT

Population: 1,767,464
Urban: 17.4 Rural: 82.6
Hindu: 88.8 Muslim: 10.4 Christian: 0.8

1952

Party	Cont	Won	LD	Pct.
CONG	10	5	0	34.4
KMPP	8	2	4	20.1
CPI	2	1	0	9.4
SP	1	0	1	1.8
HMS	3	0	3	1.6
ML	1	0	1	1.0
KLP	1	0	1	0.5
IND	(15) 9	2	7	31.2
	(41) 10	10	17	

Part: 56.4

1955

Party	Cont	Won	LD	Pct.
CONG	14	14	0	57.8
CPI	12	0	1	28.0
PSP	4	0	1	5.9
JS	1	0	1	0.3
IND	(7) 5	0	5	8.0
	(38) 14	14	8	

Part: n/a

1962

Party	Cont	Won	LD	Pct.
CONG	14	7	0	42.3
CPI	4	2	0	11.5
Swat	6	0	4	7.4
PSP	1	0	1	0.9
JS	2	0	2	0.5
IND	(20) 11	5	9	37.4
	(47) 14	14	16	

Part: 60.3

1967

Party	Cont	Won	LD	Pct.
CONG	14	7	0	43.7
Swat	3	3	0	13.4
CPM	4	1	0	8.9
CPI	5	0	3	6.5
JS	3	0	2	2.3
PSP	1	0	1	0.6
IND	(15) 10	3	6	24.6
	(45) 14	14	12	

Part: 64.0

KURNOOL DISTRICT

Population: 1,908,740
Urban: 19.2 Rural: 80.8
Hindu: 77.6 Muslim: 15.1 Christian: 7.2

1952

Party	Cont	Won	LD	Pct.
CONG	10	4	1	36.4
SP	6	1	4	11.7
KLP	5	1	3	7.3
CPI	2	1	1	5.9
KMPP	1	0	1	0.9
ML	1	0	1	0.5
IND	(20) 9	3	13	37.3
	(45) 10	10	24	

Part: 54.8

1955

Party	Cont	Won	LD	Pct.
CONG	14	11	0	46.8
CPI	10	0	1	21.8
PSP	8	1	1	9.0
KLP	1	1	0	3.7
Praja	1	0	0	2.0
IND	(14) 9	3	8	16.7
	(48) 16	16	10	

Part: n/a

1962

Party	Cont	Won	LD	Pct.
CONG	16	9*	0	50.0
CPI	3	1	0	9.9
Swat	5	1	3	4.8
JS	2	0	2	0.7
IND	(20) 11	5	11	34.6
	(46) 16	16	16	

Part: 63.0
*Uncontested: CONG (2)

1967

Party	Cont	Won	LD	Pct.
CONG	15	6	1	43.1
Swat	8	3	2	18.2
CPM	2	1	1	4.5
CPI	1	1	0	3.5
SSP	1	0	1	0.4
JS	2	0	2	0.3
IND	(21) 12	4	13	30.0
	(50) 15	15	20	

Part: 68.3

TELENGANA

Districts formerly in Hyderabad State
Population: 12,711,785
Urban: 19.3 Rural: 80.7
Hindu: 87.9 Muslim: 9.7 Christian: 2.2 Sikh: 0.1

1952

Party	Cont	Won	LD	Pct.
CONG	99	44*	5	38.2
PDF	45	36	2	26.1
SP	58	11	25	13.7
SCF	13	3	5	4.7
USCF	4	0	3	0.9
Praja	6	0	5	0.6
Repub	4	0	3	0.4
DCA	3	0	3	0.3
RRP	5	0	4	0.3
KMPP	1	0	1	0.1
PWP	1	0	1	#
IND (86)	60	7	53	14.7
(325)	101	101	110	

Part: 46.4
*Uncontested: CONG (3)

1957

Party	Cont	Won	LD	Pct.
CONG	105	68*	0	47.4
PDF	64	22	3	25.7
PSP	27	1	11	5.6
PWP	3	0	1	1.0
Praja	7	1	5	0.8
SCF	2	1	1	0.6
JS	2	0	2	0.2
IND (87)	64	12	37	18.7
(297)	105	105	60	

Part: 48.7
*Uncontested: CONG (4)

1962

Party	Cont	Won	LD	Pct.
CONG	106	64*	1	50.5
CPI	50	18	3	21.4
Swat	23	3	19	2.3
SP	11	2	8	1.9
JS	17	0	17	0.8
RPI	6	0	5	0.5
PSP	3	0	3	0.2
IND (113)	71	19	61	22.4
(329)	106	106	117	

Part: 56.5
*Uncontested: CONG (3)

1967

Party	Cont	Won	LD	Pct.
CONG	100	64*	3	45.8
CPI	42	4	19	8.9
CPM	29	4	10	8.6
JS	46	1	39	3.9
Swat	19	0	16	1.1
SSP	6	1	3	1.0
RPI	5	1	4	0.5
IND (153)	84	26	85	30.2
(400)	101	101	179	

Part: 60.4
*Uncontested: CONG (2)

MAHBUBNAGAR DISTRICT

Population: 1,590,686
Urban: 10.0 Rural: 90.0
Hindu: 90.4 Muslim: 8.7 Christian: 0.9

1952

Party	Cont	Won	LD	Pct.
CONG	14	11*	0	48.5
SP	5	0	2	6.5
USCF	2	0	1	4.3
Praja	1	0	0	3.3
SCF	1	0	0	3.1
PDF	1	1	0	1.8
DCA	1	0	1	1.0
Repub	1	0	1	0.9
IND	(15) 11	2	6	30.6
	(41) 14	14	11	

Part: 42.8
*Uncontested: CONG (1)

1957

Party	Cont	Won	LD	Pct.
CONG	14	11*	0	46.3
PDF	4	0	0	10.5
PSP	6	0	1	9.6
Praja	2	1	1	4.1
IND	(10) 8	2	3	29.5
	(36) 14	14	5	

Part: 42.6
*Uncontested: CONG (2)

1962

Party	Cont	Won	LD	Pct.
CONG	14	9*	0	52.9
CPI	3	0	0	9.7
Swat	2	1	1	3.4
IND	(12) 10	4	3	34.0
	(31) 14	14	4	

Part: 53.1
*Uncontested: CONG (1)

1967

Party	Cont	Won	LD	Pct.
CONG	12	7	0	49.8
JS	5	0	4	2.8
CPI	3	0	2	2.0
CPM	2	0	2	1.1
Swat	1	0	0	1.1
SSP	1	0	1	0.7
RPI	1	0	1	0.3
IND	(20) 12	6	10	42.2
	(45) 13	13	20	

Part: 56.2

HYDERABAD DISTRICT

Population: 2,062,995
Urban: 62.2 Rural: 37.8
Hindu: 71.0 Muslim: 26.1 Christian: 2.4 Sikh: 0.2

Party	Cont	Won	LD	Pct.
1952				
CONG	17	14*	0	57.2
PDF	7	2	1	13.8
SP	12	0	8	8.6
SCF	3	0	1	6.2
USCF	2	0	2	2.0
Repub	2	0	1	1.2
Praja	5	0	5	0.6
RRP	2	0	2	0.3
DCA	1	0	1	#
IND	(19) 12	1	18	10.1
	(70) 17	17	39	

Part: 43.6
*Uncontested: CONG (1)

Party	Cont	Won	LD	Pct.
1957				
CONG	18	17*	0	61.2
PDF	5	0	0	6.3
PSP	6	0	3	5.2
Praja	1	0	0	0.9
IND	(21) 15	1	8	26.4
	(51) 18	18	11	

Part: 42.2
*Uncontested: CONG (1)

Party	Cont	Won	LD	Pct.
1962				
CONG	18	16*	0	57.5
SP	4	0	3	3.4
CPI	2	0	0	2.9
JS	7	0	7	2.0
Swat	5	0	5	1.4
PSP	2	0	2	0.8
RPI	1	0	1	0.6
IND	(37) 15	2	27	31.4
	(76) 18	18	45	

Part: 52.2
*Uncontested: CONG (1)

Party	Cont	Won	LD	Pct.
1967				
CONG	17	11	1	47.3
JS	9	0	5	8.0
SSP	4	1	2	5.2
CPI	1	0	0	2.1
CPM	1	0	0	1.7
Swat	3	0	3	0.3
IND	(37) 17	5	23	35.4
	(72) 17	17	34	

Part: 53.7

ANDHRA PRADESH

MEDAK DISTRICT

Population: 1,227,361
Urban: 7.7 Rural: 92.3
Hindu: 86.6 Muslim: 10.2 Christian: 3.1

1952				
Party	Cont	Won	LD	Pct.
CONG	10	7	0	53.8
PDF	3	2	0	16.2
SP	5	0	1	10.6
SCF	1	0	1	1.1
IND	(9) 7	1	4	18.3
	(28) 10	10	6	
Part: 48.8				

1957				
Party	Cont	Won	LD	Pct.
CONG	11	7	0	47.3
PDF	6	1	0	17.6
SCF	1	1	0	5.1
PWP	1	0	1	1.9
IND	(14) 10	2	8	28.1
	(33) 11	11	9	
Part: 45.7				

1962				
Party	Cont	Won	LD	Pct.
CONG	11	6	1	49.7
CPI	5	2	1	18.3
Swat	4	1	2	6.9
PSP	1	0	1	0.7
RPI	1	0	1	0.2
SP	1	0	1	0.1
IND	(12) 9	2	4	24.1
	(35) 11	11	11	
Part: 52.8				

1967				
Party	Cont	Won	LD	Pct.
CONG	10	8	0	49.9
CPI	6	0	4	11.8
CPM	3	0	3	2.1
JS	2	0	2	1.1
Swat	2	0	2	0.9
RPI	1	0	1	0.4
IND	(14) 9	2	7	33.8
	(38) 10	10	19	
Part: 59.9				

NIZAMABAD DISTRICT

Population: 1,022,013
Urban: 14.5 Rural: 85.5
Hindu: 88.1 Muslim: 10.4 Christian: 1.4

1952

Party	Cont	Won	LD	Pct.
CONG	8	5*	0	53.1
SP	6	3	0	33.8
IND	(5) 3	0	2	13.1
	(19) 8	8	2	

Part: 49.2
*Uncontested: CONG (1)

1957

Party	Cont	Won	LD	Pct.
CONG	8	6*	0	46.6
PWP	2	0	0	12.6
PDF	3	0	0	12.5
PSP	1	0	0	2.7
Praja	2	0	2	1.9
IND	(8) 5	2	2	23.7
	(24) 8	8	4	

Part: 46.0
*Uncontested: CONG (1)

1962

Party	Cont	Won	LD	Pct.
CONG	8	6*	0	51.6
RPI	1	0	0	4.0
CPI	1	0	0	2.3
Swat	1	0	1	1.3
IND	(9) 6	2	2	40.8
	(20) 8	8	3	

Part: 50.4
*Uncontested: CONG (1)

1967

Party	Cont	Won	LD	Pct.
CONG	8	3*	0	40.4
RPI	1	1	0	4.7
JS	1	0	0	2.9
CPI	1	0	1	0.9
IND	(18) 7	4	12	51.1
	(29) 8	8	13	

Part: 52.6
*Uncontested: CONG (1)

ADILABAD DISTRICT

Population: 1,009,292
Urban: 15.5 Rural: 84.5
Hindu: 90.1 Muslim: 8.1 Christian: 1.1 Buddhist: 0.6

1952

Party	Cont	Won	LD	Pct.
SP	8	5	1	46.4
CONG	9	3	0	37.4
PDF	2	1	0	8.7
RRP	1	0	0	1.2
IND	(3) 3	0	2	6.3
	(23) 9	9	3	

Part: 35.7

1957

Party	Cont	Won	LD	Pct.
CONG	8	4	0	50.7
PSP	3	1	0	19.8
PDF	3	1	0	16.0
IND	(4) 3	2	0	13.5
	(18) 8	8	0	

Part: 44.5

1962

Party	Cont	Won	LD	Pct.
CONG	8	6	0	54.9
CPI	3	0	0	13.0
RPI	1	0	1	0.9
JS	1	0	1	0.8
IND	(12) 7	2	7	30.4
	(25) 8	8	9	

Part: 51.0

1967

Party	Cont	Won	LD	Pct.
CONG	8	6	0	49.6
CPI	4	1	1	13.0
JS	7	0	7	6.3
RPI	1	0	1	1.0
IND	(8) 5	1	2	30.1
	(28) 8	8	11	

Part: 58.1

KARIMNAGAR DISTRICT

Population: 1,621,515
Urban: 7.1 Rural: 92.7
Hindu: 94.7 Muslim: 4.3 Christian: 1.0

1952				
Party	Cont	Won	LD	Pct.
CONG	14	1	2	26.7
PDF	7	7	0	26.5
SP	13	2	7	23.1
SCF	3	2	0	12.7
IND (7)	4	2	2	11.0
(44)	14	14	11	

Part: 46.9

1957				
Party	Cont	Won	LD	Pct.
CONG	14	5	0	39.6
PDF	14	6	3	29.2
PSP	2	0	1	1.9
SCF	1	0	1	0.3
IND (18)	11	3	9	29.0
(49)	14	14	14	

Part: 49.0

1962				
Party	Cont	Won	LD	Pct.
CONG	14	8	0	52.3
CPI	8	0	2	11.1
SP	3	1	2	4.7
Swat	3	0	3	1.2
IND (17)	12	5	9	30.7
(45)	14	14	16	

Part: 52.5

1967				
Party	Cont	Won	LD	Pct.
CONG	13	9*	1	43.4
CPI	5	1	1	12.6
SSP	1	0	0	1.6
JS	3	0	3	0.9
Swat	1	0	1	0.2
IND (22)	12	3	10	41.3
(45)	13	13	16	

Part: 58.1
*Uncontested: CONG (1)

WARANGAL DISTRICT

Population: 1,445,435
Urban: 14.1 Rural: 85.9
Hindu: 93.5 Muslim: 5.1 Christian: 1.3

1952

Party	Cont	Won	LD	Pct.
CONG	10	3	0	35.0
PDF	8	6	1	33.3
SP	5	0	4	7.5
SCF	1	1	0	4.7
RRP	2	0	2	1.2
Repub	1	0	1	0.7
IND	(12) 9	0	7	17.6
	(39) 10	10	15	

Part: 49.2

1957

Party	Cont	Won	LD	Pct.
CONG	13	10	0	48.6
PDF	10	3	0	31.4
PSP	4	0	1	8.3
Praja	1	0	1	0.3
IND	(6) 6	0	2	11.4
	(34) 13	13	4	

Part: 53.0

1962

Party	Cont	Won	LD	Pct.
CONG	13	7	0	45.8
CPI	9	2	0	27.2
SP	1	1	0	6.0
Swat	4	1	3	4.5
JS	6	0	6	2.6
IND	(7) 6	2	3	13.9
	(40) 13	13	12	

Part: 63.2

1967

Party	Cont	Won	LD	Pct.
CONG	12	5	0	39.4
CPI	6	2	2	11.9
CPM	4	0	0	11.6
JS	6	1	5	6.6
Swat	9	0	7	5.3
IND	(14) 8	4	7	25.2
	(51) 12	12	21	

Part: 67.1

KHAMMAM DISTRICT

Population: 1,057,542
Urban: 12.1 Rural: 87.9
Hindu: 90.1 Muslim: 5.6 Christian: 4.3

1952

Party	Cont	Won	LD	Pct.
PDF	5	5	0	51.2
CONG	5	0	3	14.4
SP	2	1	0	6.3
SCF	1	0	1	2.1
KMPP	1	0	1	1.6
PWP	1	0	1	0.4
IND	(10) 7	1	6	24.0
	(25) 7	7	12	

Part: 46.2

1957

Party	Cont	Won	LD	Pct.
PDF	7	2	0	44.8
CONG	7	5	0	44.5
PSP	5	0	5	9.1
Praja	1	0	1	0.7
IND	(2) 2	0	2	0.9
	(22) 7	7	8	

Part: 61.1

1962

Party	Cont	Won	LD	Pct.
CONG	8	3	0	47.4
CPI	7	5	0	42.9
Swat	2	0	2	1.1
JS	1	0	1	0.2
IND	(5) 4	0	4	8.4
	(23) 8	8	7	

Part: 70.1

1967

Party	Cont	Won	LD	Pct.
CONG	8	7	0	48.8
CPM	7	1	0	26.1
CPI	4	0	2	7.2
JS	5	0	5	2.5
IND	(10) 6	0	6	15.4
	(34) 8	8	13	

Part: 71.2

ANDHRA PRADESH

NALGONDA DISTRICT

Population: 1,574,946
Urban: 9.3 Rural: 90.7
Hindu: 92.7 Muslim: 5.0 Christian: 2.3

1952

Party	Cont	Won	LD	Pct.
PDF	12	12	0	67.5
CONG	12	0	0	21.9
SCF	3	0	2	4.5
SP	2	0	2	1.3
DCA	1	0	1	0.9
IND	(6) 4	0	6	3.9
	(36) 12	12	11	

Part: 57.8

1957

Party	Cont	Won	LD	Pct.
PDF	12	9	0	50.2
CONG	12	3	0	43.1
JS	2	0	2	1.1
IND	(4) 4	0	3	5.6
	(30) 12	12	5	

Part: 57.3

1962

Party	Cont	Won	LD	Pct.
CPI	12	9	0	51.2
CONG	12	3	0	45.4
RPI	2	0	2	0.8
JS	2	0	2	0.8
Swat	2	0	2	0.4
SP	2	0	2	0.3
IND	(2) 2	0	2	1.1
	(34) 12	12	10	

Part: 63.4

1967

Party	Cont	Won	LD	Pct.
CONG	12	8	1	44.4
CPM	12	3	5	27.6
CPI	12	0	6	16.7
JS	8	0	8	2.7
Swat	3	0	3	0.6
RPI	1	0	1	0.6
IND	(10) 8	1	8	7.4
	(58) 12	12	32	

Part: 68.6

STATE SUMMARY

Population: 11,872,772 (excluding N.E.F.A.)
Urban: 7.7 Rural: 92.3
Hindu: 66.4 Muslim: 23.3 Christian: 6.4 Buddhist: 0.3 Other: 3.6

1952

Party	Cont	Won	LD	Pct.
CONG	92	76*	2	43.5
SP	61	4	22	13.3
KMPP	40	1	29	6.0
CPI	18	1	12	2.8
MU	3	3	0	1.2
KJD	4	1	0	1.0
TrS	3	0	1	0.9
GNC	4	3*	0	0.6
UMFO	3	0	1	0.4
JS	3	0	3	0.3
FB(R)	4	0	3	0.2
Bolsh	2	0	2	0.2
TrL	1	0	1	0.1
RSP	1	0	1	#
HMS	1	0	1	#
IND (218)	91	16	159	29.5
(458)	105	105	237	

Part: 50.1
*Uncontested: CONG (2), GNC (1)

1957

Party	Cont	Won	LD	Pct.
CONG	101	71*	1	52.4
PSP	36	8	8	12.7
CPI	22	4	3	8.1
TUP	@	9	@	@
RCPI	@	1	@	@
IND (145)	78	12	76	26.8
(304)	105	105	88	

Part: 52.5
*Uncontested: CONG (3)

1962

Party	Cont	Won	LD	Pct.
CONG	103	79	2	48.3
PSP	53	6	21	12.7
CPI	31	0	12	6.4
APHLC	15	11	1	5.5
SP	14	0	9	1.5
RCPI	8	1	5	1.2
JS	4	0	4	0.4
ACK	4	0	3	0.2
IND (177)	85	8	121	23.8
(409)	105	105	178	

Part: 49.4

1967

Party	Cont	Won	LD	Pct.
CONG	120	73*	0	43.6
PSP	36	5	20	6.9
CPI	22	7	5	5.1
APHLC	12	9*	0	3.5
SSP	17	4	7	3.3
CPM	14	0	10	2.0
JS	19	0	12	1.8
Swat	13	2	7	1.5
IND (239)	107	25	162	32.3
(492)	126	125	223	

Part: 56.9
*Uncontested: CONG (3)
                APHLC (2)
Note: For one seat no
        nomination filed.

HILL AREAS

Population: 1,315,169
Urban: 10.3 Rural: 89.7
Christian: 40.2 Hindu: 29.0 Muslim: 2.0 Buddhist: 1.6
Sikh: 0.1 Other: 27.0

1952

Party	Cont	Won	LD	Pct.
MU	3	3	0	15.6
KJD	4	1	0	13.0
CONG	3	3	0	9.9
GNC	4	3*	0	7.8
UMFO	3	0	1	4.9
JS	1	0	1	0.9
SP	1	0	1	0.2
HMS	1	0	1	0.1
FB(R)	1	0	1	0.1
IND	(24) 11	5	7	47.5
	(45) 15	15	12	

Part: 43.3
*Uncontested: GNC (1)

1957

Party	Cont	Won	LD	Pct.
CONG	11	1	1	23.1
TUP	@	9	@	@
IND	(33) 15	5	9	76.9
	(44) 15	15	10	

Part: 43.1

1962

Party	Cont	Won	LD	Pct.
APHLC	15	11	1	55.9
CONG	13	4	2	28.4
ACK	4	0	3	2.1
CPI	1	0	1	1.3
IND	(11) 6	0	6	12.3
	(44) 15	15	13	

Part: 42.3

1967

Party	Cont	Won	LD	Pct.
APHLC	12	9*	0	52.8
CONG	10	6*	0	32.1
CPI	2	0	2	1.0
IND	(9) 7	0	6	14.1
	(33) 16	15	8	

Part: 49.1
*Uncontested: CONG (2)
              APHLC (2)
Note: For one seat no
       nomination filed.

MIZO HILLS DISTRICT

Population: 266,063
Urban: 5.4 Rural: 94.6
Christian: 86.6 Buddhist: 7.0 Hindu: 5.2 Muslim: 0.1 Other: 1.1

1952				
Party	Cont	Won	LD	Pct.
MU	3	3	0	76.2
UMFO	3	0	1	23.8
	(6) 3	3	1	
Part:	42.3			

1957				
Party	Cont	Won	LD	Pct.
TUP	@	2	@	@
IND	(8) 3	1	1	100.0
	(8) 3	3	1	
Part:	39.2			

1962				
Party	Cont	Won	LD	Pct.
APHLC	3	3	0	69.1
CONG	2	0	1	16.7
IND	(2) 1	0	0	14.2
	(7) 3	3	1	
Part:	36.5			

1967				
Party	Cont	Won	LD	Pct.
CONG	2	2*	0	---
	(2) 3	2	0	---

*Uncontested: CONG (2)
Note: For third seat no
nomination was filed.

NORTH CACHAR HILLS DISTRICT

Population data includes both N.C. Hills and Mikir Hills Districts
Population: 279,726
Urban: 1.2 Rural: 98.8
Hindu: 81.2 Christian: 4.8 Muslim: 1.3 Other: 12.7

	1952			
Party	Cont	Won	LD	Pct.
IND	(2) 1	1	0	100.0
	(2) 1	1	0	
Part:	32.6			

	1957			
Party	Cont	Won	LD	Pct.
CONG	1	0	0	42.4
IND	(1) 1	1	0	57.6
	(2) 1	1	0	
Part:	41.8			

	1962			
Party	Cont	Won	LD	Pct.
CONG	1	1	0	50.1
APHLC	1	0	0	49.9
	(2) 1	1	0	
Part:	49.2			

	1967			
Party	Cont	Won	LD	Pct.
CONG	1	1	0	65.2
APHLC	1	0	0	34.8
	(2) 1	1	0	
Part:	55.1			

MIKIR HILLS DISTRICT

Population data: See North Cachar Hills, p. 28

1952

Party	Cont	Won	LD	Pct.
CONG	2	2	0	57.0
IND	(4) 2	0	1	43.0
	(6) 2	2	1	
Part:	36.6			

1957

Party	Cont	Won	LD	Pct.
CONG	2	1	0	48.8
IND	(5) 2	1	3	51.2
	(7) 2	2	3	
Part:	27.8			

1962

Party	Cont	Won	LD	Pct.
CONG	2	2	0	54.4
APHLC	2	0	1	23.4
IND	(2) 1	0	1	22.2
	(6) 2	2	2	
Part:	34.7			

1967

Party	Cont	Won	LD	Pct.
CONG	3	3	0	70.4
APHLC	2	0	0	19.6
IND	(1) 1	0	0	10.0
	(6) 3	3	0	
Part:	47.1			

UNITED KHASI AND JAINTIA HILLS DISTRICT

Population: 462,152
Urban: 23.5 Rural: 76.5
Christian: 39.7 Hindu: 19.2 Muslim: 1.3 Other: 39.8

1952

Party	Cont	Won	LD	Pct.
KJD	4	1	0	31.1
CONG	1	1	0	5.7
JS	1	0	1	2.1
SP	1	0	1	0.4
HMS	1	0	1	0.3
FB(R)	1	0	1	0.2
IND	(12) 5	3	5	60.2
	(21) 5	5	9	

Part: 47.0

1957

Party	Cont	Won	LD	Pct.
CONG	5	0	1	24.3
TUP	@	4	@	@
IND	(13) 5	1	4	75.7
	(18) 5	5	5	

Part: 56.1

1962

Party	Cont	Won	LD	Pct.
APHLC	5	5	0	61.0
CONG	4	0	1	20.5
CPI	1	0	1	2.9
IND	(7) 4	0	5	15.6
	(17) 5	5	7	

Part: 50.1

1967

Party	Cont	Won	LD	Pct.
APHLC	5	5*	0	71.0
IND	(4) 3	0	2	29.0
	(9) 5	5	2	

Part: 54.7
*Uncontested: APHLC (2)

GARO HILLS DISTRICT

Population: 307,228
Urban: 2.9 Rural: 97.1
Christian: 28.4 Hindu: 16.9 Muslim: 5.9 Other: 48.8

1952

Party	Cont	Won	LD	Pct.
GNC	4	3*	0	37.0
IND	(6) 3	1	1	63.0
	(10) 4	4	1	

Part: 44.9
*Uncontested: GNC (1)

1957

Party	Cont	Won	LD	Pct.
CONG	3	0	0	26.3
TUP	@	3	@	@
IND	(6) 4	1	1	73.7
	(9) 4	4	1	

Part: 40.8

1962

Party	Cont	Won	LD	Pct.
APHLC	4	3	0	54.6
CONG	4	1	0	34.7
ACK	4	0	3	10.7
	(12) 4	4	3	

Part: 39.3

1967

Party	Cont	Won	LD	Pct.
APHLC	4	4	0	63.3
CONG	4	0	0	29.8
CPI	2	0	2	3.0
IND	(4) 3	0	4	3.9
	(14) 4	4	6	

Part: 44.3

BRAHMAPUTRA VALLEY AND CACHAR

Population: 10,557,603
Urban: 7.4 Rural: 92.6
Hindu: 71.1 Muslim: 25.9 Christian: 2.2 Buddhist: 0.2
Jain: 0.1 Sikh: 0.1 Other: 0.4

1952

Party	Cont	Won	LD	Pct.
CONG	89	73*	2	46.3
SP	60	4	21	14.4
KMPP	40	1	29	6.5
CPI	18	1	12	3.1
TrS	3	0	1	1.0
JS	2	0	2	0.2
FB(R)	3	0	2	0.2
Bolsh	2	0	2	0.2
TrL	1	0	1	0.1
RSP	1	0	1	#
IND (194)	80	11	152	28.0
(413)	90	90	225	

Part: 50.7
*Uncontested: CONG (2)

1957

Party	Cont	Won	LD	Pct.
CONG	90	70*	0	54.9
PSP	36	8	8	13.9
CPI	22	4	3	8.8
RCPI	@	1	@	@
IND (112)	63	7	67	22.4
(260)	90	90	78	

Part: 53.6
*Uncontested: CONG (3)

1962

Party	Cont	Won	LD	Pct.
CONG	90	75	0	50.4
PSP	53	6	21	14.1
CPI	30	0	11	7.0
SP	14	0	9	1.7
RCPI	8	1	5	1.3
JS	4	0	4	0.5
IND (166)	79	8	115	25.0
(365)	90	90	165	

Part: 50.4

1967

Party	Cont	Won	LD	Pct.
CONG	110	67*	0	44.4
PSP	36	5	20	7.3
CPI	20	7	3	5.4
SSP	17	4	7	3.5
CPM	14	0	10	2.1
JS	19	0	12	2.0
Swat	13	2	7	1.6
IND (230)	100	25	156	33.7
(459)	110	110	215	

Part: 57.7
*Uncontested: CONG (1)

CACHAR DISTRICT

Population: 1,378,476
Urban: 7.0 Rural: 93.0
Hindu: 59.6 Muslim: 39.1 Christian: 1.1

1952

Party	Cont	Won	LD	Pct.
CONG	15	13	0	52.4
KMPP	10	1	6	10.6
CPI	10	0	7	10.1
SP	3	0	1	2.4
JS	2	0	2	1.5
FB(R)	3	0	2	1.3
IND (35)	10	1	31	21.7
(78)	15	15	49	

Part: 52.9

1957

Party	Cont	Won	LD	Pct.
CONG	13	10*	0	52.1
PSP	5	1	2	10.6
CPI	2	1	0	9.5
IND (14)	9	1	4	27.8
(34)	13	13	6	

Part: 56.5
*Uncontested: CONG (1)

1962

Party	Cont	Won	LD	Pct.
CONG	13	9	0	46.8
CPI	4	0	1	6.8
PSP	4	0	2	5.8
IND (27)	11	4	13	40.6
(48)	13	13	16	

Part: 56.9

1967

Party	Cont	Won	LD	Pct.
CONG	14	10	0	50.6
CPM	3	0	2	3.3
JS	4	0	3	2.8
PSP	1	0	1	0.6
CPI	1	0	1	0.5
IND (34)	14	4	21	42.2
(57)	14	14	28	

Part: 60.3

GOALPARA DISTRICT

Population: 1,543,892
Urban: 6.6 Rural: 93.4
Hindu: 50.9 Muslim: 43.3 Christian: 3.3

1952

Party	Cont	Won	LD	Pct.
CONG	12	8*	2	31.8
SP	8	0	3	12.9
TrS	2	0	1	4.7
KMPP	1	0	1	0.6
CPI	1	0	1	0.2
RSP	1	0	1	0.1
IND (38)	11	4	29	49.7
(63)	12	12	38	

Part: 56.8
*Uncontested: CONG (1)

1957

Party	Cont	Won	LD	Pct.
CONG	13	9	0	49.2
PSP	5	2	1	10.5
CPI	2	0	1	4.2
IND (20)	11	2	10	36.1
(40)	13	13	12	

Part: 45.3

1962

Party	Cont	Won	LD	Pct.
CONG	13	10	0	45.9
PSP	10	1	3	20.3
CPI	3	0	1	5.0
RCPI	1	0	1	0.4
IND (31)	13	2	23	28.4
(58)	13	13	28	

Part: 53.9

1967

Party	Cont	Won	LD	Pct.
CONG	16	8	0	38.1
PSP	4	2	1	12.5
CPM	2	0	1	2.7
CPI	1	1	0	2.2
IND (39)	15	5	23	44.5
(62)	16	16	25	

Part: 68.4

KAMRUP DISTRICT

Population: 2,062,572
Urban: 10.6 Rural: 89.4
Hindu: 69.2 Muslim: 29.4 Christian: 0.9

1952

Party	Cont	Won	LD	Pct.
CONG	16	10	0	41.2
SP	11	3	1	20.7
KMPP	12	0	9	10.9
CPI	1	1	0	1.2
TrL	1	0	1	0.5
IND (28)	15	3	19	25.5
(69)	17	17	30	

Part: 53.9

1957

Party	Cont	Won	LD	Pct.
CONG	17	9	0	51.3
PSP	10	5	0	28.0
CPI	5	2	0	10.4
IND (14)	9	1	11	10.3
(46)	17	17	11	

Part: 50.4

1962

Party	Cont	Won	LD	Pct.
CONG	17	13	0	48.9
PSP	15	4	6	23.6
CPI	8	0	4	7.1
RCPI	1	0	0	1.2
JS	1	0	1	0.3
IND (29)	14	0	20	18.9
(71)	17	17	31	

Part: 52.9

1967

Party	Cont	Won	LD	Pct.
CONG	22	11*	0	44.8
PSP	10	3	5	9.8
CPI	4	2	0	6.3
CPM	4	0	3	2.6
Swat	2	0	2	0.7
JS	2	0	2	0.7
IND (46)	19	6	31	35.1
(90)	22	22	43	

Part: 59.9
*Uncontested: CONG (1)

DARRANG DISTRICT

Population: 1,289,570
Urban: 3.9 Rural: 96.1
Hindu: 75.7 Muslim: 19.4 Christian: 4.6

1952

Party	Cont	Won	LD	Pct.
CONG	10	9*	0	52.2
SP	7	1	1	20.1
CPI	1	0	1	1.3
IND	(14) 9	0	8	26.4
	(32) 10	10	10	

Part: 51.6
*Uncontested: CONG (1)

1957

Party	Cont	Won	LD	Pct.
CONG	10	7	0	56.8
PSP	3	0	1	5.7
CPI	2	0	0	5.4
IND	(10) 7	3	3	32.1
	(25) 10	10	4	

Part: 47.4

1962

Party	Cont	Won	LD	Pct.
CONG	10	10	0	62.3
PSP	5	0	3	9.8
CPI	1	0	1	1.6
SP	2	0	2	1.3
IND	(14) 9	0	8	25.0
	(32) 10	10	14	

Part: 50.0

1967

Party	Cont	Won	LD	Pct.
CONG	13	10	0	48.1
PSP	10	0	4	16.2
CPI	1	0	1	0.7
IND	(24) 13	3	12	35.0
	(48) 13	13	17	

Part: 54.4

NOWGONG DISTRICT

Population: 1,210,761
Urban: 6.7 Rural: 93.3
Hindu: 57.9 Muslim: 41.2 Christian: 0.6

1952

Party	Cont	Won	LD	Pct.
CONG	9	8	0	46.3
KMPP	8	0	4	13.5
SP	7	0	4	12.8
CPI	1	0	0	3.5
Bolsh	1	0	1	1.4
IND (24)	9	1	21	22.5
(50)	9	9	30	

Part: 49.2

1957

Party	Cont	Won	LD	Pct.
CONG	10	10*	0	64.0
PSP	5	0	1	15.2
CPI	3	0	1	11.3
IND (14)	6	0	13	9.5
(32)	10	10	15	

Part: 49.3
*Uncontested: CONG (1)

1962

Party	Cont	Won	LD	Pct.
CONG	10	8	0	57.8
PSP	4	1	0	14.8
CPI	2	0	1	4.8
JS	1	0	1	1.9
SP	1	0	0	1.3
IND (15)	9	1	13	19.4
(33)	10	10	15	

Part: 49.6

1967

Party	Cont	Won	LD	Pct.
CONG	13	6	0	43.3
CPI	3	2	1	9.5
SSP	6	1	4	7.1
Swat	5	1	2	6.8
PSP	2	0	1	3.7
JS	3	0	1	3.6
CPM	2	0	1	2.3
IND (17)	10	3	11	23.7
(51)	13	13	21	

Part: 58.6

SIBSAGAR DISTRICT

Population: 1,808,390
Urban: 5.1 Rural: 94.9
Hindu: 91.7 Muslim: 5.8 Christian: 1.9 Buddhist: 0.3

1952

Party	Cont	Won	LD	Pct.
CONG	14	13	0	52.3
SP	14	0	5	20.3
KMPP	4	0	4	2.5
CPI	3	0	3	2.1
Bolsh	1	0	1	0.3
IND (26)	14	1	19	22.5
(62)	14	14	32	

Part: 50.5

1957

Party	Cont	Won	LD	Pct.
CONG	14	13*	0	55.2
PSP	6	0	2	13.0
CPI	3	0	1	6.0
RCPI	@	1	@	@
IND (18)	10	0	8	25.8
(41)	14	14	11	

Part: 47.7
*Uncontested: CONG (2)

1962

Party	Cont	Won	LD	Pct.
CONG	14	12	0	46.2
PSP	11	0	3	17.2
CPI	6	0	3	8.2
RCPI	6	1	4	7.9
SP	4	0	3	2.9
IND (24)	12	1	19	17.6
(65)	14	14	32	

Part: 46.0

1967

Party	Cont	Won	LD	Pct.
CONG	16	12	0	45.4
CPI	6	1	0	13.2
SSP	4	1	2	7.9
PSP	7	0	6	7.5
CPM	1	0	1	0.9
JS	1	0	1	0.1
IND (39)	14	2	32	25.0
(74)	16	16	42	

Part: 50.9

LAKHIMPUR DISTRICT

Population: 1,563,842
Urban: 9.7 Rural: 90.3
Hindu: 90.0 Muslim: 5.6 Christian: 3.5 Buddhist: 0.5

1952

Party	Cont	Won	LD	Pct.
CONG	13	12	0	52.7
SP	10	0	6	11.9
KMPP	5	0	5	3.3
TrS	1	0	0	2.4
CPI	1	0	0	2.2
IND	(29) 12	1	25	27.5
	(59) 13	13	36	

Part: 39.0

1957

Party	Cont	Won	LD	Pct.
CONG	13	12	0	62.6
CPI	5	1	0	14.5
PSP	2	0	1	2.5
IND	(22) 11	0	18	20.4
	(42) 13	13	19	

Part: 38.3

1962

Party	Cont	Won	LD	Pct.
CONG	13	13	0	49.8
CPI	6	0	0	15.2
SP	7	0	4	8.2
PSP	4	0	4	2.0
JS	2	0	2	1.8
IND	(26) 11	0	19	23.0
	(58) 13	13	29	

Part: 42.3

1967

Party	Cont	Won	LD	Pct.
CONG	16	10	0	40.9
SSP	7	2	1	14.3
CPI	4	1	0	7.9
JS	10	0	6	7.8
Swat	6	1	3	5.7
CPM	2	0	2	1.7
PSP	1	0	1	0.6
IND	(31) 15	2	26	21.1
	(77) 16	16	39	

Part: 49.4

STATE SUMMARY

Population: 66,455,610
Urban: 8.4 Rural: 91.6
Hindu: 84.7 Muslim: 12.5 Christian: 1.1 Other: 1.7

1952

Party	Cont	Won	LD	Pct.
CONG	310	235*	4	41.9
SP	264	23	108	18.8
Jhkh	51	32	4	8.3
Janata	35	11	14	3.1
KMPP	97	1	79	2.9
JS	46	0	44	1.2
FB(M)	33	1	30	1.2
CPI	22	0	15	1.1
UKS	20	0	15	0.9
RRP	27	1	26	0.6
GP	1	1	0	0.2
HMS	4	0	4	0.1
LKS	2	0	1	0.1
SCF	2	0	2	0.1
RSP	4	0	4	#
FB(R)	1	0	1	#
IND	(618)255	13	493	19.5
	(1537)318	318	844	

Part: 40.4
*Uncontested: CONG (1)

1957

Party	Cont	Won	LD	Pct.
CONG	312	210	5	42.2
PSP	220	31	88	16.0
Janata	120	23	62	7.9
Jhkh	69	30	22	6.9
CPI	60	7	22	4.9
JS	30	0	23	1.2
IND	(527)250	17	376	20.9
	(1338)318	318	598	

Part: 40.6

1962

Party	Cont	Won	LD	Pct.
CONG	318	185	9	41.3
Swat	259	50	122	17.3
PSP	199	29	102	14.2
CPI	84	12	38	6.2
SP	132	7	96	5.2
Jhkh	75	20	36	4.4
JS	75	3	61	2.8
RRP	17	0	17	0.2
HMS	3	0	3	#
IND	(367)186	12	326	8.4
	(1529)318	318	810	

Part: 44.6

1967

Party	Cont	Won	LD	Pct.
CONG	318	128	30	33.1
SSP	199	68	89	17.6
JS	270	26	191	10.4
PSP	182	18	138	7.0
CPI	98	24	47	6.9
JKD	59	13	35	3.3
Swat	126	3	114	2.3
CPM	31	4	23	1.3
RPI	2	1	1	0.2
IND	(740)276	33	630	17.9
	(2025)318	318	1298	

Part: 48.8

STATE SUMMARY (Continued)

Party	Cont	Won	LD	Pct.
		1969		
CONG	318	118	42	30.4
JS	303	34	166	15.7
SSP	191	52	87	13.7
CPI	163	25	92	10.1
PSP	98	18	58	5.7
LTCD	107	9	80	3.9
SD	123	6	102	3.6
Janata	134	13	109	3.1
BKD	112	5	98	2.1
CPM	29	3	19	1.2
HJ	32	7	20	0.9
Swat	42	3	38	0.9
Jhkh	19	6	13	0.7
RPI	19	2	16	0.5
BCP	44	0	44	0.3
PBI	63	0	63	0.3
FB	6	1	5	0.1
RSP	8	0	8	#
IND (342)	196	16	305	6.8
(2153)	318	318	1365	

Part: 51.3

PATNA DIVISION

Population: 9,815,655
Urban: 11.1 Rural: 88.9
Hindu: 91.9 Muslim: 7.9 Christian: 0.1

1952				
Party	Cont	Won	LD	Pct.
CONG	65	52	1	39.2
SP	62	10	32	18.9
KMPP	26	0	23	3.6
UKS	15	0	11	3.5
RRP	18	1	17	2.4
FB(M)	17	0	16	1.8
JS	14	0	14	1.5
SCF	2	0	2	0.3
CPI	1	0	1	0.2
HMS	1	0	1	0.1
RSP	1	0	1	#
IND (216)	61	3	180	28.5
(438)	66	66	299	

Part: 42.0

1957				
Party	Cont	Won	LD	Pct.
CONG	68	53	1	41.5
PSP	58	10	22	22.0
Janata	36	3	24	8.9
CPI	11	1	2	3.9
JS	5	0	4	0.8
IND (141)	59	1	103	22.9
(319)	68	68	156	

Part: 42.4

1962				
Party	Cont	Won	LD	Pct.
CONG	68	48	0	43.4
Swat	58	6	28	16.3
PSP	53	7	29	14.7
CPI	20	1	11	5.7
SP	38	1	30	5.6
JS	24	2	21	4.0
RRP	10	0	10	0.5
Jhkh	6	0	6	0.3
HMS	3	0	3	0.1
IND (102)	45	3	90	9.4
(382)	68	68	228	

Part: 50.2

1967				
Party	Cont	Won	LD	Pct.
CONG	67	32	2	34.3
SSP	47	14	24	16.5
JS	55	4	41	10.0
PSP	44	2	33	7.3
CPI	15	6	4	6.1
JKD	13	4	5	5.8
Swat	31	0	30	1.9
CPM	8	0	7	1.2
RPI	2	1	1	0.8
IND (166)	60	4	147	16.1
(448)	67	67	294	

Part: 51.2

1969				
Party	Cont	Won	LD	Pct.
CONG	67	20	8	26.9
JS	66	12	38	16.7
SSP	42	10	20	11.9
CPI	41	7	23	11.8
PSP	20	7	8	6.7
SD	35	2	25	5.5
Janata	31	2	26	3.1
LTCD	21	2	17	2.4
BKD	29	1	25	2.3
CPM	7	0	5	1.6

1969 (continued)				
Party	Cont	Won	LD	Pct.
BCP	23	0	23	0.8
RPI	10	0	9	0.8
Swat	11	0	11	0.7
PBI	20	0	20	0.3
FB	1	0	1	0.1
RSP	1	0	1	#
IND (97)	51	4	85	8.4
(522)	67	67	345	

Part: 53.8

PATNA DISTRICT

Population: 2,949,746
Urban: 20.1 Rural: 79.9
Hindu: 92.5 Muslim: 7.2 Christian: 0.1

1952

Party	Cont	Won	LD	Pct.
CONG	20	20	0	42.5
SP	16	0	12	11.8
FB(M)	8	0	7	3.4
KMPP	6	0	5	2.8
UKS	2	0	1	2.0
JS	5	0	5	1.6
RRP	3	0	3	0.9
SCF	2	0	2	0.9
CPI	1	0	1	0.6
HMS	1	0	1	0.2
RSP	1	0	1	0.1
IND	(80) 20	0	65	33.2
	(145) 20	20	103	

Part: 48.8

1957

Party	Cont	Won	LD	Pct.
CONG	21	15	1	43.0
PSP	12	2	6	15.9
Janata	10	3	6	13.5
CPI	3	1	0	3.3
JS	4	0	3	1.9
IND	(39) 17	0	23	22.4
	(89) 21	21	39	

Part: 44.9

1962

Party	Cont	Won	LD	Pct.
CONG	21	15	0	44.5
Swat	16	1	8	14.8
PSP	12	2	8	8.8
JS	9	1	7	7.2
CPI	7	0	5	6.0
SP	6	1	5	3.1
HMS	3	0	3	0.3
Jhkh	1	0	1	0.2
IND	(50) 18	1	45	15.1
	(125) 21	21	82	

Part: 52.2

1967

Party	Cont	Won	LD	Pct.
CONG	20	8	1	35.3
JKD	7	3	1	14.7
JS	14	3	7	13.2
SSP	14	2	12	9.4
CPI	5	2	3	4.8
PSP	7	0	5	4.7
RPI	2	1	1	2.3
CPM	3	0	3	1.1
Swat	4	0	4	0.4
IND	(45) 18	1	40	14.1
	(121) 20	20	77	

Part: 55.5

1969

Party	Cont	Won	LD	Pct.
CONG	20	9	2	27.2
JS	20	4	9	18.3
CPI	10	2	3	11.9
SSP	11	2	6	9.1
BKD	15	1	11	5.9
Janata	9	1	6	3.9
SD	11	0	9	3.5
PSP	3	1	2	3.5
LTCD	8	0	7	2.7
CPM	3	0	2	1.8

1969 (continued)

Party	Cont	Won	LD	Pct.
RPI	6	0	5	1.6
BCP	12	0	12	1.1
PBI	7	0	7	0.4
Swat	5	0	5	0.3
FB	1	0	1	0.2
RSP	1	0	1	0.1
IND	(36) 16	0	32	8.5
	(178) 20	20	120	

Part: 56.2

GAYA DISTRICT

Population: 3,647,892
Urban: 7.3 Rural: 92.7
Hindu: 90.5 Muslim: 8.9 Christian: #

Party	Cont	Won	LD	Pct.
1952				
CONG	24	15	1	42.5
SP	24	6	10	23.2
UKS	12	0	9	8.0
KMPP	6	0	6	2.2
JS	3	0	3	1.2
FB(M)	2	0	2	0.5
IND (54)	19	3	42	22.4
(125)	24	24	73	

Part: 38.5

Party	Cont	Won	LD	Pct.
1957				
CONG	25	23	0	39.9
PSP	24	1	8	20.9
Janata	13	0	8	7.9
CPI	5	0	1	4.3
JS	1	0	1	0.5
IND (59)	24	1	44	26.5
(127)	25	25	62	

Part: 37.9

Party	Cont	Won	LD	Pct.
1962				
CONG	25	16	0	43.2
Swat	23	5	13	16.8
PSP	20	2	10	15.0
CPI	5	0	0	6.9
SP	17	0	14	6.2
JS	9	1	8	3.8
RRP	1	0	1	0.1
IND (32)	15	1	28	8.0
(132)	25	25	74	

Part: 45.7

Party	Cont	Won	LD	Pct.
1967				
CONG	25	12	1	33.9
SSP	14	5	4	15.4
JS	23	1	18	10.1
CPI	6	3	0	9.3
PSP	21	2	17	7.7
JKD	2	1	0	2.2
CPM	2	0	1	1.9
Swat	12	0	12	1.2
IND (62)	22	1	52	18.3
(167)	25	25	105	

Part: 46.1

Party	Cont	Won	LD	Pct.
1969				
CONG	25	5	2	28.1
JS	24	6	14	16.8
CPI	17	3	11	14.0
SSP	15	4	8	12.0
SD	12	2	6	8.2
PSP	7	2	3	4.7
Janata	12	0	11	2.7
LTCD	8	1	7	1.9
CPM	2	0	1	1.8
PBI	6	0	6	0.2
BKD	2	0	2	0.2
BCP	5	0	5	0.1
Swat	1	0	1	#
IND (29)	18	2	24	9.3
(165)	25	25	101	

Part: 53.4

SHAHABAD DISTRICT

Population: 3,318,017
Urban: 7.2 Rural: 92.8
Hindu: 93.0 Muslim: 6.9 Christian: 0.1

<table>
<tr><td colspan="5">1952</td><td colspan="5">1957</td></tr>
<tr><td>Party</td><td>Cont</td><td>Won</td><td>LD</td><td>Pct.</td><td>Party</td><td>Cont</td><td>Won</td><td>LD</td><td>Pct.</td></tr>
<tr><td>CONG</td><td>21</td><td>17</td><td>0</td><td>33.1</td><td>CONG</td><td>22</td><td>15</td><td>0</td><td>41.5</td></tr>
<tr><td>SP</td><td>22</td><td>4</td><td>10</td><td>20.9</td><td>PSP</td><td>22</td><td>7</td><td>8</td><td>28.8</td></tr>
<tr><td>RRP</td><td>15</td><td>1</td><td>14</td><td>6.0</td><td>Janata</td><td>13</td><td>0</td><td>10</td><td>5.5</td></tr>
<tr><td>KMPP</td><td>14</td><td>0</td><td>12</td><td>5.7</td><td>CPI</td><td>3</td><td>0</td><td>1</td><td>4.1</td></tr>
<tr><td>FB(M)</td><td>7</td><td>0</td><td>7</td><td>1.8</td><td>IND (43)</td><td>18</td><td>0</td><td>36</td><td>20.1</td></tr>
<tr><td>JS</td><td>6</td><td>0</td><td>6</td><td>1.6</td><td>(103)</td><td>22</td><td>22</td><td>55</td><td></td></tr>
<tr><td>UKS</td><td>1</td><td>0</td><td>1</td><td>0.2</td><td>Part: 45.0</td><td></td><td></td><td></td><td></td></tr>
<tr><td>IND (82)</td><td>22</td><td>0</td><td>73</td><td>30.7</td><td></td><td></td><td></td><td></td><td></td></tr>
<tr><td>(168)</td><td>22</td><td>22</td><td>123</td><td></td><td></td><td></td><td></td><td></td><td></td></tr>
<tr><td>Part: 40.8</td><td></td><td></td><td></td><td></td><td></td><td></td><td></td><td></td><td></td></tr>
</table>

<table>
<tr><td colspan="5">1962</td><td colspan="5">1967</td></tr>
<tr><td>Party</td><td>Cont</td><td>Won</td><td>LD</td><td>Pct.</td><td>Party</td><td>Cont</td><td>Won</td><td>LD</td><td>Pct.</td></tr>
<tr><td>CONG</td><td>22</td><td>17</td><td>0</td><td>42.5</td><td>CONG</td><td>22</td><td>12</td><td>0</td><td>33.7</td></tr>
<tr><td>PSP</td><td>21</td><td>3</td><td>11</td><td>19.9</td><td>SSP</td><td>19</td><td>7</td><td>8</td><td>24.6</td></tr>
<tr><td>Swat</td><td>19</td><td>0</td><td>7</td><td>17.2</td><td>PSP</td><td>16</td><td>0</td><td>11</td><td>9.4</td></tr>
<tr><td>SP</td><td>15</td><td>0</td><td>11</td><td>7.5</td><td>JS</td><td>18</td><td>0</td><td>16</td><td>6.7</td></tr>
<tr><td>CPI</td><td>8</td><td>1</td><td>6</td><td>4.4</td><td>CPI</td><td>4</td><td>1</td><td>1</td><td>4.2</td></tr>
<tr><td>RRP</td><td>9</td><td>0</td><td>9</td><td>1.2</td><td>Swat</td><td>15</td><td>0</td><td>14</td><td>4.0</td></tr>
<tr><td>JS</td><td>6</td><td>0</td><td>6</td><td>1.1</td><td>CPM</td><td>3</td><td>0</td><td>3</td><td>0.7</td></tr>
<tr><td>Jhkh</td><td>5</td><td>0</td><td>5</td><td>0.6</td><td>JKD</td><td>4</td><td>0</td><td>4</td><td>0.6</td></tr>
<tr><td>IND (20)</td><td>12</td><td>1</td><td>17</td><td>5.6</td><td>IND (59)</td><td>20</td><td>2</td><td>55</td><td>16.1</td></tr>
<tr><td>(125)</td><td>22</td><td>22</td><td>72</td><td></td><td>(160)</td><td>22</td><td>22</td><td>112</td><td></td></tr>
<tr><td>Part: 53.0</td><td></td><td></td><td></td><td></td><td>Part: 52.9</td><td></td><td></td><td></td><td></td></tr>
</table>

<table>
<tr><td colspan="5">1969</td></tr>
<tr><td>Party</td><td>Cont</td><td>Won</td><td>LD</td><td>Pct.</td></tr>
<tr><td>CONG</td><td>22</td><td>6</td><td>4</td><td>25.3</td></tr>
<tr><td>JS</td><td>22</td><td>2</td><td>15</td><td>14.9</td></tr>
<tr><td>SSP</td><td>16</td><td>4</td><td>6</td><td>14.8</td></tr>
<tr><td>PSP</td><td>10</td><td>4</td><td>3</td><td>12.2</td></tr>
<tr><td>CPI</td><td>14</td><td>2</td><td>9</td><td>9.3</td></tr>
<tr><td>SD</td><td>12</td><td>0</td><td>10</td><td>4.5</td></tr>
<tr><td>LTCD</td><td>5</td><td>1</td><td>3</td><td>2.7</td></tr>
<tr><td>Janata</td><td>10</td><td>1</td><td>9</td><td>2.7</td></tr>
<tr><td>Swat</td><td>5</td><td>0</td><td>5</td><td>1.8</td></tr>
<tr><td>BCP</td><td>6</td><td>0</td><td>6</td><td>1.2</td></tr>
<tr><td>CPM</td><td>2</td><td>0</td><td>2</td><td>1.1</td></tr>
<tr><td>BKD</td><td>12</td><td>0</td><td>12</td><td>0.9</td></tr>
<tr><td>RPI</td><td>4</td><td>0</td><td>4</td><td>0.8</td></tr>
<tr><td>PBI</td><td>7</td><td>0</td><td>7</td><td>0.4</td></tr>
<tr><td>IND (32)</td><td>17</td><td>2</td><td>29</td><td>7.4</td></tr>
<tr><td>(179)</td><td>22</td><td>22</td><td>124</td><td></td></tr>
<tr><td>Part: 51.9</td><td></td><td></td><td></td><td></td></tr>
</table>

TIRHUT DIVISION

Population: 15,122,554
Urban: 4.5 Rural: 95.5
Hindu: 86.3 Muslim: 13.6 Christian: #

1952

Party	Cont	Won	LD	Pct.
CONG	110	97	0	45.6
SP	102	7	30	24.7
KMPP	35	1	26	3.4
FB(M)	7	0	7	0.9
JS	15	0	15	0.8
CPI	6	0	4	0.7
RRP	7	0	7	0.4
UKS	3	0	2	0.4
HMS	3	0	3	0.4
RSP	2	0	2	0.1
IND (204)	93	6	153	22.6
(494)	111	111	249	

Part: 37.6

1957

Party	Cont	Won	LD	Pct.
CONG	107	82	1	46.2
PSP	83	15	21	21.5
Janata	38	1	28	5.0
CPI	20	1	7	4.0
JS	13	0	11	1.5
IND (148)	79	8	88	21.8
(409)	107	107	156	

Part: 41.1

1962

Party	Cont	Won	LD	Pct.
CONG	107	73	0	42.9
PSP	81	14	29	19.8
Swat	88	7	44	15.7
CPI	21	6	6	5.6
SP	37	2	26	4.3
JS	22	1	17	2.5
RRP	5	0	5	0.1
IND (101)	58	4	85	9.1
(462)	107	107	212	

Part: 46.0

1967

Party	Cont	Won	LD	Pct.
CONG	104	41	9	34.5
SSP	72	28	22	20.9
JS	83	5	65	8.0
CPI	39	10	22	7.7
PSP	72	7	55	7.6
Swat	35	1	29	2.3
JKD	11	0	9	1.0
CPM	6	2	3	0.9
IND (192)	86	10	157	17.1
(614)	104	104	371	

Part: 52.3

1969

Party	Cont	Won	LD	Pct.
CONG	104	46	11	32.8
SSP	61	23	16	16.8
JS	96	6	58	14.2
CPI	48	6	24	8.4
PSP	36	7	21	7.1
LTCD	33	5	18	6.0
BKD	38	2	32	2.8
SD	26	2	21	2.7
Janata	27	1	23	1.5
Swat	15	3	11	1.3

1969 (continued)

Party	Cont	Won	LD	Pct.
CPM	6	0	3	0.5
PBI	20	0	20	0.2
BCP	7	0	7	0.1
RSP	3	0	3	#
FB	1	0	1	#
RPI	1	0	1	#
IND (68)	50	3	59	5.4
(590)	104	104	329	

Part: 55.3

MUZAFFARPUR DISTRICT

Population: 4,118,398
Urban: 4.6 Rural: 95.4
Hindu: 87.2 Muslim: 12.8 Christian: #

Party	Cont	1952 Won	LD	Pct.
CONG	31	24	0	44.5
SP	29	3	4	30.2
KMPP	11	0	9	3.4
UKS	2	0	1	1.0
RRP	3	0	3	0.5
JS	2	0	2	0.4
CPI	1	0	1	0.4
RSP	1	0	1	0.1
IND (44)	23	4	29	19.5
(124)	31	31	50	

Part: 44.1

Party	Cont	1957 Won	LD	Pct.
CONG	29	20	1	43.0
PSP	24	6	6	23.5
Janata	14	0	12	4.4
CPI	3	0	1	1.9
JS	3	0	3	1.5
IND (47)	22	3	28	25.7
(120)	29	29	51	

Part: 47.3

Party	Cont	1962 Won	LD	Pct.
CONG	29	18	0	39.5
PSP	22	5	8	18.5
Swat	24	0	14	11.8
SP	14	2	7	8.2
CPI	5	0	1	4.1
JS	8	0	6	1.9
RRP	2	0	2	0.1
IND (46)	21	4	38	15.9
(150)	29	29	76	

Part: 51.1

Party	Cont	1967 Won	LD	Pct.
CONG	28	16	2	39.4
SSP	22	7	6	23.2
JS	24	1	9	7.5
PSP	20	0	18	5.4
CPI	6	1	4	3.6
JKD	5	0	4	1.8
Swat	5	0	3	1.6
CPM	2	0	2	0.7
IND (47)	21	3	37	16.8
(159)	28	28	95	

Part: 59.6

Party	Cont	1969 Won	LD	Pct.
CONG	28	9	4	31.1
SSP	18	9	3	20.0
JS	24	1	14	13.3
PSP	13	2	6	10.0
LTCD	7	3	2	6.2
SD	7	1	4	4.2
CPI	5	1	3	3.2
BKD	13	1	11	3.0
Janata	7	0	6	1.3
PBI	11	0	11	0.5
BCP	4	0	4	0.2
CPM	1	0	1	0.1
RSP	1	0	1	#
Swat	1	0	1	#
IND (23)	15	1	20	6.9
(163)	28	28	91	

Part: 62.4

SARAN DISTRICT

Population: 3,584,918
Urban: 4.2 Rural: 95.8
Hindu: 88.1 Muslim: 11.9 Christian: #

1952

Party	Cont	Won	LD	Pct.
CONG	28	27	0	47.6
SP	27	0	11	21.3
KMPP	17	1	12	7.7
JS	6	0	6	1.5
CPI	2	0	2	0.9
RRP	3	0	3	0.8
RSP	1	0	1	0.3
IND	(49) 24	0	38	19.9
	(133) 28	28	73	

Part: 34.7

1957

Party	Cont	Won	LD	Pct.
CONG	26	17	0	46.0
PSP	20	6	4	25.3
Janata	8	1	4	6.7
CPI	4	0	2	2.6
JS	3	0	2	1.4
IND	(32) 18	2	16	18.0
	(93) 26	26	28	

Part: 36.4

1962

Party	Cont	Won	LD	Pct.
CONG	26	18	0	45.2
PSP	20	3	7	22.4
Swat	21	3	7	19.1
JS	5	1	4	4.1
CPI	3	1	1	3.4
SP	8	0	7	2.0
RRP	3	0	3	0.6
IND	(12) 9	0	11	3.2
	(98) 26	26	40	

Part: 45.0

1967

Party	Cont	Won	LD	Pct.
CONG	25	9	1	36.7
SSP	15	7	3	19.4
JS	20	2	13	10.4
CPI	8	1	5	5.9
PSP	12	1	9	5.6
Swat	9	0	8	1.6
JKD	3	0	2	1.4
CPM	1	1	0	0.8
IND	(45) 22	4	37	18.2
	(138) 25	25	78	

Part: 46.4

1969

Party	Cont	Won	LD	Pct.
CONG	25	14	0	37.7
SSP	17	2	8	13.2
JS	24	2	15	12.7
LTCD	9	1	5	6.6
CPI	10	1	6	6.2
BKD	13	1	10	5.8
Janata	11	1	8	4.1
PSP	4	2	2	3.5
CPM	3	0	1	1.5
SD	5	0	5	0.8
Swat	3	0	3	0.3
RSP	2	0	2	0.1
FB	1	0	1	0.1
BCP	1	0	1	#
IND	(23) 18	1	20	7.4
	(151) 25	25	87	

Part: 50.3

CHAMPARAN DISTRICT

Population: 3,006,211
Urban: 4.8 Rural: 95.2
Hindu: 83.3 Muslim: 16.6 Christian: #

1952

Party	Cont	Won	LD	Pct.
CONG	20	19	0	51.0
SP	16	1	8	14.9
FB(M)	7	0	7	5.7
JS	6	0	6	2.4
HMS	3	0	3	2.2
CPI	1	0	0	0.9
UKS	1	0	1	0.4
KMPP	1	0	1	0.2
IND	(34) 19	0	24	22.3
	(89) 20	20	50	
Part:	33.2			

1957

Party	Cont	Won	LD	Pct.
CONG	21	16	0	51.0
PSP	13	1	5	13.9
Janata	10	0	7	8.2
CPI	7	1	3	7.0
JS	3	0	2	2.6
IND	(19) 13	3	12	17.3
	(73) 21	21	29	
Part:	35.5			

1962

Party	Cont	Won	LD	Pct.
CONG	21	15	0	47.5
Swat	16	3	6	20.0
PSP	10	1	3	11.8
CPI	6	2	1	9.6
JS	2	0	1	1.4
IND	(19) 11	0	14	9.7
	(74) 21	21	25	
Part:	42.7			

1967

Party	Cont	Won	LD	Pct.
CONG	21	6	4	29.2
PSP	13	5	7	14.0
CPI	10	3	5	12.2
JS	15	2	11	9.7
SSP	11	1	7	6.5
Swat	11	0	10	4.1
CPM	2	1	0	3.5
JKD	3	0	3	0.5
IND	(37) 16	3	28	20.3
	(123) 21	21	75	
Part:	44.2			

1969

Party	Cont	Won	LD	Pct.
CONG	21	15	0	40.1
JS	21	2	9	21.6
CPI	14	1	10	10.6
PSP	8	1	5	7.3
LTCD	10	0	9	5.5
SSP	6	1	3	5.3
BKD	8	0	7	2.5
Swat	4	1	3	2.4
CPM	2	0	1	1.2
Janata	4	0	4	0.6
PBI	6	0	6	0.3
RPI	1	0	1	0.1
SD	1	0	1	0.1
BCP	1	0	1	#
IND	(11) 8	0	10	2.4
	(118) 21	21	70	
Part:	46.9			

DARBHANGA DISTRICT

Population: 4,413,027
Urban: 4.3 Rural: 95.7
Hindu: 86.3 Muslim: 13.7 Christian: #

1952				
Party	Cont	Won	LD	Pct.
CONG	31	27	0	42.8
SP	30	3	7	26.6
KMPP	6	0	4	2.2
CPI	2	0	1	0.9
RRP	1	0	1	0.3
JS	1	0	1	#
IND	(77) 27	2	62	27.2
	(148) 32	32	76	
Part:	36.9			

1957				
Party	Cont	Won	LD	Pct.
CONG	31	29	0	47.3
PSP	26	2	6	20.3
CPI	6	0	1	5.7
Janata	6	0	5	2.7
JS	4	0	4	1.1
IND	(50) 26	0	32	22.9
	(123) 31	31	48	
Part:	42.1			

1962				
Party	Cont	Won	LD	Pct.
CONG	31	22	0	42.2
PSP	29	5	11	23.8
Swat	27	1	17	14.5
CPI	7	3	3	6.7
SP	15	0	12	4.2
JS	7	0	6	2.6
IND	(24) 17	0	22	6.0
	(140) 31	31	71	
Part:	43.8			

1967				
Party	Cont	Won	LD	Pct.
CONG	30	10	2	30.5
SSP	24	13	6	26.6
CPI	15	5	8	11.1
PSP	27	1	21	8.2
JS	24	0	22	5.8
Swat	10	1	8	2.7
CPM	1	0	1	0.1
IND	(63) 27	0	55	15.0
	(194) 30	30	123	
Part:	55.1			

1969				
Party	Cont	Won	LD	Pct.
CONG	30	8	7	27.3
SSP	20	11	2	21.9
CPI	19	3	5	14.4
JS	27	1	20	12.7
PSP	11	2	8	6.6
LTCD	7	1	2	5.7
SD	13	1	11	3.8
Swat	7	2	4	3.0
BKD	4	0	4	0.4
Janata	5	0	5	0.2
PBI	3	0	3	0.1
BCP	1	0	1	0.1
IND	(11) 9	1	9	3.8
	(158) 30	30	81	
Part:	57.9			

BHAGALPUR DIVISION

Population: 12,586,115
Urban: 7.6 Rural: 92.4
Hindu: 81.1 Muslim: 17.7 Christian: 0.3 Other: 0.8

| | 1952 | | | | | 1957 | | | |
Party	Cont	Won	LD	Pct.	Party	Cont	Won	LD	Pct.
CONG	83	63*	0	45.4	CONG	82	60	1	44.7
SP	67	6	16	20.8	PSP	58	5	28	13.1
Jhkh	18	11	1	11.4	Jhkh	23	9	6	8.9
KMPP	25	0	19	2.8	CPI	20	4	7	8.4
CPI	10	0	5	2.3	Janata	15	0	7	2.8
JS	12	0	11	1.4	JS	12	0	8	1.9
FB(M)	5	1	4	1.3	IND (141)	67	5	107	20.2
Janata	2	0	2	0.3	(351)	83	83	164	
UKS	2	0	2	0.1	Part: 42.6				
RRP	1	0	1	#					
IND (114)	62	2	86	14.2					
(339)	83	83	147						

Part: 44.2
*Uncontested: CONG (1)

| | 1962 | | | | | 1967 | | | |
Party	Cont	Won	LD	Pct.	Party	Cont	Won	LD	Pct.
CONG	83	51	0	44.7	CONG	86	25	9	31.2
PSP	46	8	25	13.0	SSP	52	23	24	19.6
Swat	62	8	41	11.7	JS	72	10	48	11.8
SP	38	4	23	8.0	PSP	51	9	35	8.6
CPI	32	2	16	7.8	CPI	26	8	10	7.7
Jhkh	21	8	7	6.4	Swat	35	2	31	2.3
JS	22	0	16	3.2	JKD	18	0	16	1.6
RRP	1	0	1	0.1	CPM	9	1	7	1.5
IND (62)	41	2	58	5.1	IND (184)	72	8	158	15.7
(367)	83	83	187		(533)	86	86	338	

Part: 43.9   Part: 49.8

| | 1969 | | | | | 1969 (continued) | | | |
Party	Cont	Won	LD	Pct.	Party	Cont	Won	LD	Pct.
CONG	86	41	5	34.4	BKD	20	0	19	0.7
JS	82	4	47	14.3	RPI	5	1	4	0.6
SSP	57	14	29	14.3	Swat	9	0	9	0.4
CPI	52	8	30	12.0	PBI	13	0	13	0.2
PSP	27	4	15	5.0	FB	2	0	2	0.2
SD	41	1	36	4.5	BCP	4	0	4	#
LTCD	30	2	24	2.8	Jhkh	3	0	3	#
HJ	18	5	11	1.9	IND (94)	53	4	87	5.6
CPM	10	2	6	1.7	(576)	86	86	366	
Janata	23	0	22	1.3	Part: 52.0				

BHAGALPUR DISTRICT

Population: 1,711,136
Urban: 10.9 Rural: 89.1
Hindu: 87.5 Muslim: 12.4 Christian: #

1952

Party	Cont	Won	LD	Pct.
CONG	11	11	0	44.7
SP	10	0	4	20.3
KMPP	8	0	7	5.1
CPI	2	0	1	3.4
Jhkh	1	0	0	3.1
JS	3	0	3	2.4
FB(M)	1	0	1	0.3
UKS	1	0	1	0.2
IND	(19) 11	0	13	20.5
	(56) 11	11	30	

Part: 45.9

1957

Party	Cont	Won	LD	Pct.
CONG	12	10	0	46.0
PSP	9	0	4	14.5
CPI	5	2	1	10.5
Jhkh	4	0	2	5.8
Janata	3	0	0	5.2
JS	4	0	3	3.8
IND	(26) 9	0	23	14.2
	(63) 12	12	33	

Part: 42.2

1962

Party	Cont	Won	LD	Pct.
CONG	12	10	0	48.5
CPI	8	0	3	16.9
Swat	10	2	7	12.3
JS	7	0	4	8.0
PSP	6	0	4	7.2
SP	6	0	5	4.7
Jhkh	1	0	1	0.6
IND	(5) 4	0	5	1.8
	(55) 12	12	29	

Part: 44.6

1967

Party	Cont	Won	LD	Pct.
CONG	12	2	2	26.8
JS	12	4	7	21.6
CPI	8	3	2	20.3
SSP	7	2	5	7.9
PSP	6	1	5	7.0
JKD	3	0	2	3.1
Swat	5	0	5	2.4
IND	(28) 12	0	27	10.9
	(81) 12	12	55	

Part: 53.4

1969

Party	Cont	Won	LD	Pct.
CONG	12	5	1	29.8
CPI	11	2	5	22.3
JS	12	2	7	20.3
SSP	10	2	8	7.5
LTCD	7	0	6	3.1
SD	8	0	8	2.9
PSP	2	0	1	2.6
Janata	3	0	3	1.4
CPM	1	0	1	1.4
PBI	6	0	6	0.8
BKD	2	0	2	0.3
Swat	1	0	1	0.1
HJ	1	0	1	0.1
IND	(9) 6	1	7	7.4
	(85) 12	12	56	

Part: 58.2

MONGHYR DISTRICT

Population: 3,387,082
Urban: 11.1 Rural: 88.9
Hindu: 91.0 Muslim: 8.8 Christian: #

1952

Party	Cont	Won	LD	Pct.
CONG	24	21	0	46.1
SP	24	3	2	28.1
CPI	6	0	2	6.0
KMPP	6	0	2	4.3
JS	4	0	3	2.2
Jhkh	1	0	0	0.4
FB(M)	1	0	1	0.3
UKS	1	0	1	0.3
RRP	1	0	1	0.2
IND (28)	17	0	22	12.1
(96)	24	24	34	
Part: 48.9				

1957

Party	Cont	Won	LD	Pct.
CONG	23	18	0	50.4
CPI	8	2	2	17.7
PSP	15	2	4	13.3
JS	3	0	1	1.5
Jhkh	1	0	0	0.9
Janata	1	0	1	0.1
IND (31)	18	1	23	16.1
(82)	23	23	31	
Part: 52.3				

1962

Party	Cont	Won	LD	Pct.
CONG	23	19	0	49.1
PSP	13	1	5	11.8
CPI	11	1	3	11.8
SP	13	2	6	11.4
Swat	19	0	15	8.1
JS	6	0	4	3.9
RRP	1	0	1	0.2
Jhkh	1	0	1	0.2
IND (11)	8	0	11	3.5
(98)	23	23	46	
Part: 50.4				

1967

Party	Cont	Won	LD	Pct.
SSP	14	14	0	33.3
CONG	22	2	1	31.6
CPI	5	2	0	7.5
JS	16	0	12	7.4
PSP	13	2	11	6.6
CPM	6	1	4	4.0
Swat	3	0	3	0.4
JKD	3	0	3	0.3
IND (16)	12	1	12	8.9
(98)	22	22	46	
Part: 58.4				

1969

Party	Cont	Won	LD	Pct.
CONG	22	7	1	32.6
SSP	18	6	7	18.7
CPI	13	4	5	15.4
JS	21	1	15	10.7
SD	15	1	12	7.5
PSP	7	1	5	4.2
CPM	4	1	3	3.0
Janata	4	0	3	1.3
BKD	9	0	9	0.6
RPI	3	0	3	0.4
Swat	2	0	2	0.3
LTCD	2	0	2	0.1
PBI	2	0	2	0.1
BCP	1	0	1	#
IND (23)	15	1	22	5.1
(146)	22	22	92	
Part: 58.7				

PURNEA DISTRICT

Population: 3,089,128
Urban: 6.0 Rural: 94.0
Hindu: 62.1 Muslim: 37.7 Christian: #

		1952		
Party	Cont	Won	LD	Pct.
CONG	18	16*	0	51.4
SP	15	1	5	23.3
KMPP	6	0	6	2.9
JS	3	0	3	2.0
CPI	2	0	2	1.2
IND	(27) 12	1	16	19.2
	(71) 18	18	32	

Part: 36.5
*Uncontested: CONG (1)

		1957		
Party	Cont	Won	LD	Pct.
CONG	18	16	0	50.3
PSP	18	1	10	18.5
Janata	7	0	4	5.9
JS	2	0	1	2.4
CPI	4	0	4	1.9
Jhkh	3	0	3	1.5
IND	(20) 13	1	12	19.5
	(72) 18	18	34	

Part: 39.1

		1962		
Party	Cont	Won	LD	Pct.
CONG	18	10	0	44.7
PSP	16	4	8	24.1
Swat	12	2	6	13.9
JS	7	0	6	3.5
SP	8	0	7	3.3
CPI	3	0	3	1.1
Jhkh	1	0	1	0.2
IND	(10) 8	2	7	9.2
	(75) 18	18	38	

Part: 39.8

		1967		
Party	Cont	Won	LD	Pct.
CONG	21	12	5	30.9
PSP	20	5	9	19.7
JS	17	1	12	10.2
SSP	16	0	15	7.9
Swat	14	0	13	3.5
CPI	3	1	2	2.3
JKD	3	0	3	1.0
CPM	1	0	1	0.4
IND	(63) 21	2	56	24.1
	(158) 21	21	116	

Part: 46.6

		1969		
Party	Cont	Won	LD	Pct.
CONG	21	13	1	35.8
JS	19	0	7	17.3
PSP	13	2	5	12.2
LTCD	10	2	6	8.2
SSP	11	1	9	6.5
CPI	11	0	9	6.4
RPI	1	1	0	2.1
BKD	4	0	3	1.6
CPM	2	1	1	1.4
Swat	4	0	4	1.4
SD	6	0	6	0.7
Janata	1	0	1	0.3
PBI	2	0	2	0.2
BCP	1	0	1	0.1
HJ	1	0	1	#
IND	(22) 11	1	20	5.8
	(129) 21	21	76	

Part: 49.1

SANTHAL PARGANAS DISTRICT

Population: 2,675,203
Urban: 5.3 Rural: 94.7
Hindu: 81.4 Muslim: 13.8 Christian: 1.1 Other: 3.7

1952

Party	Cont	Won	LD	Pct.
Jhkh	16	11	1	39.7
CONG	19	6	0	39.1
SP	7	0	5	4.7
FB(M)	3	1	2	4.1
KMPP	3	0	2	1.0
Janata	2	0	2	1.0
JS	1	0	1	0.1
IND (27)	14	1	24	10.3
(78)	19	19	37	

Part: 48.5

1957

Party	Cont	Won	LD	Pct.
Jhkh	15	9	1	34.2
CONG	19	7	1	32.6
PSP	8	1	5	6.3
Janata	3	0	1	3.8
JS	3	0	3	1.8
CPI	1	0	0	0.9
IND (38)	16	2	33	20.4
(87)	19	19	44	

Part: 36.2

1962

Party	Cont	Won	LD	Pct.
CONG	19	6	0	37.6
Jhkh	18	8	4	32.7
Swat	11	3	6	13.7
CPI	6	1	4	5.5
PSP	5	1	4	3.6
JS	2	0	2	0.5
SP	1	0	1	0.1
IND (26)	14	0	25	6.3
(88)	19	19	46	

Part: 38.8

1967

Party	Cont	Won	LD	Pct.
CONG	18	4	1	29.6
JS	16	5	7	18.6
CPI	7	2	4	8.1
Swat	10	2	7	7.2
PSP	5	0	4	3.4
JKD	4	0	4	1.1
SSP	2	0	2	0.6
CPM	1	0	1	0.1
IND (53)	18	5	39	31.3
(116)	18	18	69	

Part: 36.0

1969

Party	Cont	Won	LD	Pct.
CONG	18	7	2	32.7
JS	18	1	7	20.0
HJ	16	5	9	13.0
CPI	13	2	8	10.0
SPP	5	1	3	4.5
LTCD	11	0	10	3.8
PSP	3	1	2	3.0
Janata	11	0	11	2.8
CPM	1	0	0	1.4
FB	1	0	1	0.9
SD	4	0	4	0.3
PBI	3	0	3	0.3
Swat	2	0	2	0.2
BKD	4	0	4	0.1
Jhkh	3	0	3	0.1
BCP	2	0	2	0.1
IND (28)	15	1	26	6.8
(143)	18	18	97	

Part: 38.4

SAHARSA DISTRICT

Population: 1,723,566
Urban: 3.9 Rural: 96.1
Hindu: 89.0 Muslim: 10.9 Christian: #

		1952		
Party	Cont	Won	LD	Pct.
CONG	11	9	0	48.9
SP	11	2	0	37.1
KMPP	2	0	2	0.8
JS	1	0	1	0.4
IND	(13) 8	0	11	12.8
	(38) 11	11	14	
Part:	40.2			

		1957		
Party	Cont	Won	LD	Pct.
CONG	10	9	0	40.8
PSP	8	1	5	14.5
CPI	2	0	0	4.1
Janata	1	0	1	0.1
IND	(26) 11	1	16	40.5
	(47) 11	11	22	
Part:	41.1			

		1962		
Party	Cont	Won	LD	Pct.
CONG	11	6	0	40.8
SP	10	2	4	22.7
PSP	6	2	4	16.6
Swat	10	1	7	12.6
CPI	4	0	3	3.6
IND	(10) 7	0	10	3.7
	(51) 11	11	28	
Part:	46.1			

		1967		
Party	Cont	Won	LD	Pct.
CONG	13	5	0	36.1
SSP	13	7	2	34.9
JS	11	0	10	7.9
PSP	7	1	6	4.4
JKD	5	0	4	4.2
CPI	3	0	2	3.3
Swat	3	0	3	0.5
CPM	1	0	1	0.3
IND	(24) 9	0	24	8.4
	(80) 13	13	52	
Part:	53.2			

		1969		
Party	Cont	Won	LD	Pct.
CONG	13	9	0	41.6
SSP	13	4	2	30.8
SD	8	0	6	8.8
JS	12	0	11	6.9
CPI	4	0	3	4.5
Janata	4	0	4	1.5
PSP	2	0	2	1.2
FB	1	0	1	0.4
BKD	1	0	1	0.3
CPM	2	0	2	0.2
RPI	1	0	1	0.2
IND	(12) 6	0	12	3.6
	(73) 13	13	45	
Part:	56.3			

CHOTA NAGPUR DIVISION

Population: 8,931,286
Urban: 13.3 Rural: 86.7
Hindu: 79.1 Muslim: 8.1 Christian: 5.1 Sikh: 0.4 Other: 7.3

Party	Cont	Won	LD	Pct.
	1952			
CONG	52	23	3	33.6
Jhkh	33	21	3	26.8
Janata	33	11	12	15.8
SP	33	0	30	5.7
KMPP	11	0	11	1.5
JS	5	0	4	1.2
CPI	5	0	5	0.9
GP	1	1	0	0.8
FB(M)	4	0	3	0.7
LKS	2	0	1	0.7
RSP	1	0	1	0.1
FB(R)	1	0	1	#
RRP	1	0	1	#
IND	(84) 39	2	74	12.2
	(266) 58	58	149	
Part:	38.9			

Party	Cont	Won	LD	Pct.
	1957			
CONG	55	15	2	30.7
Jhkh	46	21	16	24.8
Janata	31	19	3	20.5
CPI	9	1	6	3.6
PSP	21	1	17	3.4
IND	(97) 45	3	78	17.0
	(259) 60	60	122	
Part:	35.3			

Party	Cont	Won	LD	Pct.
	1962			
Swat	51	29	9	32.4
CONG	60	13	9	28.5
Jhkh	48	12	23	17.9
CPI	11	3	5	5.8
SP	19	0	17	1.9
PSP	19	0	19	1.9
JS	7	0	7	0.6
RRP	1	0	1	#
IND	(102) 42	3	93	11.0
	(318) 60	60	183	
Part:	36.4			

Party	Cont	Won	LD	Pct.
	1967			
CONG	61	30	10	31.0
JS	60	7	37	14.8
JKD	17	9	5	7.8
SSP	28	3	19	6.8
CPI	18	0	11	4.7
Swat	25	0	24	3.2
CPM	8	1	6	1.8
PSP	15	0	15	1.3
IND	(198) 58	11	168	28.6
	(430) 61	61	295	
Part:	37.5			

Party	Cont	Won	LD	Pct.
	1969			
CONG	61	11	18	22.3
JS	59	12	23	20.7
Janata	53	10	38	11.1
CPI	22	4	15	7.6
SSP	31	5	22	7.1
Jhkh	16	6	10	5.4
BKD	25	2	22	3.3
HJ	14	2	9	3.0
LTCD	23	0	21	2.9
PSP	15	0	14	1.5
CPM	6	1	5	1.5

Party	Cont	Won	LD	Pct.
	1969 (continued)			
SD	21	1	20	1.1
RPI	3	1	2	0.9
Swat	7	0	7	0.8
FB	2	1	1	0.5
BCP	10	0	10	0.4
PBI	10	0	10	0.2
RSP	4	0	4	0.2
IND	(83) 42	5	74	9.5
	(465) 61	61	325	
Part:	38.9			

RANCHI DISTRICT

Population: 2,138,565
Urban: 9.5 Rural: 90.5
Hindu: 63.8 Christian: 17.7 Muslim: 5.7 Sikh: 0.1 Other: 12.7

Party	Cont	Won	LD	Pct.
1952				
Jhkh	14	11	0	46.5
CONG	15	3	1	33.4
Janata	10	1	6	12.0
SP	4	0	4	1.9
FB(M)	1	0	0	0.7
CPI	1	0	1	0.6
KMPP	1	0	1	0.2
IND	(13) 8	0	13	4.7
	(59) 15	15	26	
Part: 47.3				

Party	Cont	Won	LD	Pct.
1957				
Jhkh	15	12	0	50.5
CONG	15	2	0	31.8
Janata	3	0	1	3.3
IND	(27) 12	1	25	14.4
	(60) 15	15	26	
Part: 42.6				

Party	Cont	Won	LD	Pct.
1962				
Jhkh	15	7	2	36.7
Swat	15	6	3	30.4
CONG	15	2	3	24.6
JS	1	0	1	0.5
CPI	1	0	1	0.3
IND	(26) 12	0	26	7.5
	(73) 15	15	36	
Part: 41.1				

Party	Cont	Won	LD	Pct.
1967				
CONG	15	9	3	28.7
JS	15	2	6	17.8
Swat	15	0	14	10.5
JKD	5	2	3	4.1
CPI	2	0	1	1.5
SSP	4	0	4	1.1
CPM	1	0	1	0.9
PSP	1	0	1	0.7
IND	(61) 15	2	54	34.7
	(119) 15	15	87	
Part: 36.0				

Party	Cont	Won	LD	Pct.
1969				
JS	15	7	2	31.1
CONG	15	4	3	26.1
Janata	14	0	13	6.8
Jhkh	4	1	3	3.7
SD	5	1	4	3.3
CPI	2	0	1	3.0
HJ	4	0	3	2.2
LTCD	7	0	7	1.9
SSP	6	0	6	1.5
PSP	3	0	3	1.2
Swat	3	0	3	1.1
CPM	1	0	1	0.9
PBI	5	0	5	0.7
BCP	4	0	4	0.2
RSP	1	0	1	0.1
BKD	2	0	2	0.1
IND	(26) 12	2	23	16.1
	(117) 15	15	84	
Part: 37.8				

HAZARIBAGH DISTRICT

Population: 2,396,411
Urban: 8.4 Rural: 91.6
Hindu: 87.5 Muslim: 11.8 Christian: 0.3 Sikh: 0.2

1952

Party	Cont	Won	LD	Pct.
CONG	15	7	0	44.8
Janata	12	8	0	40.3
SP	13	0	12	7.5
KMPP	3	0	3	1.6
CPI	1	0	1	0.7
IND	(12) 7	0	11	5.1
	(56) 15	15	27	

Part: 35.4

1957

Party	Cont	Won	LD	Pct.
Janata	16	16	0	58.4
CONG	16	0	1	30.3
Jhkh	8	0	8	3.7
CPI	2	0	2	2.5
PSP	5	0	5	1.1
IND	(10) 9	0	10	4.0
	(57) 16	16	26	

Part: 34.9

1962

Party	Cont	Won	LD	Pct.
Swat	16	12	0	51.9
CONG	16	4	2	33.3
SP	7	0	6	3.5
CPI	3	0	2	2.8
PSP	4	0	4	1.7
Jhkh	5	0	5	1.0
JS	4	0	4	0.9
IND	(19) 10	0	18	4.9
	(74) 16	16	41	

Part: 32.3

1967

Party	Cont	Won	LD	Pct.
CONG	16	5	2	31.7
JKD	5	5	0	14.8
JS	16	1	11	13.3
SSP	6	1	4	6.9
CPI	7	0	6	5.7
PSP	7	0	7	3.1
Swat	4	0	4	1.0
CPM	1	0	1	0.2
IND	(26) 13	4	16	23.3
	(88) 16	16	51	

Part: 39.6

1969

Party	Cont	Won	LD	Pct.
Janata	16	9	4	26.9
CONG	16	4	4	23.7
JS	16	0	6	18.5
CPI	10	1	8	10.4
SSP	10	2	7	8.8
PSP	4	0	3	2.5
BKD	5	0	5	0.9
CPM	2	0	2	0.9
HJ	1	0	1	0.3
Jhkh	3	0	3	0.3
SD	2	0	2	0.3
Swat	1	0	1	0.1
RSP	1	0	1	0.1
RPI	1	0	1	0.1
BCP	1	0	1	0.1
IND	(16) 8	0	15	6.1
	(105) 16	16	64	

Part: 36.5

PALAMAU DISTRICT

Population: 1,187,789
Urban: 4.7 Rural: 95.3
Hindu: 88.6 Muslim: 9.7 Christian: 1.7

1952

Party	Cont	Won	LD	Pct.
CONG	8	8	0	43.1
Jhkh	5	0	2	14.7
SP	6	0	4	13.3
Janata	6	0	4	10.5
KMPP	2	0	2	2.1
JS	1	0	1	1.3
IND	(10) 7	0	8	15.0
	(38) 8	8	21	

Part: 33.6

1957

Party	Cont	Won	LD	Pct.
CONG	8	4	0	33.3
Janata	8	3	1	30.8
Jhkh	8	0	3	18.3
PSP	6	1	3	12.9
IND	(6) 4	0	5	4.7
	(36) 8	8	12	

Part: 31.0

1962

Party	Cont	Won	LD	Pct.
Swat	8	7	0	57.3
CONG	8	1	2	24.4
Jhkh	7	0	5	7.5
PSP	6	0	6	3.6
SP	3	0	3	3.2
RRP	1	0	1	0.2
IND	(7) 4	0	7	3.8
	(40) 8	8	24	

Part: 34.2

1967

Party	Cont	Won	LD	Pct.
CONG	8	6	0	44.0
SSP	5	1	1	20.8
JS	8	1	5	15.4
Swat	4	0	4	2.6
JKD	2	0	2	2.1
PSP	2	0	2	0.6
IND	(19) 8	0	18	14.5
	(48) 8	8	32	

Part: 39.1

1969

Party	Cont	Won	LD	Pct.
JS	8	4	1	29.6
SSP	6	2	1	25.9
CONG	8	2	2	22.6
LTCD	4	0	3	8.1
Janata	6	0	5	5.7
BKD	3	0	3	1.9
BCP	2	0	2	1.5
Jhkh	1	0	1	1.4
HJ	1	0	1	0.7
CPI	1	0	1	0.4
PSP	1	0	1	0.4
SD	1	0	1	0.2
Swat	1	0	1	0.1
IND	(3) 3	0	3	1.5
	(46) 8	8	26	

Part: 40.4

SINGHBHUM DISTRICT

Population: 2,049,911
Urban: 21.5 Rural: 78.5
Hindu: 74.5 Muslim: 3.8 Christian: 2.1 Sikh: 0.9 Other: 18.7

1952			
Party	Cont	Won	LD	Pct.
Jhkh	12	10	1	47.6
CONG	6	1	1	14.3
SP	6	0	6	5.0
GP	1	1	0	3.5
JS	3	0	3	3.5
CPI	2	0	2	2.2
FB(M)	1	0	1	0.7
RSP	1	0	1	0.3
FB(R)	1	0	1	0.1
Janata	1	0	1	0.1
RRP	1	0	1	#
IND	(32) 11	0	27	22.7
	(67) 12	12	45	

Part: 42.7

1957			
Party	Cont	Won	LD	Pct.
Jhkh	13	9	3	33.7
CONG	9	2	1	20.9
CPI	4	1	2	7.8
PSP	6	0	6	1.9
Janata	1	0	1	0.1
IND	(38) 13	2	25	35.6
	(71) 14	14	38	

Part: 34.1

1962			
Party	Cont	Won	LD	Pct.
Jhkh	14	5	4	26.9
CONG	14	2	0	26.6
CPI	3	3	0	15.0
Swat	5	1	4	3.9
PSP	6	0	6	2.7
SP	3	0	2	1.8
IND	(36) 11	3	30	23.1
	(81) 14	14	46	

Part: 34.5

1967			
Party	Cont	Won	LD	Pct.
CONG	14	7	4	26.5
JS	13	3	9	16.2
CPI	7	0	4	8.1
SSP	9	1	6	5.9
CPM	5	0	4	4.9
PSP	4	0	4	0.9
Swat	2	0	2	0.4
IND	(67) 14	3	57	37.1
	(121) 14	14	90	

Part: 35.8

1969			
Party	Cont	Won	LD	Pct.
Jhkh	8	5	3	18.2
CONG	14	1	8	16.2
JS	13	0	8	13.2
CPI	6	2	4	12.1
HJ	5	2	1	9.3
LTCD	8	0	7	4.7
RPI	2	1	1	3.8
PSP	7	0	7	2.2
Swat	2	0	2	2.2
FB	2	1	1	2.1

1969 (continued)			
Party	Cont	Won	LD	Pct.
Janata	10	0	10	1.9
BKD	8	0	8	1.1
SSP	4	0	4	0.8
SD	6	0	6	0.6
CPM	1	0	1	0.3
PBI	4	0	4	0.3
IND	(23) 12	2	20	11.0
	(123) 14	14	95	

Part: 41.6

DHANBAD DISTRICT

Population: 1,158,610
Urban: 25.0 Rural: 75.0
Hindu: 88.3 Muslim: 10.6 Sikh: 0.5 Christian: 0.4

1952

Party	Cont	Won	LD	Pct.
CONG	8	4	1	38.3
Janata	4	2	1	13.0
Jhkh	2	0	0	7.9
KMPP	5	0	5	6.4
LKS	2	0	1	5.6
SP	4	0	4	3.6
FB(M)	2	0	2	2.8
JS	1	0	0	1.5
CPI	1	0	1	0.2
IND	(17) 6	2	15	20.7
	(46) 8	8	30	

Part: 32.5

1957

Party	Cont	Won	LD	Pct.
CONG	7	7	0	44.5
Janata	3	0	0	12.9
CPI	3	0	2	8.5
PSP	4	0	3	7.9
Jhkh	2	0	2	1.7
IND	(16) 7	0	13	24.5
	(35) 7	7	20	

Part: 31.7

1962

Party	Cont	Won	LD	Pct.
CONG	7	4	2	34.8
Swat	7	3	2	30.7
CPI	4	0	2	11.3
PSP	3	0	3	3.3
SP	6	0	6	2.3
Jhkh	7	0	7	2.3
JS	2	0	2	1.8
IND	(14) 5	0	12	13.5
	(50) 7	7	36	

Part: 41.1

1967

Party	Cont	Won	LD	Pct.
CONG	8	3	1	27.6
JKD	5	2	0	17.8
JS	8	0	6	9.5
CPI	2	0	0	7.9
CPM	1	1	0	3.7
SSP	4	0	4	3.1
PSP	1	0	1	0.3
IND	(25) 8	2	23	30.1
	(54) 8	8	35	

Part: 37.5

1969

Party	Cont	Won	LD	Pct.
CONG	8	0	1	23.3
BKD	7	2	4	17.8
JS	7	1	6	11.7
Janata	7	1	6	10.3
CPI	3	1	1	9.1
CPM	2	1	1	6.8
SSP	5	1	4	5.7
LTCD	4	0	4	1.5
HJ	3	0	3	0.9
RSP	2	0	2	0.9
SD	7	0	7	0.8
BCP	3	0	3	0.5
PBI	1	0	1	#
IND	(15) 7	1	13	10.7
	(74) 8	8	56	

Part: 40.2

STATE SUMMARY

Population: 20,633,350
Urban: 25.8 Rural: 74.2
Hindu: 89.0 Muslim: 8.5 Jain: 2.0 Christian: 0.4 Other: 0.1

1952

Party	Cont	Won	LD	Pct.
CONG	155	142*	0	56.1
SP	82	4*	54	8.6
KMPP	46	0	21	7.4
KS	36	1	11	3.1
KLP	14	1	4	2.1
RRP	14	0	8	1.7
HMS	26	0	21	1.1
SCF	6	0	5	0.6
CPI	8	0	5	0.5
FB(M)	4	0	4	0.2
JS	4	0	3	0.1
IND (150)	99	10	92	18.5
(545)	158	158	228	

Part: 50.7
*Uncontested: CONG (6), SP (1)
Note: See p. 65 for note on
       Kutch

1957

Party	Cont	Won	LD	Pct.
CONG	132	99*	1	56.5
PSP	20	3	3	4.9
JS	5	0	1	0.6
HMS	4	0	3	0.2
SCF	1	0	1	0.1
RRP	3	0	3	#
IND (153)	109	30	50	37.7
(318)	132	132	62	

Part: 53.5
*Uncontested: CONG (3)

1962

Party	Cont	Won	LD	Pct.
CONG	154	113	2	50.8
Swat	105	26	20	24.4
PSP	53	7	25	7.7
NMGJP	20	1	11	2.5
JS	26	0	23	1.3
HMS	12	0	11	0.5
RPI	13	0	12	0.4
CPI	1	0	0	0.2
SP	2	0	2	#
RRP	2	0	2	#
IND (131)	92	7	82	12.1
(519)	154	154	190	

Part: 54.6

1967

Party	Cont	Won	LD	Pct.
CONG	168	93	2	45.9
Swat	147	66	5	38.2
PSP	37	3	23	3.3
JS	16	1	8	1.9
SSP	14	0	13	0.4
RPI	4	0	4	0.1
IND (227)	124	5	195	10.2
(613)	168	168	250	

Part: 59.7

SAURASHTRA AND KUTCH

Population: 6,429,485
Urban: 30.0 Rural: 70.0
Hindu: 86.9 Muslim: 9.9 Jain: 3.1 Christian: 0.1

1952				
Party	Cont	Won	LD	Pct.
CONG	62	58*	0	63.4
KS	36	1	11	12.4
HMS	26	0	21	4.5
SP	31	2*	26	4.3
KMPP	14	0	9	2.7
CPI	3	0	1	0.7
SCF	3	0	3	0.4
JS	3	0	2	0.4
RRP	1	0	0	0.3
IND	(56) 33	2	46	10.9
	(235) 63	63	119	

Part: 47.0
*Uncontested: CONG (4), SP (1)
Note: See note on p. 65 on
       Kutch

1957				
Party	Cont	Won	LD	Pct.
CONG	41	40*	0	70.8
PSP	13	1	2	8.7
JS	4	0	0	2.1
HMS	3	0	2	0.8
SCF	1	0	1	0.6
IND	(38) 26	0	17	17.0
	(100) 41	41	22	

Part: 43.5
*Uncontested: CONG (1)

1962				
Party	Cont	Won	LD	Pct.
CONG	47	34	0	53.0
PSP	22	2	9	11.2
Swat	18	5	11	10.5
JS	12	0	9	3.5
NMGJP	7	0	3	2.9
CPI	1	0	0	0.7
HMS	4	0	4	0.2
RPI	3	0	3	0.2
SP	1	0	1	0.1
IND	(41) 28	6	21	17.7
	(156) 47	47	61	

Part: 47.8

1967				
Party	Cont	Won	LD	Pct.
CONG	52	28	1	43.2
Swat	43	22	2	36.4
JS	9	1	2	5.1
PSP	16	0	10	4.5
SSP	2	0	1	0.5
IND	(87) 43	1	77	10.3
	(209) 52	52	93	

Part: 53.6

KUTCH DISTRICT

Population: 696,440
Urban: 19.4 Rural: 80.6
Hindu: 72.2 Muslim: 18.5 Jain: 9.1 Christian: 0.1

	1952			
Party	Cont	Won	LD	Pct.
CONG	30	28*	1	63.1
SP	5	0	2	3.8
IND	(35) 28	2	11	33.1
	(70) 30	30	14	

Part: 42.7
*Uncontested: CONG (2)
Note: In 1952 Kutch elected
       an Electoral College.
       The percentage columns
       on pp. 63 and 64 in-
       clude the votes cast,
       but the "Cont-Won-LD"
       columns exclude the
       data for Kutch.

	1957			
Party	Cont	Won	LD	Pct.
CONG	5	5	0	64.7
IND	(7) 5	0	2	35.3
	(12) 5	5	2	

Part: 37.0

	1962			
Party	Cont	Won	LD	Pct.
Swat	5	5	0	61.3
CONG	5	0	5	33.8
JS	1	0	1	2.4
NMGJP	2	0	2	1.7
IND	(1) 1	0	1	0.8
	(14) 5	5	4	

Part: 57.2

	1967			
Party	Cont	Won	LD	Pct.
CONG	6	4	0	49.4
Swat	6	2	0	44.5
IND	(9) 4	0	9	6.1
	(21) 6	6	9	

Part: 54.8

SURENDRANAGAR DISTRICT

Population: 663,206
Urban: 28.0 Rural: 72.0
Hindu: 89.3 Muslim: 6.5 Jain: 4.1 Christian: 0.1

1952

Party	Cont	Won	LD	Pct.
CONG	6	6	0	67.1
HMS	4	0	2	6.7
KMPP	3	0	2	5.6
SP	4	1*	3	4.7
RRP	1	0	0	3.2
IND	(7) 5	0	5	12.7
	(25) 7	7	12	

Part: 51.8
*Uncontested: SP (1)

1957

Party	Cont	Won	LD	Pct.
CONG	4	4	0	78.4
PSP	3	0	0	19.0
HMS	1	0	0	2.6
	(8) 4	4	0	

Part: 53.4

1962

Party	Cont	Won	LD	Pct.
CONG	5	5	0	61.2
PSP	3	0	3	3.6
JS	2	0	2	1.7
HMS	1	0	1	0.8
IND	(6) 5	0	1	32.7
	(17) 5	5	7	

Part: 49.1

1967

Party	Cont	Won	LD	Pct.
Swat	5	5	0	62.2
CONG	5	0	1	30.6
PSP	1	0	1	0.2
IND	(10) 5	0	10	7.0
	(21) 5	5	12	

Part: 61.3

RAJKOT DISTRICT

Population: 1,208,519
Urban: 38.7 Rural: 61.3
Hindu: 87.2 Muslim: 10.4 Jain: 2.3 Christian: 0.1

1952

Party	Cont	Won	LD	Pct.
CONG	14	13*	0	55.1
KS	11	0	1	24.1
HMS	6	0	6	5.0
SP	4	0	4	1.3
JS	1	0	1	0.7
SCF	1	0	1	0.5
CPI	1	0	1	0.2
KMPP	1	0	1	0.1
IND (19)	9	1	15	13.0
(58)	14	14	30	

Part: 45.7
*Uncontested: CONG (1)

1957

Party	Cont	Won	LD	Pct.
CONG	8	8	0	72.6
JS	3	0	0	7.3
PSP	1	0	1	1.4
HMS	1	0	1	1.2
IND (8)	6	0	4	17.5
(21)	8	8	6	

Part: 37.8

1962

Party	Cont	Won	LD	Pct.
CONG	9	6	0	51.0
JS	3	0	2	6.4
NMGJP	2	0	0	5.9
PSP	2	0	1	2.8
Swat	2	0	2	1.0
SP	1	0	1	0.4
RPI	1	0	1	0.2
HMS	1	0	1	0.2
IND (10)	7	3	5	32.1
(31)	9	9	13	

Part: 48.7

1967

Party	Cont	Won	LD	Pct.
CONG	10	5	0	44.8
Swat	8	4	0	36.0
JS	2	1	0	9.3
PSP	2	0	1	2.3
IND (18)	8	0	17	7.6
(40)	10	10	18	

Part: 58.6

JAMNAGAR DISTRICT

Population: 828,419
Urban: 35.4 Rural: 64.6
Hindu: 84.2 Muslim: 12.2 Jain: 3.3 Christian: 0.2

1952

Party	Cont	Won	LD	Pct.
CONG	9	8	0	65.7
KS	5	0	0	13.2
KMPP	3	0	2	4.7
HMS	2	0	2	2.5
SP	3	0	3	1.8
IND	(15) 6	1	14	12.1
	(37) 9	9	21	

Part: 43.6

1957

Party	Cont	Won	LD	Pct.
CONG	5	5*	0	70.2
IND	(5) 4	0	0	29.8
	(10) 5	5	0	

Part: 51.6
*Uncontested: CONG (1)

1962

Party	Cont	Won	LD	Pct.
CONG	6	5	0	58.4
NMGJP	2	0	1	10.0
Swat	5	0	3	9.2
PSP	1	0	0	3.7
JS	1	0	1	1.5
RPI	1	0	1	0.8
HMS	1	0	1	0.1
IND	(7) 4	1	5	16.3
	(24) 6	6	12	

Part: 39.8

1967

Party	Cont	Won	LD	Pct.
Swat	7	4	0	44.9
CONG	7	3	0	39.3
PSP	2	0	2	1.0
IND	(17) 7	0	14	14.8
	(33) 7	7	16	

Part: 52.1

JUNAGADH DISTRICT

Population: 1,245,643
Urban: 28.2 Rural: 71.8
Hindu: 89.2 Muslim: 10.0 Jain: 0.7 Christian: #

1952

Party	Cont	Won	LD	Pct.
CONG	15	15	0	70.9
KS	9	0	6	7.9
HMS	9	0	7	6.5
KMPP	6	0	3	6.0
SP	9	0	9	2.5
CPI	1	0	0	1.2
SCF	1	0	1	1.1
IND	(8) 6	0	7	3.9
	(58) 15	15	33	

Part: 55.9

1957

Party	Cont	Won	LD	Pct.
CONG	9	9	0	74.6
PSP	2	0	0	4.9
JS	1	0	0	2.6
SCF	1	0	1	2.4
IND	(10) 5	0	7	15.5
	(23) 9	9	8	

Part: 44.8

1962

Party	Cont	Won	LD	Pct.
CONG	9	8	0	59.7
JS	4	0	3	6.7
PSP	3	0	2	5.5
CPI	1	0	0	3.7
Swat	2	0	2	0.5
RPI	1	0	1	0.3
IND	(9) 6	1	3	23.6
	(29) 9	9	11	

Part: 47.2

1967

Party	Cont	Won	LD	Pct.
CONG	10	5	0	44.3
Swat	7	4	0	30.5
JS	3	0	1	7.7
PSP	2	0	1	4.9
IND	(15) 8	1	12	12.6
	(37) 10	10	14	

Part: 53.1

GUJARAT

AMRELI DISTRICT

Population: 667,823
Urban: 21.3 Rural: 78.7
Hindu: 93.2 Muslim: 5.8 Jain: 0.9 Christian: 0.1

1952

Party	Cont	Won	LD	Pct.
CONG	6	5	0	57.5
KS	4	1	2	15.7
HMS	4	0	3	9.5
SP	4	0	3	8.3
IND (2)	2	0	1	9.0
(20)	6	6	9	

Part: 46.8

1957

Party	Cont	Won	LD	Pct.
CONG	3	3	0	74.7
PSP	3	0	1	18.7
HMS	1	0	1	1.1
IND (1)	1	0	1	5.5
(8)	3	3	3	

Part: 43.4

1962

Party	Cont	Won	LD	Pct.
CONG	5	5	0	68.0
PSP	5	0	0	30.5
HMS	1	0	1	0.3
IND (2)	1	0	2	1.2
(13)	5	5	3	

Part: 48.0

1967

Party	Cont	Won	LD	Pct.
CONG	5	5	0	52.1
PSP	5	0	2	20.7
Swat	5	0	2	19.5
IND (6)	5	0	5	7.7
(21)	5	5	9	

Part: 44.9

BHAVNAGAR DISTRICT

Population: 1,119,435
Urban: 31.5 Rural: 68.5
Hindu: 90.0 Muslim: 6.6 Jain: 3.2 Christian: 0.1

Party	Cont	Won	LD	Pct.
1952				
CONG	12	11*	0	61.2
KS	7	0	2	18.1
SP	7	1	4	11.1
CPI	1	0	0	2.3
JS	2	0	1	1.7
KMPP	1	0	1	0.6
SCF	1	0	1	0.4
HMS	1	0	1	0.2
IND	(5) 5	0	4	4.4
	(37) 12	12	14	

Part: 40.3
*Uncontested: CONG (1)

Party	Cont	Won	LD	Pct.
1957				
CONG	7	6	0	56.1
PSP	4	1	0	17.9
IND	(7) 5	0	3	26.0
	(18) 7	7	3	

Part: 42.8

Party	Cont	Won	LD	Pct.
1962				
CONG	8	5	0	45.6
PSP	8	2	3	33.3
Swat	4	0	4	3.8
NMGJP	1	0	0	2.8
JS	1	0	0	2.4
IND	(6) 4	1	4	12.1
	(28) 8	8	11	

Part: 45.9

Party	Cont	Won	LD	Pct.
1967				
CONG	9	6	0	43.1
Swat	5	3	0	22.2
JS	4	0	1	11.0
PSP	4	0	3	6.7
SSP	2	0	1	3.2
IND	(12) 6	0	10	13.8
	(39) 9	9	15	

Part: 49.8

FORMER BOMBAY DISTRICTS

Population: 14,203,865
Urban: 23.8 Rural: 76.2
Hindu: 89.9 Muslim: 7.8 Jain: 1.5 Christian: 0.6

1952

Party	Cont	Won	LD	Pct.
CONG	93	84*	0	53.6
SP	51	2	28	10.1
KMPP	32	0	12	9.0
KLP	14	1	4	2.8
RRP	13	0	8	2.1
SCF	3	0	2	0.7
CPI	5	0	4	0.5
FB(M)	4	0	4	0.3
JS	1	0	1	#
IND	(94) 66	8	46	20.9
	(310) 95	95	109	

Part: 52.0
*Uncontested: CONG (2)

1957

Party	Cont	Won	LD	Pct.
CONG	91	59*	1	52.3
PSP	7	2	1	3.8
JS	1	0	1	0.1
RRP	3	0	3	0.1
HMS	1	0	1	#
IND	(115) 83	30	33	43.7
	(218) 91	91	40	

Part: 57.4
*Uncontested: CONG (2)

1962

Party	Cont	Won	LD	Pct.
CONG	107	79	2	50.1
Swat	87	21	9	29.4
PSP	31	5	16	6.5
NMGJP	13	1	8	2.4
JS	14	0	14	0.7
HMS	8	0	7	0.6
RPI	10	0	9	0.5
RRP	2	0	2	#
SP	1	0	1	#
IND	(90) 64	1	61	9.8
	(363)107	107	129	

Part: 57.5

1967

Party	Cont	Won	LD	Pct.
CONG	116	65	1	47.0
Swat	104	44	3	38.8
PSP	21	3	13	2.9
JS	7	0	6	0.7
SSP	12	0	12	0.3
RPI	4	0	4	0.1
IND	(140) 81	4	118	10.2
	(404)116	116	157	

Part: 62.3

AHMEDABAD DISTRICT

Population: 2,210,199
Urban: 60.8 Rural: 39.2
Hindu: 84.1 Muslim: 11.0 Jain: 3.7 Christian: 0.9 Sikh: 0.2

1952				
Party	Cont	Won	LD	Pct.
CONG	15	15	0	57.8
SP	6	0	3	9.4
KLP	5	0	2	7.1
RRP	4	0	3	3.6
CPI	3	0	2	2.9
SCF	1	0	0	2.8
IND	(15) 11	0	10	16.4
	(49) 15	15	20	
Part:	52.9			

1957				
Party	Cont	Won	LD	Pct.
CONG	14	5	1	39.2
IND	(19) 14	9	5	60.8
	(33) 14	14	6	
Part:	67.4			

1962				
Party	Cont	Won	LD	Pct.
CONG	16	12	0	51.2
Swat	8	2	1	16.1
NMGJP	2	1	0	6.3
PSP	4	1	2	5.8
HMS	2	0	1	3.0
RPI	3	0	2	1.7
JS	6	0	6	1.6
IND	(14) 10	0	5	14.3
	(55) 16	16	17	
Part:	56.5			

1967				
Party	Cont	Won	LD	Pct.
CONG	18	7	1	41.0
Swat	13	7	2	29.3
PSP	3	1	1	5.6
JS	3	0	3	1.2
RPI	3	0	3	0.5
SSP	2	0	2	0.2
IND	(32) 14	3	24	22.2
	(74) 18	18	36	
Part:	64.0			

MEHSANA DISTRICT

Population: 1,689,963
Urban: 17.8 Rural: 82.2
Hindu: 92.5 Muslim: 5.9 Jain: 1.6 Christian: #

1952

Party	Cont	Won	LD	Pct.
CONG	13	10	0	47.9
RRP	3	0	2	3.4
SP	4	0	4	2.4
IND (22)	12	3	8	46.3
(42)	13	13	14	

Part: 56.6

1957

Party	Cont	Won	LD	Pct.
CONG	12	1	0	35.8
IND (12)	12	11	0	64.2
(24)	12	12	0	

Part: 61.3

1962

Party	Cont	Won	LD	Pct.
CONG	13	12	0	53.5
Swat	12	1	0	38.4
RPI	2	0	2	0.5
IND (10)	6	0	7	7.6
(37)	13	13	9	

Part: 61.3

1967

Party	Cont	Won	LD	Pct.
Swat	12	6	0	44.5
CONG	13	6	0	43.9
JS	1	0	0	2.7
SSP	1	0	1	0.5
RPI	1	0	1	0.3
IND (16)	9	1	13	8.1
(44)	13	13	15	

Part: 66.9

BANASKANTHA DISTRICT

Population: 966,144
Urban: 7.1 Rural: 92.9
Hindu: 89.9 Muslim: 7.0 Jain: 3.0 Christian: #

1952

Party	Cont	Won	LD	Pct.
CONG	5	5	0	63.7
SP	6	0	4	14.7
RRP	1	0	1	2.6
IND	(6) 5	1	2	19.0
	(18) 6	6	7	

Part: 31.4

1957

Party	Cont	Won	LD	Pct.
CONG	6	6	0	59.3
IND	(8) 6	0	2	40.7
	(14) 6	6	2	

Part: 33.9

1962

Party	Cont	Won	LD	Pct.
CONG	7	6	1	55.3
Swat	7	0	1	27.9
RPI	1	0	1	1.3
HMS	2	0	2	1.0
IND	(4) 3	1	3	14.5
	(21) 7	7	8	

Part: 45.6

1967

Party	Cont	Won	LD	Pct.
Swat	8	3	0	46.5
CONG	8	5	0	45.5
SSP	1	0	1	0.3
IND	(7) 3	0	6	7.7
	(24) 8	8	7	

Part: 52.3

SABARKANTHA DISTRICT

Population: 918,587
Urban: 6.7 Rural: 93.3
Hindu: 93.8 Muslim: 4.7 Jain: 1.1 Christian: 0.3

1952

Party	Cont	Won	LD	Pct.
CONG	6	5*	0	58.9
SP	4	0	4	4.9
IND (5)	4	1	1	36.2
(15)	6	6	5	

Part: 49.4
*Uncontested: CONG (1)

1957

Party	Cont	Won	LD	Pct.
CONG	6	4	0	54.0
IND (12)	6	2	6	46.0
(18)	6	6	6	

Part: 45.3

1962

Party	Cont	Won	LD	Pct.
CONG	7	6	0	53.2
Swat	7	1	0	36.0
PSP	7	0	6	7.9
RPI	2	0	2	0.9
IND (4)	3	0	4	2.0
(27)	7	7	12	

Part: 59.2

1967

Party	Cont	Won	LD	Pct.
Swat	8	8	0	57.6
CONG	8	0	0	36.6
PSP	2	0	1	3.1
IND (6)	5	0	6	2.7
(24)	8	8	7	

Part: 63.4

PANCH MAHALS DISTRICT

Population: 1,468,946
Urban: 10.5 Rural: 89.5
Hindu: 95.0 Muslim: 4.3 Christian: 0.4 Jain: 0.3

1952

Party	Cont	Won	LD	Pct.
CONG	9	6	0	51.4
SP	4	0	1	12.0
RRP	3	0	1	8.3
FB(M)	2	0	2	2.3
KMPP	1	0	1	1.4
IND (4)	3	3	1	24.6
(23)	9	9	6	

Part: 41.3

1957

Party	Cont	Won	LD	Pct.
CONG	9	7*	0	50.6
HMS	1	0	1	0.4
RRP	1	0	1	0.3
IND (17)	8	2	6	48.7
(28)	9	9	8	

Part: 47.2
*Uncontested: CONG (1)

1962

Party	Cont	Won	LD	Pct.
Swat	11	5	1	45.3
CONG	11	6	1	39.8
PSP	6	0	5	5.8
HMS	4	0	4	1.1
NMGJP	3	0	3	0.9
IND (13)	9	0	12	7.1
(48)	11	11	26	

Part: 48.0

1967

Party	Cont	Won	LD	Pct.
Swat	11	6	0	43.7
CONG	12	6	0	42.6
SSP	4	0	4	1.6
PSP	5	0	5	1.6
IND (19)	11	0	17	10.5
(51)	12	12	26	

Part: 57.0

KAIRA DISTRICT

Population: 1,917,540
Urban: 19.4 Rural: 80.6
Hindu: 88.2 Muslim: .8.9 Christian: 2.0 Jain: 0.8

1952

Party	Cont	Won	LD	Pct.
CONG	14	14	0	52.3
KMPP	12	0	0	30.2
SP	4	0	1	4.9
RRP	2	0	1	2.5
SCF	1	0	1	1.0
IND	(15) 7	0	12	9.1
	(48) 14	14	15	

Part: 60.9

1957

Party	Cont	Won	LD	Pct.
CONG	13	8	0	50.0
IND	(18) 13	5	5	50.0
	(31) 13	13	5	

Part: 62.9

1962

Party	Cont	Won	LD	Pct.
Swat	15	10	0	50.3
CONG	15	5	0	43.5
NMGJP	2	0	2	1.8
JS	2	0	2	0.4
RPI	1	0	1	0.2
IND	(8) 7	0	7	3.8
	(43) 15	15	12	

Part: 64.5

1967

Party	Cont	Won	LD	Pct.
CONG	16	9	0	50.8
Swat	16	7	0	47.0
PSP	2	0	2	0.3
IND	(9) 7	0	9	1.9
	(43) 16	16	11	

Part: 71.2

BARODA DISTRICT

Population: 1,527,326
Urban: 26.0 Rural: 74.0
Hindu: 90.8 Muslim: 7.8 Jain: 1.0 Christian: 0.4

1952

Party	Cont	Won	LD	Pct.
CONG	9	9*	0	52.3
KLP	7	1	1	19.0
SP	6	0	6	7.2
FB(M)	2	0	2	1.9
SCF	1	0	1	1.3
CPI	1	0	1	0.8
IND (10)	7	0	7	17.5
(36)	10	10	18	

Part: 48.7
*Uncontested: CONG (2)

1957

Party	Cont	Won	LD	Pct.
CONG	10	10	0	60.6
JS	1	0	1	0.8
RRP	1	0	1	0.2
IND (12)	10	0	2	38.4
(24)	10	10	4	

Part: 56.7

1962

Party	Cont	Won	LD	Pct.
CONG	12	10	0	51.3
Swat	12	2	2	29.6
PSP	4	0	2	7.1
NMGJP	3	0	2	4.2
JS	3	0	3	1.6
RRP	2	0	2	0.2
RPI	1	0	1	0.2
SP	1	0	1	0.1
IND (10)	7	0	8	5.7
(48)	12	12	21	

Part: 55.7

1967

Party	Cont	Won	LD	Pct.
CONG	13	7	0	47.1
Swat	12	5	0	38.9
PSP	3	1	1	6.0
IND (15)	9	0	13	8.0
(43)	13	13	14	

Part: 60.4

BROACH DISTRICT

Population: 891,969
Urban: 15.0 Rural: 85.0
Hindu: 82.7 Muslim: 16.0 Jain: 0.6 Christian: 0.6

1952

Party	Cont	Won	LD	Pct.
CONG	6	6	0	43.0
KMPP	4	0	2	10.9
SP	3	0	1	6.2
KLP	2	0	1	4.9
IND	(9) 6	0	2	35.0
	(24) 6	6	6	
Part:	49.9			

1957

Party	Cont	Won	LD	Pct.
CONG	6	5	0	58.4
RRP	1	0	1	0.3
IND	(6) 6	1	0	41.3
	(13) 6	6	1	
Part:	60.0			

1962

Party	Cont	Won	LD	Pct.
CONG	7	6	0	50.6
Swat	6	0	1	23.3
PSP	2	1	1	10.2
NMGJP	3	0	1	10.0
IND	(3) 3	0	2	5.9
	(21) 7	7	5	
Part:	58.4			

1967

Party	Cont	Won	LD	Pct.
CONG	7	6	0	46.8
Swat	7	1	0	34.6
PSP	3	0	3	1.9
IND	(11) 7	0	8	16.7
	(28) 7	7	11	
Part:	61.3			

SURAT DISTRICT

Population: 1,313,823
As district was divided subsequent to the 1961 Census, the rural/urban
and religious percentage data include both the present Surat District
and the Bulsar area of Bulsar and Dangs District (p. 82).
Urban: 22.1 Rural: 77.9
Hindu: 92.0 Muslim: 6.2 Jain: 0.9 Christian: 0.3

1952				
Party	Cont	Won	LD	Pct.
CONG	9	9	0	59.7
KMPP	8	0	5	12.7
SP	7	0	2	12.4
CPI	1	0	1	0.2
JS	1	0	1	0.1
IND	(6) 6	0	2	14.9
	(32) 9	9	11	

Part: 60.7

1957				
Party	Cont	Won	LD	Pct.
CONG	9	9*	0	76.8
PSP	1	0	1	3.0
IND	(10) 8	0	6	20.2
	(20) 9	9	7	

Part: 62.6
*Uncontested: CONG (1)

1962				
Party	Cont	Won	LD	Pct.
CONG	10	10	0	57.9
Swat	7	0	1	16.5
JS	3	0	3	2.1
IND	(16) 9	0	9	23.5
	(36) 10	10	13	

Part: 57.5

1967				
Party	Cont	Won	LD	Pct.
CONG	11	10	0	58.5
Swat	9	1	0	24.0
JS	2	0	2	0.6
SSP	4	0	4	0.6
IND	(20) 11	0	17	16.3
	(46) 11	11	23	

Part: 57.7

BULSAR AND DANGS DISTRICT

Population: 1,209,368
Rural/urban and religious data are for Dangs only. See note p. 81.
Urban: 0.0 Rural: 100.0
Hindu: 97.7 Muslim: 1.1 Christian: 0.9 Other: 0.3

1952				
Party	Cont	Won	LD	Pct.
CONG	7	5	0	51.4
SP	7	2	2	29.4
KMPP	7	0	4	17.0
IND	(2) 1	0	1	2.2
	(23) 7	7	7	
Part: 58.4				

1957				
Party	Cont	Won	LD	Pct.
CONG	6	4	0	58.6
PSP	6	2	0	40.1
IND	(1) 1	0	1	1.3
	(13) 6	6	1	
Part: 63.3				

1962				
Party	Cont	Won	LD	Pct.
CONG	9	6	0	49.1
PSP	8	3	0	34.2
Swat	2	0	2	2.0
IND	(8) 7	0	4	14.7
	(27) 9	9	6	
Part: 62.2				

1967				
Party	Cont	Won	LD	Pct.
CONG	10	9	0	59.1
Swat	8	0	1	26.3
PSP	3	1	0	10.3
JS	1	0	1	1.2
IND	(5) 5	0	5	3.1
	(27) 10	10	7	
Part: 58.5				

STATE SUMMARY

Population: 7,590,543
State rural/urban and religious data not available.

Party	Cont	Won	LD	Pct.
		1952		
CONG	59	51*	1	40.1
ZP	29	2	5	16.8
JS	25	2	9	6.7
SP	27	0	22	5.9
AD	2	1	1	0.7
KP	2	0	0	0.7
KMPP	1	1	0	0.2
DCL	1	0	1	0.1
CPI	1	0	1	#
IND (214)	59	4	180	28.8
(361)	61	61	220	

Part: 57.1
*Uncontested: CONG (1)

Party	Cont	Won	LD	Pct.
		1954		
CONG	14	12	0	48.7
JS	4	0	3	2.7
PSP	1	0	1	0.2
IND (56)	14	2	42	48.4
(75)	14	14	46	

Part: 62.9
Elections to PEPSU Assembly in
Jind and Mahendragarth Dis-
tricts only.

Party	Cont	Won	LD	Pct.
		1957		
CONG	55	39*	0	45.9
JS	24	4	7	12.0
CPI	14	2	7	6.7
SCF	9	4	4	5.3
PSP	7	0	6	1.8
IND (102)	45	6	64	28.3
(211)	55	55	88	

Part: 59.8
*Uncontested: CONG (1)

Party	Cont	Won	LD	Pct.
		1962		
CONG	54	31	1	40.4
JS	34	4	16	13.4
Swat	20	3	12	6.7
HLS	8	3	1	5.2
SP	7	4	3	3.8
CPI	12	0	9	2.5
PSP	5	0	3	1.1
RPI	9	0	7	1.1
AD	1	0	0	0.4
HF	1	0	0	0.2
RRP	1	0	1	0.1
IND (148)	51	9	127	25.1
(300)	54	54	180	

Part: 64.0

STATE SUMMARY (Continued)

1967					1968			
Party	Cont	Won	LD	Pct.	Party	Cont	Won	LD	Pct.
CONG	81	48	0	41.3	CONG	81	48	0	44.0
JS	48	12	21	14.4	VHP	29	11	7	11.6
SSP	23	0	17	3.6	JS	43	7	25	10.2
Swat	12	3	7	3.2	Swat	30	2	14	8.1
RPI	24	2	20	2.9	BKD	7	1	4	1.5
CPI	12	0	12	0.9	RPI	14	1	12	1.4
CPM	8	0	8	0.5	SSP	7	0	5	0.9
PSP	3	0	3	0.2	ADS	1	1	0	0.5
IND (260)	78	16	195	33.0	CPI	3	0	3	0.3
(471)	81	81	283		CPM	1	0	1	0.1
Part: 69.1					PSP	2	0	2	0.1
					Janata	1	0	1	#
					IND (179)	65	10	142	21.3
					(398)	81	81	216	
					Part: 55.5				

AMBALA DISTRICT

Population: 885,785
Rural/urban and religious data include Ruper District, Punjab, and
Union Territory of Chandigarh.
Urban: 32.0 Rural: 68.0
Hindu: 71.4 Sikh: 24.8 Muslim: 2.9 Jain: 0.4 Christian: 0.4

Party	Cont	Won	LD	Pct.
1952				
CONG	6	5	0	40.4
SP	5	0	4	12.8
JS	4	0	2	9.0
ZP	2	0	0	7.8
AD	1	0	1	1.8
IND (25)	6	1	24	28.2
(43)	6	6	31	
Part: 58.8				

Party	Cont	Won	LD	Pct.
1957				
CONG	7	7	0	61.8
JS	3	0	0	14.0
PSP	3	0	2	9.5
CPI	1	0	0	3.3
IND (5)	4	0	3	11.4
(19)	7	7	5	
Part: 55.5				

Party	Cont	Won	LD	Pct.
1962				
CONG	6	5	0	45.7
JS	5	0	1	22.8
PSP	2	0	1	5.1
CPI	1	0	0	4.1
AD	1	0	0	3.9
RPI	1	0	0	3.4
Swat	2	0	2	0.9
IND (11)	6	1	10	14.1
(29)	6	6	14	
Part: 63.4				

Party	Cont	Won	LD	Pct.
1967				
CONG	9	5	0	41.3
JS	7	2	2	23.8
RPI	2	1	0	7.5
Swat	4	0	4	2.8
PSP	1	0	1	1.3
CPI	1	0	1	1.1
IND (19)	9	1	14	22.2
(43)	9	9	22	
Part: 68.2				

Party	Cont	Won	LD	Pct.
1968				
CONG	9	7	0	49.4
JS	6	2	2	18.0
VHP	4	0	3	5.9
RPI	3	0	2	4.3
Swat	1	0	1	1.2
BKD	2	0	2	0.7
PSP	1	0	1	0.1
Janata	1	0	1	#
IND (30)	8	0	27	20.4
(57)	9	9	39	
Part: n/a				

KARNAL DISTRICT

Population: 1,490,430
Urban: 17.1 Rural: 82.9
Hindu: 86.8 Sikh: 11.8 Muslim: 0.9 Jain: 0.4 Christian: 0.1

	1952			
Party	Cont	Won	LD	Pct.
CONG	11	11	0	43.9
JS	8	0	2	14.7
ZP	5	0	2	7.9
SP	6	0	5	6.3
IND	(48) 11	0	46	27.2
	(78) 11	11	55	
Part:	56.4			

	1957			
Party	Cont	Won	LD	Pct.
CONG	11	8	0	47.4
JS	6	0	1	17.4
SCF	4	2	2	9.1
CPI	2	0	0	6.4
PSP	1	0	1	0.4
IND	(12) 8	1	7	19.3
	(36) 11	11	11	
Part:	63.6			

	1962			
Party	Cont	Won	LD	Pct.
CONG	11	8	0	43.2
Swat	8	1	3	19.2
JS	7	1	1	18.4
CPI	4	0	4	2.7
PSP	1	0	1	0.5
RRP	1	0	1	0.5
RPI	3	0	3	0.5
IND	(30) 9	1	28	15.0
	(65) 11	11	41	
Part:	66.8			

	1967			
Party	Cont	Won	LD	Pct.
CONG	16	10	0	39.3
JS	9	4	1	18.5
Swat	4	1	1	8.3
RPI	5	0	4	3.6
CPI	3	0	3	1.6
CPM	2	0	2	1.2
SSP	1	0	1	0.1
IND	(46) 16	1	35	27.4
	(86) 16	16	47	
Part:	71.4			

	1968			
Party	Cont	Won	LD	Pct.
CONG	16	9	0	41.5
JS	10	2	1	20.5
VHP	7	0	3	7.9
Swat	6	0	3	6.4
RPI	3	1	2	3.6
BKD	3	0	2	1.9
CPM	1	0	1	0.7
CPI	1	0	1	0.7
IND	(32) 13	4	27	16.8
	(79) 16	16	40	
Part:	n/a			

JIND DISTRICT

Population: 464,873
Other data not available

1952

Party	Cont	Won	LD	Pct.
CONG	6	5	1	41.7
KP	2	0	0	11.2
JS	3	0	1	7.2
KMPP	1	1	0	3.4
SP	1	0	1	0.3
IND (21)	6	0	15	36.2
(34)	6	6	18	

Part: 61.9

1954

Party	Cont	Won	LD	Pct.
CONG	6	4	0	43.1
IND (21)	6	2	12	56.9
(27)	6	6	12	

Part: 68.1

1957

Party	Cont	Won	LD	Pct.
SCF	3	2	0	46.2
CONG	3	1	0	43.5
IND (3)	2	0	3	10.3
(9)	3	3	3	

Part: 63.2

1962

Party	Cont	Won	LD	Pct.
CONG	3	0	0	35.9
Swat	2	2	0	29.1
JS	2	0	2	5.8
RPI	1	0	1	1.1
IND (9)	3	1	8	28.1
(17)	3	3	11	

Part: 67.5

1967

Party	Cont	Won	LD	Pct.
CONG	5	3	0	50.5
RPI	1	1	0	10.6
Swat	1	1	0	8.0
JS	2	0	1	7.2
CPI	1	0	1	1.9
CPM	1	0	1	0.2
IND (17)	5	0	15	21.6
(28)	5	5	18	

Part: 73.1

1968

Party	Cont	Won	LD	Pct.
CONG	5	3	0	49.4
Swat	3	1	0	22.7
VHP	1	1	0	10.0
SSP	2	0	2	3.2
JS	1	0	1	0.8
IND (9)	5	0	8	13.9
(21)	5	5	11	

Part: n/a

ROHTAK DISTRICT

Population: 1,420,391
Urban: 13.7 Rural: 86.3
Hindu: 98.5 Muslim: 0.5 Sikh: 0.5 Jain: 0.4 Christian: #

1952

Party	Cont	Won	LD	Pct.
CONG	11	9	0	36.5
ZP	10	2	0	32.7
JS	2	0	0	2.6
SP	3	0	3	2.5
IND	(42) 10	0	37	25.7
	(68) 11	11	40	

Part: 64.7

1957

Party	Cont	Won	LD	Pct.
CONG	11	5	0	39.5
CPI	5	2	2	16.3
JS	3	1	1	5.0
SCF	2	0	2	1.1
IND	(23) 10	3	12	38.1
	(44) 11	11	17	

Part: 66.3

1962

Party	Cont	Won	LD	Pct.
CONG	11	5	0	37.6
HLS	8	3	1	24.4
JS	6	2	2	13.4
HF	1	0	0	1.6
CPI	2	0	2	0.8
Swat	1	0	1	0.6
IND	(32) 11	1	30	21.6
	(61) 11	11	36	

Part: 69.6

1967

Party	Cont	Won	LD	Pct.
CONG	15	9	0	40.9
JS	10	2	6	15.4
SSP	7	0	6	2.7
RPI	6	0	6	1.0
CPM	2	0	2	0.5
CPI	3	0	3	0.4
IND	(59) 13	4	44	39.1
	(102) 15	15	67	

Part: 71.7

1968

Party	Cont	Won	LD	Pct.
CONG	15	9	0	47.1
JS	7	3	4	10.6
Swat	7	0	5	9.9
VHP	2	1	1	2.2
IND	(38) 7	2	27	30.2
	(69) 15	15	37	

Part: n/a

GURGAON DISTRICT

Population: 1,240,706
Urban: 16.6 Rural: 83.4
Hindu: 81.6 Muslim: 17.5 Sikh: 0.7 Jain: 0.2 Christian: #

1952

Party	Cont	Won	LD	Pct.
CONG	9	9*	0	49.8
ZP	7	0	1	27.4
SP	1	0	1	2.5
DCL	1	0	1	0.4
IND	(20) 8	0	19	19.9
	(38) 9	9	22	

Part: 58.3
*Uncontested: CONG (1)

1957

Party	Cont	Won	LD	Pct.
CONG	9	9*	0	53.3
JS	5	0	1	17.0
CPI	1	0	1	1.4
PSP	1	0	1	0.8
IND	(14) 7	0	7	27.5
	(30) 9	9	10	

Part: 62.5
*Uncontested: CONG (1)

1962

Party	Cont	Won	LD	Pct.
CONG	9	7	0	45.4
JS	5	0	4	11.8
CPI	2	0	1	2.9
RPI	1	0	0	1.8
Swat	1	0	1	0.4
IND	(18) 8	2	9	37.7
	(36) 9	9	15	

Part: 61.2

1967

Party	Cont	Won	LD	Pct.
CONG	13	5	0	39.2
JS	9	1	3	14.7
Swat	2	1	1	4.0
RPI	4	0	4	1.5
CPI	2	0	2	1.0
IND	(37) 12	6	25	39.6
	(67) 13	13	35	

Part: 65.8

1968

Party	Cont	Won	LD	Pct.
CONG	13	7	0	42.3
VHP	8	4	0	26.7
Swat	6	0	3	9.8
JS	8	0	7	7.0
RPI	3	0	3	0.8
CPI	1	0	1	0.7
IND	(21) 11	2	17	12.7
	(60) 13	13	31	

Part: n/a

MAHENDRAGARH DISTRICT

Population: 547,850
Urban: 9.7 Rural: 90.3
Hindu: 99.2 Sikh: 0.4 Muslim: 0.3 Christian: #

		1952		
Party	Cont	Won	LD	Pct.
CONG	7	4	0	31.4
JS	3	2	1	9.2
SP	2	0	2	1.5
IND	(32) 8	2	19	57.9
	(44) 8	8	22	
Part: 48.2				

		1954		
Party	Cont	Won	LD	Pct.
CONG	8	8	0	53.4
JS	4	0	3	5.4
PSP	1	0	1	0.4
IND	(35) 8	0	30	40.8
	(48) 8	8	34	
Part: 58.9				

		1957		
Party	Cont	Won	LD	Pct.
JS	3	3	0	36.5
CONG	4	1	0	35.2
CPI	1	0	1	0.9
IND	(5) 4	0	2	27.4
	(13) 4	4	3	
Part: 46.0				

		1962		
Party	Cont	Won	LD	Pct.
CONG	4	3	0	37.4
JS	3	1	1	16.9
CPI	1	0	0	10.1
Swat	2	0	1	7.1
SP	2	0	2	1.0
IND	(11) 4	0	10	27.5
	(23) 4	4	14	
Part: 49.2				

		1967		
Party	Cont	Won	LD	Pct.
CONG	6	2	0	34.4
SSP	3	0	2	8.9
JS	3	1	2	8.2
CPM	1	0	1	2.2
RPI	2	0	2	1.8
IND	(18) 6	3	12	44.5
	(33) 6	6	19	
Part: 63.8				

		1968		
Party	Cont	Won	LD	Pct.
VHP	5	4	0	42.6
CONG	6	2	0	35.7
SSP	1	0	0	3.9
JS	4	0	4	2.9
Swat	1	0	1	1.0
IND	(13) 6	0	11	13.9
	(30) 6	6	16	
Part: n/a				

HISSAR DISTRICT

Population: 1,540,508
Urban: 15.6 Rural: 84.4
Hindu: 89.2 Sikh: 9.9 Muslim: 0.4 Jain: 0.4 Christian: #

1952				
Party	Cont	Won	LD	Pct.
CONG	9	8	0	34.5
ZP	5	0	2	13.1
SP	9	0	6	12.3
JS	5	0	3	7.2
AD	1	1	0	3.1
CPI	1	0	1	0.3
IND	(26) 10	1	20	29.5
	(56) 10	10	32	
Part:	50.0			

1957				
Party	Cont	Won	LD	Pct.
CONG	10	8	0	39.0
CPI	4	0	3	7.0
JS	4	0	4	4.8
PSP	2	0	2	1.8
IND	(40) 10	2	30	47.4
	(60) 10	10	39	
Part:	56.4			

1962				
Party	Cont	Won	LD	Pct.
CONG	10	3	1	36.1
SP	5	4	1	18.3
JS	6	0	5	6.0
PSP	2	0	1	2.3
Swat	4	0	4	1.7
RPI	3	0	3	1.4
CPI	2	0	2	1.2
IND	(37) 10	3	32	33.0
	(69) 10	10	49	
Part:	62.8			

1967				
Party	Cont	Won	LD	Pct.
CONG	17	14	0	44.7
SSP	12	0	8	11.6
JS	8	2	6	9.0
RPI	4	0	4	0.7
CPI	2	0	2	0.5
PSP	2	0	2	0.4
Swat	1	0	1	0.3
CPM	2	0	2	0.2
IND	(64) 17	1	50	32.6
	(112) 17	17	75	
Part:	68.3			

1968				
Party	Cont	Won	LD	Pct.
CONG	17	11	0	43.5
Swat	6	1	1	8.4
BKD	2	1	0	5.0
VHP	2	1	0	4.5
JS	7	0	6	4.3
SSP	4	0	3	2.2
RPI	5	0	5	0.6
CPI	1	0	1	0.3
PSP	1	0	1	0.3
IND	(37) 15	3	25	30.9
	(82) 17	17	42	
Part:	n/a			

STATE SUMMARY

Population: 3,560,976
Urban: 16.7 Rural: 83.3
Muslim: 68.3 Hindu: 28.5 Sikh: 1.7 Buddhist: 1.4 Christian: 0.1

1952

Party	Cont	Won	LD	Pct.
NC	75	75*	0	---
	(75) 75	75		

*Uncontested: NC (75)

1957

Party	Cont	Won	LD	Pct.
NC	75	68*	0	57.4
PP	21	5	3	24.6
HM	6	1	4	6.0
PSP	8	0	6	2.4
IND	(22) 19	1	15	9.6
	(132) 75	75	28	

Part: 61.6
*Uncontested: NC (43)

1962

Party	Cont	Won	LD	Pct.
NC	75	70*	0	67.0
PP	25	3	6	17.5
DNC	20	0	15	4.3
PSP	6	0	5	1.9
HM	10	0	9	1.9
IND	(38) 27	2	33	7.4
	(174) 75	75	68	

Part: 71.0
*Uncontested: NC (34)

1967

Party	Cont	Won	LD	Pct.
CONG	75	61*	0	53.0
NC	38	8	15	17.2
JS	29	3	8	16.5
DNC	20	0	19	3.2
PSP	3	0	1	1.0
CPI	3	0	2	0.5
IND	(38) 25	3	29	8.6
	(206) 75	75	74	

Part: 56.3
*Uncontested: CONG (22)

KASHMIR PROVINCE

Population: 1,988,089
Urban: 20.2 Rural: 79.8
Muslim: 92.2 Hindu: 4.5 Buddhist: 2.4 Sikh: 0.8 Christian: #

1952

Party	Cont	Won	LD	Pct.
NC	45	45*	0	---
	(45) 45	45	0	

*Uncontested: NC (45)

1957

Party	Cont	Won	LD	Pct.
NC	45	44*	0	65.3
PSP	3	0	1	9.6
IND	(6) 6	1	2	25.1
	(54) 45	45	3	

Part: 41.8
*Uncontested: NC (37)

1962

Party	Cont	Won	LD	Pct.
NC	45	43*	0	84.4
PSP	2	0	2	1.0
DNC	4	0	4	0.8
IND	(8) 8	2	5	13.8
	(59) 45	45	11	

Part: 75.5
*Uncontested: NC (33)

1967

Party	Cont	Won	LD	Pct.
CONG	44	34*	0	51.1
NC	17	7	0	30.8
CPI	3	0	2	1.4
DNC	4	0	4	1.0
JS	3	0	2	0.9
PSP	1	0	1	#
IND	(10) 9	3	4	14.8
	(82) 44	44	13	

Part: 49.2
*Uncontested: CONG (21)

BARAMULLA DISTRICT

Population: 604,659
Urban: 9.5 Rural: 90.5
Muslim: 97.3 Hindu: 2.0 Sikh: 0.7 Christian: #

1952

Party	Cont	Won	LD	Pct.
NC	14	14*	0	---
	(14) 14	14	0	

*Uncontested: NC (14)

1957

Party	Cont	Won	LD	Pct.
NC	14	14*	0	63.5
IND	(2) 2	0	0	36.5
	(16) 14	14	0	

Part: 37.9
*Uncontested: NC (12)

1962

Party	Cont	Won	LD	Pct.
NC	14	13*	0	76.5
DNC	1	0	1	0.6
IND	(2) 2	1	1	22.9
	(17) 14	14	2	

Part: 82.0
*Uncontested: NC (11)

1967

Party	Cont	Won	LD	Pct.
CONG	13	10*	0	52.7
NC	7	3	0	41.7
DNC	1	0	1	0.9
JS	1	0	1	0.3
IND	(1) 1	0	0	4.4
	(23) 13	13	2	

Part: 52.7
*Uncontested: CONG (5)

SRINAGAR DISTRICT

Population: 640,411
Urban: 46.1 Rural: 53.9
Muslim: 90.6 Hindu: 8.3 Sikh: 1.0 Christian: #

1952

Party	Cont	Won	LD	Pct.
NC	13	13*	0	---
	(13) 13	13	0	

*Uncontested: NC (13)

1957

Party	Cont	Won	LD	Pct.
NC	13	12*	0	48.0
PSP	2	0	1	26.1
IND	(1) 1	1	0	25.9
	(16) 13	13	1	

Part: 41.4
*Uncontested: NC (11)

1962

Party	Cont	Won	LD	Pct.
NC	14	13*	0	83.3
PSP	2	0	2	1.9
DNC	2	0	2	1.0
IND	(4) 4	1	2	13.8
	(22) 14	14	6	

Part: 68.3
*Uncontested: NC (7)

1967

Party	Cont	Won	LD	Pct.
CONG	14	10*	0	50.2
NC	10	4	0	42.4
JS	2	0	1	2.5
DNC	3	0	3	1.8
CPI	2	0	2	1.6
PSP	1	0	1	#
IND	(4) 3	0	4	1.5
	(36) 14	14	11	

Part: 38.4
*Uncontested: CONG (4)

ANANTNAG DISTRICT

Population: 654,368
Urban: 7.0   Rural: 93.0
Muslim: 95.4 Hindu: 3.7 Sikh: 0.9 Christian: #

1952

Party	Cont	Won	LD	Pct.
NC	16	16*	0	---
	(16) 16	16	0	

*Uncontested: NC (16)

1957

Party	Cont	Won	LD	Pct.
NC	16	16*	0	73.4
PSP	1	0	0	6.4
IND	(3) 3	0	2	20.2
	(20) 16	16	2	

Part: 43.8
*Uncontested: NC (12)

1962

Party	Cont	Won	LD	Pct.
NC	15	15*	0	98.7
DNC	1	0	1	0.8
IND	(1) 1	0	1	0.5
	(17) 15	15	2	

Part: 85.8
*Uncontested: NC (14)

1967

Party	Cont	Won	LD	Pct.
CONG	15	13*	0	38.7
CPI	1	0	0	6.6
IND	(3) 3	2	0	54.7
	(19) 15	15	0	

Part: 57.5
*Uncontested: CONG (12)

LADAKH DISTRICT

Population: 88,651
Urban: 4.2 Rural: 95.8
Buddhist: 53.8 Muslim: 45.4 Hindu: 0.6 Sikh: 0.1 Christian: #

Party	Cont	Won	LD	Pct.
1952				
NC	2	2*	0	---
	(2) 2	2	0	

*Uncontested: NC (2)

Party	Cont	Won	LD	Pct.
1957				
NC	2	2*	0	---
	(2) 2	2	0	

*Uncontested: NC (2)

Party	Cont	Won	LD	Pct.
1962				
NC	2	2*	0	97.3
IND	(1) 1	0	1	2.7
	(3) 2	2	1	

Part: 90.0
*Uncontested: NC (1)

Party	Cont	Won	LD	Pct.
1967				
CONG	2	1	0	61.9
IND	(2) 2	1	0	38.1
	(4) 2	2	0	

Part: 73.5

JAMMU PROVINCE

Population: 1,572,887
Urban: 12.2 Rural: 87.8
Hindu: 58.7 Muslim: 38.1 Sikh: 2.9 Christian: 0.2

1952				
Party	Cont	Won	LD	Pct.
NC	30	30*	0	---
	(30) 30	30	0	

*Uncontested: NC (30)

1957				
Party	Cont	Won	LD	Pct.
NC	30	24*	0	56.2
PP	21	5	3	28.4
HM	6	1	4	7.0
PSP	5	0	5	1.3
IND	(16) 13	0	13	7.1
	(78) 30	30	25	

Part: 66.4
*Uncontested: NC (6)

1962				
Party	Cont	Won	LD	Pct.
NC	30	27*	0	60.0
PP	25	3	6	24.4
DNC	16	0	11	5.7
HM	10	0	9	2.6
PSP	4	0	3	2.3
IND	(30) 19	0	28	5.0
	(115) 30	30	57	

Part: 69.4
*Uncontested: NC (1)

1967				
Party	Cont	Won	LD	Pct.
CONG	31	27*	0	54.2
JS	26	3	6	25.9
NC	21	1	15	8.9
DNC	16	0	15	4.7
PSP	2	0	0	1.6
IND	(28) 16	0	25	4.7
	(124) 31	31	61	

Part: 61.8
*Uncontested: CONG (1)

DODA DISTRICT

Population: 268,403
Urban: 5.8 Rural: 94.2
Muslim: 65.0 Hindu: 34.6 Buddhist: 0.2 Sikh: 0.2 Christian: #

1952

Party	Cont	Won	LD	Pct.
NC	5	5*	0	---
(5)	5	5	0	

*Uncontested: NC (5)

1957

Party	Cont	Won	LD	Pct.
NC	5	5*	0	81.3
PP	4	0	2	16.7
IND	(1) 1	0	1	2.0
(10)	5	5	3	

Part: 64.3
*Uncontested: NC (1)

1962

Party	Cont	Won	LD	Pct.
NC	5	5	0	81.9
PP	4	0	2	12.6
PSP	1	0	1	3.3
IND	(1) 1	0	1	2.2
(11)	5	5	4	

Part: 69.1

1967

Party	Cont	Won	LD	Pct.
CONG	6	5	0	54.1
NC	3	1	0	21.6
JS	3	0	2	8.7
PSP	1	0	0	4.2
IND	(2) 2	0	0	11.4
(15)	6	6	2	43.3

Part: 43.3

UDHAMPUR DISTRICT

Population: 254,061
Urban: 6.5 Rural: 93.5
Hindu: 65.1 Muslim: 33.9 Sikh: 0.9 Christian: 0.1

1952

Party	Cont	Won	LD	Pct.
NC	5	5*	0	---
	(5) 5	5	0	

*Uncontested: NC (5)

1957

Party	Cont	Won	LD	Pct.
NC	5	5*	0	50.4
PP	4	0	1	41.5
PSP	1	0	1	1.5
IND	(4) 3	0	4	6.6
	(14) 5	5	6	

Part: 59.3
*Uncontested: NC (1)

1962

Party	Cont	Won	LD	Pct.
NC	5	3	0	61.2
PP	5	2	1	33.8
DNC	2	0	2	1.4
HM	2	0	2	1.0
IND	(7) 4	0	7	2.6
	(21) 5	5	12	

Part: 67.3

1967

Party	Cont	Won	LD	Pct.
CONG	5	4	0	60.5
JS	4	1	0	29.4
NC	3	0	3	2.6
DNC	2	0	2	1.7
IND	(6) 3	0	5	5.8
	(20) 5	5	10	

Part: 63.4

KATHUA DISTRICT

Population: 207,430
Urban: 7.5 Rural: 92.5
Hindu: 85.7 Muslim: 13.0 Sikh: 1.2 Christian: #

1952

Party	Cont	Won	LD	Pct.
NC	4	4*	0	---
	(4)	4	4	0

*Uncontested: NC (4)

1957

Party	Cont	Won	LD	Pct.
NC	4	3	0	57.7
PP	4	1	0	33.0
HM	2	0	2	5.0
IND	(2) 2	0	1	4.3
	(12) 4	4	3	

Part: 68.3

1962

Party	Cont	Won	LD	Pct.
NC	4	4	0	55.8
PP	4	0	0	34.6
DNC	3	0	3	2.7
HM	1	0	1	1.9
IND	(6) 3	0	6	5.0
	(18) 4	4	10	

Part: 67.2

1967

Party	Cont	Won	LD	Pct.
CONG	4	4	0	55.9
JS	4	0	0	34.1
NC	4	0	4	5.6
DNC	1	0	1	1.0
IND	(4) 3	0	4	3.4
	(17) 4	4	9	

Part: 66.1

JAMMU AND KASHMIR

JAMMU DISTRICT

Population: 516,932
Urban: 24.7 Rural: 75.3
Hindu: 83.0 Muslim: 10.0 Sikh: 6.3 Christian: 0.4 Jain: 0.3

1952

Party	Cont	Won	LD	Pct.
NC	11	11*	0	---
(11)	11	11	0	

*Uncontested: NC (11)

1957

Party	Cont	Won	LD	Pct.
NC	11	6	0	50.1
PP	8	4	0	27.7
HM	4	1	2	11.2
PSP	3	0	3	1.3
IND	(9) 7	0	7	9.7
(35)	11	11	12	

Part: 67.5

1962

Party	Cont	Won	LD	Pct.
NC	11	10	0	46.9
PP	11	1	2	31.4
DNC	8	0	5	9.2
HM	7	0	6	6.2
PSP	1	0	1	0.4
IND	(14) 9	0	13	5.9
(52)	11	11	27	

Part: 71.8

1967

Party	Cont	Won	LD	Pct.
CONG	11	9	0	48.5
JS	11	2	2	29.4
NC	10	0	7	10.9
DNC	9	0	9	7.1
IND	(16) 8	0	16	4.1
(57)	11	11	34	

Part: 71.3

POONCH DISTRICT

Population: 326,061
Urban: 5.0 Rural: 95.0
Muslim: 79.5 Hindu: 18.0 Sikh: 2.5 Christian: #

1952

Party	Cont	Won	LD	Pct.
NC	5	5*	0	---
(5)	5	5	0	

*Uncontested: NC (5)

1957

Party	Cont	Won	LD	Pct.
NC	5	5*	0	70.5
PP	1	0	0	21.5
PSP	1	0	1	8.0
(7)	5	5	1	

Part: 75.4
*Uncontested: NC (4)

1962

Party	Cont	Won	LD	Pct.
NC	5	5*	0	67.9
DNC	3	0	1	11.9
PSP	2	0	1	10.2
PP	1	0	1	2.0
IND (2)	2	0	1	8.0
(13)	5	5	4	

Part: 69.0
*Uncontested: NC (1)

1967

Party	Cont	Won	LD	Pct.
CONG	5	5*	0	60.4
JS	4	0	2	16.9
DNC	4	0	3	11.2
PSP	1	0	0	8.0
NC	1	0	1	3.5
(15)	5	5	6	

Part: 56.2
*Uncontested: CONG (1)

STATE SUMMARY

Population: 16,903,715
Urban: 15.1 Rural: 84.9
Hindu: 60.8 Christian: 21.2 Muslim: 17.9

1952

Party	Cont	Won	LD	Pct.
CONG	125	49*	3	35.8
SP	82	13*	41	14.3
CPI**	13	6	1	5.7
KMPP	11	7	1	4.5
ML	9	5	0	3.7
RSP	10	6	1	2.5
KSP	10	1	1	1.6
Cochin	12	1	5	1.3
TTNC	5	1	1	1.2
Repub	7	0	2	1.2
CPI***	@	19	@	@
IND	(214)101	20	134	28.5
	(498)128	128	190	

Part: 66.7
*Uncontested: CONG (3), SP (1)
**Malabar area only
***Travancore-Cochin area

1954

Party	Cont	Won	LD	Pct.
CONG	106	45	2	47.0
CPI	33	23	0	17.3
PSP	36	18	0	16.7
RSP	12	9	0	5.9
TTNC	7	4	1	2.8
JS	1	0	1	#
IND	(44) 36	8	19	10.3
	(239)107	107	23	

Part: 74.0

1957

Party	Cont	Won	LD	Pct.
CONG	125	44	5	38.4
CPI	100	60	3	35.4
PSP	62	9	28	10.4
RSP	28	0	22	3.2
ML	@	7	@	@
IND	(74) 59	6*	30	12.6
	(389)126	126	88	

Part: 66.0
*Uncontested: IND (1)

1960

Party	Cont	Won	LD	Pct.
CPI	108	29	0	39.1
CONG	80	63	0	34.4
PSP	33	20	0	14.3
ML	12	11	0	4.9
JS	3	0	3	0.1
IND	(76) 60	3	52	7.2
	(312)126	126	55	

Part: 84.4

STATE SUMMARY (Continued)

	1965					1967			
Party	Cont	Won	LD	Pct.	Party	Cont	Won	LD	Pct.
CONG	133	36	6	33.6	CONG	133	9	9	35.4
CPM	73	40	9	19.7	CPM	59	52	0	23.5
KC	57	24	12	13.0	CPI	22	19	0	8.6
CPI	78	3	54	8.3	SSP	21	19	0	8.4
SSP	29	13	4	8.1	KC	61	5	38	7.6
ML	21	11	2	5.8	ML	15	14	0	6.7
RSP	11	0	6	1.2	RSP	6	6	0	2.7
Swat	12	1	11	0.7	JS	24	0	24	0.9
JS	16	0	16	0.5	PSP	7	0	7	0.2
PSP	8	0	8	0.4	Swat	6	0	6	0.2
DMK	1	0	1	0.1	IND (69) 59		9	55	5.8
RPI	3	0	3	0.1	(423)133		133	139	
FB	2	0	2	#	Part: 72.9				
IND (114) 72		5	87	8.5					
(558)133		133	221						
Part: n/a									

KERALA

MALABAR

Population: 6,174,049
Urban: 14.7 Rural: 85.3
Hindu: 62.7 Muslim: 33.0 Christian: 4.3

1952				
Party	Cont	Won	LD	Pct.
CONG	32	7	0	31.9
CPI	13	6	1	16.3
SP	23	4	14	15.2
KMPP	11	7	1	12.8
ML	9	5	0	10.5
KSP	2	0	0	0.6
IND	(29) 19	3	19	12.7
	(119) 32	32	35	
Part:	60.0			

1954				
Party	Cont	Won	LD	Pct.
CONG	2	1	0	48.5
PSP	2	1	0	44.6
TTNC	1	0	1	2.8
IND	(1) 1	0	1	4.1
	(6) 2	2	2	
Part:	61.8			

See note, p. 109, Palghat
District

1957				
Party	Cont	Won	LD	Pct.
CONG	46	12	0	36.1
CPI	36	20	2	30.7
PSP	15	4	2	10.7
RSP	1	0	1	0.1
ML	@	7	@	@
IND	(37) 28	4*	4	22.4
	(135) 47	47	9	
Part:	57.7			

*Uncontested: IND (1)

1960				
Party	Cont	Won	LD	Pct.
CPI	38	13	0	36.4
CONG	22	15	0	27.6
ML	12	11	0	13.6
PSP	12	7	0	13.5
JS	2	0	2	0.1
IND	(14) 13	1	3	8.8
	(100) 47	47	5	
Part:	80.3			

1965				
Party	Cont	Won	LD	Pct.
CONG	48	2	2	32.6
CPM	31	23	1	28.3
ML	18	8	2	13.1
SSP	10	10	0	12.4
CPI	25	1	23	4.2
JS	15	0	15	1.3
Swat	6	0	6	0.5
KC	3	0	3	0.3
IND	(21) 16	4	15	6.3
	(177) 48	48	67	
Part:	n/a			

1967				
Party	Cont	Won	LD	Pct.
CONG	48	0	3	32.8
CPM	24	23	0	29.8
ML	12	11	0	16.2
SSP	10	10	0	13.0
JS	19	0	19	2.3
KC	7	0	7	0.4
Swat	3	0	3	0.3
PSP	1	0	1	0.1
IND	(13) 13	4	9	5.1
	(137) 48	48	42	
Part:	68.1			

CANNANORE DISTRICT

Population: 1,780,294
Urban: 16.9 Rural: 83.1
Hindu: 69.5 Muslim: 23.5 Christian: 6.9

Party	Cont	Won	LD	Pct.
		1952		
CPI	4	4	0	28.5
CONG	8	1	0	28.1
KMPP	3	2	0	17.0
SP	6	0	5	10.8
ML	1	0	0	2.2
IND (8)	7	1	5	13.4
(30)	8	8	10	
Part: 71.2				

Party	Cont	Won	LD	Pct.
		1957		
CPI	10	7	0	42.7
CONG	11	1	0	30.9
PSP	6	2	1	16.1
IND (5)	5	2*	0	10.3
(32)	12	12	1	
Part: 61.4				
*Uncontested: IND (1)				

Party	Cont	Won	LD	Pct.
		1960		
CPI	10	2	0	39.1
CONG	7	6	0	29.2
PSP	4	3	0	20.1
IND (5)	4	1	1	11.6
(26)	12	12	1	
Part: 85.1				

Party	Cont	Won	LD	Pct.
		1965		
CONG	14	1	0	37.1
CPM	8	7	0	30.8
SSP	3	3	0	13.0
ML	4	2	1	10.0
CPI	7	0	7	2.6
JS	4	0	4	1.5
KC	1	0	1	0.2
IND (4)	3	1	2	4.8
(45)	14	14	15	
Part: n/a				

Party	Cont	Won	LD	Pct.
		1967		
CPM	8	7	0	33.6
CONG	14	0	2	31.6
SSP	3	3	0	13.4
ML	2	1	0	8.0
JS	3	0	3	1.0
KC	5	0	5	0.9
PSP	1	0	1	0.3
IND (4)	4	3	1	11.2
(40)	14	14	12	
Part: 73.6				

KOZHIKODE DISTRICT

Population: 2,617,189
Urban: 16.5 Rural: 83.5
Hindu: 53.0 Muslim: 42.7 Christian: 4.2

1952				
Party	Cont	Won	LD	Pct.
CONG	12	3	0	35.7
SP	9	3	5	21.0
ML	5	4	0	17.4
KMPP	4	2	1	10.3
CPI	5	0	1	10.1
IND	(5) 4	0	3	5.5
	(40) 12	12	10	
Part: 64.5				

1957				
Party	Cont	Won	LD	Pct.
CONG	20	8	0	38.9
CPI	12	3	2	17.1
PSP	6	2	1	9.8
ML	@	6	@	@
IND	(21) 16	1	1	34.2
	(59) 20	20	4	
Part: 60.4				

1960				
Party	Cont	Won	LD	Pct.
CONG	8	7	0	30.5
CPI	13	1	0	23.0
ML	8	8	0	22.4
PSP	4	4	0	11.2
JS	1	0	1	0.1
IND	(7) 7	0	0	12.8
	(41) 20	20	1	
Part: 80.2				

1965				
Party	Cont	Won	LD	Pct.
CONG	20	0	0	31.8
CPM	12	6	1	21.4
ML	10	6	0	18.5
SSP	5	5	0	15.3
CPI	7	0	7	1.3
JS	8	0	8	1.2
Swat	3	0	3	0.3
IND	(12) 9	3	8	10.2
	(77) 20	20	27	
Part: n/a				

1967				
Party	Cont	Won	LD	Pct.
CONG	20	0	0	34.1
ML	8	8	0	24.8
CPM	6	6	0	19.5
SSP	5	5	0	15.5
JS	11	0	11	2.9
Swat	1	0	1	0.3
KC	2	0	2	0.2
IND	(6) 6	1	5	2.7
	(59) 20	20	19	
Part: 70.8				

PALGHAT DISTRICT

Population: 1,776,566
Urban: 9.7 Rural: 90.3
Hindu: 70.1 Muslim: 28.0 Christian: 1.9

1952

Party	Cont	Won	LD	Pct.
CONG	12	3	0	29.9
CPI	4	2	0	14.9
KMPP	4	3	0	12.9
SP	8	1	4	11.3
ML	3	1	0	8.0
KSP	2	0	0	1.7
IND (16)	8	2	11	21.3
(49)	12	12	15	

Part: 49.9

1954

Party	Cont	Won	LD	Pct.
CONG	2	1	0	48.5
PSP	2	1	0	44.6
TTNC	1	0	1	2.8
IND (1)	1	0	1	4.1
(6)	2	2	2	

Part: 61.8

Note: The area polled in 1954
was then a part of
Travancore-Cochin and
became a part of
Palghat after the ex-
change of enclaves
with Trichur.

1957

Party	Cont	Won	LD	Pct.
CPI	14	10	0	40.8
CONG	15	3	0	36.4
PSP	3	0	0	7.1
RSP	1	0	1	0.4
ML	@	1	@	@
IND (11)	9	1	3	15.3
(44)	15	15	4	

Part: 51.3

1960

Party	Cont	Won	LD	Pct.
CPI	15	10	0	53.8
CONG	7	2	0	21.8
ML	4	3	0	13.2
PSP	4	0	0	10.8
JS	1	0	1	0.3
IND (2)	2	0	2	0.1
(33)	15	15	3	

Part: 77.6

1965

Party	Cont	Won	LD	Pct.
CPM	11	10	0	37.4
CONG	14	1	2	28.8
CPI	11	1	9	11.5
SSP	2	2	0	8.5
ML	4	0	1	7.9
Swat	3	0	3	1.9
JS	3	0	3	1.5
KC	2	0	2	1.4
IND (5)	4	0	5	1.1
(55)	14	14	25	

Part: n/a

1967

Party	Cont	Won	LD	Pct.
CPM	10	10	0	43.5
CONG	14	0	1	32.1
ML	2	2	0	11.3
SSP	2	2	0	8.2
JS	5	0	5	3.0
Swat	2	0	2	0.7
IND (3)	3	0	3	1.2
(38)	14	14	11	

Part: 58.3

TRAVANCORE-COCHIN

Population: 10,729,666
Urban: 15.4 Rural: 84.6
Hindu: 59.8 Christian: 30.9 Muslim: 9.2

1952

Party	Cont	Won	LD	Pct.
CONG	93	42*	3	37.8
SP	59	9*	27	13.8
RSP	10	6	1	3.8
KSP	8	1	1	2.1
Cochin	12	1	5	2.0
TTNC	5	1	1	1.8
Repub	7	0	2	1.8
CPI	@	22	@	@
IND (185)	82	14	115	36.9
(379)	96	96	155	

Part: 71.0
*Uncontested: CONG (3), SP (1)

1954

Party	Cont	Won	LD	Pct.
CONG	104	44	2	46.9
CPI	33	23	0	17.6
PSP	34	17	0	16.3
RSP	12	9	0	5.9
TTNC	6	4	0	2.9
JS	1	0	1	#
IND (43)	35	8	18	10.4
(233)	105	105	21	

Part: 74.2

1957

Party	Cont	Won	LD	Pct.
CONG	79	32	5	39.7
CPI	64	40	1	37.8
PSP	47	5	26	10.3
RSP	27	0	21	4.9
IND (37)	31	2	26	7.3
(254)	79	79	79	

Part: 71.3

1960

Party	Cont	Won	LD	Pct.
CPI	70	16	0	40.7
CONG	58	48	0	38.3
PSP	21	13	0	14.5
JS	1	0	1	#
IND (62)	47	2	49	6.5
(212)	79	79	50	

Part: 86.7

1965

Party	Cont	Won	LD	Pct.
CONG	85	34	4	34.2
KC	54	24	9	19.3
CPM	42	17	8	15.0
CPI	53	2	31	10.6
SSP	19	3	4	5.6
RSP	11	0	6	1.9
ML	3	3	0	1.7
Swat	6	1	5	0.8
PSP	8	0	8	0.6
DMK	1	0	1	0.1
RPI	3	0	3	0.1
FB	2	0	2	0.1
JS	1	0	1	#
IND (93)	56	1	72	9.9
(381)	85	85	154	

Part: n/a

1967

Party	Cont	Won	LD	Pct.
CONG	85	9	6	36.8
CPM	35	29	0	20.2
CPI	22	19	0	13.1
KC	54	5	31	11.4
SSP	11	9	0	6.0
RSP	6	6	0	4.2
ML	3	3	0	1.7
PSP	6	0	6	0.3
Swat	3	0	3	0.2
JS	5	0	5	0.1
IND (56)	46	5	46	6.0
(286)	85	85	97	

Part: 75.8

TRICHUR DISTRICT

Population: 1,639,862
Urban: 11.3 Rural: 88.7
Hindu: 63.1 Christian: 25.1 Muslim: 11.7

<table>
<tr><td colspan="5">1952</td><td colspan="5">1954</td></tr>
<tr><td>Party</td><td>Cont</td><td>Won</td><td>LD</td><td>Pct.</td><td>Party</td><td>Cont</td><td>Won</td><td>LD</td><td>Pct.</td></tr>
<tr><td>CONG</td><td>12</td><td>6</td><td>1</td><td>31.8</td><td>CONG</td><td>14</td><td>9</td><td>0</td><td>51.4</td></tr>
<tr><td>SP</td><td>13</td><td>1</td><td>5</td><td>21.9</td><td>CPI</td><td>7</td><td>3</td><td>0</td><td>24.7</td></tr>
<tr><td>Cochin</td><td>10</td><td>1</td><td>3</td><td>13.8</td><td>PSP</td><td>4</td><td>1</td><td>0</td><td>15.7</td></tr>
<tr><td>KSP</td><td>1</td><td>0</td><td>0</td><td>1.4</td><td>IND (3)</td><td>3</td><td>1</td><td>0</td><td>8.2</td></tr>
<tr><td>CPI</td><td>@</td><td>4</td><td>@</td><td>@</td><td>(28)</td><td>14</td><td>14</td><td>0</td><td></td></tr>
<tr><td>IND (18)</td><td>12</td><td>2</td><td>7</td><td>31.1</td><td colspan="5">Part: 72.6</td></tr>
<tr><td>(54)</td><td>14</td><td>14</td><td>·16</td><td></td><td colspan="5"></td></tr>
<tr><td colspan="5">Part: 57.4</td><td colspan="5"></td></tr>
</table>

<table>
<tr><td colspan="5">1957</td><td colspan="5">1960</td></tr>
<tr><td>Party</td><td>Cont</td><td>Won</td><td>LD</td><td>Pct.</td><td>Party</td><td>Cont</td><td>Won</td><td>LD</td><td>Pct.</td></tr>
<tr><td>CONG</td><td>12</td><td>3</td><td>0</td><td>44.0</td><td>CPI</td><td>11</td><td>1</td><td>0</td><td>43.2</td></tr>
<tr><td>CPI</td><td>8</td><td>6</td><td>0</td><td>32.1</td><td>CONG</td><td>9</td><td>9</td><td>0</td><td>36.6</td></tr>
<tr><td>PSP</td><td>7</td><td>1</td><td>4</td><td>14.6</td><td>PSP</td><td>3</td><td>2</td><td>0</td><td>16.1</td></tr>
<tr><td>IND (5)</td><td>5</td><td>2</td><td>2</td><td>9.3</td><td>JS</td><td>1</td><td>0</td><td>1</td><td>0.2</td></tr>
<tr><td>(32)</td><td>12</td><td>12</td><td>6</td><td></td><td>IND (7)</td><td>5</td><td>0</td><td>6</td><td>3.9</td></tr>
<tr><td colspan="5">Part: 68.7</td><td>(31)</td><td>12</td><td>12</td><td>7</td><td></td></tr>
<tr><td colspan="5"></td><td colspan="5">Part: 86.2</td></tr>
</table>

<table>
<tr><td colspan="5">1965</td><td colspan="5">1967</td></tr>
<tr><td>Party</td><td>Cont</td><td>Won</td><td>LD</td><td>Pct.</td><td>Party</td><td>Cont</td><td>Won</td><td>LD</td><td>Pct.</td></tr>
<tr><td>CONG</td><td>13</td><td>7</td><td>0</td><td>41.9</td><td>CONG</td><td>13</td><td>3</td><td>0</td><td>46.5</td></tr>
<tr><td>CPI</td><td>11</td><td>1</td><td>5</td><td>17.1</td><td>CPM</td><td>5</td><td>5</td><td>0</td><td>19.6</td></tr>
<tr><td>CPM</td><td>3</td><td>2</td><td>0</td><td>9.9</td><td>CPI</td><td>5</td><td>3</td><td>0</td><td>19.1</td></tr>
<tr><td>SSP</td><td>2</td><td>1</td><td>1</td><td>4.6</td><td>SSP</td><td>1</td><td>1</td><td>0</td><td>3.7</td></tr>
<tr><td>KC</td><td>5</td><td>0</td><td>5</td><td>3.3</td><td>ML</td><td>1</td><td>1</td><td>0</td><td>3.3</td></tr>
<tr><td>ML</td><td>1</td><td>1</td><td>0</td><td>3.2</td><td>KC</td><td>6</td><td>0</td><td>6</td><td>1.8</td></tr>
<tr><td>PSP</td><td>1</td><td>0</td><td>1</td><td>0.1</td><td>PSP</td><td>2</td><td>0</td><td>2</td><td>0.3</td></tr>
<tr><td>IND (20)</td><td>12</td><td>1</td><td>13</td><td>19.9</td><td>IND (6)</td><td>6</td><td>0</td><td>5</td><td>5.6</td></tr>
<tr><td>(56)</td><td>13</td><td>13</td><td>25</td><td></td><td>(39)</td><td>13</td><td>13</td><td>13</td><td></td></tr>
<tr><td colspan="5">Part: n/a</td><td colspan="5">Part: 77.0</td></tr>
</table>

ERNAKULAM DISTRICT

Population: 1,859,913
Urban: 21.3 Rural: 78.7
Hindu: 46.0 Christian: 42.6 Muslim: 11.3

1952

Party	Cont	Won	LD	Pct.
CONG	17	8	0	45.5
KSP	3	0	0	6.5
SP	7	0	5	6.3
Cochin	2	0	2	0.5
CPI	@	3	@	@
IND	(37) 17	6	23	41.2
	(66) 17	17	30	
Part: 72.3				

1954

Party	Cont	Won	LD	Pct.
CONG	18	15	0	56.4
PSP	4	1	0	14.0
CPI	5	1	0	10.9
RSP	1	0	0	0.9
IND	(11) 10	1	3	17.8
	(39) 18	18	3	
Part: 76.5				

1957

Party	Cont	Won	LD	Pct.
CONG	14	10	0	50.5
CPI	12	4	0	37.9
PSP	9	0	9	3.8
RSP	1	0	1	0.1
IND	(6) 5	0	4	7.7
	(42) 14	14	14	
Part: 71.4				

1960

Party	Cont	Won	LD	Pct.
CONG	14	13	0	57.7
CPI	10	1	0	31.5
IND	(14) 11	0	10	10.8
	(38) 14	14	10	
Part: 88.3				

1965

Party	Cont	Won	LD	Pct.
CONG	15	5	0	37.2
KC	9	5	2	17.3
CPM	6	3	0	16.1
ML	2	2	0	6.8
SSP	3	0	1	5.7
CPI	7	0	6	4.2
Swat	3	0	3	1.2
PSP	1	0	1	0.5
JS	1	0	1	0.3
IND	(20) 10	0	15	10.6
	(67) 15	15	29	
Part: n/a				

1967

Party	Cont	Won	LD	Pct.
CONG	15	2	1	37.6
CPM	8	8	0	26.6
KC	12	0	7	12.1
CPI	2	1	0	5.9
ML	1	1	0	3.8
SSP	1	0	0	1.8
JS	3	0	3	0.5
Swat	1	0	1	0.1
IND	(10) 8	3	6	11.6
	(53) 15	15	18	
Part: 78.5				

KOTTAYAM DISTRICT

Population: 1,732,880
Urban: 9.5 Rural: 90.5
Hindu: 48.9 Christian: 47.2 Muslim: 3.8

1952

Party	Cont	Won	LD	Pct.
CONG	16	11*	1	44.1
Repub	6	0	2	8.3
TTNC	2	1	0	7.9
SP	4	0	2	7.3
CPI	@	3	@	@
IND	(34) 13	1	24	32.4
	(62) 16	16	29	

Part: 76.4
*Uncontested: CONG (2)

1954

Party	Cont	Won	LD	Pct.
CONG	18	11	0	52.8
PSP	7	1	0	16.3
TTNC	2	2	0	8.4
CPI	3	3	0	8.3
RSP	1	0	0	1.6
IND	(8) 8	1	3	12.6
	(39) 18	18	3	

Part: 75.1

1957

Party	Cont	Won	LD	Pct.
CONG	13	9	0	47.5
CPI	8	3	0	29.2
PSP	4	1	2	6.3
RSP	4	0	4	2.6
IND	(11) 8	0	8	14.4
	(40) 13	13	14	

Part: 67.6

1960

Party	Cont	Won	LD	Pct.
CONG	11	10	0	43.8
CPI	12	2	0	40.6
PSP	2	1	0	12.1
IND	(7) 5	0	6	3.5
	(32) 13	13	6	

Part: 85.6

1965

Party	Cont	Won	LD	Pct.
KC	13	7	2	34.9
CONG	14	1	4	23.8
CPM	7	5	2	13.7
CPI	6	0	3	7.6
Swat	2	1	1	3.6
SSP	1	0	0	1.7
DMK	1	0	1	0.8
RSP	1	0	1	0.2
IND	(21) 11	0	16	13.7
	(66) 14	14	30	

Part: n/a

1967

Party	Cont	Won	LD	Pct.
KC	12	4	3	27.3
CONG	14	1	4	25.3
CPM	8	4	0	24.1
CPI	4	4	0	15.3
SSP	1	1	0	3.2
IND	(12) 10	0	11	4.8
	(51) 14	14	18	

Part: 72.9

ALLEPPEY DISTRICT

Population: 1,811,252
Urban: 17.1 Rural: 82.9
Hindu: 65.4 Christian: 28.5 Muslim: 6.1

		1952						1954		
Party	Cont	Won	LD	Pct.		Party	Cont	Won	LD	Pct.
CONG	16	6*	0	35.5		CONG	21	7	0	45.3
SP	9	1	6	10.7		CPI	8	7	0	22.9
RSP	2	2	0	6.0		PSP	8	4	0	18.7
KSP	1	0	0	1.4		RSP	3	2	0	7.3
CPI	@	4	@	@		IND	(8) 5	1	5	5.8
IND	(32) 14	3	20	46.4			(48) 21	21	5	
	(60) 16	16	26			Part: 76.4				

Part: 74.6
*Uncontested: CONG (1)

		1957						1960		
Party	Cont	Won	LD	Pct.		Party	Cont	Won	LD	Pct.
CPI	13	9	0	43.0		CONG	13	8	0	50.6
CONG	14	5	0	41.5		CPI	11	6	0	39.8
PSP	10	0	7	8.7		PSP	1	0	0	3.2
RSP	4	0	4	2.9		IND	(3) 3	0	0	6.4
IND	(3) 3	0	2	3.9			(28) 14	14	0	
	(44) 14	14	13			Part: 88.0				

Part: 72.8

		1965						1967		
Party	Cont	Won	LD	Pct.		Party	Cont	Won	LD	Pct.
KC	12	6	0	30.6		CONG	14	1	0	36.3
CONG	14	4	0	30.3		CPM	8	7	0	27.6
CPM	9	4	0	20.1		KC	11	1	6	13.6
CPI	10	0	9	6.9		SSP	4	3	0	12.8
SSP	3	0	1	4.2		CPI	1	1	0	4.1
RSP	2	0	2	0.3		Swat	1	0	1	0.7
IND	(14) 9	0	11	7.6		PSP	1	0	1	0.2
	(64) 14	14	23			JS	2	0	2	0.2
Part: n/a						IND	(12) 9	1	11	4.5
							(54) 14	14	21	

Part: 77.3

QUILON DISTRICT

Population: 1,941,228
Urban: 7.4 Rural: 92.6
Hindu: 64.1 Christian: 24.3 Muslim: 11.6

1952

Party	Cont	Won	LD	Pct.
CONG	19	8	0	35.8
SP	12	2	5	15.5
RSP	6	3	1	9.2
Repub	1	0	0	1.5
CPI	@	5	@	@
IND	(42) 16	1	29	38.0
	(80) 19	19	35	
Part:	74.8			

1954

Party	Cont	Won	LD	Pct.
CONG	16	1	0	39.9
CPI	5	5	0	24.6
RSP	6	6	0	21.4
PSP	3	3	0	8.5
IND	(6) 6	1	4	5.6
	(36) 16	16	4	
Part:	77.7			

1957

Party	Cont	Won	LD	Pct.
CPI	13	10	0	41.2
CONG	14	4	0	33.9
RSP	12	0	8	13.6
PSP	7	0	3	8.1
IND	(4) 3	0	3	3.2
	(50) 14	14	14	
Part:	77.7			

1960

Party	Cont	Won	LD	Pct.
CPI	14	4	0	42.9
CONG	8	6	0	28.6
PSP	6	3	0	19.1
IND	(20) 13	1	17	9.4
	(48) 14	14	17	
Part:	89.0			

1965

Party	Cont	Won	LD	Pct.
CONG	15	7	0	28.8
KC	11	6	0	24.3
CPI	10	1	1	18.7
CPM	10	0	6	9.8
RSP	5	0	1	7.9
SSP	3	1	1	4.1
FB	2	0	2	0.4
RPI	1	0	1	0.3
IND	(12) 9	0	11	5.7
	(69) 15	15	23	
Part:	n/a			

1967

Party	Cont	Won	LD	Pct.
CONG	15	0	1	31.5
CPI	8	8	0	26.4
RSP	5	5	0	19.4
KC	13	0	9	12.7
SSP	1	1	0	4.0
CPM	1	1	0	3.9
IND	(7) 6	0	6	2.1
	(50) 15	15	16	
Part:	77.8			

TRIVANDRUM DISTRICT

Population: 1,744,531
Urban: 25.7 Rural: 74.3
Hindu: 71.5 Christian: 17.7 Muslim: 10.8

1952				
Party	Cont	Won	LD	Pct.
CONG	13	3	1	31.6
SP	14	5*	4	26.0
RSP	2	1	0	5.9
KSP	3	1	1	4.7
TTNC	3	0	1	4.2
CPI	@	3	@	@
IND	(22) 10	1	12	27.6
	(57) 14	14	19	

Part: 72.7
*Uncontested: SP (1)

1954				
Party	Cont	Won	LD	Pct.
CONG	17	1	2	34.9
PSP	8	7	0	25.9
CPI	5	4	0	14.9
TTNC	4	2	0	8.6
RSP	1	1	0	2.6
JS	1	0	1	0.1
IND	(7) 6	3	3	13.0
	(43) 18	18	6	

Part: 66.4

1957				
Party	Cont	Won	LD	Pct.
CPI	10	8	1	38.3
PSP	10	3	1	25.2
CONG	12	1	5	21.4
RSP	6	0	4	7.9
IND	(8) 7	0	7	7.2
	(46) 12	12	18	

Part: 68.5

1960				
Party	Cont	Won	LD	Pct.
CPI	12	2	0	45.8
PSP	9	7	0	37.4
CONG	3	2	0	12.4
IND	(11) 10	1	10	4.4
	(35) 12	12	10	

Part: 82.7

1965				
Party	Cont	Won	LD	Pct.
CONG	14	10	0	44.2
CPM	7	3	0	20.1
SSP	7	1	0	13.8
CPI	9	0	7	8.3
KC	4	0	0	6.5
PSP	6	0	6	3.1
RSP	3	0	2	2.4
RPI	2	0	2	0.4
Swat	1	0	1	0.1
IND	(6) 5	0	6	1.1
	(59) 14	14	24	

Part: n/a

1967				
Party	Cont	Won	LD	Pct.
CONG	14	2	0	44.8
CPM	5	4	0	20.0
SSP	3	3	0	10.8
CPI	2	2	0	7.4
RSP	1	1	0	4.5
ML	1	1	0	3.6
PSP	3	0	3	1.4
Swat	1	0	1	0.1
IND	(9) 7	1	7	7.4
	(39) 14	14	11	

Part: 70.6

STATE SUMMARY

Population: 32,372,408
Urban: 14.3 Rural: 85.7
Hindu: 94.0 Muslim: 4.1 Jain: 0.8 Christian: 0.6 Buddhist: 0.4
Sikh: 0.1

Party	Cont	Won	LD	Pct.
	1952			
CONG	325	258*	7	46.6
SP	200	16*	138	8.8
KMPP	109	10	61	6.0
JS	127	6	68	5.7
RRP	84	7	46	4.9
HMS	47	13	6	4.2
SCF	15	0	10	0.9
CPI	22	0	19	0.6
FB(M)	5	0	1	0.6
FB(R)	10	0	8	0.4
KMM	11	0	7	0.2
BLC	2	0	2	0.1
KS	6	0	6	#
IND	(513)247	28*	402	21.0
	(1476)338	338	781	

Part: 36.9
*Uncontested: CONG (5), SP (1)
                IND (4)

Party	Cont	Won	LD	Pct.
	1957			
CONG	288	232*	6	49.8
PSP	154	12	58	13.2
JS	127	10	65	9.9
HMS	43	7	9	4.7
RRP	51	5	33	3.1
CPI	25	2	12	1.6
SCF	24	0	17	1.2
SP	@	6	@	@
IND	(317)197	14	204	16.5
	(1029)288	288	404	

Part: 36.8
*Uncontested: CONG (9)

Party	Cont	Won	LD	Pct.
	1962			
CONG	288	142*	12	38.5
JS	195	41	91	16.7
PSP	140	33	64	10.7
SP	86	14	55	4.7
RRP	75	10	46	3.8
HMS	50	6	31	3.2
CPI	42	1	34	2.0
RPI	33	0	27	1.3
Swat	43	2	39	1.2
FB	9	0	8	0.3
IND	(374)191	39	280	17.6
	(1335)288	288	687	

Part: 41.7
*Uncontested: CONG (3)

Party	Cont	Won	LD	Pct.
	1967			
CONG	296	167	25	40.7
JS	265	78	75	28.3
SSP	114	10	81	5.3
PSP	110	9	82	4.7
Swat	21	7	11	2.6
JC	33	2	22	1.5
CPI	33	1	30	1.1
RPI	38	0	36	0.8
CPM	9	0	9	0.2
IND	(634)232	22	570	14.8
	(1553)296	296	941	

Part: 49.7

MADHYA BHARAT AND BHOPAL

Population: 10,875,630
Urban: 21.2 Rural: 78.8
Hindu: 90.5 Muslim: 7.5 Jain: 1.3 Sikh: 0.3 Christian: 0.2
Buddhist: 0.2

Party	Cont	Won	LD	Pct.
1952				
CONG	128	100*	2	47.6
HMS	43	13	5	12.3
JS	52	4	20	9.2
SP	62	4	52	6.7
RRP	39	2	17	6.5
CPI	18	0	15	1.8
KMM	11	0	7	0.6
KMPP	8	0	8	0.4
IND (175)	91	7	136	14.9
(536)	130	130	262	

Part: 35.1
*Uncontested: CONG (2)

Party	Cont	Won	LD	Pct.
1957				
CONG	98	73*	0	46.8
JS	52	8	17	15.8
HMS	41	7	9	12.7
PSP	25	2	14	4.4
CPI	19	2	8	4.0
RRP	16	0	12	2.2
SCF	3	0	3	0.2
SP	3	@	1	@	@
IND (89)	64	5	58	13.9
(343)	98	98	121	

Part: 39.6
*Uncontested: CONG (2)

Party	Cont	Won	LD	Pct.
1962				
CONG	98	38	4	38.6
JS	70	26	29	21.3
HMS	42	6	23	8.1
SP	45	8	34	5.2
PSP	26	6	14	4.8
CPI	20	1	13	3.2
Swat	32	0	30	2.1
RRP	6	0	6	0.3
RPI	3	0	3	0.3
IND (119)	62	13	84	16.1
(461)	98	98	240	

Part: 46.2

Party	Cont	Won	LD	Pct.
1967				
JS	84	54	6	37.4
CONG	102	26	19	32.3
Swat	16	7	7	6.4
SSP	37	6	24	5.9
CPI	19	1	16	2.2
PSP	19	1	17	1.2
JC	5	0	2	0.7
RPI	12	0	12	0.6
CPM	4	0	4	0.4
IND (254)	75	7	239	12.9
(552)	102	102	346	

Part: 54.6

MORENA DISTRICT

Population: 783,348
Urban: 8.6 Rural: 91.4
Hindu: 96.0 Muslim: 3.5 Jain: 0.4 Christian: #

Party	Cont	Won	LD	Pct.
1952				
CONG	9	8	0	39.9
RRP	4	1	1	14.3
SP	9	0	8	12.0
HMS	3	0	1	8.2
KMPP	1	0	1	0.5
JS	1	0	1	0.4
IND	(19) 8	0	16	24.7
	(46) 9	9	28	
Part: 28.8				

Party	Cont	Won	LD	Pct.
1957				
CONG	7	5	0	38.7
HMS	5	1	2	20.3
PSP	3	0	1	9.1
RRP	4	0	2	9.1
CPI	3	0	1	7.1
SCF	1	0	1	1.0
SP	@	1	@	@
IND	(7) 6	0	6	14.7
	(30) 7	7	13	
Part: 39.0				

Party	Cont	Won	LD	Pct.
1962				
CONG	7	0	3	23.6
PSP	4	3	1	17.7
CPI	4	0	1	8.4
HMS	2	1	1	7.5
SP	7	0	6	7.2
JS	5	0	4	5.9
Swat	4	0	4	1.9
RRP	2	0	2	0.7
IND	(17) 7	3	12	27.1
	(52) 7	7	34	
Part: 42.8				

Party	Cont	Won	LD	Pct.
1967				
CONG	7	0	5	17.9
JS	2	2	0	10.7
SSP	6	0	6	6.6
CPI	5	0	5	6.3
JC	1	0	0	3.6
PSP	2	0	2	1.8
RPI	3	0	3	1.7
IND	(47) 7	5	41	51.4
	(73) 7	7	62	
Part: 50.3				

BHIND DISTRICT

Population: 641,169
Urban: 7.4 Rural: 92.6
Hindu: 95.2 Muslim: 3.0 Jain: 1.5 Sikh: 0.3 Christian: #

	1952			
Party	Cont	Won	LD	Pct.
CONG	7	6	0	43.9
SP	7	0	5	16.1
RRP	5	1	2	13.3
JS	3	0	2	4.8
CPI	2	0	2	2.4
IND	(7) 6	0	3	19.5
	(31) 7	7	14	
Part:	34.7			

	1957			
Party	Cont	Won	LD	Pct.
CONG	6	4	0	37.1
PSP	5	2	0	26.8
JS	4	0	2	12.0
RRP	2	0	1	4.8
HMS	4	0	4	3.7
CPI	1	0	0	2.1
IND	(6) 5	0	4	13.5
	(28) 6	6	11	
Part:	41.2			

	1962			
Party	Cont	Won	LD	Pct.
CONG	6	4	0	37.8
PSP	6	1	1	29.3
JS	4	0	4	5.8
Swat	2	0	2	4.2
RRP	4	0	4	3.5
RPI	2	0	2	3.1
CPI	1	0	1	2.7
HMS	3	0	3	1.1
SP	1	0	1	0.6
IND	(11) 5	1	10	11.9
	(40) 6	6	28	
Part:	51.1			

	1967			
Party	Cont	Won	LD	Pct.
JS	4	4	0	25.4
CONG	6	0	3	19.8
SSP	2	1	1	11.3
PSP	2	1	0	8.7
RPI	3	0	3	3.3
CPI	2	0	2	2.0
CPM	1	0	1	0.3
IND	(27) 6	0	25	29.2
	(47) 6	6	35	
Part:	58.1			

GWALIOR DISTRICT

Population: 657,876
Urban: 49.3 Rural: 50.7
Hindu: 91.9 Muslim: 6.0 Jain: 1.0 Sikh: 0.9 Christian: #

1952						1957				
Party	Cont	Won	LD	Pct.		Party	Cont	Won	LD	Pct.
CONG	5	3	0	28.7		CONG	6	5	0	41.9
HMS	5	2	1	27.2		HMS	6	0	0	28.1
SP	5	0	5	8.8		PSP	3	0	1	13.8
CPI	2	0	1	5.7		CPI	2	1	0	8.4
JS	1	0	1	2.8		JS	2	0	2	4.2
KMPP	1	0	1	1.7		IND	(5) 3	0	5	3.6
IND	(24) 5	0	23	25.1			(24) 6	6	8	
	(43) 5	5	32			Part: 38.4				
Part: 36.6										

1962						1967				
Party	Cont	Won	LD	Pct.		Party	Cont	Won	LD	Pct.
CONG	6	6	0	41.2		JS	6	6	0	51.3
CPI	3	0	1	11.3		CONG	6	0	3	16.0
HMS	5	0	3	10.7		CPI	2	0	1	7.1
JS	4	0	3	9.0		RPI	4	0	4	4.2
PSP	6	0	5	6.8		PSP	5	0	5	1.8
Swat	4	0	4	3.8		CPM	1	0	1	1.8
SP	4	0	4	1.2		SSP	1	0	1	0.1
IND	(10) 6	0	8	16.0		IND	(28) 6	0	27	17.7
	(42) 6	6	28				(53) 6	6	42	
Part: 53.9						Part: 56.7				

SHIVPURI DISTRICT

Population: 557,954
Urban: 7.0 Rural: 93.0
Hindu: 96.9 Muslim: 2.1 Jain: 0.9 Sikh: 0.1 Christian: #

1952

Party	Cont	Won	LD	Pct.
CONG	6	3	0	41.0
HMS	5	3	0	35.4
RRP	2	0	2	3.6
KMPP	3	0	3	1.9
SP	1	0	1	0.7
IND	(11) 6	0	10	17.4
	(28) 6	6	16	

Part: 32.6

1957

Party	Cont	Won	LD	Pct.
CONG	5	3	0	40.9
HMS	5	1	0	33.2
JS	3	0	3	5.2
IND	(3) 3	1	1	20.7
	(16) 5	5	4	

Part: 36.2

1962

Party	Cont	Won	LD	Pct.
CONG	5	4	0	40.1
HMS	4	1	1	26.0
JS	3	0	2	8.6
Swat	2	0	1	4.6
SP	4	0	4	3.5
IND	(9) 4	0	7	17.2
	(27) 5	5	15	

Part: 37.6

1967

Party	Cont	Won	LD	Pct.
JS	3	3	0	44.8
Swat	2	2	0	32.1
CONG	5	0	4	13.2
SSP	3	0	3	2.0
IND	(16) 5	0	16	7.9
	(29) 5	5	23	

Part: 56.3

GUNA DISTRICT

Population: 595,825
Urban: 14.6 Rural: 87.4
Hindu: 94.1 Muslim: 3.7 Jain: 1.8 Sikh: 0.3 Christian: #

1952

Party	Cont	Won	LD	Pct.
CONG	6	4	1	38.1
HMS	4	1	0	25.6
SP	2	0	2	1.9
JS	1	0	1	1.4
IND	(10) 5	1	7	33.0
	(23) 6	6	11	

Part: 34.9

1957

Party	Cont	Won	LD	Pct.
CONG	5	4	0	44.7
HMS	4	1	0	26.4
CPI	3	0	3	7.9
PSP	1	0	0	4.2
JS	1	0	1	2.8
IND	(6) 3	0	4	14.0
	(20) 5	5	8	

Part: 35.0

1962

Party	Cont	Won	LD	Pct.
CONG	5	2	0	33.8
HMS	5	1	3	17.2
PSP	2	1	1	11.6
JS	4	0	3	10.5
CPI	1	0	1	2.3
IND	(10) 4	1	8	24.6
	(27) 5	5	16	

Part: 43.4

1967

Party	Cont	Won	LD	Pct.
Swat	5	5	0	72.8
CONG	5	0	3	17.6
PSP	2	0	2	2.1
IND	(15) 5	0	15	7.5
	(27) 5	5	20	

Part: 56.0

VIDISHA DISTRICT

Population: 489,213
Urban: 13.1 Rural: 86.9
Hindu: 89.3 Muslim: 9.1 Jain: 1.5 Sikh: 0.1 Christian: #

1952

Party	Cont	Won	LD	Pct.
HMS	5	4	0	45.3
CONG	5	1	0	42.6
SP	2	0	2	2.7
RRP	2	0	2	2.3
CPI	2	0	2	2.1
JS	1	0	1	0.7
IND	(5) 3	0	5	4.3
	(22) 5	5	12	

Part: 32.0

1957

Party	Cont	Won	LD	Pct.
CONG	4	3	0	53.5
HMS	4	1	0	38.1
RRP	3	0	3	2.2
IND	(4) 3	0	4	6.2
	(15) 4	4	7	

Part: 41.9

1962

Party	Cont	Won	LD	Pct.
CONG	4	2	0	46.7
HMS	4	2	0	40.5
CPI	2	0	2	1.8
JS	3	0	3	1.5
SP	2	0	2	0.7
PSP	1	0	1	0.5
Swat	1	0	1	0.3
IND	(3) 3	0	2	8.0
	(20) 4	4	11	

Part: 45.1

1967

Party	Cont	Won	LD	Pct.
JS	4	4	0	64.8
CONG	4	0	0	23.5
SSP	1	0	1	0.2
IND	(16) 4	0	16	11.5
	(25) 4	4	17	

Part: 56.8

RAJGARH DISTRICT

Population: 516,871
Urban: 9.5 Rural: 90.5
Hindu: 94.7 Muslim: 5.1 Jain: 0.2 Christian: #

1952

Party	Cont	Won	LD	Pct.
CONG	6	4	1	47.1
RRP	6	0	3	16.9
SP	3	0	3	4.3
JS	1	0	0	2.5
IND	(10) 4	2	3	29.2
	(26) 6	6	10	

Part: 28.7

1957

Party	Cont	Won	LD	Pct.
CONG	5	3	0	47.3
CPI	2	0	0	13.0
JS	2	0	1	10.6
PSP	1	0	1	2.3
HMS	1	0	1	1.5
IND	(7) 3	2	3	25.3
	(18) 5	5	6	

Part: 30.9

1962

Party	Cont	Won	LD	Pct.
CONG	5	0	1	25.0
JS	2	1	1	11.0
PSP	1	1	0	5.3
CPI	3	0	3	3.2
SP	1	0	1	2.1
IND	(14) 5	3	9	53.4
	(26) 5	5	15	

Part: 35.8

1967

Party	Cont	Won	LD	Pct.
CONG	5	2	1	30.6
JS	5	2	2	26.5
JC	1	0	0	4.1
CPI	2	0	2	2.6
PSP	1	0	1	2.5
Swat	1	0	1	0.9
IND	(33) 4	1	32	32.8
	(48) 5	5	39	

Part: 41.9

SHAJAPUR DISTRICT

Population: 526,135
Urban: 10.1 Rural: 89.9
Hindu: 89.9 Muslim: 8.7 Jain: 1.4 Christian: #

1952

Party	Cont	Won	LD	Pct.
CONG	5	5	0	41.4
RRP	4	0	0	21.6
JS	5	0	2	20.9
KMPP	1	0	1	1.5
SP	2	0	2	1.3
HMS	1	0	1	0.2
IND (5)	5	0	4	13.1
(23)	5	5	10	

Part: 34.3

1957

Party	Cont	Won	LD	Pct.
CONG	5	2	0	45.3
JS	5	3	1	38.4
RRP	3	0	3	5.0
HMS	2	0	2	4.3
IND (4)	3	0	3	7.0
(19)	5	5	9	

Part: 46.3

1962

Party	Cont	Won	LD	Pct.
JS	5	4	0	45.5
CONG	5	1	0	38.7
SP	3	0	2	7.8
Swat	3	0	3	4.8
IND (2)	1	0	2	3.2
(18)	5	5	7	

Part: 48.8

1967

Party	Cont	Won	LD	Pct.
JS	5	5	0	51.2
CONG	5	0	0	39.4
SSP	3	0	2	7.1
IND (4)	3	0	4	2.3
(17)	5	5	6	

Part: 60.9

UJJAIN DISTRICT

Population: 661,720
Urban: 32.4 Rural: 67.6
Hindu: 87.5 Muslim: 10.1 Jain: 1.7 Sikh: 0.4 Christian: 0.2
Buddhist: 0.1

1952

Party	Cont	Won	LD	Pct.
CONG	7	7	0	55.8
JS	6	0	2	15.3
RRP	5	0	4	8.9
CPI	4	0	3	8.0
SP	4	0	4	3.7
IND (14)	5	0	14	8.3
(40)	7	7	27	

Part: 34.6

1957

Party	Cont	Won	LD	Pct.
CONG	6	5	0	50.6
JS	4	0	1	14.5
RRP	2	0	1	10.3
HMS	1	1	0	7.1
CPI	2	0	1	4.7
PSP	3	0	3	0.8
SCF	1	0	1	0.3
IND (4)	3	0	2	11.7
(23)	6	6	9	

Part: 40.5

1962

Party	Cont	Won	LD	Pct.
CONG	6	3	0	40.9
JS	4	1	1	22.7
SP	1	1	0	7.6
Swat	2	0	2	2.1
HMS	2	0	2	1.8
IND (8)	4	1	4	24.9
(23)	6	6	9	

Part: 52.3

1967

Party	Cont	Won	LD	Pct.
JS	5	5	0	45.9
CONG	6	0	0	31.2
SSP	3	1	2	12.6
CPM	1	0	1	2.9
CPI	2	0	2	1.9
RPI	2	0	2	0.7
IND (13)	5	0	13	4.8
(32)	6	6	20	

Part: 64.9

MADHYA PRADESH

INDORE DISTRICT

Population: 753,594
Urban: 60.0 Rural: 40.0
Hindu: 85.5 Muslim: 10.4 Jain: 2.5 Sikh: 0.7 Christian: 0.7
Buddhist: 0.2

1952				
Party	Cont	Won	LD	Pct.
CONG	7	7	0	59.5
JS	4	0	1	11.2
HMS	3	0	1	10.3
SP	6	0	5	7.4
CPI	5	0	5	7.1
RRP	1	0	1	0.1
KMPP	1	0	1	#
IND	(9) 5	0	9	4.4
	(36) 7	7	23	
Part: 42.9				

1957				
Party	Cont	Won	LD	Pct.
CONG	7	6	0	60.8
JS	4	0	1	11.8
PSP	1	0	1	1.4
IND	(6) 5	1	2	26.0
	(18) 7	7	4	
Part: 41.3				

1962				
Party	Cont	Won	LD	Pct.
CONG	7	6	0	47.5
JS	4	0	1	11.4
SP	6	1	5	6.7
HMS	4	0	4	1.0
RPI	1	0	1	0.8
IND	(12) 5	0	6	32.6
	(34) 7	7	17	
Part: 57.7				

1967				
Party	Cont	Won	LD	Pct.
CONG	7	3	0	38.6
JS	7	1	2	24.2
SSP	4	2	0	18.9
PSP	2	0	2	0.7
Swat	2	0	2	0.3
IND	(8) 4	1	6	17.3
	(30) 7	7	12	
Part: 61.1				

DEWAS DISTRICT

Population: 446,901
Urban: 15.1 Rural: 84.9
Hindu: 89.8 Muslim: 9.1 Jain: 0.7 Sikh: 0.2 Christian: 0.1

1952

Party	Cont	Won	LD	Pct.
CONG	5	4	0	48.4
HMS	3	1	0	19.4
SP	4	0	4	8.3
JS	1	0	0	7.7
RRP	1	0	0	3.2
IND (7)	4	0	6	13.0
(21)	5	5	10	

Part: 40.3

1957

Party	Cont	Won	LD	Pct.
CONG	4	3	0	45.2
JS	3	1	0	36.0
PSP	4	0	4	10.6
HMS	1	0	0	4.7
IND (2)	2	0	2	3.5
(14)	4	4	6	

Part: 44.4

1962

Party	Cont	Won	LD	Pct.
CONG	4	1	0	39.2
JS	3	2	0	38.3
PSP	2	0	1	5.9
Swat	1	0	1	2.5
CPI	1	0	1	1.3
IND (4)	3	1	3	12.8
(15)	4	4	6	

Part: 50.8

1967

Party	Cont	Won	LD	Pct.
JS	4	3	0	46.4
CONG	4	1	0	43.1
PSP	1	0	1	2.0
JC	1	0	1	0.8
CPM	1	0	1	0.3
IND (4)	3	0	3	7.4
(15)	4	4	6	

Part: 60.5

NIMAR (KHARGONE) DISTRICT

Population: 990,464
Urban: 13.9 Rural: 86.1
Hindu: 93.4 Muslim: 5.6 Jain: 0.5 Sikh: 0.3 Christian: 0.1
Buddhist: 0.1

1952

Party	Cont	Won	LD	Pct.
CONG	9	6	0	55.5
JS	7	3	0	29.5
SP	1	0	0	2.4
IND	(9) 6	0	5	12.6
	(26) 9	9	5	

Part: 31.3

1957

Party	Cont	Won	LD	Pct.
CONG	8	7	0	48.8
JS	8	1	1	37.7
IND	(7) 7	0	4	13.5
	(23) 8	8	5	

Part: 37.6

1962

Party	Cont	Won	LD	Pct.
JS	7	7	0	48.9
CONG	8	0	0	37.6
SP	5	0	5	4.0
IND	(2) 2	1	1	9.5
	(22) 8	8	6	

Part: 42.5

1967

Party	Cont	Won	LD	Pct.
CONG	9	7	0	53.2
JS	9	2	0	42.5
SSP	2	0	2	2.6
IND	(3) 3	0	3	1.7
	(23) 9	9	5	

Part: 47.9

DHAR DISTRICT

Population: 643,744
Urban: 10.3 Rural: 89.7
Hindu: 93.9 Muslim: 4.8 Jain: 1.2 Sikh: 0.1 Christian: #

1952

Party	Cont	Won	LD	Pct.
CONG	6	5	0	48.1
HMS	3	1	0	31.5
JS	3	0	0	11.3
SP	3	0	3	4.9
KMPP	1	0	1	1.1
IND	(3) 2	0	3	3.1
	(19) 6	6	7	
Part: 41.1				

1957

Party	Cont	Won	LD	Pct.
CONG	6	4	0	53.4
HMS	2	2	0	18.8
JS	4	0	0	18.7
CPI	1	0	1	1.6
IND	(6) 4	0	6	7.5
	(19) 6	6	7	
Part: 43.9				

1962

Party	Cont	Won	LD	Pct.
CONG	6	2	0	43.2
JS	4	4	0	32.0
HMS	3	0	1	14.4
SP	4	0	3	5.9
Swat	2	0	2	1.2
IND	(3) 2	0	3	3.3
	(22) 6	6	9	
Part: 44.1				

1967

Party	Cont	Won	LD	Pct.
CONG	6	3	0	45.2
JS	6	3	0	44.1
SSP	4	0	4	4.4
CPI	1	0	1	0.8
IND	(2) 2	0	1	5.5
	(19) 6	6	6	
Part: 51.6				

MADHYA PRADESH

JHABUA DISTRICT

Population: 514,384
Urban: 6.9 Rural: 93.1
Hindu: 96.1 Muslim: 2.0 Jain: 1.0 Christian: 0.9

1952

Party	Cont	Won	LD	Pct.
SP	4	4	0	54.4
CONG	4	0	0	39.7
RRP	2	0	2	5.9
(10)	4	4	2	

Part: 38.2

1957

Party	Cont	Won	LD	Pct.
CONG	4	3	0	49.5
PSP	2	0	1	5.4
SP	@	1	@	@
IND (7)	4	0	3	45.1
(13)	4	4	4	

Part: 33.1

1962

Party	Cont	Won	LD	Pct.
SP	4	4	0	52.9
CONG	4	0	0	27.3
Swat	3	0	2	8.5
JS	3	0	3	7.2
PSP	1	0	1	0.1
IND (1)	1	0	0	4.0
(16)	4	4	6	

Part: 31.4

1967

Party	Cont	Won	LD	Pct.
CONG	5	3	0	41.1
SSP	5	2	1	33.3
Swat	5	0	3	16.7
JS	2	0	1	6.5
IND (1)	1	0	1	2.4
(18)	5	5	6	

Part: 38.0

RATLAM DISTRICT

Population: 483,521
Urban: 28.6 Rural: 71.4
Hindu: 86.4 Muslim: 9.8 Jain: 3.1 Christian: 0.5 Sikh: 0.1

1952

Party	Cont	Won	LD	Pct.
CONG	5	5*	0	58.7
JS	2	0	1	8.5
RRP	1	0	0	6.9
CPI	2	0	1	5.0
HMS	1	0	0	3.9
SP	2	0	2	1.6
IND	(7) 4	0	8	15.4
	(20) 5	5	12	

Part: 38.5
*Uncontested: CONG (1)

1957

Party	Cont	Won	LD	Pct.
CONG	4	4*	0	58.2
CPI	1	0	0	10.1
JS	2	0	1	7.7
RRP	2	0	2	5.1
IND	(2) 2	0	1	18.9
	(11) 4	4	4	

Part: 37.8
*Uncontested: CONG (1)

1962

Party	Cont	Won	LD	Pct.
CONG	4	1	0	39.6
JS	1	1	0	14.1
SP	2	1	1	11.4
Swat	3	0	3	5.6
CPI	1	0	1	4.9
HMS	1	0	1	0.4
IND	(5) 3	1	3	24.0
	(17) 4	4	9	

Part: 44.4

1967

Party	Cont	Won	LD	Pct.
CONG	4	3	0	46.0
JS	4	1	1	36.2
SSP	2	0	0	13.0
Swat	1	0	1	2.4
IND	(4) 2	0	4	2.4
	(15) 4	4	6	

Part: 53.3

MANDSAUR DISTRICT

Population: 752,085
Urban: 21.2 Rural: 78.8
Hindu: 89.5 Muslim: 7.8 Jain: 2.4 Sikh: 0.2 Christian: 0.1

1952

Party	Cont	Won	LD	Pct.
CONG	8	7	0	53.9
JS	7	1	2	19.4
RRP	6	0	0	19.4
SP	5	0	5	3.3
CPI	1	0	1	0.4
HMS	1	0	1	0.3
IND	(3) 3	0	2	3.3
	(31) 8	8	11	

Part: 37.0

1957

Party	Cont	Won	LD	Pct.
CONG	7	4	0	50.1
JS	7	3	2	38.1
HMS	1	0	0	2.2
PSP	1	0	1	0.3
IND	(4) 3	0	2	9.3
	(20) 7	7	5	

Part: 41.2

1962

Party	Cont	Won	LD	Pct.
JS	7	6	0	52.0
CONG	7	1	0	43.0
Swat	4	0	4	2.2
PSP	1	0	1	0.2
IND	(3) 3	0	3	2.6
	(22) 7	7	8	

Part: 54.7

1967

Party	Cont	Won	LD	Pct.
JS	7	6	0	52.0
CONG	7	1	0	41.1
JC	2	0	1	4.2
IND	(7) 5	0	7	2.7
	(23) 7	7	8	

Part: 61.0

SEHORE DISTRICT

Population: 754,684
Urban: 36.0 Rural: 64.0
Hindu: 81.6 Muslim: 16.7 Jain: 0.8 Sikh: 0.4 Christian: 0.3
Buddhist: 0.2

1952

Party	Cont	Won	LD	Pct.
CONG	17	16*	0	53.3
HMS	6	1	0	16.2
KMM	7	0	4	6.7
JS	5	0	3	5.8
SP	2	0	1	1.2
IND	(17) 12	1	11	16.8
	(54) 18	18	19	

Part: 39.2
*Uncontested: CONG (1)

1957

Party	Cont	Won	LD	Pct.
CONG	6	5	0	39.6
JS	3	0	1	17.7
HMS	3	0	0	16.5
CPI	4	1	2	13.7
SCF	1	0	1	0.7
PSP	1	0	1	0.2
IND	(6) 4	0	4	11.6
	(24) 6	6	9	

Part: 42.8

1962

Party	Cont	Won	LD	Pct.
CONG	6	3	0	36.0
HMS	6	1	2	24.5
JS	4	0	2	16.2
CPI	4	1	2	15.5
PSP	2	0	2	0.6
IND	(3) 2	1	2	7.2
	(25) 6	6	10	

Part: 47.3

1967

Party	Cont	Won	LD	Pct.
JS	7	5	0	47.8
CONG	7	1	0	31.7
CPI	5	1	3	12.2
PSP	1	0	1	0.2
IND	(18) 6	0	18	8.1
	(38) 7	7	22	

Part: 54.5

MADHYA PRADESH

RAISEN DISTRICT

Population: 411,426
Urban: 5.3 Rural: 94.7
Hindu: 90.4 Muslim: 8.2 Jain: 1.0 Sikh: 0.2 Christian: 0.1

1952

Party	Cont	Won	LD	Pct.
CONG	11	9	0	49.8
HMS	3	0	0	10.4
JS	4	0	3	3.4
KMM	4	0	3	3.3
IND	(15) 8	3	7	33.1
	(37) 12	12	13	

Part: 36.6

1957

Party	Cont	Won	LD	Pct.
CONG	3	3*	0	55.1
HMS	2	0	0	20.6
IND	(3) 1	0	2	24.3
	(8) 3	3	2	

Part: 42.2
*Uncontested: CONG (1)

1962

Party	Cont	Won	LD	Pct.
CONG	3	2	0	46.7
JS	3	0	2	19.2
HMS	3	0	2	12.2
SP	1	1	0	12.1
Swat	1	0	1	0.8
IND	(2) 2	0	1	9.0
	(13) 3	3	6	

Part: 36.3

1967

Party	Cont	Won	LD	Pct.
JS	4	2	0	42.5
CONG	4	2	0	41.3
PSP	3	0	3	2.3
SSP	1	0	1	0.4
IND	(8) 4	0	7	13.5
	(20) 4	4	11	

Part: 49.6

VINDHYA PRADESH

Population: 4,451,509
Urban: 6.6 Rural: 93.4
Hindu: 97.1 Muslim: 2.4 Jain: 0.3 Christian: #

1952

Party	Cont	Won	LD	Pct.
CONG	56	40	2	39.6
SP	46	11*	17	18.8
KMPP	48	3	24	15.9
JS	33	2	16	9.9
RRP	17	2	12	4.5
HMS	3	0	1	1.1
SCF	1	0	0	0.6
KS	6	0	6	0.4
IND (43)	30	2	29	9.2
(253)	60	60	107	

Part: 28.4
*Uncontested: SP (1)

1957

Party	Cont	Won	LD	Pct.
CONG	39	26	5	40.2
PSP	30	3	18	14.0
JS	25	2	14	12.1
RRP	17	1	9	6.4
HMS	2	0	0	1.5
CPI	1	0	0	0.5
SP	@	3	@	@
IND (70)	33	4	42	25.3
(184)	39	39	88	

Part: 30.5

1962

Party	Cont	Won	LD	Pct.
CONG	39	18	3	37.1
SP	25	5	10	14.5
PSP	28	7	18	13.5
JS	28	5	16	12.6
RRP	9	0	7	2.4
CPI	6	0	5	1.3
HMS	2	0	2	0.1
Swat	1	0	1	0.1
IND (43)	19	4	36	18.4
(181)	39	39	98	

Part: 39.8

1967

Party	Cont	Won	LD	Pct.
CONG	40	30	1	45.3
JS	39	1	24	17.4
PSP	27	4	17	10.8
SSP	22	0	15	8.4
JC	10	1	9	2.2
RPI	2	0	2	0.4
CPI	3	0	3	0.3
CPM	2	0	2	0.1
IND (77)	31	4	69	15.1
(222)	40	40	142	

Part: 48.5

MADHYA PRADESH

DATIA DISTRICT

Population: 200,467
Urban: 14.7 Rural: 85.3
Hindu: 96.9 Muslim: 3.3 Jain: 0.2 Sikh: 0.2 Christian: #

		1952		
Party	Cont	Won	LD	Pct.
CONG	3	3	0	40.0
HMS	3	0	1	18.5
KMPP	1	0	0	12.0
SCF	1	0	0	9.7
JS	2	0	1	9.5
IND (2)	2	0	1	10.3
(12)	3	3	3	
Part: 31.9				

		1957		
Party	Cont	Won	LD	Pct.
CONG	2	2	0	53.6
HMS	2	0	0	37.6
PSP	1	0	1	2.3
JS	1	0	1	2.1
IND (2)	2	0	2	4.4
(8)	2	2	4	
Part: 37.4				

		1962		
Party	Cont	Won	LD	Pct.
CONG	2	1	0	39.5
PSP	2	0	2	2.3
Swat	1	0	1	1.4
IND (9)	2	1	7	56.8
(14)	2	2	10	
Part: 46.5				

		1967		
Party	Cont	Won	LD	Pct.
CONG	2	0	0	29.3
JC	1	1	0	16.8
RPI	2	0	2	8.1
JS	1	0	1	1.1
IND (6)	2	1	4	44.7
(12)	2	2	7	
Part: 56.1				

TIKAMGARH DISTRICT

Population: 455,662
Urban: 4.5 Rural: 95.5
Hindu: 96.4 Muslim: 2.2 Jain: 1.3 Christian: #

Party		Cont	Won	LD	Pct.
CONG		5	5	0	46.6
SP		7	1*	2	29.3
KMPP		6	1	4	19.5
JS		2	0	2	3.6
IND	(1)	1	0	1	1.0
	(21)	7	7	9	

Part: 36.6
*Uncontested: SP (1),

Party		Cont	Won	LD	Pct.
CONG		4	3	0	45.3
PSP		3	1	1	38.0
JS		2	0	2	4.2
CPI		1	0	0	3.3
IND	(3)	2	0	1	9.2
	(13)	4	4	4	

Part: 41.8

1962

Party		Cont	Won	LD	Pct.
PSP		2	2	0	26.1
CONG		4	0	2	22.5
CPI		1	0	1	0.8
IND	(3)	2	2	1	50.6
	(10)	4	4	4	

Part: 53.7

1967

Party		Cont	Won	LD	Pct.
CONG		4	4	0	53.3
PSP		3	0	0	23.6
JS		4	0	4	6.0
JC		2	0	2	4.7
CPM		1	0	1	0.7
IND	(7)	3	0	7	11.7
	(21)	4	4	14	

Part: 55.4

CHHATARPUR DISTRICT

Population: 587,373
Urban: 9.6 Rural: 90.4
Hindu: 96.4 Muslim: 2.7 Jain: 0.7 Sikh: 0.1 Christian: 0.1

Party	Cont	Won	LD	Pct.
CONG	7	7	0	48.6
JS	7	0	2	19.9
KMPP	7	0	5	15.8
SP	2	0	2	3.8
IND (5)	3	0	3	11.9
(28)	7	7	12	

Part: 27.7

1952

Party	Cont	Won	LD	Pct.
CONG	5	5	0	51.0
JS	4	0	0	28.7
PSP	3	0	0	10.5
IND (3)	2	0	2	9.8
(15)	5	5	2	

Part: 30.2

1957

Party	Cont	Won	LD	Pct.
CONG	5	1	1	34.1
JS	3	2	1	22.0
PSP	4	1	2	19.2
IND (2)	1	1	1	24.7
(14)	5	5	5	

Part: 42.6

1962

Party	Cont	Won	LD	Pct.
CONG	5	3	1	33.1
JS	5	0	3	18.5
PSP	3	0	3	4.1
JC	4	0	4	3.8
IND (10)	5	2	7	40.5
(27)	5	5	18	

Part: 45.3

1967

PANNA DISTRICT

Population: 331,257
Urban: 5.1 Rural: 94.9
Hindu: 96.5 Muslim: 2.8 Jain: 0.6 Christian: #

1952						1957			
Party	Cont	Won	LD	Pct.	Party	Cont	Won	LD	Pct.
CONG	5	5	0	62.9	CONG	3	2	0	47.4
JS	4	0	1	17.8	JS	3	0	0	25.2
KMPP	3	0	1	13.1	PSP	2	0	1	9.3
IND	(4) 3	0	4	6.2	IND	(2) 2	1	1	18.1
	(16) 5	5	6			(10) 3	3	2	
Part: 24.9					Part: 29.3				

1962						1967			
Party	Cont	Won	LD	Pct.	Party	Cont	Won	LD	Pct.
CONG	3	2	0	51.9	CONG	3	3	0	48.7
JS	3	1	0	30.3	JS	3	0	0	29.6
CPI	1	0	0	9.2	JC	2	0	2	2.4
SP	1	0	0	4.7	IND	(7) 3	0	6	19.3
PSP	1	0	1	3.9		(15) 3	3	8	
	(9) 3	3	1		Part: 43.5				
Part: 32.6									

SATNA DISTRICT

Population: 694,370
Urban: 9.1 Rural: 90.9
Hindu: 97.5 Muslim: 2.3 Jain: 0.1 Sikh: 0.1 Christian: #

1952				
Party	Cont	Won	LD	Pct.
CONG	10	8	0	44.7
RRP	7	1	3	16.6
SP	10	0	7	13.4
KMPP	9	0	7	11.7
JS	7	1	5	8.3
KS	1	0	1	0.4
IND	(7) 5	0	6	4.9
	(51) 10	10	29	
Part:	32.6			

1957				
Party	Cont	Won	LD	Pct.
CONG	6	4	0	36.2
RRP	6	1	3	17.7
JS	4	1	2	12.2
PSP	4	0	4	3.6
IND	(17) 6	0	15	30.3
	(37) 6	6	24	
Part:	35.0			

1962				
Party	Cont	Won	LD	Pct.
CONG	6	4	0	40.9
JS	6	2	1	24.0
SP	6	0	5	12.5
RRP	4	0	2	8.4
PSP	4	0	4	2.2
IND	(11) 5	0	10	12.0
	(37) 6	6	22	
Part:	44.2			

1967				
Party	Cont	Won	LD	Pct.
CONG	6	4	0	40.6
JS	6	1	0	37.2
SSP	3	0	2	6.7
PSP	3	1	2	5.1
IND	(13) 5	0	12	10.4
	(31) 6	6	16	
Part:	59.5			

REWA DISTRICT

Population: 772,602
Urban: 5.6 Rural: 94.4
Hindu: 97.1 Muslim: 2.8 Christian: #

Party	Cont	Won	LD	Pct.
1952				
CONG	11	5	0	25.8
SP	11	3	3	25.3
KMPP	10	1	4	17.8
RRP	10	1	9	10.5
JS	4	0	4	3.0
KS	5	0	5	2.3
IND	(15) 9	1	12	15.3
	(66) 11	11	37	
Part:	31.3			

Party	Cont	Won	LD	Pct.
1957				
CONG	7	3	1	24.8
RRP	7	0	3	13.7
PSP	7	0	6	9.5
JS	3	1	2	4.5
SP	@	1	@	@
IND	(23) 7	2	13	47.5
	(47) 7	7	25	
Part:	32.8			

Party	Cont	Won	LD	Pct.
1962				
CONG	7	6	0	42.2
SP	7	0	2	25.0
PSP	7	1	6	13.3
JS	6	0	5	6.5
RRP	3	0	3	3.2
CPI	3	0	3	2.0
HMS	2	0	2	0.5
IND	(8) 5	0	7	7.3
	(43) 7	7	28	
Part:	44.9			

Party	Cont	Won	LD	Pct.
1967				
CONG	7	5	0	45.0
SSP	7	0	2	25.9
PSP	7	1	6	10.7
JS	7	0	6	10.5
CPI	1	0	1	0.7
IND	(11) 4	1	10	7.2
	(40) 7	7	25	
Part:	53.2			

SIDHI DISTRICT

Population: 580,129
Urban: 0.9 Rural: 99.1
Hindu: 97.9 Muslim: 2.1 Christian: #

1952

Party	Cont	Won	LD	Pct.
SP	8	6	1	42.2
CONG	7	1	2	20.6
JS	6	1	0	19.6
KMPP	6	0	3	15.4
IND	(1) 1	0	0	2.1
	(28) 8	8	6	

Part: 24.8

1957

Party	Cont	Won	LD	Pct.
PSP	5	2	1	22.6
CONG	5	0	4	16.6
RRP	3	0	2	9.7
JS	3	0	2	8.5
SP	@	2	@	@
IND	(13) 5	1	7	42.6
	(29) 5	5	16	

Part: 23.3

1962

Party	Cont	Won	LD	Pct.
CONG	5	2	0	30.0
PSP	5	2	1	27.9
SP	5	1	3	22.3
JS	4	0	4	6.4
RRP	2	0	2	2.4
CPI	1	0	1	2.3
IND	(9) 3	0	9	8.7
	(31) 5	5	20	

Part: 31.1

1967

Party	Cont	Won	LD	Pct.
CONG	5	3	0	39.7
PSP	5	2	1	33.6
SSP	4	0	3	9.9
JS	5	0	4	8.1
IND	(16) 3	0	16	8.7
	(35) 5	5	24	

Part: 42.4

SHAHDOL DISTRICT

Population: 829,649
Urban: 7.0 Rural: 93.0
Hindu: 97.7 Muslim: 2.0 Christian: 0.1 Jain: 0.1 Sikh: 0.1

Party	Cont	Won	LD	Pct.
1952				
CONG	8	6	0	40.0
SP	8	1	2	21.3
KMPP	6	1	0	19.7
JS	1	0	1	1.1
IND	(8) 6	1	2	17.9
	(31) 9	9	5	
Part: 23.4				

Party	Cont	Won	LD	Pct.
1957				
CONG	7	6	0	50.3
PSP	5	0	4	11.0
JS	5	0	5	8.7
RRP	1	0	1	2.8
SP	@	1	@	@
IND	(7) 7	0	1	27.2
	(25) 7	7	11	
Part: 23.4				

Party	Cont	Won	LD	Pct.
1962				
CONG	7	2	0	41.4
SP	6	4	0	39.5
JS	6	0	5	11.2
PSP	3	1	2	7.3
IND	(1) 1	0	1	0.6
	(23) 7	7	8	
Part: 27.8				

Party	Cont	Won	LD	Pct.
1967				
CONG	8	8	0	66.3
JS	8	0	6	15.9
SSP	8	0	8	6.3
PSP	6	0	5	5.0
CPI	2	0	2	0.7
JC	1	0	1	0.6
CPM	1	0	1	0.1
IND	(7) 6	0	7	5.1
	(41) 8	8	30	
Part: 37.1				

MAHAKOSHAL

Population: 17,045,269
Urban: 11.9 Rural: 88.1
Hindu: 95.4 Muslim: 2.3 Christian: 0.9 Buddhist: 0.6 Jain: 0.5
Sikh: 0.2

1952

Party	Cont	Won	LD	Pct.
CONG	141	118*	3	47.2
SP	92	1	69	8.3
KMPP	53	7	29	7.4
RRP	28	3	17	4.2
JS	42	0	32	3.0
SCF	14	0	10	1.5
FB(M)	5	0	1	1.0
FB(R)	10	0	8	0.7
HMS	1	0	0	0.2
BLC	2	0	2	0.1
CPI	4	0	4	0.1
IND	(295)126	19*	237	26.3
	(687)148	148	412	

Part: 40.0
*Uncontested: CONG (3), IND (4)

1957

Party	Cont	Won	LD	Pct.
CONG	151	133*	1	53.9
PSP	99	7	26	18.8
JS	50	0	34	5.5
RRP	18	4	12	3.0
SCF	21	0	14	2.2
CPI	5	0	4	0.3
SP	@	2	@	@
IND	(158)100	5	104	16.3
	(502)151	151	195	

Part: 36.7
*Uncontested: CONG (7)

1962

Party	Cont	Won	LD	Pct.
CONG	151	86*	5	38.9
PSP	86	20	32	14.7
JS	97	10	46	14.1
RRP	60	10	33	7.0
RPI	30	0	24	2.4
SP	16	1	11	1.6
CPI	16	0	16	1.3
Swat	10	2	8	0.8
FB	9	0	8	0.5
HMS	6	0	6	0.2
IND	(212)110	22	160	18.5
	(693)151	151	349	

Part: 39.2
*Uncontested: CONG (3)

1967

Party	Cont	Won	LD	Pct.
CONG	154	111	5	45.9
JS	142	23	45	24.1
PSP	64	4	48	5.7
SSP	55	4	42	3.9
JC	18	1	11	2.0
RPI	24	0	22	1.1
CPI	11	0	11	0.5
Swat	5	0	4	0.2
CPM	3	0	3	0.2
IND	(303)126	11	262	16.4
	(779)154	154	453	

Part: 46.6

SURGUJA DISTRICT

Population: 1,036,738
Urban: 4.2 Rural: 95.8
Hindu: 97.3 Muslim: 1.7 Christian: 0.8 Sikh: 0.1

1952

Party	Cont	Won	LD	Pct.
CONG	7	4*	0	41.0
SP	1	0	0	3.3
IND	(17) 7	4*	9	55.7
	(25) 8	8	9	

Part: 31.4
*Uncontested: CONG (1), IND (1)

1957

Party	Cont	Won	LD	Pct.
CONG	9	9	0	43.7
PSP	9	0	7	13.4
JS	6	0	6	7.6
IND	(23) 9	0	16	35.3
	(47) 9	9	29	

Part: 21.5

1962

Party	Cont	Won	LD	Pct.
CONG	9	4	0	34.6
JS	9	1	6	18.7
PSP	7	1	4	13.7
RRP	9	1	6	13.4
SP	2	0	2	2.5
IND	(9) 7	2	5	17.1
	(45) 9	9	23	

Part: 27.6

1967

Party	Cont	Won	LD	Pct.
CONG	10	7	0	49.2
JS	10	3	1	26.5
PSP	9	0	9	7.9
SSP	8	0	6	7.6
RPI	7	0	7	2.9
IND	(16) 6	0	16	5.9
	(60) 10	10	39	

Part: 37.3

RAIGARH DISTRICT

Population: 1,041,226
Urban: 5.8 Rural: 94.2
Hindu: 90.6 Christian: 8.7 Muslim: 0.6

1952				
Party	Cont	Won	LD	Pct.
CONG	9	7	0	46.8
RRP	7	1	2	21.7
KMPP	7	1	3	18.8
SP	4	0	4	2.7
FB(R)	1	0	1	0.4
IND	(11) 8	0	10	9.6
	(39) 9	9	20	
Part: 45.2				

1957				
Party	Cont	Won	LD	Pct.
CONG	9	8	0	65.2
PSP	7	1	0	16.5
JS	4	0	4	4.7
CPI	1	0	1	0.6
IND	(7) 6	0	5	13.0
	(28) 9	9	10	
Part: 36.1				

1962				
Party	Cont	Won	LD	Pct.
CONG	9	5	2	30.9
RRP	9	4	3	27.0
PSP	7	0	5	11.7
JS	4	0	4	3.7
Swat	2	0	2	0.9
SP	2	0	2	0.8
CPI	1	0	1	0.7
IND	(18) 8	0	12	24.3
	(51) 9	9	31	
Part: 39.3				

1967				
Party	Cont	Won	LD	Pct.
CONG	9	6	0	48.3
JS	9	2	2	26.1
PSP	4	1	1	11.6
JC	2	0	1	2.7
IND	(13) 7	0	13	11.3
	(37) 9	9	17	
Part: 44.3				

BILASPUR DISTRICT

Population: 2,021,793
Urban: 8.3 Rural: 91.7
Hindu: 98.0 Muslim: 1.3 Christian: 0.5 Jain: 0.1 Sikh: 0.1

1952

Party	Cont	Won	LD	Pct.
CONG	18	16	0	39.4
SP	17	0	17	8.2
RRP	5	1	3	5.5
JS	6	0	5	2.4
KMPP	3	0	3	2.2
IND	(68) 20	3	64	42.3
	(117) 20	20	92	

Part: 31.0

1957

Party	Cont	Won	LD	Pct.
CONG	19	14*	1	43.9
JS	14	0	6	15.9
RRP	6	3	3	14.0
PSP	8	1	5	8.0
IND	(26) 15	1	20	18.2
	(73) 19	19	35	

Part: 30.2
*Uncontested: CONG (1)

1962

Party	Cont	Won	LD	Pct.
CONG	19	16	0	47.1
JS	19	1	6	24.3
RRP	12	1	8	9.8
PSP	5	0	4	2.0
Swat	4	0	4	1.2
SP	1	0	1	1.0
CPI	1	0	1	0.3
IND	(35) 16	1	31	14.3
	(96) 19	19	55	

Part: 32.7

1967

Party	Cont	Won	LD	Pct.
CONG	19	17	0	54.5
JS	18	1	1	28.4
JC	9	0	6	6.0
SSP	2	0	1	1.0
CPI	1	0	1	0.1
IND	(30) 14	1	28	10.0
	(79) 19	19	37	

Part: 44.1

MADHYA PRADESH

RAIPUR DISTRICT

Population: 2,002,004
Urban: 11.4 Rural: 88.6
Hindu: 97.2 Muslim: 1.6 Christian: 0.6 Jain: 0.3 Sikh: 0.2
Buddhist: 0.1

1952

Party	Cont	Won	LD	Pct.
CONG	19	16	0	48.2
KMPP	19	3	7	23.8
SP	15	0	10	11.9
SCF	5	0	3	3.9
JS	6	0	4	3.8
RRP	5	0	4	2.4
CPI	2	0	2	0.3
IND (15)	10	0	13	5.7
(86)	19	19	43	

Part: 40.1

1957

Party	Cont	Won	LD	Pct.
CONG	18	14*	0	44.1
PSP	15	2	3	25.9
JS	7	0	5	9.0
SCF	10	0	5	8.5
CPI	1	0	1	0.3
IND (15)	9	2	11	12.2
(66)	18	18	25	

Part: 37.9
*Uncontested: CONG (2)

1962

Party	Cont	Won	LD	Pct.
CONG	18	9	0	38.8
PSP	16	5	3	24.1
JS	12	3	7	20.0
RPI	11	0	8	6.2
CPI	1	0	1	1.3
FB	1	0	1	0.1
Swat	1	0	1	0.1
IND (22)	13	1	19	9.4
(82)	18	18	40	

Part: 40.1

1967

Party	Cont	Won	LD	Pct.
CONG	18	16	0	50.6
JS	18	1	9	24.0
SSP	10	0	9	4.5
JC	1	1	0	3.8
PSP	11	0	11	3.7
RPI	3	0	3	0.3
CPI	1	0	1	0.2
IND (44)	16	0	41	12.9
(106)	18	18	74	

Part: 46.4

BASTAR DISTRICT

Population: 1,167,501
Urban: 2.3 Rural: 97.7
Hindu: 99.0 Muslim: 0.4 Christian: 0.4 Jain: 0.1

1952

Party	Cont	Won	LD	Pct.
CONG	7	2*	3	14.4
SP	1	0	1	3.7
RRP	1	0	1	1.3
IND	(10) 8	8*	2	80.6
	(19) 10	10	7	

Part: 60.9
*Uncontested: CONG (2), IND (3)

1957

Party	Cont	Won	LD	Pct.
CONG	10	10	0	72.0
PSP	2	0	1	6.0
IND	(11) 9	0	4	22.0
	(23) 10	10	5	

Part: 48.6

1962

Party	Cont	Won	LD	Pct.
CONG	10	1*	3	23.7
PSP	2	0	1	2.2
CPI	1	0	1	1.0
IND	(21) 9	9	9	73.1
	(34) 10	10	14	

Part: 43.7
*Uncontested: CONG (1)

1967

Party	Cont	Won	LD	Pct.
JS	10	2	4	29.0
CONG	11	2	5	20.0
SSP	5	1	4	7.3
PSP	2	1	1	3.6
CPI	1	0	1	0.5
JC	1	0	1	0.5
IND	(28) 11	5	20	39.1
	(58) 11	11	36	

Part: 43.7

DURG DISTRICT

Population: 1,885,236
Urban: 12.5 Rural: 87.5
Hindu: 96.2 Muslim: 1.4 Buddhist: 0.8 Christian: 0.4 Jain: 0.4
Sikh: 0.4 Other: 0.4

1952

Party	Cont	Won	LD	Pct.
CONG	16	12	0	50.7
SP	13	1	11	10.5
RRP	8	1	5	9.4
KMPP	7	0	5	5.2
FB(R)	3	0	2	2.2
JS	2	0	2	1.1
SCF	2	0	2	0.6
CPI	1	0	1	0.1
IND	(19) 13	2	11	20.2
	(71) 16	16	39	

Part: 43.8

1957

Party	Cont	Won	LD	Pct.
CONG	16	13*	0	50.0
PSP	11	2	2	27.6
RRP	6	1	5	10.4
SCF	4	0	4	2.1
JS	2	0	1	1.5
IND	(8) 6	0	4	8.4
	(47) 16	16	16	

Part: 38.2
*Uncontested: CONG (1)

1962

Party	Cont	Won	LD	Pct.
CONG	16	13	0	41.4
PSP	16	2	3	30.2
RRP	6	1	3	9.5
JS	10	0	9	6.9
CPI	5	0	5	2.9
RPI	5	0	4	2.6
IND	(14) 7	0	13	6.5
	(72) 16	16	37	

Part: 39.1

1967

Party	Cont	Won	LD	Pct.
CONG	17	11	0	46.1
JS	13	0	7	13.5
SSP	11	2	7	10.5
CPI	5	0	5	2.4
PSP	4	0	4	1.9
CPM	1	0	1	1.0
RPI	1	0	1	0.7
IND	(20) 11	4	12	23.9
	(72) 17	17	37	

Part: 47.8

BALAGHAT DISTRICT

Population: 806,702
Urban: 5.7 Rural: 94.3
Hindu: 91.1 Buddhist: 6.1 Muslim: 2.1 Jain: 0.3 Christian: 0.2
Sikh: 0.1

Party	Cont	Won	LD	Pct.
	1952			
CONG	8	8	0	60.2
SP	7	0	3	15.0
SCF	1	0	0	4.6
JS	1	0	1	0.5
RRP	1	0	1	0.1
IND	(23) 8	0	23	19.6
	(41) 8	8	28	
Part:	42.4			

Party	Cont	Won	LD	Pct.
	1957			
CONG	8	8	0	53.2
PSP	6	0	2	19.2
SCF	2	0	1	7.2
CPI	1	0	1	1.2
IND	(10) 7	0	5	19.2
	(27) 8	8	9	
Part:	44.7			

Party	Cont	Won	LD	Pct.
	1962			
CONG	8	3	0	38.9
PSP	5	2	0	22.4
RPI	5	0	2	11.9
CPI	2	0	2	2.7
IND	(8) 7	3	3	24.1
	(28) 8	8	7	
Part:	41.3			

Party	Cont	Won	LD	Pct.
	1967			
CONG	8	8	0	50.6
JS	6	0	4	10.9
RPI	4	0	2	8.9
PSP	4	0	2	8.1
CPI	2	0	2	2.9
IND	(22) 7	0	20	18.6
	(46) 8	8	30	
Part:	52.7			

MANDLA DISTRICT

Population: 684,503
Urban: 4.8 Rural: 95.2
Hindu: 98.4 Muslim: 0.9 Christian: 0.4 Jain: 0.2

1952				
Party	Cont	Won	LD	Pct.
CONG	6	6	0	64.4
SP	6	0	6	8.9
JS	2	0	1	4.9
IND (16)	6	0	13	21.8
(30)	6	6	20	
Part: 38.6				

1957				
Party	Cont	Won	LD	Pct.
CONG	6	6*	0	66.6
PSP	5	0	1	31.3
RRP	1	0	1	0.7
IND (1)	1	0	1	1.4
(13)	6	6	3	
Part: 32.2				

*Uncontested: CONG (1)

1962				
Party	Cont	Won	LD	Pct.
CONG	6	4	0	35.2
PSP	6	1	2	27.2
RRP	6	1	2	20.6
IND (11)	5	0	9	17.0
(29)	6	6	13	
Part: 26.2				

1967				
Party	Cont	Won	LD	Pct.
CONG	6	5	0	38.7
PSP	6	1	4	19.9
JS	4	0	3	8.9
SSP	3	0	2	6.3
IND (19)	6	0	17	26.2
(38)	6	6	26	
Part: 33.9				

JABALPUR DISTRICT

Population: 1,273,825
Urban: 37.1 Rural: 62.9
Hindu: 92.5 Muslim: 4.5 Christian: 1.1 Jain: 1.1 Sikh: 0.6
Buddhist: 0.1

1952

Party	Cont	Won	LD	Pct.
CONG	11	11	0	54.0
SP	10	0	4	16.5
KMPP	6	0	4	7.9
JS	8	0	7	5.4
BLC	1	0	1	1.6
SCF	1	0	1	0.5
CPI	1	0	1	0.2
IND	(23) 9	0	20	13.9
	(61) 11	11	38	

Part: 45.8

1957

Party	Cont	Won	LD	Pct.
CONG	12	11*	0	53.8
PSP	6	0	0	20.0
JS	6	0	4	8.6
RRP	2	0	2	1.5
CPI	1	0	0	1.3
SCF	2	0	2	0.3
SP	@	1	@	@
IND	(12) 8	0	10	14.5
	(41) 12	12	18	

Part: 41.4
*Uncontested: CONG (1)

1962

Party	Cont	Won	LD	Pct.
CONG	12	10	0	46.9
JS	11	1	2	22.1
SP	9	1	4	14.6
RRP	7	0	6	5.1
CPI	2	0	2	2.0
IND	(16) 9	0	14	9.3
	(57) 12	12	28	

Part: 48.2

1967

Party	Cont	Won	LD	Pct.
CONG	12	9	0	43.9
JS	12	1	3	27.6
SSP	7	1	4	8.9
RPI	2	0	2	0.3
IND	(29) 10	1	24	19.3
	(62) 12	12	33	

Part: 54.9

DAMOH DISTRICT

Population: 438,343
Urban: 12.7 Rural: 87.3
Hindu: 94.4 Muslim: 3.2 Jain: 2.1 Christian: 0.2 Sikh: 0.1

1952				
Party	Cont	Won	LD	Pct.
CONG	4	4	0	53.2
JS	2	0	0	13.2
SP	2	0	1	10.8
HMS	1	0	0	5.8
IND (10)	4	0	10	17.0
(19)	4	4	11	
Part: 39.3				

1957				
Party	Cont	Won	LD	Pct.
CONG	4	4	0	60.5
SCF	2	0	2	5.8
CPI	1	0	1	3.1
JS	1	0	1	1.2
IND (5)	3	0	2	29.4
(13)	4	4	6	
Part: 31.4				

1962				
Party	Cont	Won	LD	Pct.
CONG	4	1	0	33.2
JS	2	0	1	8.6
HMS	2	0	2	3.2
CPI	1	0	1	2.4
IND (10)	4	3	6	52.6
(19)	4	4	10	
Part: 40.9				

1967				
Party	Cont	Won	LD	Pct.
CONG	4	4	0	45.1
JS	4	0	2	18.1
RPI	3	0	3	3.8
JC	2	0	2	3.5
IND (22)	4	0	19	29.5
(35)	4	4	26	
Part: 52.5				

SAGAR DISTRICT

Population: 796,547
Urban: 22.7 Rural: 77.3
Hindu: 91.6 Muslim: 4.0 Jain: 3.5 Christian: 0.4 Sikh: 0.3
Buddhist: 0.2

		1952		
Party	Cont	Won	LD	Pct.
CONG	6	6	0	49.1
JS	6	0	4	12.2
SP	3	0	3	5.2
KMPP	3	0	3	3.3
SCF	1	0	1	2.1
IND	(17) 5	0	14	28.1
	(36) 6	6	25	
Part:	39.3			

		1957		
Party	Cont	Won	LD	Pct.
CONG	7	7	0	49.8
PSP	6	0	2	17.0
JS	6	0	5	9.6
IND	(12) 7	0	9	23.6
	(31) 7	7	16	
Part:	41.4			

		1962		
Party	Cont	Won	LD	Pct.
CONG	7	4	0	38.2
JS	7	2	0	34.2
PSP	5	1	4	6.7
CPI	1	0	1	2.8
HMS	4	0	4	1.8
IND	(14) 6	0	11	16.3
	(38) 7	7	20	
Part:	43.2			

		1967		
Party	Cont	Won	LD	Pct.
JS	7	5	0	41.4
CONG	7	2	0	39.9
PSP	3	0	1	9.1
SSP	4	0	4	1.3
CPM	1	0	1	0.9
CPI	1	0	1	0.2
IND	(11) 7	0	11	7.2
	(34) 7	7	18	
Part:	50.8			

MADHYA PRADESH

NARSIMHAPUR DISTRICT

Population: 412,406
Urban: 11.9 Rural: 88.1
Hindu: 96.2 Muslim: 2.7 Jain: 0.9 Christian: 0.1 Sikh: 0.1

1952

Party	Cont	Won	LD	Pct.
CONG	4	3	0	44.5
KMPP	4	1	2	25.6
JS	1	0	0	8.0
IND	(5) 3	0	3	21.9
	(14) 4	4	5	

Part: 44.2

1957

Party	Cont	Won	LD	Pct.
CONG	4	4	0	53.8
PSP	4	0	0	38.5
RRP	1	0	1	2.3
JS	1	0	1	1.5
IND	(2) 1	0	2	3.9
	(12) 4	4	4	

Part: 45.3

1962

Party	Cont	Won	LD	Pct.
PSP	4	4	0	56.0
CONG	4	0	0	32.7
RRP	3	0	2	8.2
JS	2	0	2	3.1
	(13) 4	4	4	

Part: 47.2

1967

Party	Cont	Won	LD	Pct.
CONG	4	4	0	50.7
PSP	4	0	2	19.8
JS	4	0	3	13.2
IND	(5) 4	0	3	16.3
	(17) 4	4	8	

Part: 54.4

SEONI DISTRICT

Population: 523,741
Urban: 5.8 Rural: 94.2
Hindu: 94.2 Muslim: 4.6 Buddhist: 0.6 Jain: 0.5 Christian: 0.1

1952

Party	Cont	Won	LD	Pct.
CONG	4	4	0	55.0
SP	3	0	2	9.1
RRP	1	0	1	1.1
JS	1	0	1	1.0
IND (8)	4	0	4	33.8
(17)	4	4	8	

Part: 27.2

1957

Party	Cont	Won	LD	Pct.
CONG	5	5	0	55.6
PSP	4	0	0	23.3
RRP	2	0	0	11.7
IND (4)	3	0	4	9.4
(15)	5	5	4	

Part: 29.6

1962

Party	Cont	Won	LD	Pct.
CONG	5	2*	0	34.6
RRP	3	2	0	31.9
PSP	1	1	0	14.3
JS	1	0	0	2.9
RPI	1	0	1	2.3
IND (6)	3	0	6	14.0
(17)	5	5	7	

Part: 37.3
*Uncontested: CONG (1)

1967

Party	Cont	Won	LD	Pct.
CONG	5	5	0	52.8
JS	5	0	1	19.6
PSP	2	0	1	10.1
RPI	1	0	1	1.8
IND (6)	4	0	4	15.7
(19)	5	5	7	

Part: 40.7

CHHINDWARA DISTRICT

Population: 785,535
Urban: 12.5 Rural: 87.5
Hindu: 93.1 Muslim: 4.0 Buddhist: 2.1 Jain: 0.5 Christian: 0.3

1952

Party	Cont	Won	LD	Pct.
CONG	6	6	0	48.2
JS	2	0	2	5.9
FB(M)	3	0	1	5.3
SCF	1	0	1	3.2
FB(R)	1	0	0	2.1
BLC	1	0	1	0.1
IND	(19) 7	1	14	35.2
	(33) 7	7	19	

Part: 34.1

1957

Party	Cont	Won	LD	Pct.
CONG	7	7	0	58.5
PSP	5	0	2	18.4
SCF	1	0	0	4.7
IND	(7) 5	0	1	18.4
	(20) 7	7	3	

Part: 34.4

1962

Party	Cont	Won	LD	Pct.
CONG	7	4*	0	37.1
JS	4	0	2	10.3
RPI	3	0	3	3.8
FB	4	0	4	3.4
PSP	1	0	1	1.6
RRP	1	0	1	1.1
IND	(12) 6	3	9	42.7
	(32) 7	7	20	

Part: 37.6
*Uncontested: CONG (1)

1967

Party	Cont	Won	LD	Pct.
CONG	7	6	0	46.7
JS	7	1	2	22.5
JC	2	0	1	9.0
PSP	4	0	4	2.9
RPI	1	0	1	1.9
SSP	1	0	1	0.2
IND	(23) 7	0	23	16.8
	(45) 7	7	32	

Part: 40.4

BETUL DISTRICT

Population: 560,412
Urban: 8.4 Rural: 91.6
Hindu: 96.7 Muslim: 1.6 Buddhist: 1.0 Christian: 0.3 Jain: 0.3
Sikh: 0.1

		1952		
Party	Cont	Won	LD	Pct.
CONG	5	5	0	48.6
FB(M)	2	0	0	17.2
FB(R)	3	0	3	5.0
SCF	1	0	1	4.5
SP	2	0	2	3.2
IND	(9) 5	0	7	21.5
	(22) 5	5	13	
Part: 51.1				

		1957		
Party	Cont	Won	LD	Pct.
CONG	5	3	0	55.5
PSP	3	0	0	21.7
IND	(3) 3	3	2	1	22.8
	(11) 5	5	1	
Part: 33.7				

		1962		
Party	Cont	Won	LD	Pct.
CONG	5	3	0	44.1
JS	5	2	2	21.2
FB	4	0	3	11.9
RPI	3	0	3	6.6
PSP	2	0	2	3.9
IND	(7) 4	0	6	12.3
	(26) 5	5	16	
Part: 35.7				

		1967		
Party	Cont	Won	LD	Pct.
CONG	5	2	0	40.0
JS	4	3	0	38.5
RPI	2	0	2	3.0
IND	(4) 4	0	2	18.5
	(15) 5	5	4	
Part: 42.0				

HOSHANGABAD DISTRICT

Population: 618,293
Urban: 19.3 Rural: 80.7
Hindu: 94.6 Muslim: 4.0 Christian: 0.4 Jain: 0.4 Sikh: 0.3
Buddhist: 0.2

1952

Party	Cont	Won	LD	Pct.
CONG	5	3	0	43.7
KMPP	4	2	2	25.7
SP	5	0	4	8.3
JS	4	0	4	4.6
FB(R)	2	0	2	2.0
SCF	1	0	1	0.9
IND (18)	4	0	18	14.8
(39)	5	5	31	

Part: 33.6

1957

Party	Cont	Won	LD	Pct.
CONG	6	6	0	49.7
PSP	4	0	0	13.3
JS	1	0	1	0.8
IND (10)	6	0	7	36.2
(21)	6	6	8	

Part: 36.8

1962

Party	Cont	Won	LD	Pct.
CONG	6	4	0	37.8
PSP	6	2	2	26.4
RRP	4	0	2	10.9
JS	5	0	4	8.3
CPI	1	0	1	1.6
SP	2	0	2	1.2
IND (6)	4	0	4	13.8
(30)	6	6	15	

Part: 39.7

1967

Party	Cont	Won	LD	Pct.
CONG	6	5	0	49.0
PSP	6	1	4	21.3
JS	5	0	3	12.6
JC	1	0	0	3.9
SSP	4	0	4	1.9
Swat	2	0	2	1.2
CPM	1	0	1	0.1
IND (7)	6	0	5	10.0
(32)	6	6	19	

Part: 49.5

NIMAR (KHANDWA) DISTRICT

Population: 685,150
Urban: 22.5 Rural: 77.5
Hindu: 84.5 Muslim: 12.4 Buddhist: 1.9 Jain: 0.5
Christian: 0.4 Sikh: 0.3

1952

Party	Cont	Won	LD	Pct.
CONG	6	5	0	50.3
SP	3	0	1	13.1
SCF	1	0	0	4.1
JS	1	0	1	1.0
IND	(7) 5	1	2	31.5
	(18) 6	6	4	

Part: 46.4

1957

Party	Cont	Won	LD	Pct.
CONG	6	5*	0	62.7
PSP	4	1	1	22.8
JS	2	0	0	12.0
IND	(2) 2	0	2	2.5
	(14) 6	6	3	

Part: 54.5
*Uncontested: CONG (1)

1962

Party	Cont	Won	LD	Pct.
CONG	6	3	0	44.6
JS	6	0	1	25.0
PSP	3	1	1	14.3
Swat	3	2	1	10.9
RPI	3	0	3	4.1
IND	(3) 2	0	3	1.1
	(24) 6	6	9	

Part: 54.8

1967

Party	Cont	Won	LD	Pct.
CONG	6	2	0	42.3
JS	6	4	0	42.3
PSP	5	0	4	9.3
Swat	3	0	2	3.5
IND	(4) 2	0	4	2.6
	(24) 6	6	10	

Part: 58.9

STATE SUMMARY

Population: 39,553,718
Urban: 28.2 Rural: 71.8
Hindu: 82.2 Muslim: 7.7 Buddhist: 7.1 Christian: 1.4 Jain: 1.2
Sikh: 0.1 Other: 0.3

1952						1957			
Party	Cont	Won	LD	Pct.		Party	Cont	Won	LD	Pct.
CONG	301	244*	0	47.3		CONG	264	135	6	45.3
SP	190	7	75	12.7		PSP	78	33	16	10.7
PWP	103	23	32	8.5		PWP	55	31	0	9.6
SCF	72	3	27	6.0		SCF	47	13	2	8.9
CPI+PDF	51	7	17	3.4		CPI	32	13	1	5.2
KKP	33	2	14	2.4		JS	18	4	6	2.0
JS	36	0	31	1.3		HMS	6	1	3	0.5
SKP	19	2	14	1.0		RRP	7	0	7	0.1
KMPP	24	1	21	0.7		IND	(247)153	34	150	17.7
RRP	32	0	31	0.6			(754)264	264	191	
HMS	9	0	7	0.3		Part: 53.6				
FB(R)	6	0	5	0.2						
KLP	2	0	2	0.1						
DCA	2	0	2	0.1						
FB(M)	2	0	2	#						
IND	(475)220	12	406	15.4						
	(1357)301	301	686							

Part: 50.4
*Uncontested: CONG (1)

1962						1967			
Party	Cont	Won	LD	Pct.		Party	Cont	Won	LD	Pct.
CONG	264	215	1	51.2		CONG	270	203*	0	47.0
PWP	79	15	29	7.5		JS	165	4	115	8.2
PSP	100	9	47	7.2		PWP	58	19	11	7.8
CPI	56	6	13	5.9		RPI	79	5	29	6.7
RPI	66	3	27	5.4		CPI	41	10	7	4.9
JS	127	0	98	5.0		SSP	47	4	14	4.6
SP	14	1	12	0.5		PSP	66	8	40	4.1
Swat	9	0	5	0.4		Swat	41	0	36	1.1
HMS	5	0	5	0.1		CPM	11	1	3	1.1
RRP	3	0	3	#		IND	(464)212	16	392	14.5
IND	(438)209	15	347	16.8			(1242)270	270	647	
	(1161)264	264	587			Part: 60.4				

Part: 56.5

BOMBAY DIVISION

Population: 13,662,321
Urban: 43.9 Rural: 56.1
Hindu: 81.5 Muslim: 8.6 Buddhist: 4.6 Christian: 2.8 Jain: 1.6
Sikh: 0.2 Other: 0.7

1952				
Party	Cont	Won	LD	Pct.
CONG	100	89	0	45.2
SP	79	6	14	19.3
PWP	40	2	16	8.4
SCF	15	1	6	4.5
KKP	16	0	9	3.1
CPI	11	0	6	2.3
RRP	19	0	19	1.0
HMS	5	0	4	0.4
KLP	2	0	2	0.4
KMPP	4	0	4	0.1
IND (162)	84	2	141	15.3
(453)	100	100	221	
Part: 49.5				

1957				
Party	Cont	Won	LD	Pct.
CONG	90	28	4	41.6
PSP	34	22	0	17.8
PWP	14	12	0	9.1
CPI	13	8	0	8.4
SCF	8	6	0	6.6
JS	4	3	0	2.2
HMS	2	0	0	0.5
RRP	3	0	3	0.1
IND (61)	39	11	39	13.7
(229)	90	90	46	
Part: 56.1				

1962				
Party	Cont	Won	LD	Pct.
CONG	90	76	0	49.5
PSP	60	6	31	12.6
CPI	28	2	8	8.6
JS	65	0	49	7.6
PWP	23	4	10	5.1
RPI	21	0	13	4.1
SP	12	1	10	1.4
Swat	5	0	1	1.1
HMS	2	0	2	0.1
RRP	2	0	2	#
IND (100)	63	1	82	9.9
(408)	90	90	208	
Part: 55.1				

1967				
Party	Cont	Won	LD	Pct.
CONG	93	64	0	43.0
JS	67	1	40	12.0
PSP	50	7	28	9.9
PWP	15	9	4	6.1
CPI	13	5	1	5.1
RPI	19	2	9	4.6
SSP	18	1	7	4.5
Swat	28	0	26	2.4
CPM	7	0	2	1.8
IND (124)	63	4	107	10.6
(434)	93	93	224	
Part: 60.0				

MAHARASHTRA

RATNAGIRI DISTRICT

Population: 1,827,203
Urban: 8.1 Rural: 91.9
Hindu: 87.5 Muslim: 6.0 Buddhist: 5.5 Christian: 0.9 Jain: 0.1

1952

Party	Cont	Won	LD	Pct.
CONG	15	15	0	43.0
SP	11	0	2	17.6
PWP	10	0	6	8.7
SCF	3	0	2	4.6
HMS	1	0	1	0.6
IND	(37) 15	0	32	25.5
	(77) 15	15	43	

Part: 38.4

1957

Party	Cont	Won	LD	Pct.
PSP	5	5	0	23.7
CONG	14	0	4	23.2
PWP	3	2	0	11.8
SCF	2	2	0	10.5
JS	2	2	0	9.4
CPI	1	1	0	7.1
IND	(5) 5	2	2	14.3
	(32) 14	14	6	

Part: 46.8

1962

Party	Cont	Won	LD	Pct.
CONG	14	9	0	45.4
PSP	12	5	3	24.8
JS	13	0	7	13.8
PWP	6	0	5	4.2
RPI	3	0	3	2.0
HMS	2	0	2	1.3
CPI	1	0	1	0.9
IND	(9) 9	0	8	7.6
	(60) 14	14	29	

Part: 43.2

1967

Party	Cont	Won	LD	Pct.
CONG	13	8	0	43.2
PSP	9	4	2	22.4
JS	9	0	4	14.4
SSP	2	0	1	3.2
PWP	2	1	1	2.8
RPI	3	0	3	1.6
Swat	1	0	1	0.2
IND	(15) 10	0	13	12.2
	(54) 13	13	25	

Part: 55.4

KOLABA DISTRICT

Population: 1,508,855
Urban: 10.1 Rural: 89.9
Hindu: 89.0 Muslim: 5.9 Buddhist: 4.4 Jain: 0.4 Other: 0.2
Christian: 0.1

	1952			
Party	Cont	Won	LD	Pct.
CONG	9	8	0	48.5
PWP	7	0	0	23.3
SP	8	1	5	18.3
SCF	1	0	0	5.2
HMS	2	0	2	1.8
IND	(3) 3	0	3	2.9
	(30) 9	9	10	
Part:	49.2			

	1957			
Party	Cont	Won	LD	Pct.
PWP	5	5	0	42.1
CONG	8	0	0	31.9
PSP	2	2	0	15.3
IND	(2) 1	1	1	10.7
	(17) 8	8	1	
Part:	51.3			

	1962			
Party	Cont	Won	LD	Pct.
CONG	8	5	0	44.7
PWP	6	3	1	31.4
PSP	6	0	4	11.2
JS	8	0	8	5.7
RPI	2	0	2	2.1
IND	(4) 4	0	3	4.9
	(34) 8	8	18	
Part:	54.7			

	1967			
Party	Cont	Won	LD	Pct.
PWP	6	5	0	43.9
CONG	7	2	0	41.5
PSP	2	0	1	6.5
JS	7	0	7	6.2
RPI	1	0	1	0.6
IND	(3) 3	0	3	1.4
	(26) 7	7	12	
Part:	62.7			

BOMBAY DISTRICT

Population: 4,152,056
Urban: 100.0 Rural: 0.0
Hindu: 69.1 Muslim: 13.0 Christian: 6.9 Buddhist: 4.6
Jain: 3.8 Sikh: 0.6 Other: 2.0

Party	1952 Cont	Won	LD	Pct.
CONG	27	23	0	46.0
SP	25	3	1	29.8
SCF	2	1	0	4.7
CPI	4	0	1	3.8
RRP	14	0	14	2.4
PWP	2	0	2	0.5
KMPP	4	0	4	0.3
HMS	1	0	1	0.2
IND	(48) 23	0	45	12.3
	(127) 27	27	68	
Part: 52.4				

Party	1957 Cont	Won	LD	Pct.
CONG	24	13	0	46.9
PSP	8	3	0	15.4
SCF	3	3	0	11.1
CPI	2	2	0	8.3
JS	1	0	0	2.1
HMS	2	0	0	1.7
RRP	1	0	1	#
IND	(22) 12	3	15	14.5
	(63) 24	24	16	
Part: 66.4				

Party	1962 Cont	Won	LD	Pct.
CONG	24	21	0	48.7
CPI	10	1	2	11.7
PSP	11	1	7	8.3
RPI	5	0	0	6.7
JS	18	0	18	5.9
Swat	5	0	1	3.1
SP	8	0	7	2.3
PWP	1	0	1	0.4
RRP	1	0	1	#
IND	(31) 17	1	24	12.9
	(114) 24	24	61	
Part: 59.7				

Party	1967 Cont	Won	LD	Pct.
CONG	28	20	0	37.7
JS	24	1	18	11.7
CPI	7	3	0	8.6
PSP	17	1	12	7.7
RPI	8	1	2	7.5
Swat	22	0	20	6.3
SSP	5	0	1	4.3
CPM	2	0	0	2.4
PWP	1	0	0	1.2
IND	(56) 21	2	51	12.6
	(170) 28	28	104	
Part: 64.5				

THANA DISTRICT

Population: 1,652,678
Urban: 30.2 Rural: 69.8
Hindu: 87.7 Muslim: 5.1 Christian: 3.9 Buddhist: 2.4 Jain: 0.5
Sikh: 0.2 Other: 0.2

<table>
<tr><td colspan="5">1952</td></tr>
<tr><th>Party</th><th>Cont</th><th>Won</th><th>LD</th><th>Pct.</th></tr>
<tr><td>CONG</td><td>13</td><td>9</td><td>0</td><td>38.5</td></tr>
<tr><td>SP</td><td>11</td><td>2</td><td>2</td><td>22.2</td></tr>
<tr><td>PWP</td><td>5</td><td>0</td><td>2</td><td>6.0</td></tr>
<tr><td>KLP</td><td>2</td><td>0</td><td>2</td><td>2.5</td></tr>
<tr><td>CPI</td><td>2</td><td>0</td><td>2</td><td>1.8</td></tr>
<tr><td>SCF</td><td>1</td><td>0</td><td>1</td><td>1.7</td></tr>
<tr><td>KKP</td><td>1</td><td>0</td><td>0</td><td>1.1</td></tr>
<tr><td>HMS</td><td>1</td><td>0</td><td>0</td><td>0.9</td></tr>
<tr><td>RRP</td><td>2</td><td>0</td><td>2</td><td>0.1</td></tr>
<tr><td>IND (26)</td><td>12</td><td>2</td><td>19</td><td>25.2</td></tr>
<tr><td>(64)</td><td>13</td><td>13</td><td>30</td><td></td></tr>
</table>

Part: 50.8

		1957		
Party	Cont	Won	LD	Pct.
CONG	11	4	0	45.2
PWP	4	4	0	19.7
PSP	4	3	0	16.8
CPI	3	0	0	13.4
IND (4)	3	0	3	4.9
(26)	11	11	3	

Part: 57.6

		1962		
Party	Cont	Won	LD	Pct.
CONG	11	8	0	42.9
PSP	9	0	4	16.1
PWP	6	1	2	12.4
CPI	3	1	0	9.6
JS	6	0	3	7.9
SP	1	1	0	4.0
RPI	1	0	1	0.7
RRP	1	0	1	0.1
IND (11)	7	0	10	6.3
(49)	11	11	21	

Part: 56.7

		1967		
Party	Cont	Won	LD	Pct.
CONG	11	7	0	40.9
PSP	6	1	2	15.5
JS	10	0	5	13.5
PWP	2	2	0	9.9
CPM	4	0	2	6.0
RPI	1	0	0	2.8
SSP	2	0	1	2.3
Swat	1	0	1	0.1
IND (12)	8	1	10	9.0
(49)	11	11	21	

Part: 58.5

NASIK DISTRICT

Population: 1,855,246
Urban: 25.6 Rural: 74.4
Hindu: 85.0 Muslim: 7.5 Buddhist: 6.0 Jain: 0.8 Christian: 0.5
Sikh: 0.2

1952 Party	Cont	Won	LD	Pct.
CONG	12	12	0	41.9
SP	7	0	0	13.9
KKP	9	0	6	13.1
PWP	6	0	4	7.9
SCF	3	0	0	5.8
RRP	3	0	3	2.7
CPI	1	0	1	1.5
IND (20)	11	0	19	13.2
(61)	12	12	33	

Part: 48.5

1957 Party	Cont	Won	LD	Pct.
CONG	12	1	0	37.6
PSP	5	4	0	20.0
CPI	4	4	0	17.7
SCF	1	1	0	6.2
PWP	1	1	0	5.6
RRP	2	0	2	1.2
IND (17)	10	1	14	11.7
(42)	12	12	16	

Part: 52.8

1962 Party	Cont	Won	LD	Pct.
CONG	12	12	0	50.5
CPI	8	0	2	16.5
PSP	8	0	5	13.0
RPI	3	0	1	5.0
JS	4	0	4	3.6
PWP	1	0	0	1.3
SP	1	0	1	0.2
IND (23)	11	0	20	9.9
(60)	12	12	33	

Part: 56.6

1967 Party	Cont	Won	LD	Pct.
CONG	13	9	0	46.3
SSP	3	1	0	8.6
RPI	3	1	0	8.4
JS	3	0	1	6.5
PWP	2	1	1	4.3
PSP	3	1	2	4.2
CPI	1	0	0	2.4
CPM	1	0	0	2.1
Swat	1	0	1	#
IND (20)	9	0	14	17.2
(50)	13	13	19	

Part: 58.2

DHULIA DISTRICT

Population: 1,351,236
Urban: 16.0 Rural: 84.0
Hindu: 91.0 Muslim: 5.6 Buddhist: 2.3 Jain: 0.8 Christian: 0.3

1952				
Party	Cont	Won	LD	Pct.
CONG	10	8	0	43.3
PWP	7	2	0	20.6
SP	7	0	1	14.7
SCF	2	0	1	4.9
CPI	1	0	0	3.7
IND	(9) 8	0	6	12.8
	(36) 10	10	9	
Part: 50.7				

1957				
Party	Cont	Won	LD	Pct.
CONG	9	3	0	43.3
PSP	4	2	0	17.5
SCF	1	0	0	3.7
CPI	1	0	0	1.1
IND	(8) 6	4	4	34.4
	(23) 9	9	4	
Part: 47.5				

1962				
Party	Cont	Won	LD	Pct.
CONG	9	9	0	56.3
JS	7	0	3	12.7
PSP	5	0	5	5.4
CPI	2	0	0	5.1
RPI	4	0	4	3.4
PWP	1	0	0	2.4
IND	(15) 9	0	12	14.7
	(43) 9	9	24	
Part: 49.7				

1967				
Party	Cont	Won	LD	Pct.
CONG	9	7	0	52.3
JS	5	0	0	20.6
CPI	3	2	0	14.1
PSP	2	0	1	3.9
SSP	1	0	0	3.7
RPI	1	0	1	0.5
IND	(10) 6	0	10	4.9
	(31) 9	9	12	
Part: 53.8				

JALGAON DISTRICT

Population: 1,765,047
Urban: 22.5 Rural: 77.5
Hindu: 83.4 Muslim: 9.7 Buddhist: 5.8 Jain: 0.9 Christian: 0.2

1952

Party	Cont	Won	LD	Pct.
CONG	14	14	0	54.8
SP	10	0	4	12.2
KKP	6	0	3	5.1
SCF	3	0	1	4.7
PWP	3	0	1	4.2
CPI	3	0	2	3.0
IND	(19) 12	0	17	16.0
	(58) 14	14	28	

Part: 54.0

1957

Party	Cont	Won	LD	Pct.
CONG	12	7	0	49.0
PSP	6	3	0	19.4
CPI	2	1	0	6.3
PWP	1	0	0	6.2
SCF	1	0	0	5.9
JS	1	1	0	3.7
IND	(3) 2	0	0	9.5
	(26) 12	12	0	

Part: 57.6

1962

Party	Cont	Won	LD	Pct.
CONG	12	12	0	58.1
PSP	9	0	3	17.2
JS	9	0	6	8.8
CPI	4	0	3	4.5
RPI	3	0	2	2.9
PWP	2	0	1	2.2
SP	2	0	2	0.8
IND	(7) 6	0	5	5.5
	(48) 12	12	22	

Part: 56.5

1967

Party	Cont	Won	LD	Pct.
CONG	12	11	0	51.4
JS	9	0	5	12.5
PSP	11	0	8	11.3
SSP	5	0	4	7.6
CPI	2	0	1	3.9
PWP	2	0	2	2.4
RPI	2	0	2	1.9
Swat	3	0	3	0.7
IND	(8) 6	1	6	8.3
	(54) 12	12	31	

Part: 57.9

NAGPUR DIVISION (VIDARBHA)

Population: 9,233,742
Urban: 22.4 Rural: 77.6
Hindu: 78.6 Buddhist: 14.1 Muslim: 6.3 Jain: 0.5 Christian: 0.3

1952				
Party	Cont	Won	LD	Pct.
CONG	83	75	0	51.5
SP	50	1	21	11.0
SCF	31	0	12	7.6
JS	34	0	29	4.4
SKP	19	2	14	3.4
KMPP	19	1	16	2.4
CPI	8	0	6	0.8
FB(R)	6	0	5	0.6
RRP	6	0	6	0.2
FB(M)	1	0	1	#
IND (174)	61	4	144	18.1
(431)	83	83	254	
Part: 58.9				

1957				
Party	Cont	Won	LD	Pct.
CONG	63	55	0	51.7
SCF	25	2	2	12.3
PSP	29	2	15	8.1
PWP	5	1	0	3.4
JS	9	0	3	2.9
CPI	4	0	1	2.0
RRP	4	0	4	0.2
HMS	2	0	2	0.1
IND (93)	49	3	65	19.3
(234)	63	63	92	
Part: 60.0				

1962				
Party	Cont	Won	LD	Pct.
CONG	63	45	1	44.5
RPI	26	3	5	10.4
JS	36	0	27	5.9
PSP	7	2	1	3.3
PWP	7	1	3	3.0
CPI	6	0	1	2.4
SP	1	0	1	#
HMS	1	0	1	#
RRP	1	0	1	#
IND (166)	62	12	124	30.4
(314)	63	63	165	
Part: 63.3				

1967				
Party	Cont	Won	LD	Pct.
CONG	63	48	0	45.2
RPI	43	3	14	15.5
JS	41	2	26	9.2
SSP	9	0	2	3.3
PWP	5	0	1	2.5
CPI	7	0	4	1.5
CPM	2	1	1	0.9
PSP	4	0	4	0.3
Swat	2	0	2	#
IND (169)	61	9	143	21.6
(345)	63	63	197	
Part: 64.3				

BULDANA DISTRICT

Population: 1,059,689
Urban: 16.6 Rural: 83.4
Hindu: 76.2 Buddhist: 13.1 Muslim: 9.4 Jain: 0.7 Christian: 0.5

	1952			
Party	Cont	Won	LD	Pct.
CONG	9	6	0	45.9
SKP	6	2	2	21.8
JS	5	0	4	5.9
SCF	1	0	0	3.0
SP	2	0	2	1.5
IND (13)	9	1	9	21.9
(36)	9	9	17	
Part: 56.5				

	1957			
Party	Cont	Won	LD	Pct.
CONG	7	5	0	42.9
PWP	2	1	0	16.2
JS	3	0	1	7.4
SCF	2	1	1	7.3
HMS	1	0	1	0.6
RRP	1	0	1	0.5
IND (13)	7	0	9	25.1
(29)	7	7	13	
Part: 62.6				

	1962			
Party	Cont	Won	LD	Pct.
CONG	7	6	0	48.7
JS	6	0	2	15.4
PWP	3	1	2	10.3
RPI	3	0	2	4.8
HMS	1	0	1	0.1
IND (17)	7	0	14	20.7
(32)	7	7	21	
Part: 66.6				

	1967			
Party	Cont	Won	LD	Pct.
CONG	7	7	0	48.0
JS	7	0	2	21.3
RPI	6	0	2	20.3
PWP	1	0	0	5.6
Swat	2	0	2	0.3
PSP	1	0	1	0.1
IND (15)	7	0	15	4.4
(39)	7	7	22	
Part: 69.4				

AKOLA DISTRICT

Population: 1,189,354
Urban: 22.1 Rural: 77.9
Hindu: 70.7 Buddhist: 16.7 Muslim: 11.5 Jain: 0.9 Christian: 0.2

1952

Party	Cont	Won	LD	Pct.
CONG	10	10	0	52.5
JS	4	0	3	8.3
SP	6	0	3	8.1
SKP	7	0	7	5.7
SCF	1	0	0	4.4
RRP	1	0	1	0.8
CPI	1	0	1	0.2
IND	(21) 10	0	18	20.0
	(51) 10	10	33	
Part:	77.6			

1957

Party	Cont	Won	LD	Pct.
CONG	8	8	0	54.2
SCF	3	0	1	8.8
PWP	2	0	0	5.2
JS	3	0	1	4.9
PSP	3	0	2	3.3
RRP	1	0	1	0.2
IND	(13) 7	0	10	23.4
	(33) 8	8	15	
Part:	61.5			

1962

Party	Cont	Won	LD	Pct.
CONG	8	7	0	50.8
RPI	3	0	0	8.4
PWP	2	0	1	5.6
JS	4	0	3	5.6
CPI	1	0	0	2.6
IND	(19) 8	1	13	27.0
	(37) 8	8	17	
Part:	59.4			

1967

Party	Cont	Won	LD	Pct.
CONG	8	7	0	55.7
RPI	5	1	0	19.9
JS	3	0	1	10.1
PWP	1	0	0	3.8
CPM	1	0	1	1.9
CPI	1	0	1	0.1
IND	(20) 7	0	19	8.5
	(39) 8	8	22	
Part:	63.6			

AMRAVATI DISTRICT

Population: 1,232,780
Urban: 26.1 Rural: 73.9
Hindu: 75.0 Buddhist: 14.3 Muslim: 9.7 Jain: 0.6 Christian: 0.3

Party	1952 Cont	Won	LD	Pct.
CONG	12	11	0	46.9
SCF	10	0	5	11.6
SP	7	0	5	5.9
CPI	4	0	2	4.5
KMPP	3	0	2	3.1
JS	3	0	3	2.8
FB(R)	3	0	3	0.8
RRP	1	0	1	0.1
IND	(33) 11	1	25	24.3
	(76) 12	12	46	
Part:	56.0			

Party	1957 Cont	Won	LD	Pct.
CONG	8	8	0	50.3
SCF	2	0	0	10.9
CPI	3	0	1	8.8
PSP	3	0	3	3.6
RRP	2	0	2	0.6
IND	(17) 7	0	12	25.8
	(35) 8	8	18	
Part:	64.7			

Party	1962 Cont	Won	LD	Pct.
CONG	8	4	0	45.1
RPI	3	1	0	15.8
CPI	1	0	0	4.2
JS	3	0	3	2.6
RRP	1	0	1	0.1
IND	(24) 8	3	20	32.2
	(40) 8	8	24	
Part:	70.7			

Party	1967 Cont	Won	LD	Pct.
CONG	8	7	0	47.0
RPI	5	1	1	23.2
CPI	3	0	1	8.4
JS	6	0	6	5.7
PWP	1	0	0	5.5
SSP	1	0	0	4.5
PSP	1	0	1	0.1
IND	(10) 7	0	10	5.6
	(35) 8	8	19	
Part:	64.9			

WARDHA DISTRICT

Population: 634,277
Urban: 23.6 Rural: 76.4
Hindu: 80.6 Buddhist: 15.1 Muslim: 3.5 Jain: 0.6
Christian: 0.1 Sikh: 0.1

		1952		
Party	Cont	Won	LD	Pct.
CONG	6	6	0	55.3
SP	4	0	3	9.1
SCF	2	0	0	8.3
FB(R)	2	0	2	3.3
JS	2	0	2	2.1
KMPP	1	0	1	0.8
IND (16)	6	0	13	21.1
(33)	6	6	21	
Part: 57.5				

		1957		
Party	Cont	Won	LD	Pct.
CONG	4	4	0	61.4
PWP	1	0	0	12.4
SCF	1	0	0	12.4
IND (5)	2	0	4	13.8
(11)	4	4	4	
Part: 63.9				

		1962		
Party	Cont	Won	LD	Pct.
CONG	4	2	0	40.8
RPI	2	0	1	10.2
CPI	1	0	0	5.1
JS	3	0	3	4.8
IND (12)	4	2	9	39.1
(22)	4	4	13	
Part: 66.5				

		1967		
Party	Cont	Won	LD	Pct.
CONG	4	2	0	38.6
RPI	3	0	1	12.3
CPM	1	1	0	8.8
JS	1	0	1	1.6
IND (20)	4	1	16	38.7
(29)	4	4	18	
Part: 67.9				

NAGPUR DISTRICT

Population: 1,512,807
Urban: 52.1 Rural: 47.9
Hindu: 77.0 Buddhist: 15.5 Muslim: 5.8 Christian: 0.9
Jain: 0.5 Sikh: 0.3

	1952			
Party	Cont	Won	LD	Pct.
CONG	13	12	0	51.3
SP	8	0	4	10.7
SCF	7	0	3	10.1
KMPP	7	1	6	6.8
JS	10	0	9	6.3
FB(R)	1	0	0	1.6
CPI	2	0	2	0.6
RRP	2	0	2	0.3
FB(M)	1	0	1	0.2
SKP	1	0	1	0.2
IND (35)	11	0	32	11.9
(87)	13	13	60	

Part: 57.5

	1957			
Party	Cont	Won	LD	Pct.
CONG	10	8	0	50.7
SCF	4	1	0	15.3
PSP	5	0	0	11.7
JS	1	0	1	0.8
HMS	1	0	1	0.3
IND (18)	8	1	13	21.2
(39)	10	10	15	

Part: 57.3

	1962			
Party	Cont	Won	LD	Pct.
CONG	10	7	0	35.8
RPI	3	1	0	8.8
JS	8	0	8	7.0
CPI	2	0	1	3.7
PSP	2	0	1	3.6
IND (31)	10	2	21	41.1
(56)	10	10	31	

Part: 64.1

	1967			
Party	Cont	Won	LD	Pct.
CONG	10	9	0	45.9
RPI	6	0	1	13.5
JS	6	0	4	8.9
PSP	1	0	1	0.5
SSP	2	0	2	0.5
PWP	1	0	1	0.3
CPI	1	0	1	0.2
IND (46)	10	1	41	30.2
(73)	10	10	51	

Part: 62.4

BHANDARA DISTRICT

Population: 1,268,286
Urban: 10.7 Rural: 89.3
Hindu: 81.1 Buddhist: 16.9 Muslim: 1.8 Christian: 0.1 Jain: 0.1

1952				
Party	Cont	Won	LD	Pct.
CONG	12	11	0	45.2
SP	8	1	0	18.3
SCF	4	0	1	9.1
KMPP	6	0	6	3.6
JS	3	0	2	1.7
RRP	1	0	1	0.1
CPI	1	0	1	0.1
IND	(35) 11	0	32	21.9
	(70) 12	12	43	
Part:	55.7			

1957				
Party	Cont	Won	LD	Pct.
CONG	9	8	0	45.9
SCF	7	0	0	22.7
PSP	9	1	4	19.1
JS	1	0	0	5.6
IND	(11) 6	0	10	6.7
	(37) 9	9	14	
Part:	53.9			

1962				
Party	Cont	Won	LD	Pct.
CONG	9	6	0	38.2
RPI	5	1	0	18.3
PSP	3	2	0	13.7
JS	5	0	2	8.2
PWP	1	0	0	2.9
SP	1	0	1	0.3
IND	(31) 9	0	28	18.4
	(55) 9	9	31	
Part:	55.1			

1967				
Party	Cont	Won	LD	Pct.
CONG	9	5	0	37.5
RPI	8	1	1	20.5
JS	8	2	4	14.7
SSP	3	0	0	8.6
IND	(23) 9	1	20	18.7
	(51) 9	9	25	
Part:	63.7			

CHANDA AND RAJURA DISTRICT

Population: 1,238,070
Urban: 7.7 Rural: 92.3
Hindu: 85.7 Buddhist: 11.9 Muslim: 1.9 Christian: 0.2
Jain: 0.1 Sikh: 0.1

Party	Cont	Won	LD	Pct.
1952				
CONG	11	10	0	61.7
SP	7	0	1	15.7
SCF	4	0	2	6.4
JS	5	0	4	5.3
KMPP	2	0	1	2.2
RRP	1	0	1	0.3
IND	(7) 5	1	4	8.4
	(37) 11	11	13	
Part:	58.9			

Party	Cont	Won	LD	Pct.
1957				
CONG	9	7	0	48.1
PSP	6	1	5	15.9
SCF	4	0	0	10.2
JS	1	0	0	4.6
IND	(9) 7	1	4	21.2
	(29) 9	9	9	
Part:	57.9			

Party	Cont	Won	LD	Pct.
1962				
CONG	9	6	1	42.6
RPI	4	0	0	11.3
PSP	2	0	0	7.8
JS	3	0	2	3.2
IND	(14) 8	3	7	35.1
	(32) 9	9	10	
Part:	60.1			

Party	Cont	Won	LD	Pct.
1967				
CONG	9	6	0	42.3
SSP	3	0	0	11.2
RPI	4	0	2	7.4
JS	3	0	1	6.2
PSP	1	0	1	1.6
IND	(22) 9	3	16	31.3
	(42) 9	9	20	
Part:	57.1			

YEOTMAL DISTRICT

Population: 1,098,470
Urban: 12.6 Rural: 87.4
Hindu: 84.2 Buddhist: 8.8 Muslim: 6.3 Jain: 0.5 Christian: 0.1

	1952			
Party	Cont	Won	LD	Pct.
CONG	10	9	0	54.6
SP	8	0	3	15.3
SCF	2	0	1	6.1
SKP	5	0	4	4.1
JS	2	0	2	1.8
IND	(14) 9	1	11	18.1
	(41) 10	10	21	

Part: 56.7

	1957			
Party	Cont	Won	LD	Pct.
CONG	8	7	0	62.5
SCF	2	0	0	9.2
CPI	1	0	0	6.9
PSP	3	0	1	5.2
IND	(7) 5	1	3	16.2
	(21) 8	8	4	

Part: 62.5

	1962			
Party	Cont	Won	LD	Pct.
CONG	8	7	0	56.0
PWP	1	0	0	5.9
RPI	3	0	2	5.1
CPI	1	0	0	3.5
JS	4	0	4	1.0
IND	(18) 8	1	12	28.5
	(35) 8	8	18	

Part: 68.8

	1967			
Party	Cont	Won	LD	Pct.
CONG	8	5	0	45.1
RPI	6	0	6	5.3
PWP	1	0	0	4.8
CPI	2	0	1	2.5
JS	7	0	7	2.4
IND	(13) 8	3	6	39.9
	(37) 8	8	20	

Part: 69.1

AURANGABAD DIVISION (MARATHWADA)

Population: 6,297,373
Urban: 12.6 Rural: 87.4
Hindu: 80.8 Muslim: 11.1 Buddhist: 7.3 Jain: 0.5 Christian: 0.3

1952

Party	Cont	Won	LD	Pct.
CONG	48	30*	0	45.5
PWP	19	10	3	16.4
PDF	28	6	5	15.9
SCF	10	2	3	8.1
SP	25	0	20	6.0
DCA	2	0	2	0.5
RRP	2	0	2	0.3
HMS	2	0	2	0.2
JS	2	0	2	0.2
IND	(26) 23	0	23	6.9
	(164) 48	48	62	

Part: 38.3
*Uncontested: CONG (1)

1957

Party	Cont	Won	LD	Pct.
CONG	42	35	0	53.3
PWP	15	4	0	15.0
CPI	11	2	0	7.6
SCF	5	0	0	6.4
PSP	6	1	0	6.2
JS	3	0	3	0.7
IND	(23) 20	0	11	10.8
	(105) 42	42	14	

Part: 36.9

1962

Party	Cont	Won	LD	Pct.
CONG	42	33	0	53.6
PWP	19	7	3	18.2
CPI	11	2	0	9.9
PSP	11	0	6	4.1
RPI	6	0	1	3.2
JS	1	0	1	0.1
IND	(54) 29	0	45	10.9
	(144) 42	42	56	

Part: 46.1

1967

Party	Cont	Won	LD	Pct.
CONG	43	33	0	49.6
PWP	16	3	3	14.4
CPI	10	4	0	10.7
SSP	6	3	1	5.1
JS	27	0	22	5.0
RPI	7	0	1	3.3
Swat	3	0	2	0.9
CPM	1	0	0	0.9
IND	(61) 34	0	52	10.1
	(174) 43	43	81	

Part: 50.0

NANDED DISTRICT

Population: 1,079,674
Urban: 14.4 Rural: 85.6
Hindu: 81.2 Muslim: 10.9 Buddhist: 7.5 Sikh: 0.3 Jain: 0.1
Christian: #

1952

Party	Cont	Won	LD	Pct.
CONG	9	8	0	55.4
PDF	8	1	1	26.0
SP	6	0	3	10.8
RRP	1	0	1	0.8
SCF	1	0	1	0.3
IND	(5) 5	0	4	6.7
	(30) 9	9	10	

Part: 30.1

1957

Party	Cont	Won	LD	Pct.
CONG	7	5	0	49.5
PWP	2	1	0	13.5
CPI	2	1	0	9.5
SCF	1	0	0	4.3
PSP	1	0	0	4.1
JS	1	0	1	0.7
IND	(5) 4	0	2	18.4
	(19) 7	7	3	

Part: 34.8

1962

Party	Cont	Won	LD	Pct.
CONG	7	6	0	56.7
PWP	2	1	0	12.3
CPI	2	0	0	9.6
PSP	1	0	0	3.7
RPI	1	0	1	1.8
JS	1	0	1	0.7
IND	(14) 6	0	11	15.2
	(28) 7	7	13	

Part: 48.8

1967

Party	Cont	Won	LD	Pct.
CONG	7	6	0	52.2
PWP	2	1	0	14.1
CPI	2	0	0	10.3
RPI	2	0	0	8.2
SSP	1	0	0	4.9
JS	5	0	5	3.2
IND	(11) 6	0	11	7.1
	(30) 7	7	16	

Part: 49.0

PARBHANI DISTRICT

Population: 1,206,236
Urban: 13.8   Rural: 86.1
Hindu: 77.9   Buddhist: 11.1 Muslim: 10.4   Jain: 0.5 Christian: 0.1

<table>
<tr><td colspan="5">1952</td></tr>
<tr><td>Party</td><td>Cont</td><td>Won</td><td>LD</td><td>Pct.</td></tr>
<tr><td>PWP</td><td>7</td><td>6</td><td>0</td><td>38.5</td></tr>
<tr><td>CONG</td><td>9</td><td>1</td><td>0</td><td>28.5</td></tr>
<tr><td>SCF</td><td>2</td><td>2</td><td>0</td><td>11.0</td></tr>
<tr><td>PDF</td><td>4</td><td>0</td><td>3</td><td>6.1</td></tr>
<tr><td>SP</td><td>6</td><td>0</td><td>6</td><td>5.3</td></tr>
<tr><td>RRP</td><td>1</td><td>0</td><td>1</td><td>1.0</td></tr>
<tr><td>DCA</td><td>1</td><td>0</td><td>1</td><td>1.0</td></tr>
<tr><td>IND (4)</td><td>4</td><td>0</td><td>3</td><td>8.6</td></tr>
<tr><td>(34)</td><td>9</td><td>9</td><td>14</td><td></td></tr>
</table>

Part: 34.3

<table>
<tr><td colspan="5">1957</td></tr>
<tr><td>Party</td><td>Cont</td><td>Won</td><td>LD</td><td>Pct.</td></tr>
<tr><td>CONG</td><td>8</td><td>7</td><td>0</td><td>56.8</td></tr>
<tr><td>PWP</td><td>5</td><td>1</td><td>0</td><td>22.9</td></tr>
<tr><td>SCF</td><td>2</td><td>0</td><td>0</td><td>13.0</td></tr>
<tr><td>CPI</td><td>1</td><td>0</td><td>0</td><td>4.9</td></tr>
<tr><td>IND (2)</td><td>2</td><td>0</td><td>1</td><td>2.4</td></tr>
<tr><td>(18)</td><td>8</td><td>8</td><td>1</td><td></td></tr>
</table>

Part: 31.4

<table>
<tr><td colspan="5">1962</td></tr>
<tr><td>Party</td><td>Cont</td><td>Won</td><td>LD</td><td>Pct.</td></tr>
<tr><td>CONG</td><td>8</td><td>6</td><td>0</td><td>51.9</td></tr>
<tr><td>PWP</td><td>6</td><td>2</td><td>0</td><td>27.5</td></tr>
<tr><td>PSP</td><td>2</td><td>0</td><td>1</td><td>5.5</td></tr>
<tr><td>RPI</td><td>1</td><td>0</td><td>0</td><td>3.3</td></tr>
<tr><td>IND (15)</td><td>8</td><td>0</td><td>14</td><td>11.8</td></tr>
<tr><td>(32)</td><td>8</td><td>8</td><td>15</td><td></td></tr>
</table>

Part: 39.8

<table>
<tr><td colspan="5">1967</td></tr>
<tr><td>Party</td><td>Cont</td><td>Won</td><td>LD</td><td>Pct.</td></tr>
<tr><td>CONG</td><td>8</td><td>5</td><td>0</td><td>48.2</td></tr>
<tr><td>PWP</td><td>5</td><td>1</td><td>1</td><td>20.8</td></tr>
<tr><td>CPI</td><td>1</td><td>1</td><td>0</td><td>8.2</td></tr>
<tr><td>SSP</td><td>1</td><td>1</td><td>0</td><td>7.1</td></tr>
<tr><td>JS</td><td>4</td><td>0</td><td>4</td><td>3.2</td></tr>
<tr><td>RPI</td><td>1</td><td>0</td><td>0</td><td>2.1</td></tr>
<tr><td>Swat</td><td>1</td><td>0</td><td>1</td><td>0.1</td></tr>
<tr><td>IND (17)</td><td>7</td><td>0</td><td>16</td><td>10.3</td></tr>
<tr><td>(38)</td><td>8</td><td>8</td><td>22</td><td></td></tr>
</table>

Part: 44.9

AURANGABAD DISTRICT

Population: 1,532,341
Urban: 14.1 Rural: 85.9
Hindu: 75.6 Muslim: 13.9 Buddhist: 8.6 Christian: 1.1 Jain: 0.8

	1952			
Party	Cont	Won	LD	Pct.
CONG	11	9	0	48.9
PDF	8	2	1	22.1
SCF	4	0	2	11.7
SP	7	0	5	9.0
DCA	1	0	1	1.1
PWP	2	0	2	0.9
JS	2	0	2	0.8
IND	(6) 5	0	6	5.5
	(41) 11	11	19	
Part:	39.7			

	1957			
Party	Cont	Won	LD	Pct.
CONG	10	8	0	54.2
PSP	3	1	0	12.3
CPI	3	1	0	9.5
PWP	2	0	0	4.7
JS	2	0	2	2.8
IND	(10) 8	0	7	16.5
	(30) 10	10	9	
Part:	34.2			

	1962			
Party	Cont	Won	LD	Pct.
CONG	10	9	0	55.4
PWP	3	1	2	11.0
PSP	4	0	1	8.8
CPI	3	0	0	7.9
RPI	1	0	0	2.7
IND	(11) 7	0	8	14.2
	(32) 10	10	11	
Part:	44.3			

	1967			
Party	Cont	Won	LD	Pct.
CONG	11	10	0	56.5
JS	6	0	2	11.1
SSP	3	1	1	6.4
CPI	2	0	0	5.4
RPI	2	0	1	3.4
Swat	1	0	0	2.8
PWP	1	0	1	1.0
IND	(14) 8	0	10	13.4
	(40) 11	11	15	
Part:	48.0			

BHIR DISTRICT

Population: 1,001,466
Urban: 9.9 Rural: 90.1
Hindu: 88.1 Muslim: 9.1 Buddhist: 2.2 Jain: 0.5 Christian: #

		1952						1957		
Party	Cont	Won	LD	Pct.		Party	Cont	Won	LD	Pct.
CONG	8	4	0	41.3		CONG	7	7	0	51.1
PDF	7	3	0	32.2		CPI	4	0	0	17.5
PWP	3	1	1	14.1		PSP	1	0	0	10.3
SCF	1	0	0	7.2		SCF	1	0	0	9.3
SP	1	0	1	1.5		PWP	1	0	0	5.8
IND	(6) 4	0	6	3.7		IND	(2) 2	0	1	6.0
	(26) 8	8	8				(16) 7	7	1	
Part:	36.8					Part:	33.7			

		1962						1967		
Party	Cont	Won	LD	Pct.		Party	Cont	Won	LD	Pct.
CONG	7	5	0	51.1		CONG	7	4	0	40.9
CPI	5	2	0	36.1		CPI	4	3	0	31.7
PWP	1	0	0	4.1		JS	5	0	4	5.6
RPI	1	0	0	2.1		CPM	1	0	0	5.6
PSP	1	0	1	0.9		PWP	1	0	0	4.3
IND	(8) 4	0	8	5.7		RPI	1	0	0	2.6
	(23) 7	7	9			IND	(8) 5	0	6	9.3
Part:	39.6						(27) 7	7	10	
						Part:	48.9			

OSMANABAD DISTRICT

Population: 1,477,656
Urban: 10.6 Rural: 89.4
Hindu: 83.2 Muslim: 10.1 Buddhist: 6.2 Jain: 0.4 Christian: 0.1

1952

Party	Cont	Won	LD	Pct.
CONG	11	8*	0	50.8
PWP	7	3	0	25.7
SCF	2	0	0	7.8
SP	5	0	5	3.5
PDF	1	0	0	2.4
HMS	2	0	2	0.8
IND	(5) 5	0	4	9.0
	(33) 11	11	11	

Part: 49.6
*Uncontested: CONG (1)

1957

Party	Cont	Won	LD	Pct.
CONG	10	8	0	53.7
PWP	5	2	0	21.6
SCF	1	0	0	6.3
PSD	1	0	0	5.5
CPI	1	0	0	2.3
IND	(4) 4	0	0	10.6
	(22) 10	10	0	

Part: 47.7

1962

Party	Cont	Won	LD	Pct.
CONG	10	7	0	52.4
PWP	7	3	1	29.6
RPI	2	0	0	5.0
CPI	1	0	0	4.4
PSP	3	0	3	1.4
IND	(6) 4	0	4	7.2
	(29) 10	10	8	

Part: 55.2

1967

Party	Cont	Won	LD	Pct.
CONG	10	8	0	48.1
PWP	7	1	1	28.0
SSP	1	1	0	5.8
CPI	1	0	0	4.3
JS	7	0	7	1.9
RPI	1	0	0	1.2
Swat	1	0	1	1.0
IND	(11) 8	0	9	9.7
	(39) 10	10	18	

Part: 57.8

POONA DIVISION

Population: 10,360,282
Urban: 22.3 Rural: 77.7
Hindu: 87.3 Muslim: 5.5 Buddhist: 3.9 Jain: 1.9 Christian: 1.2
Other: 0.2

1952

Party	Cont	Won	LD	Pct.
CONG	70	50	0	46.3
PWP	44	11	13	14.8
SP	36	0	20	8.2
KKP	17	2	5	5.5
SCF	16	0	6	5.3
CPI	4	1	0	1.7
RRP	5	0	4	0.7
HMS	2	0	1	0.5
KMPP	1	0	1	0.1
FB(M)	1	0	1	#
IND (113)	52	6	98	16.9
(309)	70	70	149	

Part: 51.1

1957

Party	Cont	Won	LD	Pct.
CONG	69	17	2	39.1
PWP	21	14	0	15.2
SCF	9	5	0	9.1
PSP	9	8	1	6.1
CPI	4	3	0	3.6
HMS	2	1	1	1.3
JS	2	1	0	1.2
IND (70)	45	20	35	24.4
(186)	69	69	39	

Part: 54.4

1962

Party	Cont	Won	LD	Pct.
CONG	69	61	0	59.4
PWP	30	3	13	10.0
PSP	22	1	9	5.9
CPI	11	2	4	4.2
JS	25	0	21	3.1
RPI	13	0	8	2.6
Swat	4	0	4	0.3
HMS	2	0	2	0.2
SP	1	0	1	0.1
IND (118)	55	2	96	14.2
(295)	69	69	158	

Part: 58.4

1967

Party	Cont	Won	LD	Pct.
CONG	71	58*	0	52.8
PWP	22	7	3	11.8
SSP	14	0	4	5.8
CPI	11	1	2	4.9
JS	30	1	27	3.8
PSP	12	1	8	2.4
RPI	10	0	5	2.4
Swat	8	0	6	0.6
CPM	1	0	0	0.4
IND (110)	54	3	90	15.1
(289)	71	71	145	

Part: 64.2
*Uncontested: CONG (1)

SHOLAPUR DISTRICT

Population: 1,860,119
Urban: 27.9 Rural: 72.1
Hindu: 86.5 Muslim: 9.2 Buddhist: 3.4 Jain: 0.8 Christian: 0.1

1952

Party	Cont	Won	LD	Pct.
CONG	13	6	0	41.2
PWP	10	5	1	27.0
SCF	5	0	2	10.3
SP	3	0	3	2.6
RRP	2	0	2	0.9
IND	(18) 11	2	15	18.0
	(51) 13	13	23	

Part: 52.0

1957

Party	Cont	Won	LD	Pct.
CONG	12	10	0	46.5
PWP	4	0	0	11.3
SCF	3	0	0	9.4
PSP	2	1	1	4.8
CPI	1	0	0	3.5
HMS	1	0	1	1.0
IND	(16) 10	1	10	23.6
	(39) 12	12	12	

Part: 48.3

1962

Party	Cont	Won	LD	Pct.
CONG	12	9	0	54.3
PWP	3	1	0	8.7
CPI	1	1	0	4.9
RPI	4	0	3	4.6
PSP	1	0	0	2.3
JS	2	0	1	1.9
HMS	1	0	1	0.6
IND	(29) 12	1	22	22.7
	(53) 12	12	27	

Part: 54.2

1967

Party	Cont	Won	LD	Pct.
CONG	13	9	0	50.5
PWP	4	2	0	14.0
Swat	5	0	4	3.5
SSP	1	0	0	3.5
RPI	2	0	1	2.9
CPI	1	0	0	2.6
JS	3	0	3	0.8
IND	(22) 11	2	15	22.2
	(51) 13	13	23	

Part: 62.1

AHMEDNAGAR DISTRICT

Population: 1,757,969
Urban: 10.5 Rural: 89.5
Hindu: 87.7 Muslim: 5.3 Buddhist: 2.9 Christian: 2.7 Jain: 1.3

		1952		
Party	Cont	Won	LD	Pct.
CONG	11	9	0	47.8
KKP	7	1	0	23.3
CPI	4	1	0	11.6
SP	5	0	0	9.9
SCF	2	0	1	3.0
PWP	1	0	0	2.5
HMS	1	0	1	0.4
FB(M)	1	0	1	0.1
IND	(5) 3	0	5	1.4
	(37) 11	11	8	

Part: 40.5

		1957		
Party	Cont	Won	LD	Pct.
CONG	12	1	1	33.7
IND	(21) 12	11	7	66.3
	(33) 12	12	8	

Part: 45.3

		1962		
Party	Cont	Won	LD	Pct.
CONG	12	10	0	51.0
CPI	4	1	0	12.7
PSP	4	0	1	5.1
RPI	2	0	0	3.5
JS	2	0	2	1.7
IND	(16) 11	1	9	26.0
	(40) 12	12	12	

Part: 54.1

		1967		
Party	Cont	Won	LD	Pct.
CONG	12	10	0	48.5
CPI	7	1	0	24.1
SSP	1	0	0	4.9
JS	6	0	5	4.2
PSP	1	0	0	2.3
RPI	2	0	1	1.7
IND	(16) 8	1	12	14.3
	(45) 12	12	18	

Part: 60.1

POONA DISTRICT

Population: 2,466,880
Urban: 38.1 Rural: 61.9
Hindu: 86.8 Buddhist: 5.2 Muslim: 4.4 Christian: 1.8
Jain: 1.3 Sikh: 0.4 Other: 0.1

1952				
Party	Cont	Won	LD	Pct.
CONG	15	14	0	53.4
SP	12	0	6	14.1
PWP	13	0	6	12.3
SCF	4	0	2	4.0
RRP	3	0	2	2.7
HMS	1	0	0	2.6
KKP	2	0	2	0.4
IND	(18) 10	1	17	10.5
	(68) 15	15	35	
Part: 48.0				

1957				
Party	Cont	Won	LD	Pct.
CONG	16	1	0	37.3
PSP	6	6	0	20.6
SCF	2	2	0	11.2
PWP	2	2	0	8.9
HMS	1	1	0	5.3
CPI	1	1	0	4.2
JS	1	1	0	2.8
IND	(10) 8	2	6	9.7
	(39) 16	16	6	
Part: 52.4				

1962				
Party	Cont	Won	LD	Pct.
CONG	16	15	0	54.0
PSP	10	1	3	16.0
JS	12	0	9	9.0
PWP	8	0	7	5.0
RPI	4	0	4	1.9
CPI	2	0	2	1.4
HMS	1	0	1	0.7
Swat	1	0	1	0.3
SP	1	0	1	0.2
IND	(35) 11	0	32	11.5
	(90) 16	16	60	
Part: 54.1				

1967				
Party	Cont	Won	LD	Pct.
CONG	17	14	0	51.8
SSP	10	0	3	14.4
JS	11	1	9	10.6
PSP	10	1	7	9.1
PWP	4	1	2	6.1
RPI	3	0	2	2.8
Swat	2	0	2	0.1
IND	(27) 13	0	26	5.1
	(84) 17	17	51	
Part: 61.9				

SATARA DISTRICT

Population: 1,430,105
Urban: 11.1 Rural: 88.9
Hindu: 89.1 Buddhist: 6.8 Muslim: 3.4 Jain: 0.5 Christian: 0.1

		1952						1957		
Party	Cont	Won	LD	Pct.	Party	Cont	Won	LD	Pct.
CONG	11	8	0	45.9	CONG	10	3	0	40.9
PWP	9	2	4	21.6	PWP	5	3	0	22.7
KKP	5	1	1	9.5	CPI	1	1	0	10.0
SCF	2	0	1	2.8	SCF	1	1	0	8.6
SP	3	0	3	2.5	PSP	1	1	0	6.0
IND	(25) 9	0	22	17.7	IND	(5) 3	1	2	11.8
	(55) 11	11	31			(23) 10	10	2	
Part:	56.9					Part:	61.6			

		1962						1967		
Party	Cont	Won	LD	Pct.	Party	Cont	Won	LD	Pct.
CONG	10	10	0	70.6	CONG	10	10*	0	68.2
PWP	6	0	4	10.3	PWP	4	0	1	10.0
PSP	2	0	1	4.0	CPI	3	0	2	3.9
CPI	2	0	1	3.5	RPI	1	0	0	3.1
Swat	3	0	3	1.5	SSP	1	0	0	2.3
RPI	1	0	1	0.9	JS	3	0	3	2.1
JS	1	0	1	0.6	IND	(13) 6	0	12	10.4
IND	(17) 7	0	15	8.6		(35) 10	10	18	
	(42) 10	10	26			Part:	65.6			
Part:	64.5					*Uncontested: CONG (1)				

SANGLI DISTRICT

Population: 1,230,716
Urban: 15.6 Rural: 84.4
Hindu: 84.5 Muslim: 6.2 Buddhist: 4.6 Jain: 3.9 Christian: 0.8

		1952		
Party	Cont	Won	LD	Pct.
CONG	9	8	0	53.1
SP	4	0	2	6.9
PWP	4	0	2	6.8
SCF	1	0	0	5.7
KKP	2	0	1	3.4
KMPP	1	0	1	0.7
IND	(16) 8	1	14	23.4
	(37) 9	9	20	
Part: 58.3				

		1957		
Party	Cont	Won	LD	Pct.
CONG	8	2	0	43.5
PWP	4	4	0	30.0
SCF	2	1	0	14.1
JS	1	0	0	4.2
IND	(6) 3	1	5	8.2
	(21) 8	8	5	
Part: 65.4				

		1962		
Party	Cont	Won	LD	Pct.
CONG	8	8	0	70.1
PWP	6	0	1	17.3
PSP	4	0	4	3.0
RPI	1	0	0	2.7
JS	6	0	6	2.4
CPI	1	0	1	1.5
IND	(7) 6	0	7	3.0
	(33) 8	8	19	
Part: 67.6				

		1967		
Party	Cont	Won	LD	Pct.
CONG	8	8	0	57.6
PWP	4	0	0	15.6
SSP	1	0	1	1.2
JS	6	0	6	1.1
RPI	1	0	1	0.3
PSP	1	0	1	0.1
IND	(14) 6	0	10	24.1
	(35) 8	8	19	
Part: 69.0				

KOLHAPUR DISTRICT

Population: 1,596,493
Urban: 19.3 Rural: 80.7
Hindu: 89.2 Muslim: 4.8 Jain: 4.6 Christian: 0.8 Buddhist: 0.6

1952

Party	Cont	Won	LD	Pct.
CONG	11	5	0	37.7
PWP	7	4	0	14.5
SP	9	0	6	12.8
SCF	2	0	0	4.6
KKP	1	0	1	0.7
IND (31)	11	2	25	29.7
(61)	11	11	32	
Part: 55.8				

1957

Party	Cont	Won	LD	Pct.
CONG	11	0	1	31.8
PWP	6	5	0	22.4
SCF	1	1	0	10.8
CPI	1	1	0	3.5
IND (12)	9	4	5	31.5
(31)	11	11	6	
Part: 61.5				

1962

Party	Cont	Won	LD	Pct.
CONG	11	9	0	59.5
PWP	7	2	1	20.3
RPI	1	0	0	2.5
CPI	1	0	0	2.2
PSP	1	0	0	1.6
JS	2	0	2	1.0
IND (14)	8	0	11	12.9
(37)	11	11	14	
Part: 61.4				

1967

Party	Cont	Won	LD	Pct.
CONG	11	7	0	45.3
PWP	6	4	0	26.5
SSP	1	0	0	4.2
RPI	1	0	0	2.9
CPM	1	0	0	2.4
JS	1	0	1	0.7
IND (18)	10	0	15	18.0
(39)	11	11	16	
Part: 69.8				

STATE SUMMARY

Population: 23,586,772
Urban: 22.3 Rural: 77.7
Hindu: 87.3 Muslim: 9.9 Christian: 2.1 Jain: 0.7

1952

Party	Cont	Won	LD	Pct.
CONG	211	163*	0	51.4
KMPP	95	9	32	13.1
SP	81	4	43	7.2
SCF	12	2	7	1.5
PDF+CPI	20	1	14	1.5
JS	26	0	21	1.3
PWP	3	1	0	0.9
Repub	2	0	1	0.1
FB(M)	3	0	3	0.1
DCA	1	0	1	#
HMS	1	0	1	#
IND	(283)162	31	162	22.8
	(738)211	211	285	

Part: 56.1
*Uncontested: CONG (1)

1957

Party	Cont	Won	LD	Pct.
CONG	206	149*	1	51.9
PSP	78	18	18	14.1
CPI	20	1	9	1.9
JS	20	0	14	1.3
SCF	6	2	1	1.3
PWP	2	2	0	0.6
IND	(229)158	36*	91	28.9
	(561)208	208	134	

Part: 52.6
*Uncontested: CONG (5)
                 IND (1)

1962

Party	Cont	Won	LD	Pct.
CONG	208	138*	0	50.2
PSP	83	20	14	14.1
Swat	60	9	24	7.2
LSS	17	4	4	2.5
JS	63	0	56	2.3
CPI	31	3	22	2.3
MES	6	6	0	2.2
SP	8	1	4	0.9
RPI	19	0	14	0.8
DMK	4	0	4	0.1
IND	(180)120	27	108	17.4
	(679)208	208	250	

Part: 56.0
*Uncontested: CONG (2)

1967

Party	Cont	Won	LD	Pct.
CONG	216	126*	1	48.6
PSP	52	20	10	8.9
Swat	45	16	12	6.6
JS	37	4	24	2.8
SSP	17	6	5	2.5
CPM	10	1	4	1.1
RPI	12	1	9	0.8
CPI	6	1	3	0.5
IND	(332)172	41	200	28.2
	(727)216	216	268	

Part: 59.3
*Uncontested: CONG (2)

BOMBAY, MADRAS AND HYDERABAD KARNATAK

Population: 11,926,522
Urban: 20.6 Rural: 79.4
Hindu: 84.2 Muslim: 12.3 Christian: 2.3 Jain: 1.2

1952

Party	Cont	Won	LD	Pct.
CONG	87	73	0	56.0
KMPP	36	1	7	12.6
SP	34	1	21	6.1
PDF+CPI	13	0	9	2.0
PWP	3	1	0	1.8
SCF	5	0	3	1.3
JS	3	0	3	0.4
Repub	2	0	1	0.3
FB(M)	3	0	3	0.2
DCA	1	0	1	0.1
HMS	1	0	1	#
IND (94)	56	11	59	19.2
(282)	87	87	108	

Part: 62.6

1957

Party	Cont	Won	LD	Pct.
CONG	105	81*	1	54.4
PSP	27	5	5	10.2
CPI	9	0	1	2.2
SCF	3	1	0	1.7
JS	10	0	6	1.5
PWP	2	2	0	1.2
IND (107)	81	17*	39	28.8
(263)	106	106	52	

Part: 53.0
*Uncontested: CONG (3)
                      IND (1)

1962

Party	Cont	Won	LD	Pct.
CONG	106	78*	0	54.0
Swat	38	7	10	11.0
PSP	31	6	6	10.2
LSS	17	4	4	5.2
MES	6	6	0	4.5
CPI	15	2	8	3.0
JS	30	0	25	2.5
RPI	12	0	9	1.1
SP	1	0	1	#
IND (59)	45	3	39	8.5
(315)	106	106	102	

Part: 54.3
*Uncontested: CONG (1)

1967

Party	Cont	Won	LD	Pct.
CONG	108	67	0	51.9
Swat	29	10	8	8.7
PSP	21	10	6	7.1
JS	18	3	8	3.8
CPM	6	0	2	1.4
RPI	7	1	5	1.0
CPI	5	1	3	0.9
SSP	4	1	1	0.7
IND (126)	81	15	70	24.5
(324)	108	108	103	

Part: 58.8
*Uncontested: CONG (2)

BIDAR DISTRICT

Population: 663,172
Urban: 12.3 Rural: 87.7
Hindu: 79.2 Muslim: 18.1 Christian: 2.4 Buddhist: 0.3

1952

Party	Cont	Won	LD	Pct.
CONG	5	5	0	63.9
SP	5	0	2	21.8
PDF	5	0	4	9.0
SCF	1	0	1	3.8
DCA	1	0	1	1.5
(17)	5	5	8	

Part: 44.6

1957

Party	Cont	Won	LD	Pct.
PSP	6	1	1	34.8
CONG	6	3	1	33.0
IND (5)	5	2	0	32.2
(17)	6	6	2	

Part: 44.8

1962

Party	Cont	Won	LD	Pct.
CONG	6	4	0	47.0
PSP	5	1	2	20.9
CPI	1	0	0	7.8
RPI	2	0	1	5.9
IND (3)	3	1	0	18.4
(17)	6	6	3	

Part: 45.4

1967

Party	Cont	Won	LD	Pct.
CONG	6	3	0	47.1
JS	1	1	0	10.1
CPI	1	1	0	7.5
RPI	1	0	0	5.0
PSP	2	0	2	2.5
IND (6)	5	1	2	27.8
(17)	6	6	4	

Part: 58.4

GULBARGA DISTRICT

Population: 1,399,457
Urban: 16.2 Rural: 83.8
Hindu: 81.8 Muslim: 17.3 Christian: 0.6 Jain: 0.2

1952

Party	Cont	Won	LD	Pct.
CONG	12	11	0	60.4
SP	7	0	5	7.7
Repub	2	0	1	3.7
PDF	1	0	1	1.2
HMS	1	0	1	0.1
IND	(11) 8	1	5	26.9
	(34) 12	12	13	

Part: 31.0

1957

Party	Cont	Won	LD	Pct.
CONG	12	10*	0	51.9
PSP	3	0	1	9.6
CPI	4	0	0	7.2
IND	(10) 10	3*	1	31.3
	(29) 13	13	2	

Part: 38.8
*Uncontested: CONG (2)
                       IND (1)

1962

Party	Cont	Won	LD	Pct.
CONG	13	8	0	51.0
Swat	8	3	0	30.7
CPI	3	1	1	7.0
LSS	1	1	0	5.5
PSP	4	0	2	3.4
RPI	3	0	3	2.0
SP	1	0	1	0.1
IND	(1) 1	0	1	0.3
	(34) 13	13	8	

Part: 42.4

1967

Party	Cont	Won	LD	Pct.
CONG	13	8	0	57.4
Swat	7	3	1	19.8
PSP	1	1	0	4.1
CPM	1	0	0	3.4
SSP	2	0	1	1.7
CPI	2	0	2	1.3
JS	1	0	1	0.5
RPI	1	0	1	0.3
IND	(6) 6	1	2	11.5
	(34) 13	13	8	

Part: 49.2

RAICHUR DISTRICT

Population: 1,100,895
Urban: 14.6 Rural: 86.4
Hindu: 86.8 Muslim: 11.9 Christian: 1.1 Jain: 0.2

1952

Party		Cont	Won	LD	Pct.
CONG		9	3	0	43.5
SP		2	0	2	1.3
IND	(13)	9	6	4	55.2
	(24)	9	9	6	

Part: 44.2

1957

Party		Cont	Won	LD	Pct.
CONG		10	10	0	57.0
PSP		1	0	1	0.4
IND	(19)	10	0	8	42.6
	(30)	10	10	9	

Part: 39.1

1962

Party		Cont	Won	LD	Pct.
CONG		10	7	0	55.0
LSS		10	3	1	41.9
Swat		2	0	1	2.9
IND	(1)	1	0	1	0.2
	(23)	10	10	3	

Part: 41.3

1967

Party		Cont	Won	LD	Pct.
CONG		10	7	0	51.0
Swat		2	1	0	9.6
SSP		1	1	0	4.9
JS		1	0	1	0.7
IND	(11)	8	1	4	33.8
	(25)	10	10	5	

Part: 48.0

BELLARY DISTRICT

Population: 915,261
Urban: 22.6 Rural: 77.4
Hindu: 88.5 Muslim: 10.6 Christian: 0.6 Jain: 0.3

		1952						1957		
Party	Cont	Won	LD	Pct.		Party	Cont	Won	LD	Pct.
CONG	5	3	0	46.2		CONG	8	5	0	50.4
SP	2	0	2	2.3		PSP	4	2	0	31.3
KMPP	1	0	1	0.9		JS	1	0	1	0.6
IND (9)	5	2	3	50.6		IND (6)	4	1	2	17.7
(17)	5	5	6			(19)	8	8	3	

Part: 59.4   Part: 63.9

		1962						1967		
Party	Cont	Won	LD	Pct.		Party	Cont	Won	LD	Pct.
CONG	8	4	0	49.0		CONG	8	7*	0	54.4
PSP	4	2	1	24.8		Swat	3	1	0	21.3
Swat	3	1	1	15.0		PSP	2	0	1	6.6
IND (8)	6	1	6	11.2		IND (6)	4	0	3	17.7
(23)	8	8	8			(19)	8	8	4	

Part: 59.4   Part: 62.0
                                          *Uncontested: CONG (1)

SOUTH KANARA (MANGALORE) DISTRICT

Population: 1,563,837
Urban: 17.9 Rural: 82.1
Hindu: 79.1 Christian: 10.4 Muslim: 9.7 Jain: 0.7

1952

Party	Cont	Won	LD	Pct.
CONG	9	8	0	52.9
KMPP	5	1	0	22.8
SP	5	0	3	10.2
CPI	2	0	0	5.4
JS	2	0	2	1.8
SCF	1	0	1	0.6
IND	(5) 4	0	3	6.3
	(29) 9	9	9	
Part:	62.0			

1957

Party	Cont	Won	LD	Pct.
CONG	14	12	0	59.0
PSP	6	2	0	19.3
CPI	4	0	0	11.5
JS	3	0	1	5.9
IND	(3) 3	0	2	4.3
	(30) 14	14	3	
Part:	52.8			

1962

Party	Cont	Won	LD	Pct.
CONG	14	9	0	46.6
PSP	7	3	0	20.3
Swat	7	1	2	13.8
CPI	6	1	2	11.3
JS	9	0	8	4.7
IND	(8) 8	0	8	3.3
	(51) 14	14	20	
Part:	57.8			

1967

Party	Cont	Won	LD	Pct.
CONG	14	6	0	41.2
PSP	7	4	1	19.4
Swat	7	2	4	8.9
JS	4	1	1	8.8
CPM	2	0	0	4.5
CPI	1	0	1	0.7
IND	(21) 11	1	17	16.5
	(56) 14	14	24	
Part:	65.9			

NORTH KANARA (KARWAR) DISTRICT

Population: 689,549
Urban: 17.5 Rural: 82.5
Hindu: 87.8 Muslim: 7.7 Christian: 4.2 Jain: 0.3

1952 Party	Cont	Won	LD	Pct.
CONG	5	4	0	47.8
SP	5	1	0	28.9
CPI	3	0	3	5.3
FB(M)	1	0	1	0.5
IND (12)	4	0	10	17.5
(26)	5	5	14	
Part: 58.6				

1957 Party	Cont	Won	LD	Pct.
CONG	5	5	0	52.3
PSP	5	0	1	26.4
IND (8)	5	0	7	21.3
(18)	5	5	8	
Part: 58.2				

1962 Party	Cont	Won	LD	Pct.
CONG	5	4	0	52.4
PSP	4	0	0	24.8
MES	1	1	0	12.7
Swat	1	0	0	4.4
CPI	2	0	2	2.9
JS	2	0	2	1.4
IND (4)	3	0	4	1.4
(19)	5	5	8	
Part: 54.0				

1967 Party	Cont	Won	LD	Pct.
CONG	6	1	0	34.8
PSP	3	3	0	21.5
Swat	2	0	1	5.6
JS	1	0	0	3.6
CPM	1	0	1	0.7
IND (6)	4	2	2	33.8
(19)	6	6	4	
Part: 57.3				

DHARWAR DISTRICT

Population: 1,950,362
Urban: 26.9 Rural: 73.1
Hindu: 83.4 Muslim: 14.7 Christian: 0.9 Jain: 0.9

<table>
<tr><th colspan="5">1952</th><th colspan="5">1957</th></tr>
<tr><th>Party</th><th>Cont</th><th>Won</th><th>LD</th><th>Pct.</th><th>Party</th><th>Cont</th><th>Won</th><th>LD</th><th>Pct.</th></tr>
<tr><td>CONG</td><td>14</td><td>14</td><td>0</td><td>58.5</td><td>CONG</td><td>17</td><td>16</td><td>0</td><td>65.2</td></tr>
<tr><td>KMPP</td><td>10</td><td>0</td><td>0</td><td>21.8</td><td>JS</td><td>3</td><td>0</td><td>2</td><td>2.1</td></tr>
<tr><td>SCF</td><td>1</td><td>0</td><td>0</td><td>1.7</td><td>IND (24)</td><td>17</td><td>1</td><td>13</td><td>32.7</td></tr>
<tr><td>SP</td><td>4</td><td>0</td><td>4</td><td>1.6</td><td>(44)</td><td>17</td><td>17</td><td>15</td><td></td></tr>
<tr><td>JS</td><td>1</td><td>0</td><td>1</td><td>0.9</td><td>Part: 56.9</td><td></td><td></td><td></td><td></td></tr>
<tr><td>FB(M)</td><td>1</td><td>0</td><td>1</td><td>0.3</td><td></td><td></td><td></td><td></td><td></td></tr>
<tr><td>IND (15)</td><td>9</td><td>0</td><td>11</td><td>15.2</td><td></td><td></td><td></td><td></td><td></td></tr>
<tr><td>(46)</td><td>14</td><td>14</td><td>17</td><td></td><td></td><td></td><td></td><td></td><td></td></tr>
<tr><td>Part: 58.9</td><td></td><td></td><td></td><td></td><td></td><td></td><td></td><td></td><td></td></tr>
</table>

<table>
<tr><th colspan="5">1962</th><th colspan="5">1967</th></tr>
<tr><th>Party</th><th>Cont</th><th>Won</th><th>LD</th><th>Pct.</th><th>Party</th><th>Cont</th><th>Won</th><th>LD</th><th>Pct.</th></tr>
<tr><td>CONG</td><td>17</td><td>16</td><td>0</td><td>59.5</td><td>CONG</td><td>18</td><td>10*</td><td>0</td><td>51.9</td></tr>
<tr><td>PSP</td><td>4</td><td>0</td><td>0</td><td>9.4</td><td>PSP</td><td>4</td><td>2</td><td>1</td><td>10.4</td></tr>
<tr><td>Swat</td><td>6</td><td>1</td><td>2</td><td>8.9</td><td>JS</td><td>5</td><td>1</td><td>2</td><td>6.2</td></tr>
<tr><td>JS</td><td>9</td><td>0</td><td>7</td><td>5.2</td><td>Swat</td><td>2</td><td>1</td><td>0</td><td>5.3</td></tr>
<tr><td>LSS</td><td>1</td><td>0</td><td>0</td><td>2.2</td><td>CPM</td><td>1</td><td>0</td><td>0</td><td>1.9</td></tr>
<tr><td>CPI</td><td>2</td><td>0</td><td>2</td><td>0.9</td><td>CPI</td><td>1</td><td>0</td><td>0</td><td>1.3</td></tr>
<tr><td>IND (11)</td><td>9</td><td>0</td><td>5</td><td>13.9</td><td>SSP</td><td>1</td><td>0</td><td>0</td><td>0.8</td></tr>
<tr><td>(50)</td><td>17</td><td>17</td><td>16</td><td></td><td>RPI</td><td>1</td><td>0</td><td>1</td><td>0.1</td></tr>
<tr><td>Part: 61.1</td><td></td><td></td><td></td><td></td><td>IND (21)</td><td>13</td><td>4</td><td>14</td><td>22.1</td></tr>
<tr><td></td><td></td><td></td><td></td><td></td><td>(54)</td><td>18</td><td>18</td><td>18</td><td></td></tr>
<tr><td></td><td></td><td></td><td></td><td></td><td>Part: 64.6</td><td></td><td></td><td></td><td></td></tr>
<tr><td></td><td></td><td></td><td></td><td></td><td colspan="5">*Uncontested: CONG (1)</td></tr>
</table>

BELGAUM DISTRICT

Population: 1,983,811
Urban: 18.0 Rural: 82.0
Hindu: 85.6 Muslim: 9.0 Jain: 4.6 Christian: 0.7 Buddhist: 0.1

1952						1957				
Party	Cont	Won	LD	Pct.		Party	Cont	Won	LD	Pct.
CONG	15	12	0	54.2		CONG	18	7*	0	47.5
KMPP	9	0	3	13.2		SCF	2	1	0	7.8
PWP	3	1	0	9.0		PWP	2	2	0	5.9
SP	3	0	2	3.1		PSP	2	0	1	1.7
SCF	1	0	0	2.7		JS	1	0	0	1.1
CPI	1	0	1	0.4		IND (14)	12	8	4	36.0
IND (14)	8	2	9	17.4		(39)	18	18	5	
(46)	15	15	15			Part: 61.3				
Part: 65.0						*Uncontested: CONG (1)				

1962						1967				
Party	Cont	Won	LD	Pct.		Party	Cont	Won	LD	Pct.
CONG	18	12	0	55.0		CONG	18	14	0	59.0
MES	5	5	0	20.2		RPI	3	0	3	1.6
PSP	3	0	1	3.6		Swat	2	0	2	0.9
LSS	2	0	1	3.3		JS	2	0	1	0.9
RPI	3	0	2	2.6		PSP	1	0	1	0.4
Swat	2	0	1	1.4		IND (31)	18	4	14	37.2
IND (12)	8	1	6	13.9		(57)	18	18	21	
(45)	18	18	11			Part: 63.2				
Part: 62.0										

BIJAPUR DISTRICT

Population: 1,660,178
Urban: 18.9 Rural: 81.1
Hindu: 86.6 Muslim: 12.4 Jain: 0.9 Christian: 0.1

1952					1957				
Party	Cont	Won	LD	Pct.	Party	Cont	Won	LD	Pct.
CONG	13	13	0	68.1	CONG	15	13	0	58.3
KMPP	11	0	3	17.9	SCF	1	0	0	1.6
CPI	1	0	0	1.5	JS	2	0	2	0.9
SCF	1	0	1	1.3	CPI	1	0	1	0.5
FB(M)	1	0	1	0.8	IND	(18) 15	2	2	38.7
SP	1	0	1	0.5		(37) 15	15	5	
IND	(15) 9	0	14	9.9	Part:	54.4			
	(43) 13	13	20						
Part:	52.9								

1962					1967				
Party	Cont	Won	LD	Pct.	Party	Cont	Won	LD	Pct.
CONG	15	14*	0	61.9	CONG	15	11	0	57.2
Swat	9	1	3	18.8	Swat	4	2	0	11.9
JS	10	0	8	6.6	JS	3	0	2	3.6
LSS	3	0	2	4.2	RPI	1	1	0	3.0
RPI	4	0	3	1.2	PSP	1	0	0	1.6
CPI	1	0	1	#	CPM	1	0	1	0.7
IND	(11) 6	0	8	7.3	IND	(18) 12	1	12	22.0
	(53) 15	15	25			(43) 15	15	15	
Part:	53.8				Part:	56.0			
*Uncontested:	CONG (1)								

"OLD MYSORE" AND COORG

Population: 11,660,250
Urban: 24.1 Rural: 75.9
Hindu: 90.4 Muslim: 7.4 Christian: 1.9 Jain: 0.3

1952

Party	Cont	Won	LD	Pct.
CONG	124	90*	0	46.8
KMPP	59	8	25	13.6
SP	47	3	22	8.4
JS	23	0	18	2.2
SCF	7	2	4	1.7
CPI	7	1	5	0.9
IND	(189) 106	20	103	26.4
	(456) 124	124	177	

Part: 50.7
*Uncontested: CONG (1)

1957

Party	Cont	Won	LD	Pct.
CONG	101	68*	0	49.7
PSP	51	13	13	17.5
CPI	11	1	8	1.7
JS	10	0	8	1.2
SCF	3	1	1	0.9
IND	(122) 77	19	52	29.0
	(298) 102	102	82	

Part: 52.3
*Uncontested: CONG (2)

1962

Party	Cont	Won	LD	Pct.
CONG	102	60*	0	46.6
PSP	52	14	8	17.7
Swat	22	2	14	3.7
JS	33	0	31	2.1
SP	7	1	3	1.8
CPI	16	1	14	1.6
RPI	7	0	5	0.5
DMK	4	0	4	0.3
IND	(121) 75	24	69	25.7
	(364) 102	102	148	

Part: 57.8
*Uncontested: CONG (1)

1967

Party	Cont	Won	LD	Pct.
CONG	108	59	1	45.1
PSP	31	10	4	10.6
Swat	16	6	4	4.6
SSP	13	5	4	4.2
JS	19	1	16	1.9
CPM	4	1	2	0.8
RPI	5	0	4	0.5
CPI	1	0	0	0.2
IND	(206) 91	26	130	32.1
	(403) 108	108	165	

Part: 59.8

CHITRADURGA DISTRICT

Population: 1,094,284
Urban: 17.4 Rural: 82.6
Hindu: 92.3 Muslim: 7.1 Christian: 0.3 Jain: 0.2

Party	Cont	Won	LD	Pct.
1952				
CONG	10	8	0	50.5
SP	7	1	4	13.7
KMPP	3	1	2	7.0
SCF	2	0	2	1.1
CPI	1	0	1	0.3
IND (16)	8	0	10	27.4
(39)	10	10	19	
Part: 58.4				

Party	Cont	Won	LD	Pct.
1957				
CONG	9	5	0	51.3
PSP	5	3	1	20.0
IND (8)	6	1	3	28.7
(22)	9	9	4	
Part: 57.6				

Party	Cont	Won	LD	Pct.
1962				
CONG	9	7	0	50.9
PSP	8	2	0	36.8
JS	3	0	3	2.5
CPI	1	0	1	0.6
Swat	1	0	1	0.2
IND (11)	5	0	9	9.0
(33)	9	9	14	
Part: 62.4				

Party	Cont	Won	LD	Pct.
1967				
CONG	10	7	0	49.2
PSP	6	0	0	25.8
Swat	1	1	0	4.5
RPI	1	0	1	0.3
SSP	1	0	1	#
IND (14)	8	2	9	20.2
(33)	10	10	11	
Part: 65.2				

TUMKUR DISTRICT

Population: 1,367,402
Urban: 10.2   Rural: 89.8
Hindu: 93.4   Muslim: 6.1   Christian: 0.2   Jain: 0.2

	1952			
Party	Cont	Won	LD	Pct.
CONG	13	11	0	46.6
SP	12	0	4	17.5
KMPP	10	1	4	14.9
JS	5	0	4	3.4
IND	(17) 9	1	12	17.6
	(57) 13	13	24	

Part: 55.5

	1957			
Party	Cont	Won	LD	Pct.
CONG	11	7	0	49.4
PSP	8	3	0	28.8
JS	3	0	3	4.0
CPI	3	0	3	0.9
IND	(13) 6	2	7	16.9
	(38) 12	12	13	

Part: 49.8

	1962			
Party	Cont	Won	LD	Pct.
CONG	12	5	0	43.1
PSP	10	4	1	31.7
JS	4	0	4	1.8
CPI	1	0	1	0.8
IND	(11) 8	3	5	22.6
	(38) 12	12	11	

Part: 57.3

	1967			
Party	Cont	Won	LD	Pct.
CONG	13	9	0	46.1
PSP	8	3	0	21.8
Swat	2	0	1	1.5
JS	1	0	1	1.0
CPM	1	0	1	0.8
IND	(22) 13	1	13	28.8
	(47) 13	13	16	

Part: 56.9

KOLAR DISTRICT

Population: 1,290,144
Urban: 22.7   Rural: 77.3
Hindu: 87.5   Muslim: 9.6   Christian: 2.6   Jain: 0.2

1952

Party	Cont	Won	LD	Pct.
CONG	13	7*	0	43.0
CPI	2	1	1	5.7
SCF	1	1	0	5.2
SP	5	1	4	5.1
IND	(28) 12	3	17	41.0
	(49) 13	13	22	

Part: 48.0
*Uncontested: CONG (1)

1957

Party	Cont	Won	LD	Pct.
CONG	12	5	0	42.8
CPI	1	1	0	4.6
SCF	1	1	0	4.5
PSP	1	0	1	0.5
JS	1	0	1	0.2
IND	(18) 12	5	7	47.4
	(34) 12	12	9	

Part: 50.7

1962

Party	Cont	Won	LD	Pct.
CONG	12	5	0	45.9
RPI	5	0	4	3.0
CPI	2	1	1	2.6
DMK	1	0	1	0.3
IND	(15) 12	6	4	48.2
	(35) 12	12	10	

Part: 57.7

1967

Party	Cont	Won	LD	Pct.
CONG	12	8	0	50.3
RPI	1	0	0	3.6
CPM	1	0	0	2.2
IND	(22) 11	4	11	43.9
	(36) 12	12	11	

Part: 60.2

BANGALORE URBAN DISTRICT

Population: 1,302,419
Urban: 100.0 Rural: 0.0
Hindu: 85.8 Muslim: 9.7 Christian: 4.1 Jain: 0.4

1952				
Party	Cont	Won	LD	Pct.
CONG	7	7	0	48.0
KMPP	6	0	4	12.1
SP	5	0	3	9.8
JS	5	0	5	4.0
CPI	2	0	2	1.4
IND (18)	8	0	14	24.7
(43)	7	7	28	
Part: 49.6				

1957				
Party	Cont	Won	LD	Pct.
CONG	8	6	0	50.4
CPI	2	0	2	3.9
SCF	1	0	1	0.9
JS	1	0	1	0.4
IND (15)	8	2	6	44.4
(27)	8	8	10	
Part: 43.2				

1962				
Party	Cont	Won	LD	Pct.
CONG	10	8	0	39.7
Swat	7	0	5	10.5
CPI	4	0	4	3.9
PSP	3	0	2	3.4
DMK	3	0	3	2.8
JS	7	0	7	2.7
RPI	2	0	1	2.3
SP	1	0	1	0.6
IND (23)	9	2	15	34.1
(60)	10	10	38	
Part: 54.2				

1967				
Party	Cont	Won	LD	Pct.
CONG	12	7	0	34.0
CPM	2	1	1	4.2
Swat	3	0	2	2.5
JS	2	0	2	1.6
PSP	1	0	1	1.2
RPI	2	0	2	0.6
IND (58)	12	4	44	55.9
(80)	12	12	52	
Part: 48.7				

BANGALORE RURAL DISTRICT

Population: 1,202,043
Urban: 4.6 Rural: 95.4
Religious data included in Bangalore Urban District

1952				
Party	Cont	Won	LD	Pct.
CONG	14	14	0	50.8
KMPP	14	0	6	26.5
SP	4	0	2	3.2
JS	3	0	2	3.1
SCF	1	0	1	0.6
IND	(19) 11	0	13	15.8
	(55) 14	14	24	
Part:	42.9			

1957				
Party	Cont	Won	LD	Pct.
CONG	15	12	0	53.1
PSP	9	3	3	22.8
CPI	3	0	2	2.4
JS	2	0	1	1.7
IND	(16) 10	0	8	20.0
	(45) 15	15	14	
Part:	48.6			

1962				
Party	Cont	Won	LD	Pct.
CONG	13	7	0	45.9
PSP	4	1	1	11.1
Swat	3	1	1	7.2
CPI	1	0	1	0.9
SP	1	0	1	0.3
JS	1	0	1	0.3
IND	(13) 9	4	5	34.3
	(36) 13	13	10	
Part:	61.7			

1967				
Party	Cont	Won	LD	Pct.
CONG	11	6	0	47.3
PSP	2	1	0	6.3
Swat	1	0	0	3.4
JS	1	0	1	0.5
SSP	1	0	1	0.2
IND	(26) 11	4	17	42.3
	(42) 11	11	19	
Part:	61.4			

MANDYA DISTRICT

Population: 899,210
Urban: 11.1 Rural: 88.9
Hindu: 95.9 Muslim: 3.5 Christian: 0.4 Jain: 0.1

1952				
Party	Cont	Won	LD	Pct.
CONG	8	5	0	45.3
KMPP	5	1	0	20.3
SCF	1	1	0	6.1
IND	(9) 7	1	2	28.3
	(23) 8	8	2	

Part: 53.6

1957				
Party	Cont	Won	LD	Pct.
CONG	8	5	0	53.2
PSP	5	1	1	21.1
SCF	1	0	0	3.6
IND	(7) 5	2	3	22.1
	(21) 8	8	4	

Part: 57.6

1962				
Party	Cont	Won	LD	Pct.
CONG	8	4	0	52.0
PSP	3	0	0	9.3
SP	1	0	1	0.7
IND	(9) 7	4	3	38.0
	(21) 8	8	4	

Part: 63.9

1967				
Party	Cont	Won	LD	Pct.
CONG	8	5	0	49.8
PSP	2	0	0	9.0
RPI	1	0	1	0.4
IND	(15) 8	3	8	40.8
	(26) 8	8	9	

Part: 66.1

MYSORE DISTRICT

Population: 1,671,399
Urban: 24.8 Rural: 75.2
Hindu: 92.8 Muslim: 5.7 Christian: 1.2 Jain: 0.3

1952				
Party	Cont	Won	LD	Pct.
CONG	15	6	0	33.1
KMPP	10	3	6	12.5
SP	5	0	4	3.4
SCF	2	0	1	2.3
JS	4	0	4	1.0
IND (32)	15	6	16	47.7
(68)	15	15	31	
Part: 45.7				

1957				
Party	Cont	Won	LD	Pct.
CONG	16	11	0	47.6
PSP	12	1	3	22.4
JS	1	0	1	1.2
CPI	1	0	1	0.2
IND (19)	12	4	7	28.6
(49)	16	16	12	
Part: 50.1				

1962				
Party	Cont	Won	LD	Pct.
CONG	16	10*	0	48.7
PSP	8	2	1	16.9
Swat	5	1	3	7.2
JS	4	0	4	2.0
CPI	3	0	3	1.9
SP	1	0	0	0.9
IND (21)	12	3	16	22.4
(58)	16	16	27	
Part: 57.7				
*Uncontested: CONG (1)				

1967				
Party	Cont	Won	LD	Pct.
CONG	16	9	1	45.6
SSP	3	1	1	3.9
PSP	2	0	0	3.5
JS	7	0	7	3.4
Swat	3	0	1	3.0
IND (31)	15	6	16	40.6
(62)	16	16	26	
Part: 61.2				

COORG DISTRICT

Population: 322,829
Urban: 13.2 Rural: 86.8
Hindu: 85.9 Muslim: 10.8 Christian: 3.3

1952

Party	Cont	Won	LD	Pct.
CONG	24	15	0	55.6
CPI	2	0	1	1.6
IND	(34) 24	9	11	42.8
	(60) 24	24	12	

Part: 63.6

1957

Party	Cont	Won	LD	Pct.
CONG	2	2	0	53.2
PSP	1	0	0	20.8
CPI	1	0	0	20.8
IND	(1) 1	0	1	5.2
	(5) 2	2	1	

Part: 69.4

1962

Party	Cont	Won	LD	Pct.
CONG	2	2	0	49.7
Swat	2	0	1	19.0
CPI	2	0	1	16.6
JS	2	0	2	3.8
PSP	1	0	1	1.0
IND	(1) 1	0	0	9.9
	(10) 2	2	5	

Part: 60.8

1967

Party	Cont	Won	LD	Pct.
CONG	3	1	0	44.3
Swat	1	1	0	20.2
JS	1	1	0	15.1
CPI	1	0	0	6.3
PSP	1	0	1	1.9
IND	(3) 1	0	2	12.2
	(10) 3	3	3	

Part: 62.5

HASSAN DISTRICT

Population: 895,847
Urban: 12.0 Rural: 88.0
Hindu: 93.8 Muslim: 4.8 Christian: 1.0 Jain: 0.3

1952				
Party	Cont	Won	LD	Pct.
CONG	8	8	0	62.4
KMPP	5	0	1	25.5
SP	2	0	0	4.7
IND (5)	5	0	2	7.4
(20)	8	8	3	
Part: 50.4				

1957				
Party	Cont	Won	LD	Pct.
CONG	8	4	0	46.8
PSP	3	2	1	13.0
IND (12)	7	2	4	40.2
(23)	8	8	5	
Part: 59.5				

1962				
Party	Cont	Won	LD	Pct.
CONG	8	4	0	44.1
PSP	7	3	1	31.8
JS	5	0	4	5.9
Swat	4	0	3	5.5
CPI	1	0	1	1.1
IND (7)	5	1	5	11.6
(32)	8	8	14	
Part: 51.5				

1967				
Party	Cont	Won	LD	Pct.
CONG	8	2	0	42.3
Swat	5	4	0	32.1
PSP	2	1	0	14.5
JS	3	0	3	1.3
IND (3)	2	1	1	9.8
(21)	8	8	4	
Part: 61.8				

CHIKMAGALUR DISTRICT

Population: 597,305
Urban: 15.0 Rural: 85.0
Hindu: 90.1 Muslim: 6.7 Christian: 2.9 Jain: 0.3

1952

Party	Cont	Won	LD	Pct.
CONG	6	5	0	50.9
JS	4	0	2	11.5
SP	3	0	1	10.9
KMPP	3	1	1	10.3
IND (8)	4	0	5	16.4
(24)	6	6	9	

Part: 45.6

1957

Party	Cont	Won	LD	Pct.
CONG	5	4*	0	46.2
PSP	3	0	2	15.0
IND (5)	4	1	1	38.8
(13)	5	5	3	

Part: 49.1
*Uncontested: CONG (1)

1962

Party	Cont	Won	LD	Pct.
CONG	5	3	0	49.0
PSP	3	1	0	23.2
JS	1	0	1	0.8
IND (6)	5	1	3	27.0
(15)	5	5	4	

Part: 51.8

1967

Party	Cont	Won	LD	Pct.
CONG	6	1	0	41.3
PSP	5	4	1	40.3
JS	1	0	0	6.5
IND (3)	3	1	1	11.9
(15)	6	6	2	

Part: 57.1

SHIMOGA DISTRICT

Population: 1,017,368
Urban: 25.6 Rural: 74.4
Hindu: 89.2 Muslim: 9.0 Christian: 1.5 Jain: 0.3

Party	Cont	Won	LD	Pct.
		1952		
CONG	6	4	0	46.0
SP	4	1	0	21.4
KMPP	3	1	1	16.1
JS	2	0	1	5.0
IND	(3) 3	0	1	11.5
	(18) 6	6	3	

Part: 66.7

Party	Cont	Won	LD	Pct.
		1957		
CONG	7	7*	0	58.0
PSP	4	0	1	17.1
JS	2	0	1	2.9
IND	(8) 6	0	5	22.0
	(21) 7	7	7	

Part: 57.0
*Uncontested: CONG (1)

Party	Cont	Won	LD	Pct.
		1962		
CONG	7	5	0	45.9
PSP	5	1	1	23.6
SP	3	1	0	20.3
JS	6	0	5	6.5
CPI	1	0	1	0.4
IND	(4) 2	0	4	3.3
	(26) 7	7	11	

Part: 54.7

Party	Cont	Won	LD	Pct.
		1967		
SSP	8	4	1	41.6
CONG	9	4	0	41.6
PSP	2	1	1	4.9
JS	3	0	2	3.3
IND	(9) 5	0	8	8.6
	(31) 9	9	12	

Part: 63.0

1952:   Three seats allotted to Naga Hills-Tuensang Area in the Assam
        Legislative Assembly; however, no nominations were filed and
        the seats were not filled.

1957:   Three seats in the Assam Legislative Assembly were filled by
        independents who were elected unopposed.

1961:   State of Nagaland formed from Naga Hills-Tuensang Area.
        Interim Body of 45 members formed by indirect elections by
        Tribal Councils pending direct elections in Kohima and
        Mokokchung districts.

1964:   Elections held in Kohima and Mokokchung districts; six members
        from Tuensang District elected by Regional Council. According
        to the official Government of Nagaland report all candidates
        ran as independents. According to India, 1964, the members
        sat as follows after the Assembly convened:

Total:	NNO:	32	DPN:	12	IND:	2
Kohima:		12		6		1
Mokokchung:		14		6		1
Tuensang:		6		0		0

1969 ELECTION

STATE SUMMARY

Population: 369,200
Urban: 5.2 Rural: 94.8
Christian: 53.0 Hindu: 9.4
Muslim: 0.2 Other: 37.4

Party	Cont	Won	LD	Pct.
NNO	40	22	5	38.8
UNF	31	11	7	22.9
IND	(73) 34	7	28	38.3
	(144) 40	40	40	

Part: 78.0 (36 seats)

KOHIMA DISTRICT

Population: 108,924
Urban: 11.9 Rural: 88.1
Christian: 38.3 Hindu: 22.4
Muslim: 0.6 Other: 38.7

Party	Cont	Won	LD	Pct.
NNO	19	8	3	38.3
UNF	17	6	4	28.7
IND	(35) 13	5	16	33.0
	(71) 19	19	23	

Part: 74.4

MOKOKCHUNG DISTRICT

Population: 126,001
Urban: 4.9 Rural: 95.1
Christian: 85.9 Hindu: 5.2
Muslim: # Other: 8.9

Party	Cont	Won	LD	Pct.
NNO	21	14	2	39.3
UNF	14	5	3	17.7
IND	(38) 21	2	12	43.0
	(73) 21	21	17	

Part: 82.6 (17 seats)

TUENSANG DISTRICT

Population: 134,275
Urban: 0.0 Rural: 100.0
Christian: 34.0 Hindu: 2.8
Muslim: 0.1 Other: 63.1

12 members elected by Regional
Council. All associated with
NNO.

STATE SUMMARY

Population: 17,548,846
Urban: 6.3 Rural: 93.7
Hindu: 97.6 Muslim: 1.2 Christian: 1.1

1952					1957				
Party	Cont	Won	LD	Pct.	Party	Cont	Won	LD	Pct.
CONG	136	67*	13	38.1	CONG	140	56*	11	38.2
GP	58	31	10	20.5	GP	110	51	20	29.3
SP	79	10	39	11.8	PSP	44	11	14	9.8
CPI	33	7	14	5.6	CPI	43	9	18	8.4
KMPP	7	0	7	0.5	IND (171)	125	13	137	14.3
FB(M)	2	1	1	0.4	(508)	140	140	200	
FB(R)	1	0	1	0.1	Part: 34.3				
IND (206)	99	24	138	23.0	*Uncontested: CONG (1)				
(522)	140	140	223						

Part: 32.5
*Uncontested: CONG (5)

1961					1967				
Party	Cont	Won	LD	Pct.	Party	Cont	Won	LD	Pct.
CONG	140	83	2	43.1	CONG	140	31	15	30.7
GP	120	36	39	22.2	Swat	101	49	17	22.6
PSP	46	10	16	11.1	JC	47	26	12	13.5
CPI	34	4	9	8.0	PSP	33	21	7	12.2
Jhkh	21	0	16	1.4	CPI	31	7	16	5.3
SP	6	1	3	0.7	SSP	9	2	3	1.5
Swat	9	0	8	0.5	CPM	10	1	5	1.2
IND (156)	87	6	131	13.0	JS	19	0	19	0.5
(532)	140	140	224		IND (213)	101	3	188	12.5
					(603)	140	140	282	

Part: 34.5

Part: 40.8

WESTERN ORISSA

Population: 7,836,363
Urban: 5.7 Rural: 94.3
Hindu: 97.7 Christian: 1.8 Muslim: 0.4

1952				
Party	Cont	Won	LD	Pct.
GP	39	23	3	38.6
CONG	59	22*	8	30.2
SP	25	5	14	7.6
CPI	3	2	1	1.4
FB(R)	1	0	1	0.2
IND (76)	40	9	46	22.0
(203)	61	61	73	

Part: 31.3
*Uncontested: CONG (4)

1957				
Party	Cont	Won	LD	Pct.
GP	62	44	6	49.5
CONG	62	7	11	25.6
PSP	15	2	10	3.4
CPI	11	2	5	2.9
IND (114)	47	7	97	18.6
(264)	62	62	129	

Part: 31.3

1961				
Party	Cont	Won	LD	Pct.
GP	59	31	4	42.5
CONG	62	25	1	36.5
PSP	15	3	9	4.2
Jhkh	20	0	15	3.8
CPI	8	1	3	3.5
SP	3	1	1	1.3
Swat	3	0	3	0.2
IND (70)	40	1	67	8.0
(240)	62	62	103	

Part: 28.8

1967				
Party	Cont	Won	LD	Pct.
Swat	55	41	2	41.8
CONG	63	7	8	26.4
JC	15	9	5	8.2
PSP	9	4	4	4.0
CPI	11	1	7	3.0
SSP	8	1	3	2.6
JS	15	0	15	1.1
IND (114)	50	0	106	12.9
(290)	63	63	150	

Part: 35.6

PHULBANI (BAUDH KHONDMALS) DISTRICT

Population: 514,427
Urban: 1.2 Rural: 97.8
Hindu: 96.7 Christian: 3.2 Muslim: 0.1

1952

Party	Cont	Won	LD	Pct.
CONG	4	1*	1	20.3
IND	(10) 3	3	2	79.7
	(14) 4	4	3	

Part: 19.9
*Uncontested: CONG (1)

1957

Party	Cont	Won	LD	Pct.
GP	4	4	0	51.3
CONG	4	0	1	24.1
IND	(13) 3	0	13	24.6
	(21) 4	4	14	

Part: 24.5

1961

Party	Cont	Won	LD	Pct.
GP	4	2	0	49.4
CONG	4	2	0	41.5
Swat	2	0	2	3.3
IND	(3) 2	0	3	5.8
	(13) 4	4	5	

Part: 15.9

1967

Party	Cont	Won	LD	Pct.
Swat	4	3	0	37.5
CONG	4	0	0	26.6
JC	2	1	1	16.4
JS	4	0	4	4.1
IND	(8) 4	0	8	15.4
	(22) 4	4	13	

Part: 24.5

KALAHANDI DISTRICT

Population: 1,009,654
Urban: 2.8 Rural: 97.2
Hindu: 99.5 Muslim: 0.2 Christian: 0.1 Jain: 0.1

1952

Party	Cont	Won	LD	Pct.
GP	5	4	0	64.2
CONG	7	3	2	27.6
SP	1	0	1	1.4
FB(R)	1	0	1	0.9
IND	(5) 2	0	4	5.9
	(19) 7	7	8	

Part: 39.3

1957

Party	Cont	Won	LD	Pct.
GP	8	6	0	60.8
CONG	8	2	3	27.4
PSP	2	0	2	2.4
IND	(8) 5	0	8	9.4
	(26) 8	8	13	

Part: 36.0

1961

Party	Cont	Won	LD	Pct.
GP	7	6	0	60.5
CONG	8	1	0	31.1
Swat	1	0	1	0.5
IND	(6) 4	1	5	7.9
	(22) 8	8	6	

Part: 24.0

1967

Party	Cont	Won	LD	Pct.
Swat	8	6	0	62.9
CONG	8	2	1	28.3
JS	3	0	3	1.4
PSP	1	0	1	0.6
IND	(5) 4	0	4	6.8
	(25) 8	8	9	

Part: 37.4

BOLANGIR DISTRICT

Population: 1,068,686
Urban: 4.6 Rural: 95.4
Hindu: 99.2 Christian: 0.5 Muslim: 0.2

1952

Party	Cont	Won	LD	Pct.
GP	8	8	0	72.7
CONG	8	0	4	18.0
SP	5	0	5	4.9
IND	(5) 4	0	5	4.4
	(26) 8	8	14	

Part: 29.7

1957

Party	Cont	Won	LD	Pct.
GP	9	9	0	68.8
CONG	9	0	1	22.7
PSP	3	0	3	4.5
IND	(3) 2	0	3	4.0
	(24) 9	9	7	

Part: 31.0

1961

Party	Cont	Won	LD	Pct.
GP	9	9	0	68.0
CONG	9	0	0	26.0
PSP	2	0	2	1.5
IND	(7) 6	0	7	4.5
	(27) 9	9	9	

Part: 29.0

1967

Party	Cont	Won	LD	Pct.
Swat	9	9	0	64.5
CONG	9	0	1	27.2
JS	3	0	3	1.4
CPI	1	0	1	1.4
IND	(9) 3	0	9	5.5
	(31) 9	9	14	

Part: 41.1

SAMBALPUR DISTRICT

Population: 1,508,686
Urban: 7.6 Rural: 92.4
Hindu: 98.7 Christian: 0.8 Muslim: 0.4

1952

Party	Cont	Won	LD	Pct.
GP	13	6	2	38.0
CONG	14	6	0	36.0
SP	2	1	0	2.4
CPI	1	0	1	0.6
IND (24)	13	1	17	23.0
(54)	14	14	20	

Part: 28.3

1957

Party	Cont	Won	LD	Pct.
GP	12	9	1	40.9
CONG	12	2	0	28.3
CPI	5	1	3	6.7
IND (35)	12	0	34	24.1
(64)	12	12	38	

Part: 28.6

1961

Party	Cont	Won	LD	Pct.
CONG	12	8	0	43.2
GP	12	2	2	33.6
CPI	2	1	0	7.6
SP	2	1	0	5.1
Jhkh	2	0	2	1.4
PSP	1	0	1	0.4
IND (16)	7	0	16	8.7
(47)	12	12	21	

Part: 29.0

1967

Party	Cont	Won	LD	Pct.
Swat	10	6	1	33.3
CONG	12	4	0	31.2
SSP	7	0	3	10.3
CPI	6	1	4	9.4
JC	4	1	3	4.5
JS	2	0	2	0.8
IND (16)	9	0	14	10.5
(57)	12	12	27	

Part: 34.6

SUNDARGARH DISTRICT

Population: 658,617
Urban: 17.9 Rural: 82.1
Hindu: 84.4 Christian: 13.9 Muslim: 1.4 Sikh: 0.1

1952

Party	Cont	Won	LD	Pct.
CONG	5	3	0	42.4
GP	4	2	0	28.4
SP	3	0	3	2.8
IND (9)	5	0	6	26.4
(21)	5	5	9	

Part: 46.8

1957

Party	Cont	Won	LD	Pct.
GP	5	3	1	50.4
CONG	5	0	1	25.1
PSP	2	0	2	2.0
IND (7)	5	2	3	22.5
(19)	5	5	7	

Part: 50.3

1961

Party	Cont	Won	LD	Pct.
GP	5	4	0	45.4
CONG	5	1	1	25.1
Jhkh	5	0	4	10.5
PSP	2	0	2	1.9
IND (7)	4	0	5	17.1
(24)	5	5	12	

Part: 35.7

1967

Party	Cont	Won	LD	Pct.
Swat	6	5	0	40.2
CONG	6	0	0	25.8
PSP	2	1	0	9.6
JS	3	0	3	3.4
CPI	1	0	1	0.5
IND (18)	6	0	17	20.5
(36)	6	6	21	

Part: 42.4

KEONJHAR DISTRICT

Population: 743,315
Urban: 4.3 Rural: 95.7
Hindu: 99.4 Muslim: 0.3 Christian: 0.1 Sikh: 0.1

1952

Party	Cont	Won	LD	Pct.
GP	4	2	1	25.7
CONG	4	0	0	20.5
SP	1	0	1	2.2
IND	(6) 3	3	3	51.6
	(15) 5	5	5	

Part: 28.2

1957

Party	Cont	Won	LD	Pct.
GP	6	5	0	40.1
CONG	6	0	1	24.6
IND	(18) 6	1	14	35.3
	(30) 6	6	15	

Part: 26.1

1961

Party	Cont	Won	LD	Pct.
GP	6	4	0	43.5
CONG	6	2	0	42.6
PSP	2	0	2	2.8
Jhkh	3	0	3	1.9
CPI	1	0	1	1.5
IND	(11) 5	0	11	7.7
	(29) 6	6	17	

Part: 23.4

1967

Party	Cont	Won	LD	Pct.
Swat	6	5	0	45.3
CONG	6	0	1	25.4
JC	1	1	0	9.4
IND	(14) 6	0	12	19.9
	(27) 6	6	13	

Part: 24.7

DHENKANAL DISTRICT

Population: 1,028,935
Urban: 4.6 Rural: 95.4
Hindu: 99.7 Muslim: 0.2 Christian: #

1952

Party	Cont	Won	LD	Pct.
CONG	7	5*	0	38.3
SP	4	0	2	20.0
CPI	2	2	0	14.4
GP	2	0	0	8.7
IND	(6) 4	1	3	18.6
	(21) 8	8	5	

Part: 28.4
*Uncontested: CONG (2)

1957

Party	Cont	Won	LD	Pct.
GP	8	5	2	51.3
CONG	8	1	2	25.3
CPI	2	1	0	6.7
IND	(12) 4	1	10	16.7
	(30) 8	8	14	

Part: 33.9

1961

Party	Cont	Won	LD	Pct.
CONG	8	4	0	45.3
GP	8	4	1	38.2
CPI	3	0	1	8.6
SP	1	0	1	1.5
IND	(10) 5	0	10	6.4
	(30) 8	8	13	

Part: 35.1

1967

Party	Cont	Won	LD	Pct.
Swat	5	3	0	29.9
JC	4	4	0	27.3
CONG	8	0	3	18.7
CPI	2	0	0	4.0
SSP	1	1	0	3.7
PSP	1	0	1	0.7
IND	(22) 8	0	22	15.7
	(43) 8	8	26	

Part: 39.2

MAYURBHANJ DISTRICT

Population: 1,204,043
Urban: 2.4 Rural: 97.6
Hindu: 99.2 Muslim: 0.6 Christian: 0.1 Other: 0.1

Party	Cont	Won	LD	Pct.
1952				
SP	9	4	2	33.2
CONG	10	4*	1	29.7
GP	3	1	0	12.9
IND	(11) 6	1	6	24.2
	(33) 10	10	9	

Part: 29.8
*Uncontested: CONG (1)

Party	Cont	Won	LD	Pct.
1957				
CONG	10	2	2	24.3
GP	10	3	2	24.2
PSP	8	2	3	19.7
CPI	4	0	2	6.8
IND	(18) 10	3	12	25.0
	(50) 10	10	21	

Part: 25.4

Party	Cont	Won	LD	Pct.
1961				
CONG	10	7	0	36.3
PSP	8	3	2	22.7
GP	8	0	1	17.7
Jhkh	10	0	6	14.8
CPI	2	0	1	2.5
IND	(10) 7	0	10	6.0
	(48) 10	10	20	

Part: 27.3

Party	Cont	Won	LD	Pct.
1967				
CONG	10	1	2	25.8
Swat	7	4	1	24.6
PSP	5	3	2	18.5
JC	4	2	1	12.9
CPI	1	0	1	1.1
IND	(22) 10	0	20	17.1
	(49) 10	10	27	

Part: 34.3

COASTAL ORISSA

Population: 9,712,483
Urban: 6.9 Rural: 93.1
Hindu: 97.5 Muslim: 1.9 Christian: 0.6

	1952			
Party	Cont	Won	LD	Pct.
CONG	77	45*	5	44.4
SP	54	5	25	15.1
CPI	30	5	13	8.9
GP	19	8	7	6.2
KMPP	7	0	7	0.8
FB(M)	2	1	1	0.6
IND (130)	59	15	92	24.0
(319)	79	79	150	

Part: 33.5
*Uncontested: CONG (1)

	1957			
Party	Cont	Won	LD	Pct.
CONG	78	49*	0	47.7
PSP	29	9	4	14.6
GP	48	7	14	14.1
CPI	32	7	13	12.5
IND (57)	34	6	40	11.1
(244)	78	78	71	

Part: 37.1
*Uncontested: CONG (1)

	1961			
Party	Cont	Won	LD	Pct.
CONG	78	58	1	46.8
PSP	31	7	7	14.8
GP	61	5	35	11.1
CPI	26	3	6	10.4
Swat	6	0	5	0.6
SP	3	0	2	0.4
Jhkh	1	0	1	#
IND (86)	47	5	64	15.9
(292)	78	78	121	

Part: 38.6

	1967			
Party	Cont	Won	LD	Pct.
CONG	77	24	7	33.1
PSP	24	17	3	17.1
JC	32	17	7	16.6
Swat	46	8	15	11.2
CPI	20	6	9	6.6
CPM	10	1	5	1.8
SSP	1	1	0	0.9
JS	4	0	4	0.2
IND (99)	51	3	82	12.5
(313)	77	77	132	

Part: 44.6

KORAPUT DISTRICT

Population: 1,498,271
Urban: 5.1 Rural: 94.9
Hindu: 97.7 Christian: 2.1 Muslim: 0.2

1952

Party	Cont	Won	LD	Pct.
CONG	10	4*	0	46.7
GP	10	7	0	44.4
SP	4	0	2	5.5
IND	(3) 2	0	2	3.4
	(27) 11	11	4	

Part: 29.9
*Uncontested: CONG (1)

1957

Party	Cont	Won	LD	Pct.
CONG	12	7	0	46.6
GP	12	5	0	39.3
CPI	10	0	9	9.4
PSP	1	0	1	0.2
IND	(7) 4	0	7	4.5
	(42) 12	12	17	

Part: 20.6

1961

Party	Cont	Won	LD	Pct.
CONG	12	10	0	51.7
GP	12	2	1	39.8
CPI	3	0	2	4.9
IND	(5) 4	0	4	3.6
	(32) 12	12	7	

Part: 18.7

1967

Party	Cont	Won	LD	Pct.
Swat	12	5	0	45.1
CONG	12	7	0	44.8
CPM	3	0	2	2.7
JC	1	0	0	2.6
CPI	1	0	1	0.4
IND	(6) 6	0	4	4.4
	(35) 12	12	7	

Part: 23.5

GANJAM DISTRICT

Population: 1,872,530
Urban: 8.3 Rural: 91.7
Hindu: 98.8 Christian: 0.9 Muslim: 0.3

1952

Party	Cont	Won	LD	Pct.
CONG	14	4	3	23.3
CPI	7	4	1	15.6
SP	6	1	3	10.4
FB(M)	2	1	1	3.7
KMPP	1	0	1	1.2
IND	(47) 15	5	35	45.8
	(77) 15	15	44	
Part:	29.8			

1957

Party	Cont	Won	LD	Pct.
CONG	16	11	0	48.8
CPI	7	3	1	19.8
GP	10	0	5	10.1
PSP	4	0	1	5.2
IND	(16) 7	2	10	16.1
	(53) 16	16	17	
Part:	33.8			

1961

Party	Cont	Won	LD	Pct.
CONG	16	14	1	50.6
CPI	5	1	0	14.4
GP	10	0	9	5.9
PSP	3	0	1	5.2
SP	1	0	0	1.7
Swat	1	0	1	0.9
IND	(25) 14	1	19	21.3
	(61) 16	16	31	
Part:	39.7			

1967

Party	Cont	Won	LD	Pct.
CONG	15	9	0	42.1
Swat	12	1	3	16.6
CPI	6	3	2	13.3
JC	5	0	3	5.6
SSP	1	1	0	5.0
PSP	2	1	1	3.4
IND	(23) 13	0	19	14.0
	(64) 15	15	28	
Part:	41.8			

PURI DISTRICT

Population: 1,865,439
Urban: 7.2 Rural: 92.8
Hindu: 98.0 Muslim: 1.9 Christian: 0.1

Party	Cont	Won	LD	Pct.
1952				
CONG	15	8	2	48.0
CPI	8	1	1	16.8
SP	8	1	6	7.7
IND	(24) 12	5	15	27.5
	(55) 15	15	24	
Part:	37.4			

Party	Cont	Won	LD	Pct.
1957				
CONG	15	8*	0	47.4
CPI	6	3	1	25.6
GP	6	1	1	10.7
PSP	3	1	2	4.3
IND	(9) 7	2	6	12.0
	(39) 15	15	10	
Part:	39.2			
*Uncontested:	CONG (1)			

Party	Cont	Won	LD	Pct.
1961				
CONG	15	10	0	46.4
CPI	8	2	1	21.1
GP	13	2	9	10.7
PSP	3	0	2	3.0
Swat	1	0	1	0.3
SP	1	0	1	0.1
IND	(26) 11	1	22	18.4
	(67) 15	15	36	
Part:	38.7			

Party	Cont	Won	LD	Pct.
1967				
CONG	15	5	2	32.8
JC	10	5	1	23.9
CPI	6	2	3	11.1
Swat	7	1	4	7.1
CPM	6	0	3	4.7
PSP	1	1	0	4.6
JS	1	0	1	0.4
IND	(23) 11	1	18	15.4
	(69) 15	15	32	
Part:	44.0			

CUTTACK DISTRICT

Population: 3,060,320
Urban: 6.8 Rural: 93.2
Hindu: 96.8 Muslim: 3.0 Christian: 0.1

1952

Party	Cont	Won	LD	Pct.
CONG	26	18	0	43.7
SP	26	3	11	23.5
CPI	10	0	7	5.4
KMPP	6	0	6	1.8
GP	2	1	1	1.5
IND (48)	23	4	35	24.1
(118)	26	26	60	
Part: 39.1				

1957

Party	Cont	Won	LD	Pct.
CONG	24	15	0	46.3
PSP	16	6	0	26.1
GP	14	1	6	12.0
CPI	7	1	2	6.6
IND (19)	12	1	14	9.0
(80)	24	24	22	
Part: 42.8				

1961

Party	Cont	Won	LD	Pct.
CONG	24	18	0	46.6
PSP	18	4	4	23.5
GP	17	0	9	9.2
CPI	6	0	2	5.3
SP	1	0	1	0.2
Swat	3	0	3	0.2
IND (24)	14	2	17	15.0
(93)	24	24	36	
Part: 44.5				

1967

Party	Cont	Won	LD	Pct.
PSP	15	11	1	30.8
CONG	24	2	2	29.8
JC	11	8	2	14.8
CPI	5	1	2	4.3
Swat	7	0	3	3.9
JS	3	0	3	0.3
IND (42)	17	2	36	16.1
(107)	24	24	49	
Part: 51.9				

BALASORE DISTRICT

Population: 1,415,923
Urban: 6.5 Rural: 93.5
Hindu: 96.6 Muslim: 3.2 Christian: 0.1

1952

Party	Cont	Won	LD	Pct.
CONG	12	11	0	61.5
SP	10	0	3	16.7
CPI	5	0	4	6.1
GP	7	0	6	5.1
IND	(8) 7	1	5	10.6
	(42) 12	12	18	
Part:	27.6			

1957

Party	Cont	Won	LD	Pct.
CONG	11	8	0	51.3
PSP	5	2	0	15.9
GP	6	0	2	13.8
CPI	2	0	0	5.6
IND	(6) 4	1	3	13.4
	(30) 11	11	5	
Part:	43.2			

1961

Party	Cont	Won	LD	Pct.
CONG	11	6	0	41.0
PSP	7	3	0	27.0
GP	9	1	7	9.1
CPI	4	0	1	7.0
Swat	1	0	0	1.9
Jhkh	1	0	1	0.1
IND	(6) 4	1	2	13.9
	(39) 11	11	11	
Part:	44.4			

1967

Party	Cont	Won	LD	Pct.
JC	5	4	1	29.7
CONG	11	1	3	26.5
PSP	6	4	1	22.7
Swat	8	1	5	11.4
CPM	1	1	0	4.2
CPI	2	0	1	2.8
IND	(5) 4	0	5	2.7
	(38) 11	11	16	
Part:	54.1			

STATE SUMMARY

Population: 11,135,069
Rural/urban and religion data not available.

1952				
Party	Cont	Won	LD	Pct.
CONG	101	60	11	31.3
AD	87	31	13	24.0
CPI	35	6	16	6.1
JS	51	0	39	4.0
SCF	16	1	5	3.8
SP	50	0	47	3.0
FB	29	1	24	2.2
CP(L)	14	2	7	2.1
DCL	4	0	3	0.8
KMPP	14	0	14	0.4
RRP	1	0	0	0.2
IND	(362)104	9	311	22.1
	(764)110	110	490	
Part:	58.1			

1954				
Party	Cont	Won	LD	Pct.
CONG	43	22	0	40.4
ADM	33	10	1	27.6
ADR	22	2	10	9.9
CPI	10	4	0	8.1
JS	7	0	7	0.6
PSP	3	0	3	0.1
IND	(79) 37	5	69	13.3
	(197) 43	43	90	
Part:	63.1			

1957				
Party	Cont	Won	LD	Pct.
CONG	86	71	0	48.6
CPI	50	3	9	17.7
JS	35	5	19	7.2
SCF	15	1	3	6.2
PSP	7	0	5	0.9
IND	(129) 58	6	93	19.4
	(322) 86	86	129	
Part:	59.4			

1962				
Party	Cont	Won	LD	Pct.
CONG	86	49	0	45.7
AD	45	19	3	20.7
CPI	30	9	12	9.8
JS	41	4	27	7.6
RPI	13	0	7	2.8
Swat	20	0	16	2.4
PSP	3	0	1	0.7
HMS	1	0	1	#
RRP	3	0	3	#
SP	1	0	1	#
IND	(145) 74	5	132	10.1
	(388) 86	86	203	
Part:	64.6			

STATE SUMMARY (Continued)

Party	1967 Cont	Won	LD	Pct.	Party	1969 Cont	Won	LD	Pct.
CONG	102	48	1	37.5	CONG	103	38	4	39.2
ADS	58	24	9	20.5	AD	66	43	3	29.5
JS	49	9	26	9.8	JS	31	8	7	9.0
CPI	19	5	5	5.2	CPI	29	4	18	5.0
ADM	62	2	55	4.2	CPM	9	2	1	2.9
CPM	13	3	5	3.3	Janata	15	1	11	1.7
RPI	17	3	14	1.8	RPI	22	0	22	1.1
SSP	8	1	6	0.7	Swat	7	1	5	0.9
PSP	9	0	8	0.5	SSP	7	2	5	0.8
Swat	10	0	9	0.5	RPI-A	11	0	10	0.5
IND	(255) 95	9	229	16.0	PSP	3	1	2	0.5
	(602)104	104	367		PBI	6	0	6	#
Part:	67.5				HMS	1	0	1	#
					IND	(161) 70	4	144	8.8
						(471)104	104	239	
					Part:	70.4			

FEROZEPUR DISTRICT

Population: 1,619,116
Urban: 20.1 Rural: 79.9
Sikh: 57.9 Hindu: 40.6 Christian: 1.2 Muslim: 0.2

Party	Cont	Won	LD	Pct.
1952				
CONG	12	3	1	27.1
AD	9	5	2	22.5
JS	8	0	5	8.0
CPI	2	1	0	4.7
SCF	1	0	0	2.6
FB	4	0	4	2.0
SP	5	0	5	1.9
CP(L)	1	1	0	1.8
DCL	1	0	1	0.1
IND	(56) 12	3	46	29.3
	(99) 13	13	64	
Part:	55.2			

Party	Cont	Won	LD	Pct.
1957				
CONG	12	11	0	50.9
CPI	8	0	1	22.3
JS	6	1	2	8.4
SCF	1	0	0	1.4
PSP	1	0	1	0.3
IND	(18) 7	0	14	16.7
	(46) 12	12	18	
Part:	62.1			

Party	Cont	Won	LD	Pct.
1962				
CONG	12	4	0	42.0
AD	7	3	1	22.5
CPI	4	2	1	12.3
JS	7	2	4	12.3
RPI	3	0	3	0.6
IND	(26) 11	1	24	10.3
	(59) 12	12	33	
Part:	63.5			

Party	Cont	Won	LD	Pct.
1967				
CONG	15	7	0	39.4
ADS	9	4	0	23.9
JS	10	1	6	12.1
CPI	4	2	1	8.0
SSP	1	0	0	1.9
ADM	8	0	8	1.6
CPM	1	0	1	1.1
RPI	2	0	2	0.3
IND	(42) 15	1	40	11.7
	(92) 15	15	58	
Part:	67.8			

Party	Cont	Won	LD	Pct.
1969				
CONG	15	6	2	36.4
AD	8	4	0	25.3
JS	6	2	0	13.3
CPI	4	1	1	6.7
Janata	1	1	0	4.1
SSP	2	1	1	3.0
CPM	1	0	1	1.0
RPI-A	3	0	3	0.4
RPI	1	0	1	0.1
Swat	1	0	1	#
IND	(21) 11	0	17	9.7
	(63) 15	15	27	
Part:	71.6			

AMRITSAR DISTRICT

Population: 1,534,916
Urban: 30.2 Rural: 69.8
Sikh: 64.5 Hindu: 33.0 Christian: 2.2 Jain: 0.1 Muslim: 0.2

Party		Cont	Won	LD	Pct.
		1952			
CONG		14	11	0	36.8
AD		10	1	3	20.6
CPI		6	2	0	12.6
CP(L)		2	0	1	2.5
JS		3	0	1	2.2
SP		5	0	4	2.1
RRP		1	0	0	1.6
FB		2	0	1	1.1
IND	(44)	13	0	39	20.5
	(87)	14	14	49	
Part:	53.4				

Party		Cont	Won	LD	Pct.
		1957			
CONG		13	9	0	49.0
CPI		8	1	0	19.4
JS		7	2	5	11.6
PSP		2	0	2	1.5
IND	(25)	10	1	21	18.5
	(55)	13	13	28	
Part:	61.5				

Party		Cont	Won	LD	Pct.
		1962			
CONG		13	7	0	46.4
AD		6	2	1	17.2
CPI		5	1	2	10.1
JS		4	2	1	8.6
Swat		3	0	2	3.1
PSP		1	0	0	2.0
HMS		1	0	1	0.2
RRP		2	0	2	0.1
IND	(23)	12	1	20	12.3
	(58)	13	13	29	
Part:	68.0				

Party		Cont	Won	LD	Pct.
		1967			
CONG		13	5	1	36.9
ADS		8	4	0	25.0
JS		6	3	3	11.3
CPM		2	1	0	5.6
CPI		2	1	0	5.3
PSP		1	0	0	2.8
ADM		7	0	7	1.3
IND	(35)	12	0	33	11.8
	(74)	14	14	44	
Part:	66.5				

Party		Cont	Won	LD	Pct.
		1969			
CONG		14	4	0	38.0
AD		9	6	1	28.3
JS		5	1	2	8.9
CPM		2	1	0	6.8
CPI		4	1	2	6.2
PSP		1	1	0	3.1
Janata		3	0	2	2.2
Swat		1	0	1	#
IND	(37)	13	0	36	6.5
	(76)	14	14	44	
Part:	70.4				

GURDASPUR DISTRICT

Population: 979,415
Urban: 20.2 Rural: 79.8
Hindu: 50.1 Sikh: 42.9 Christian: 6.3 Muslim: 0.6
Buddhist: 0.1

1952

Party	Cont	Won	LD	Pct.
CONG	8	8	0	41.5
AD	6	0	0	23.3
JS	6	0	4	8.1
SP	4	0	4	1.9
FB	3	0	3	1.2
CP(L)	1	0	1	0.6
IND	(26) 8	1	23	23.4
	(54) 9	9	35	

Part: 54.7

1957

Party	Cont	Won	LD	Pct.
CONG	8	8	0	40.8
CPI	6	0	3	19.4
JS	7	0	2	18.1
IND	(23) 7	0	19	21.7
	(44) 8	8	24	

Part: 62.5

1962

Party	Cont	Won	LD	Pct.
CONG	8	5	0	48.4
AD	5	3	0	23.8
JS	7	0	3	15.6
CPI	3	0	3	3.5
Swat	2	0	2	0.8
RRP	1	0	1	0.1
IND	(13) 8	0	12	7.8
	(39) 8	8	21	

Part: 63.4

1967

Party	Cont	Won	LD	Pct.
CONG	9	7	0	39.2
JS	7	1	2	21.2
ADS	6	1	0	18.2
ADM	6	0	6	4.4
CPI	1	0	1	1.8
Swat	2	0	2	0.5
IND	(26) 9	0	25	14.7
	(57) 9	9	36	

Part: 67.7

1969

Party	Cont	Won	LD	Pct.
CONG	9	3	0	43.2
AD	5	4	0	27.0
JS	4	2	0	17.8
CPI	2	0	1	3.8
RPI	1	0	1	0.1
PBI	2	0	2	0.1
IND	(12) 5	0	10	8.0
	(35) 9	9	14	

Part: 70.6

HOSHIARPUR DISTRICT

Population: 872,594
Urban: 11.9 Rural: 88.1
Hindu: 67.7 Sikh: 31.0 Christian: 0.6 Muslim: 0.6
(Rural/urban and religion data include area transferred to
Himachal Pradesh.)

Party	1952 Cont	Won	LD	Pct.
CONG	8	7	0	37.2
AD	3	0	0	8.2
SP	6	0	5	7.9
CPI	3	1	2	6.1
JS	5	0	4	5.9
CP(L)	2	0	1	3.4
FB	1	0	0	2.5
DCL	1	0	1	0.1
IND	(31) 7	0	25	28.7
	(60) 8	8	38	
Part: 58.0				

Party	1957 Cont	Won	LD	Pct.
CONG	7	4	0	44.8
SCF	3	1	0	17.6
CPI	2	1	0	11.8
JS	2	0	1	5.6
PSP	1	0	1	1.0
IND	(8) 4	1	5	19.2
	(23) 7	7	7	
Part: 63.1				

Party	1962 Cont	Won	LD	Pct.
CONG	7	7	0	48.3
RPI	4	0	1	15.5
CPI	3	0	1	8.5
PSP	1	0	0	5.1
JS	2	0	2	3.4
Swat	4	0	4	1.4
IND	(13) 6	0	10	17.8
	(34) 7	7	18	
Part: 62.1				

Party	1967 Cont	Won	LD	Pct.
CONG	8	4	0	35.8
JS	4	0	3	8.6
ADS	3	0	2	6.0
RPI	3	1	2	5.6
SSP	1	1	0	4.7
CPI	1	0	0	4.0
CPM	1	0	0	3.3
ADM	1	0	0	3.1
PSP	1	0	1	0.2
Swat	1	0	1	0.1
IND	(17) 8	2	13	28.6
	(41) 8	8	22	
Part: 65.9				

Party	1969 Cont	Won	LD	Pct.
CONG	8	5	0	37.9
JS	5	0	2	15.6
AD	2	2	0	11.5
CPI	3	0	2	7.3
Swat	1	0	0	4.8
RPI	5	0	5	4.8
SSP	1	1	0	4.5
Janata	1	0	0	4.0
CPM	1	0	0	2.6
RPI-A	3	0	3	1.9
IND	(7) 5	0	6	5.1
	(37) 8	8	18	
Part: 66.1				

KAPURTHALA DISTRICT

Population: 343,778
Urban: 23.0 Rural: 77.0
Sikh: 58.2 Hindu: 41.0 Christian: 0.4 Muslim: 0.2 Jain: 0.1

1952

Party	Cont	Won	LD	Pct.
AD	5	1	1	28.3
CONG	3	3	0	26.8
FB	5	0	4	8.7
SCF	1	0	0	8.1
CP(L)	2	0	2	5.5
CPI	2	1	1	5.3
JS	1	0	1	1.1
SP	1	0	1	1.1
KMPP	1	0	1	0.7
IND	(9) 4	0	7	14.4
	(30) 5	5	18	

Part: 53.8

1954

Party	Cont	Won	LD	Pct.
CONG	5	3	0	44.4
ADM	3	2	0	26.8
CPI	2	0	0	13.5
JS	2	0	2	3.2
ADR	1	0	1	1.5
IND	(7) 5	0	6	10.6
	(20) 5	5	9	

Part: 57.5

1957

Party	Cont	Won	LD	Pct.
CONG	3	3	0	57.8
CPI	2	0	0	20.3
SCF	1	0	0	9.7
IND	(3) 1	0	2	12.2
	(9) 3	3	2	

Part: 50.3

1962

Party	Cont	Won	LD	Pct.
CONG	3	1	0	46.4
AD	2	1	0	26.9
Swat	1	0	1	1.8
IND	(2) 2	1	1	24.9
	(8) 3	3	2	

Part: 65.2

1967

Party	Cont	Won	LD	Pct.
CONG	3	3	0	38.8
ADM	2	0	1	15.4
CPI	1	0	0	6.8
JS	1	0	1	5.8
RPI	1	0	1	4.0
ADS	1	0	1	2.5
PSP	1	0	1	0.6
IND	(8) 3	0	5	26.1
	(18) 3	3	10	

Part: 67.8

1969

Party	Cont	Won	LD	Pct.
CONG	3	1	0	39.2
AD	2	2	0	35.8
JS	1	0	0	13.7
CPI	1	0	1	4.5
RPI-A	1	0	1	0.8
IND	(4) 3	0	4	6.0
	(12) 3	3	6	

Part: 70.7

JULLUNDUR DISTRICT

Population: 1,227,367
Urban: 28.5   Rural: 71.5
Hindu: 54.0   Sikh: 44.8   Christian: 0.7   Muslim: 0.3   Jain: 0.2

1952

Party	Cont	Won	LD	Pct.
CONG	11	11	0	37.1
AD	9	0	1	20.7
SCF	5	0	0	11.4
CPI	4	0	3	5.3
JS	7	0	5	4.3
CP(L)	3	0	1	3.9
SP	8	0	8	3.1
FB	4	0	4	1.8
DCL	1	0	1	1.6
IND	(36) 11	0	35	10.8
	(88) 11	11	58	

Part: 57.8

1957

Party	Cont	Won	LD	Pct.
CONG	10	8	0	46.3
SCF	5	0	1	16.0
CPI	5	0	1	12.1
JS	7	1	5	11.9
PSP	1	0	0	1.8
IND	(10) 5	1	8	11.9
	(38) 10	10	15	

Part: 60.0

1962

Party	Cont	Won	LD	Pct.
CONG	10	8	0	53.2
RPI	3	0	0	12.1
AD	4	1	0	11.4
JS	3	0	1	6.8
CPI	2	0	1	5.8
Swat	3	0	3	0.9
PSP	1	0	1	0.3
IND	(15) 7	1	14	9.5
	(41) 10	10	20	

Part: 62.6

1967

Party	Cont	Won	LD	Pct.
CONG	12	5	0	39.8
JS	3	2	1	9.6
ADS	5	1	3	8.3
CPI	2	0	0	7.1
RPI	6	1	5	6.4
CPM	2	1	0	5.9
ADM	6	0	6	2.2
PSP	3	0	3	0.3
SSP	2	0	2	0.3
IND	(34) 11	2	29	20.1
	(75) 12	12	49	

Part: 68.5

1969

Party	Cont	Won	LD	Pct.
CONG	12	8	0	44.8
AD	6	1	1	19.1
JS	3	1	1	7.0
CPM	2	0	0	5.8
CPI	3	1	2	4.6
RPI	8	0	8	4.5
RPI-A	3	0	2	2.4
Janata	3	0	3	0.5
PBI	1	0	1	#
IND	(19) 9	1	16	11.3
	(60) 12	12	34	

Part: 73.8

LUDHIANA DISTRICT

Population: 1,022,519
Urban: 30.8 Rural: 69.2
Sikh: 63.0 Hindu: 35.7 Christian: 0.3 Muslim: 0.5 Jain: 0.5

1952

Party	Cont	Won	LD	Pct.
AD	7	5	1	34.1
CONG	8	2	4	22.1
SCF	2	0	1	6.2
FB	3	0	2	5.2
CPI	3	0	2	4.3
JS	4	0	4	3.0
SP	6	0	6	2.9
IND	(30) 8	1	25	22.2
	(63) 8	8	45	
Part:	55.7			

1957

Party	Cont	Won	LD	Pct.
CONG	8	7	0	50.8
CPI	3	0	1	14.6
SCF	2	0	0	11.7
JS	3	1	1	6.4
PSP	1	0	0	3.0
IND	(10) 5	0	6	13.5
	(27) 8	8	8	
Part:	59.2			

1962

Party	Cont	Won	LD	Pct.
CONG	8	3	0	39.6
AD	6	4	0	34.8
JS	4	0	3	7.2
CPI	4	0	4	5.6
RPI	1	0	1	1.2
Swat	1	0	1	0.1
IND	(13) 8	1	12	11.5
	(37) 8	8	21	
Part:	66.1			

1967

Party	Cont	Won	LD	Pct.
CONG	10	4	0	38.2
ADS	7	3	0	33.9
JS	3	2	1	9.0
ADM	10	0	9	6.7
RPI	3	1	2	4.0
CPI	1	0	1	0.8
CPM	1	0	1	0.7
PSP	3	0	3	0.5
Swat	1	0	1	0.2
SSP	2	0	2	0.1
IND	(14) 6	0	14	5.9
	(55) 10	10	34	
Part:	70.0			

1969

Party	Cont	Won	LD	Pct.
AD	8	6	0	42.4
CONG	9	3	1	35.2
JS	2	0	0	7.2
Janata	1	0	0	3.4
CPI	2	0	2	2.0
RPI	3	0	3	0.3
SSP	1	0	1	0.3
RPI-A	1	0	1	0.3
PBI	3	0	3	0.1
PSP	1	0	1	0.1
HMS	1	0	1	#
IND	(14) 8	1	13	8.7
	(46) 10	10	26	
Part:	67.7			

RUPAR DISTRICT

Population: 471,594
Rural/urban and religion data not available.

1952

Party	Cont	Won	LD	Pct.
AD	2	1	0	28.0
CONG	2	1	0	21.5
DCL	1	0	0	11.8
SP	3	0	3	9.8
CPI	3	0	3	7.9
FB	1	1	0	6.1
JS	2	0	0	4.3
SCF	1	0	1	1.3
IND	(7) 3	0	7	9.3
	(22) 3	3	14	

Part: 88.5

1957

Party	Cont	Won	LD	Pct.
CONG	3	2	0	43.2
CPI	2	0	2	11.3
IND	(4) 3	1	1	45.5
	(9) 3	3	3	

Part: 87.8

1962

Party	Cont	Won	LD	Pct.
CONG	3	1	0	48.5
AD	1	1	0	16.5
CPI	1	1	0	11.4
JS	1	0	1	3.0
IND	(6) 3	0	5	20.6
	(12) 3	3	6	

Part: 64.0

1967

Party	Cont	Won	LD	Pct.
CONG	5	4	0	42.2
ADS	2	1	0	13.7
JS	3	0	1	10.0
CPI	2	0	1	9.2
CPM	2	0	1	8.9
ADM	3	0	3	3.2
IND	(11) 5	0	10	12.8
	(28) 5	5	16	

Part: 67.9

1969

Party	Cont	Won	LD	Pct.
CONG	5	1	0	39.0
AD	3	3	0	33.5
JS	1	1	0	5.3
CPM	1	0	0	4.5
CPI	2	0	2	2.6
PSP	1	0	1	1.5
Swat	1	0	1	0.7
RPI	1	0	1	0.3
IND	(10) 5	0	9	12.6
	(25) 5	5	14	

Part: 70.9

PATIALA DISTRICT

Population: 1,048,778
Urban: 24.7 Rural: 75.3
Sikh: 52.8 Hindu: 45.8 Muslim: 1.1 Jain: 0.2 Christian: 0.1

1952

Party	Cont	Won	LD	Pct.
CONG	11	7	0	35.7
AD	12	4	4	24.5
SCF	1	1	0	6.8
KMPP	6	0	6	2.2
SP	6	0	6	1.7
JS	5	0	5	1.3
CPI	1	0	1	0.9
FB(M)	1	0	1	0.1
IND	(42) 13	1	36	26.8
	(85) 13	13	59	
Part: 60.7				

1954

Party	Cont	Won	LD	Pct.
CONG	13	7	0	47.0
ADM	7	2	0	21.0
ADR	5	0	4	3.3
JS	2	0	2	0.4
PSP	2	0	2	0.3
IND	(41) 12	4	36	28.0
	(70) 13	13	44	
Part: 60.1				

1957

Party	Cont	Won	LD	Pct.
CONG	7	7	0	57.6
SCF	3	0	2	8.0
CPI	2	0	0	6.8
JS	2	0	2	2.4
IND	(9) 6	0	4	25.2
	(23) 7	7	8	
Part: 50.2				

1962

Party	Cont	Won	LD	Pct.
CONG	7	7	0	47.2
AD	4	0	0	23.9
Swat	3	0	1	11.0
JS	5	0	4	7.5
CPI	1	0	0	4.7
RPI	1	0	1	0.3
SP	1	0	1	0.1
IND	(16) 6	0	16	5.3
	(38) 7	7	23	
Part: 63.4				

1967

Party	Cont	Won	LD	Pct.
CONG	8	4	0	30.5
ADM	5	2	1	14.6
ADS	5	0	3	8.7
JS	4	0	1	8.3
Swat	3	0	2	4.1
CPI	1	0	1	0.9
CPM	1	0	1	0.9
RPI	2	0	2	0.4
SSP	2	0	2	0.3
IND	(24) 9	3	19	31.3
	(55) 9	9	32	
Part: 67.7				

1969

Party	Cont	Won	LD	Pct.
CONG	9	0	1	33.1
AD	6	5	1	28.8
JS	4	1	2	10.7
Swat	3	1	2	6.1
CPI	2	0	2	2.2
RPI	2	0	2	0.8
Janata	5	0	5	0.4
SSP	3	0	3	0.2
IND	(19) 7	2	16	17.7
	(53) 9	9	34	
Part: 71.8				

SANGRUR DISTRICT

Population: 959,815 (Including Jind District, Haryana)
Urban: 16.9 Rural: 83.1
Hindu: 51.9 Sikh: 43.7 Muslim: 3.9 Christian: 0.5

1952				
Party	Cont	Won	LD	Pct.
AD	11	6	0	33.3
CONG	12	4	3	24.5
CPI	3	1	0	7.2
CP(L)	3	1	1	4.7
SCF	4	0	2	4.6
JS	5	0	5	1.9
KMPP	2	0	2	1.3
FB(M)	2	0	2	0.7
SP	1	0	1	0.1
IND	(35) 13	1	31	21.7
	(78) 13	13	47	
Part:	62.6			

1954				
Party	Cont	Won	LD	Pct.
CONG	12	7	0	40.5
ADM	11	4	1	32.6
CPI	5	1	0	12.3
ADR	6	0	3	9.4
JS	2	0	2	0.6
PSP	1	0	1	0.1
IND	(12) 10	0	11	4.5
	(49) 12	12	18	
Part:	62.2			

1957				
Party	Cont	Won	LD	Pct.
CONG	7	5	0	42.7
CPI	6	1	1	26.9
JS	1	0	1	0.7
IND	(12) 5	1	9	29.7
	(26) 7	7	11	
Part:	54.1			

1962				
Party	Cont	Won	LD	Pct.
CONG	7	3	0	47.2
AD	5	1	1	25.6
CPI	3	3	0	19.8
JS	3	0	3	2.6
RPI	1	0	1	0.6
Swat	1	0	1	0.5
IND	(9) 6	0	9	3.7
	(29) 7	7	15	
Part:	66.5			

1967				
Party	Cont	Won	LD	Pct.
CONG	9	3	0	35.5
ADS	5	4	0	27.1
CPM	3	1	1	10.6
CPI	2	1	0	6.4
JS	3	0	2	4.7
ADM	6	0	6	1.9
Swat	2	0	2	1.0
IND	(20) 8	0	18	12.8
	(50) 9	9	29	
Part:	67.1			

1969				
Party	Cont	Won	LD	Pct.
CONG	9	3	0	42.6
AD	7	5	0	40.9
CPM	2	1	0	10.1
CPI	2	0	1	1.8
IND	(7) 5	0	7	4.6
	(27) 9	9	8	
Part:	69.2			

BHATINDA DISTRICT

Population: 1,055,177
Urban: 21.2 Rural: 78.8
Sikh: 72.3 Hindu: 27.1 Muslim: 0.3 Jain: 0.2 Christian: 0.1

1952

Party	Cont	Won	LD	Pct.
AD	13	8	1	32.8
CONG	12	3	3	21.7
CPI	8	0	4	10.6
SP	5	0	4	2.5
FB	3	0	3	1.6
KMPP	5	0	5	1.3
JS	5	0	5	1.1
SCF	1	0	1	0.5
IND	(46) 12	2	37	27.9
	(98) 13	13	63	

Part: 63.5

1954

Party	Cont	Won	LD	Pct.
CONG	13	5	0	33.1
ADM	12	2	0	29.9
ADR	10	2	2	18.6
CPI	3	3	0	10.1
JS	1	0	1	0.1
IND	(19) 10	1	16	8.2
	(58) 13	13	19	

Part: 69.2

1957

Party	Cont	Won	LD	Pct.
CONG	8	7	0	54.4
CPI	6	0	0	29.0
PSP	1	0	1	0.4
IND	(7) 5	1	4	16.2
	(22) 8	8	5	

Part: 53.7

1962

Party	Cont	Won	LD	Pct.
CONG	8	3	0	39.1
AD	5	3	0	26.7
CPI	4	2	0	19.8
Swat	2	0	1	6.2
JS	5	0	5	5.3
IND	(9) 5	0	9	2.9
	(33) 8	8	15	

Part: 64.6

1967

Party	Cont	Won	LD	Pct.
CONG	10	2	0	36.6
ADS	7	6	0	35.5
CPI	2	1	0	8.1
JS	5	0	5	3.4
ADM	8	0	8	2.4
Swat	1	0	1	0.1
IND	(24) 9	1	23	13.9
	(57) 10	10	37	

Part: 65.4

1969

Party	Cont	Won	LD	Pct.
CONG	10	4	0	42.7
AD	10	5	0	40.0
CPI	4	1	2	9.5
Janata	1	0	1	0.9
RPI	1	0	1	0.5
IND	(11) 4	0	10	6.4
	(37) 10	10	14	

Part: 71.0

STATE SUMMARY

Population: 20,155,602
Urban: 16.3 Rural: 83.7
Hindu: 90.0 Muslim: 6.5 Jain: 2.0 Sikh: 1.4 Christian: 0.1

		1952						1957		
Party	Cont	Won	LD	Pct.		Party	Cont	Won	LD	Pct.
CONG	185	102*	10	39.8		CONG	176	119*	2	45.1
RRP	59	24	14	11.5		RRP	57	17	11	9.9
KLP	46	7	19	7.8		JS	46	6	24	5.4
JS	64	11	34	6.3		CPI	24	1	14	3.0
SP	52	1	40	3.9		PSP	25	1	10	2.5
HMS	5	1	1	0.7		SP	@	2	@	@
CPI	13	0	11	0.6		IND	(325)144	30	200	34.1
KMPP	6	1	4	0.5			(653)176	176	261	
PP	6	3	2	0.5		Part: 39.1				
SCF	1	0	1	0.2		*Uncontested: CONG (5)				
KJSP	6	0	6	0.2						
FB	1	0	1	#						
IND	(307)140	39	207	28.0						
	(751)189	189	350							

Part: 36.8
*Uncontested: CONG (6)

		1962						1967		
Party	Cont	Won	LD	Pct.		Party	Cont	Won	LD	Pct.
CONG	176	88*	4	40.0		CONG	182	89	3	41.4
Swat	93	36	33	17.1		Swat	107	48	18	22.1
JS	94	15	55	9.1		JS	63	22	11	11.7
CPI	45	5	25	5.4		SSP	38	8	18	4.8
SP	40	5	25	3.7		CPM	22	0	19	1.2
RRP	23	3	13	2.0		CPI	20	1	17	1.0
PSP	22	2	14	1.5		PSP	16	0	13	0.8
HMS	7	0	6	0.3		Janata	4	0	0	0.7
IND	(390)147	22	322	20.9		RPI	5	0	5	0.1
	(890)176	176	497			IND	(435)159	16	388	16.2
							(892)184	184	492	

Part: 50.2
*Uncontested: CONG (1)

Part: 55.4

GANGANAGAR DISTRICT

Population: 1,037,423
Urban: 14.5 Rural: 85.5
Hindu: 75.7 Sikh: 20.7 Muslim: 3.4 Jain: 0.2 Christian: #

1952

Party	Cont	Won	LD	Pct.
CONG	6	6	0	50.6
SCF	1	0	1	3.7
RRP	3	0	3	3.4
KMPP	1	0	0	3.3
SP	1	0	1	2.8
KJSP	1	0	1	1.7
JS	2	0	2	1.1
IND	(14) 5	0	10	33.4
	(29) 6	6	18	

Part: 51.2

1957

Party	Cont	Won	LD	Pct.
CONG	7	5*	0	47.8
PSP	1	0	0	5.3
JS	1	0	1	1.3
CPI	1	0	1	0.9
IND	(12) 6	2	6	44.7
	(22) 7	7	8	

Part: 55.9
*Uncontested: CONG (1)

1962

Party	Cont	Won	LD	Pct.
CONG	7	1	0	38.0
CPI	2	2	0	19.9
JS	5	0	5	2.6
IND	(13) 6	4	7	39.5
	(27) 7	7	12	

Part: 60.9

1967

Party	Cont	Won	LD	Pct.
CONG	9	7	0	41.1
Swat	6	1	1	21.6
SSP	4	1	2	10.8
CPM	3	0	1	6.4
JS	2	0	1	3.1
CPI	1	0	1	0.5
IND	(20) 7	0	17	16.5
	(45) 9	9	23	

Part: 60.1

BIKANER DISTRICT

Population: 444,515
Urban: 42.3 Rural: 57.7
Hindu: 84.6 Muslim: 11.3 Jain: 3.8 Sikh: 0.2 Christian: #

1952

Party	Cont	Won	LD	Pct.
CONG	3	0	0	23.9
RRP	1	0	0	6.7
SP	2	0	2	5.8
JS	1	0	1	3.1
FB	1	0	1	2.0
IND (11)	3	3	6	58.5
(19)	3	3	10	
Part: 43.1				

1957

Party	Cont	Won	LD	Pct.
CONG	4	1	0	23.6
PSP	2	1	0	21.0
JS	1	0	1	1.3
IND (14)	5	2	8	54.1
(21)	4	4	9	
Part: 34.5				

1962

Party	Cont	Won	LD	Pct.
CONG	4	1	0	28.6
PSP	3	2	1	20.4
CPI	1	0	0	5.8
JS	3	0	3	3.7
Swat	1	0	1	2.0
IND (18)	4	1	15	39.5
(30)	4	4	20	
Part: 45.0				

1967

Party	Cont	Won	LD	Pct.
CONG	4	3	0	32.7
PSP	2	0	1	9.5
Swat	3	0	2	9.3
SSP	1	0	0	6.5
JS	1	0	0	5.3
CPI	1	0	1	1.0
CPM	1	0	1	0.3
IND (21)	4	1	19	35.4
(34)	4	4	24	
Part: 48.5				

CHURU DISTRICT

Population: 659,011
Urban: 31.6 Rural: 68.4
Hindu: 88.8 Muslim: 8.0 Jain: 3.1 Christian: #

Party		Cont	Won	LD	Pct.
		1957			
CONG		5	3	0	40.7
KLP		3	0	1	12.3
JS		2	0	2	4.8
RRP		1	0	1	4.1
SP		2	0	2	2.8
IND	(14)	5	2	11	35.3
	(27)	5	5	17	
Part:	42.3				

Party		Cont	Won	LD	Pct.
		1957			
CONG		6	3	1	30.8
JS		2	0	0	7.6
IND	(18)	6	3	7	61.6
	(26)	6	6	8	
Part:	39.6				

Party		Cont	Won	LD	Pct.
		1962			
CONG		6	4	0	37.6
CPI		4	0	3	9.6
JS		2	0	2	2.6
PSP		1	0	1	0.7
IND	(16)	6	2	9	49.5
	(29)	6	6	15	
Part:	55.0				

Party		Cont	Won	LD	Pct.
		1967			
CONG		6	1	1	31.1
JS		3	1	1	13.7
CPM		2	0	1	4.2
Janata		1	0	0	3.9
Swat		1	0	1	2.7
CPI		1	0	1	1.0
PSP		2	0	2	0.7
IND	(21)	5	4	16	42.7
	(37)	6	6	23	
Part:	60.3				

JHUNJHUNU DISTRICT

Population: 719,650
Urban: 17.7 Rural: 82.3
Hindu: 93.1 Muslim: 6.7 Jain: 0.1 Christian: #

Party	Cont	Won	LD	Pct.
CONG	6	3	0	37.6
RRP	4	3	1	25.9
KLP	6	0	2	23.1
SP	1	0	1	2.4
JS	1	0	0	2.1
IND	(4) 2	0	3	8.9
	(22) 6	6	7	

Part: 44.3

Party	Cont	Won	LD	Pct.
CONG	7	5	0	43.6
CPI	6	1	4	19.2
JS	4	0	4	5.7
RRP	3	0	2	4.8
IND	(11) 7	1	7	26.7
	(31) 7	7	17	

Part: 45.6

Party	Cont	Won	LD	Pct.
CONG	7	3	0	37.4
Swat	5	3	0	24.6
CPI	7	0	3	14.3
JS	4	0	4	2.8
IND	(9) 6	1	6	20.9
	(32) 7	7	13	

Part: 58.1

Party	Cont	Won	LD	Pct.
CONG	7	3	0	42.5
Swat	6	4	0	38.1
CPM	4	0	4	2.4
JS	1	0	1	1.7
IND	(18) 6	0	17	15.3
	(36) 7	7	22	

Part: 63.2

SIKAR DISTRICT

Population: 820,286
Urban: 17.5 Rural: 82.5
Hindu: 91.3 Muslim: 8.1 Jain: 0.5 Christian: #

Party	Cont	Won	LD	Pct.
CONG	8	4	0	41.5
KLP	8	2	1	35.1
RRP	3	1	0	11.4
JS	2	1	1	7.2
IND	(2) 2	0	1	4.8
	(23) 8	8	3	

1952

Part: 39.1

Party	Cont	Won	LD	Pct.
CONG	8	5	0	36.8
RRP	5	1	2	15.0
CPI	6	0	5	8.2
JS	2	2	0	6.6
IND	(25) 8	0	22	33.4
	(46) 8	8	29	

1957

Part: 46.4

Party	Cont	Won	LD	Pct.
CONG	8	7	0	38.7
CPI	7	0	3	14.5
JS	6	0	2	13.5
Swat	7	0	5	9.0
SP	2	0	1	2.1
IND	(29) 7	1	27	22.2
	(59) 8	8	38	

1962

Part: 55.5

Party	Cont	Won	LD	Pct.
CONG	7	2	0	40.2
JS	3	2	0	20.6
Swat	2	2	0	10.6
PSP	1	0	0	6.6
CPM	4	0	4	4.9
IND	(13) 5	1	10	17.1
	(30) 7	7	14	

1967

Part: 59.7

JAIPUR DISTRICT

Population: 1,901,756
Urban: 26.3 Rural: 73.7
Hindu: 92.4 Muslim: 5.9 Jain: 1.3 Sikh: 0.2 Christian: 0.1

1952						1957				
Party	Cont	Won	LD	Pct.		Party	Cont	Won	LD	Pct.
CONG	16	11*	0	46.1		CONG	17	7	0	37.9
RRP	10	4	1	26.0		RRP	9	4	3	21.7
KLP	8	0	6	6.6		JS	2	2	0	5.4
CPI	5	0	5	1.9		PSP	1	0	1	0.3
JS	2	0	1	1.8		CPI	1	0	1	0.3
SP	5	0	5	1.8		IND	(34) 12	4	20	34.4
IND	(18) 11	1	11	15.8			(64) 17	17	25	
	(64) 16	16	29			Part: 34.1				

Part: 28.5
*Uncontested: CONG (1)

1962						1967				
Party	Cont	Won	LD	Pct.		Party	Cont	Won	LD	Pct.
Swat	15	13	0	51.6		Swat	14	10	1	40.2
CONG	17	2	4	27.9		CONG	17	4	0	34.5
JS	12	2	8	13.2		JS	2	2	0	7.3
HMS	1	0	0	2.6		Janata	3	0	0	5.7
CPI	5	0	5	0.6		PSP	4	0	4	0.4
RRP	4	0	4	0.6		CPI	1	0	1	0.3
SP	8	0	8	0.3		CPM	1	0	1	0.1
PSP	2	0	2	0.2		SSP	1	0	1	0.1
IND	(45) 13	0	45	3.0		IND	(47) 14	1	46	11.4
	(109) 17	17	76				(90) 17	17	54	

Part: 56.7   Part: 53.5

ALWAR DISTRICT

Population: 1,090,026
Urban: 8.1 Rural: 91.9
Hindu: 89.8 Muslim: 7.6 Sikh: 2.1 Jain: 0.5 Christian: #

1952

Party	Cont	Won	LD	Pct.
CONG	9	9*	0	55.6
KLP	5	0	1	21.7
RRP	4	0	2	11.0
HMS	2	0	1	4.7
SP	4	0	4	3.6
CPI	1	0	1	2.3
IND	(2) 2	0	2	1.1
	(27) 9	9	11	

Part: 50.5
*Uncontested: CONG (2)

1957

Party	Cont	Won	LD	Pct.
CONG	10	8*	0	48.9
CPI	4	0	0	16.6
RRP	1	1	0	4.4
IND	(19) 9	1	9	30.1
	(34) 10	10	9	

Part: 46.1
*Uncontested: CONG (1)

1962

Party	Cont	Won	LD	Pct.
CONG	10	6	0	43.6
CPI	4	2	1	18.4
SP	1	0	0	3.7
JS	1	0	0	3.1
Swat	3	0	3	1.7
IND	(34) 10	2	28	29.5
	(53) 10	10	32	

Part: 58.1

1967

Party	Cont	Won	LD	Pct.
CONG	10	5	0	36.9
Swat	7	1	4	12.0
SSP	3	1	0	11.0
CPI	4	1	1	9.1
JS	3	1	0	8.8
CPM	2	0	2	2.5
IND	(36) 10	1	33	19.7
	(65) 10	10	40	

Part: 57.6

BHARATPUR DISTRICT

Population: 1,149,883
Urban: 13.7 Rural: 86.3
Hindu: 90.2 Muslim: 8.2 Sikh: 1.3 Jain: 0.3 Christian: #

1952

Party	Cont	Won	LD	Pct.
CONG	10	6	0	37.5
KLP	7	4	2	23.4
SP	4	0	2	8.8
RRP	2	0	1	1.9
KMPP	1	0	1	0.3
IND (19)	9	0	11	28.1
(43)	10	10	17	

Part: 49.0

1957

Party	Cont	Won	LD	Pct.
CONG	10	6	0	42.3
JS	1	0	1	0.6
IND (27)	10	4	11	57.1
(38)	10	10	12	

Part: 56.2

1962

Party	Cont	Won	LD	Pct.
CONG	10	2	0	33.9
SP	8	3	2	22.0
Swat	8	2	4	17.2
CPI	2	0	1	3.3
JS	2	0	2	0.6
IND (32)	10	3	28	23.0
(62)	10	10	37	

Part: 60.1

1967

Party	Cont	Won	LD	Pct.
CONG	10	4	1	28.3
SSP	8	4	1	23.2
Swat	6	0	6	7.8
RPI	4	0	4	2.0
CPI	1	0	1	1.7
JS	2	0	2	1.2
IND (44)	10	2	40	35.8
(75)	10	10	55	

Part: 62.1

SAWAI MADHOPUR DISTRICT

Population: 943,574
Urban: 10.2 Rural: 89.8
Hindu: 93.2 Muslim: 5.9 Jain: 0.8 Christian: #

		1952		
Party	Cont	Won	LD	Pct.
CONG	8	6	0	50.0
JS	6	0	3	19.1
RRP	2	1	1	6.7
HMS	1	0	0	3.1
IND	(9) 7	1	5	21.1
	(26) 8	8	9	
Part:	33.6			

		1957		
Party	Cont	Won	LD	Pct.
CONG	8	5	0	42.4
JS	4	0	2	8.2
IND	(18) 8	3	10	49.4
	(30) 8	8	12	
Part:	35.7			

		1962		
Party	Cont	Won	LD	Pct.
CONG	8	3*	0	37.2
Swat	5	2	2	24.6
JS	6	3	3	22.0
RRP	2	0	1	3.8
CPI	1	0	1	0.6
IND	(14) 6	0	13	11.8
	(36) 8	8	20	
Part:	46.5			
*Uncontested:	CONG (1)			

		1967		
Party	Cont	Won	LD	Pct.
CONG	9	4	0	41.7
Swat	4	3	0	22.6
JS	5	2	2	16.2
SSP	2	0	2	1.2
IND	(30) 9	0	29	18.3
	(50) 9	9	33	
Part:	47.9			

TONK DISTRICT

Population: 497,729
Urban: 14.7 Rural: 85.3
Hindu: 89.4 Muslim: 8.5 Jain: 2.0 Christian: #

1952

Party	Cont	Won	LD	Pct.
CONG	4	3	0	43.8
SP	4	0	2	22.7
RRP	1	1	0	12.4
JS	1	0	0	10.0
KLP	1	0	1	3.1
IND	(3) 3	0	3	8.0
	(14) 4	4	6	

Part: 27.7

1957

Party	Cont	Won	LD	Pct.
CONG	4	3*	0	48.5
PSP	3	0	1	19.3
RRP	1	1	0	14.6
IND	(2) 2	0	1	17.6
	(10) 4	4	2	

Part: 32.0
*Uncontested: CONG (1)

1962

Party	Cont	Won	LD	Pct.
Swat	4	4	0	61.3
CONG	4	0	0	30.6
JS	3	0	3	3.7
PSP	1	0	1	2.8
IND	(4) 2	0	4˙	1.6
	(16) 4	4	8	

Part: 62.3

1967

Party	Cont	Won	LD	Pct.
CONG	5	3	0	51.2
Swat	5	2	0	44.6
IND	(10) 5	0	10	4.2
	(20) 5	5	10	

Part: 64.1

AJMER DISTRICT

Population: 976,547
Urban: 37.4 Rural: 62.6
Hindu: 87.3 Muslim: 8.5 Jain: 2.8 Christian: 0.8 Sikh: 0.4
Other: 0.2

		1952		
Party	Cont	Won	LD	Pct.
CONG	31	21	0	43.8
JS	15	3	4	11.1
PP	6	3	2	6.3
CPI	2	0	0	1.4
SP	2	0	2	0.3
IND	(80) 30	4	58	37.1
	(136) 31	31	66	
Part:	49.1			

		1957		
Party	Cont	Won	LD	Pct.
CONG	9	7	0	48.3
RRP	2	0	0	8.4
CPI	1	0	0	4.4
JS	1	0	1	1.6
IND	(24) 9	2	17	37.3
	(37) 9	9	18	
Part:	54.5			

		1962		
Party	Cont	Won	LD	Pct.
CONG	9	6	0	43.0
Swat	8	2	2	24.4
JS	6	0	3	11.9
CPI	1	1	0	4.5
RRP	1	0	1	0.2
SP	1	0	1	0.2
HMS	2	0	2	0.1
IND	(27) 9	0	25	15.7
	(55) 9	9	34	
Part:	55.5			

		1967		
Party	Cont	Won	LD	Pct.
CONG	9	2	1	37.9
Swat	5	5	0	32.3
JS	4	2	0	17.9
CPI	2	0	2	2.0
SSP	3	0	3	0.3
RPI	1	0	1	0.1
IND	(23) 8	0	22	9.5
	(47) 9	9	29	
Part:	60.3			

BUNDI DISTRICT

Population: 338,010
Urban: 15.3   Rural: 84.7
Hindu: 93.1 Muslim: 5.0   Jain: 1.4 Sikh: 0.3 Christian: #

1952

Party	Cont	Won	LD	Pct.
RRP	2	2	0	52.0
CONG	3	0	1	22.2
KMPP	2	1	1	18.9
SP	2	0	2	2.3
IND (3)	2	0	3	4.6
(12)	3	3	7	

Part: 23.5

1957

Party	Cont	Won	LD	Pct.
CONG	3	3	0	61.0
PSP	3	0	0	29.7
JS	2	0	2	5.8
IND (1)	1	0	0	3.5
(9)	3	3	2	

Part: 31.3

1962

Party	Cont	Won	LD	Pct.
CONG	3	2	0	37.4
JS	2	1	0	32.2
PSP	3	0	1	17.4
SP	1	0	1	3.0
Swat	2	0	2	2.1
IND (4)	3	0	4	7.9
(15)	3	3	8	

Part: 38.8

1967

Party	Cont	Won	LD	Pct.
CONG	3	2	0	42.7
JS	3	1	0	36.6
SSP	2	0	1	7.7
PSP	1	0	0	6.8
IND (4)	3	0	4	6.2
(13)	3	3	5	

Part: 49.2

KOTAH DISTRICT

Population: 848,389
Urban: 18.9 Rural: 81.1
Hindu: 90.8 Muslim: 7.7 Jain: 0.9 Sikh: 0.4 Christian: 0.2

1952

Party	Cont	Won	LD	Pct.
CONG	8	4	0	34.9
RRP	7	4	0	27.9
JS	5	0	4	9.4
SP	7	0	6	9.4
IND	(17) 7	0	16	18.4
	(44) 8	8	26	

Part: 21.3

1957

Party	Cont	Won	LD	Pct.
CONG	7	5*	0	39.4
JS	5	2	0	31.7
IND	(10) 5	0	5	28.9
	(22) 7	7	5	

Part: 29.9
*Uncontested: CONG (1)

1962

Party	Cont	Won	LD	Pct.
CONG	7	3	0	46.8
JS	7	4	1	34.9
SP	5	0	4	7.1
Swat	4	0	4	2.5
IND	(16) 7	0	16	8.7
	(39) 7	7	25	

Part: 45.9

1967

Party	Cont	Won	LD	Pct.
JS	8	8	0	53.4
CONG	8	0	0	36.6
SSP	1	0	1	1.2
IND	(22) 8	0	22	8.8
	(39) 8	8	23	

Part: 51.7

JHALAWAR DISTRICT

Population: 490,609
Urban: 7.7 Rural: 92.3
Hindu: 92.7 Muslim: 6.0 Jain: 1.2 Christian: #

Party	Cont	Won	LD	Pct.
		1952		
CONG	4	3	0	37.7
RRP	3	1	0	34.7
JS	2	0	2	7.4
SP	3	0	2	6.1
IND	(4) 3	0	2	14.1
	(16) 4	4	6	
Part:	22.6			

Party	Cont	Won	LD	Pct.
		1957		
CONG	5	5	0	78.0
IND	(5) 5	0	2	22.0
	(10) 5	5	2	
Part:	33.5			

Party	Cont	Won	LD	Pct.
		1962		
CONG	5	3	0	55.9
JS	5	1	2	23.0
SP	5	0	4	7.4
Swat	1	0	1	0.3
IND	(6) 4	1	5	13.4
	(22) 5	5	12	
Part:	43.4			

Party	Cont	Won	LD	Pct.
		1967		
JS	2	2	0	26.7
CONG	4	0	0	22.3
Swat	2	2	0	19.0
SSP	3	0	3	2.0
IND	(9) 4	1	6	30.0
	(20) 5	5	9	
Part:	49.7			

CHITTORGARH DISTRICT

Population: 710,132
Urban: 9.5 Rural: 90.5
Hindu: 93.3 Muslim: 4.1 Jain: 2.5 Christian: #

1952				
Party	Cont	Won	LD	Pct.
CONG	6	4*	0	47.7
JS	4	2	1	34.8
SP	3	0	0	11.0
IND (1)	1	0	0	6.5
(14)	6	6	1	

Part: 27.0
*Uncontested: CONG (1)

1957				
Party	Cont	Won	LD	Pct.
CONG	7	7	0	46.9
RRP	5	0	0	24.4
JS	3	0	1	12.3
PSP	1	0	1	1.7
IND (9)	5	0	7	14.7
(25)	7	7	9	

Part: 31.5

1962				
Party	Cont	Won	LD	Pct.
CONG	7	5	0	42.0
JS	5	1	2	18.4
Swat	2	1	1	12.0
SP	1	0	0	4.1
PSP	2	0	1	4.1
IND (9)	5	0	5	19.4
(26)	7	7	9	

Part: 41.4

1967				
Party	Cont	Won	LD	Pct.
CONG	7	6	0	47.6
JS	4	0	0	17.9
Swat	3	0	2	9.3
SSP	1	0	0	3.2
CPM	1	0	1	0.3
IND (12)	6	1	6	21.7
(28)	7	7	9	

Part: 48.7

BANSWARA DISTRICT

Population: 475,245
Urban: 5.2 Rural: 94.8
Hindu: 95.4 Muslim: 2.6 Jain: 1.5 Christian: 0.4

1952

Party	Cont	Won	LD	Pct.
SP	2	1	0	37.8
CONG	2	2*	0	35.3
RRP	1	0	0	11.0
IND	(1) 1	0	0	15.9
	(6) 3	3	0	

Part: 27.4
*Uncontested: CONG (1)

1957

Party	Cont	Won	LD	Pct.
CONG	4	2	0	46.5
SP	@	2	@	@
IND	(4) 4	0	0	53.5
	(8) 4	4	0	

Part: 45.5

1962

Party	Cont	Won	LD	Pct.
CONG	4	2	0	35.7
Swat	4	0	1	18.5
SP	4	2	0	45.8
	(12) 4	4	1	

Part: 58.0

1967

Party	Cont	Won	LD	Pct.
CONG	4	2	0	48.2
SSP	4	2	0	47.0
JS	2	0	2	2.0
IND	(3) 3	0	3	2.8
	(13) 4	4	5	

Part: 67.5

DUNGARPUR DISTRICT

Population: 406,944
Urban: 5.3 Rural: 94.7
Hindu: 95.9 Muslim: 2.5 Jain: 1.6 Christian: #

1952

Party	Cont	Won	LD	Pct.
CONG	3	3	0	62.1
IND	(3) 3	0	0	37.9
	(6) 3	3	0	

Part: 42.3

1957

Party	Cont	Won	LD	Pct.
CONG	3	2*	0	45.5
IND	(4) 2	1	2	54.5
	(7) 3	3	2	

Part: 46.7
*Uncontested: CONG (1)

1962

Party	Cont	Won	LD	Pct.
CONG	3	1	0	48.1
Swat	3	2	0	47.1
SP	3	0	3	2.9
CPI	2	0	2	1.9
	(11) 3	3	5	

Part: 58.4

1967

Party	Cont	Won	LD	Pct.
CONG	4	3	0	59.1
Swat	4	1	0	38.0
CPI	3	0	3	1.8
IND	(2) 2	0	2	1.1
	(13) 4	4	5	

Part: 68.3

UDAIPUR DISTRICT

Population: 1,464,276
Urban: 10.9 Rural: 89.1
Hindu: 92.6 Jain: 4.3 Muslim: 2.8 Sikh: 0.1 Christian: 0.1

1952

Party	Cont	Won	LD	Pct.
CONG	13	7*	1	40.4
JS	7	4	1	22.5
SP	6	0	5	7.7
KLP	2	1	0	7.1
RRP	2	0	1	5.3
CPI	1	0	1	1.6
KJSP	2	0	2	0.7
IND	(12) 6	1	9	14.7
	(45) 13	13	20	

Part: 22.9
*Uncontested: CONG (2)

1957

Party	Cont	Won	LD	Pct.
CONG	13	12	0	63.4
JS	7	0	4	11.7
PSP	9	0	5	9.7
RRP	6	0	4	5.9
IND	(6) 3	1	4	9.3
	(41) 13	13	17	

Part: 33.0

1962

Party	Cont	Won	LD	Pct.
CONG	13	5	0	47.3
Swat	7	5	1	21.2
JS	6	3	0	18.5
PSP	5	0	4	4.0
CPI	1	0	1	0.9
RRP	1	0	1	0.6
HMS	1	0	1	0.2
SP	1	0	1	0.1
IND	(12) 9	0	10	7.2
	(47) 13	13	19	

Part: 41.5

1967

Party	Cont	Won	LD	Pct.
CONG	13	12	0	56.4
JS	6	0	0	18.1
Swat	7	1	1	17.0
SSP	1	0	1	0.9
PSP	1	0	1	0.3
CPI	1	0	1	0.3
IND	(14) 9	0	13	7.0
	(43) 13	13	17	

Part: 55.8

BHILWARA DISTRICT

Population: 865,797
Urban: 7.3 Rural: 92.7
Hindu: 93.7 Muslim: 3.6 Jain: 2.5 Christian: 0.1 Sikh: 0.1

1952 Party	Cont	Won	LD	Pct.
CONG	8	3	0	36.9
JS	2	1	0	10.8
HMS	2	1	0	7.0
KLP	3	0	2	3.6
SP	1	0	1	2.8
RRP	2	0	2	2.0
CPI	1	0	1	0.8
IND	(10) 8	3	4	36.1
	(29) 8	8	10	
Part: 25.0				

1957 Party	Cont	Won	LD	Pct.
CONG	8	6	0	48.1
RRP	6	2	0	27.0
JS	3	0	2	4.5
PSP	2	0	0	3.6
CPI	2	0	2	3.2
IND	(13) 6	0	13	13.6
	(34) 8	8	17	
Part: 31.8				

1962 Party	Cont	Won	LD	Pct.
CONG	8	7	0	49.8
JS	3	0	2	6.3
Swat	3	0	2	5.1
PSP	2	0	1	3.6
CPI	1	0	0	2.5
HMS	3	0	3	1.7
RRP	2	0	2	0.7
IND	(18) 8	1	13	30.3
	(40) 8	8	23	
Part: 35.8				

1967 Party	Cont	Won	LD	Pct.
CONG	8	7	0	55.9
Swat	3	0	0	12.8
JS	4	0	2	9.1
SSP	3	0	2	7.5
PSP	2	0	2	1.5
CPM	1	0	1	0.7
IND	(10) 7	1	8	12.5
	(31) 8	8	15	
Part: 47.0				

PALI DISTRICT

Population: 805,682
Urban: 9.5 Rural: 90.5
Hindu: 89.7 Jain: 5.7 Muslim: 4.5 Christian: #

1952

Party	Cont	Won	LD	Pct.
CONG	5	0	3	12.1
JS	4	0	4	3.8
CPI	1	0	1	1.3
KMPP	1	0	1	0.9
SP	1	0	1	0.5
IND	(21) 7	7	12	81.4
	(33) 7	7	22	

Part: 46.0

1957

Party	Cont	Won	LD	Pct.
CONG	7	4	0	40.9
RRP	2	0	0	8.7
JS	3	0	2	5.4
CPI	1	0	0	3.7
IND	(12) 6	3	6	41.3
	(25) 7	7	8	

Part: 37.5

1962

Party	Cont	Won	LD	Pct.
CONG	7	5	0	41.5
Swat	4	1	0	20.7
CPI	6	0	5	9.1
JS	4	0	4	5.0
IND	(20) 5	1	18	23.7
	(41) 7	7	27	

Part: 45.2

1967

Party	Cont	Won	LD	Pct.
Swat	7	5	0	45.3
CONG	7	2	0	41.0
CPM	2	0	2	3.1
CPI	1	0	1	0.6
IND	(15) 6	0	14	10.0
	(32) 7	7	17	

Part: 56.2

SIROHI DISTRICT

Population: 352,303
Urban: 16.4 Rural: 83.6
Hindu: 92.4 Jain: 4.9 Muslim: 2.4 Christian: 0.2

1952				
Party	Cont	Won	LD	Pct.
CONG	3	0	0	30.0
JS	2	0	2	4.6
IND	(5) 3	3	2	65.4
	(10) 3	3	4	
Part: 38.3				

1957				
Party	Cont	Won	LD	Pct.
CONG	3	1	0	52.2
RRP	1	0	0	17.1
IND	(2) 2	2	0	30.7
	(6) 3	3	0	
Part: 38.2				

1962				
Party	Cont	Won	LD	Pct.
CONG	3	3	0	49.5
JS	3	0	3	8.2
RRP	1	0	1	3.1
IND	(6) 3	0	3	39.2
	(13) 3	3	7	
Part: 34.2				

1967				
Party	Cont	Won	LD	Pct.
CONG	3	2	0	39.0
Swat	2	1	0	28.6
JS	1	0	0	8.5
IND	(9) 4	0	8	23.9
	(15) 3	3	8	
Part: 41.8				

JALORE DISTRICT

Population: 547,072
Urban: 4.5 Rural: 95.5
Hindu: 91.7 Jain: 5.2 Muslim: 3.1 Christian: #

1952

Party	Cont	Won	LD	Pct.
CONG	5	0	0	26.2
RRP	1	1	0	16.1
JS	1	0	1	1.6
KMPP	1	0	1	0.8
IND	(8) 5	4	4	55.3
	(16) 5	5	6	

Part: 44.6

1957

Party	Cont	Won	LD	Pct.
CONG	5	1	0	37.1
RRP	4	4	0	32.4
JS	1	0	1	2.4
IND	(8) 4	0	5	28.1
	(18) 5	5	6	

Part: 26.2

1962

Party	Cont	Won	LD	Pct.
CONG	5	4	0	43.5
RRP	4	1	1	25.4
JS	3	0	3	3.8
Swat	1	0	1	0.9
IND	(9) 4	0	6	26.4
	(22) 5	5	11	

Part: 38.0

1967

Party	Cont	Won	LD	Pct.
CONG	5	2	0	39.0
Swat	4	3	0	36.0
JS	1	0	0	10.3
IND	(10) 5	0	10	14.7
	(20) 5	5	10	

Part: 44.1

BARMER DISTRICT

Population: 649,794
Urban: 6.1 Rural: 93.9
Hindu: 82.7 Muslim: 14.1 Jain: 3.1 Christian: #

1952

Party	Cont	Won	LD	Pct.
RRP	2	2	0	36.4
CONG	3	0	1	23.4
JS	1	0	1	3.8
IND	(7) 3	2	4	36.4
	(13) 4	4	6	

Part: 32.2

1957

Party	Cont	Won	LD	Pct.
RRP	5	2	0	41.3
CONG	5	3	0	38.3
JS	1	0	1	3.6
IND	(7) 5	0	6	16.8
	(18) 5	5	7	

Part: 30.3

1962

Party	Cont	Won	LD	Pct.
CONG	5	2	0	43.9
RRP	2	1	0	13.8
JS	1	0	1	0.9
IND	(11) 5	2	6	41.4
	(19) 5	5	7	

Part: 37.1

1967

Party	Cont	Won	LD	Pct.
CONG	5	4	0	49.0
Swat	3	1	0	18.8
JS	1	0	0	4.7
CPI	1	0	1	0.6
IND	(13) 5	1	10	26.9
	(23) 6	6	11	

Part: 41.4

JAISALMER DISTRICT

Population: 140,338
Urban: 9.7 Rural: 90.3
Hindu: 73.1 Muslim: 26.4 Jain: 0.4 Christian: #

	1952			
Party	Cont	Won	LD	Pct.
CONG	1	0	1	3.8
IND	(4) 1	1	3	96.2
	(5) 1	1	4	
Part:	27.7			

	1957			
Party	Cont	Won	LD	Pct.
CONG	1	0	1	15.0
IND	(1) 1	1	0	85.0
	(2) 1	1	1	
Part:	34.4			

	1962			
Party	Cont	Won	LD	Pct.
CONG	1	1	0	57.9
RRP	1	0	0	31.0
PSP	1	0	1	2.4
IND	(2) 1	0	2	8.7
	(5) 1	1	3	
Part:	36.0			

	1967			
Party	Cont	Won	LD	Pct.
Swat	1	1	0	52.1
CONG	1	0	0	40.3
PSP	1	0	1	3.4
IND	(2) 1	0	2	4.2
	(5) 1	1	3	
Part:	32.7			

JODHPUR DISTRICT

Population: 885,663
Urban: 29.9 Rural: 70.1
Hindu: 88.1 Muslim: 9.0 Jain: 2.4 Christian: 0.3 Sikh: 0.2

1952

Party	Cont	Won	LD	Pct.
CONG	7	0	3	20.1
KLP	1	0	1	1.6
CPI	2	0	2	1.5
SP	2	0	2	1.3
RRP	1	0	1	0.5
JS	1	0	1	0.1
IND	(24) 7	7	17	74.9
	(38) 7	7	27	
Part:	46.5			

1957

Party	Cont	Won	LD	Pct.
CONG	7	5	0	39.8
RRP	3	2	0	22.6
PSP	2	0	1	5.1
CPI	2	0	1	3.6
JS	1	0	1	1.9
IND	(24) 6	0	22	27.0
	(39) 7	7	25	
Part:	37.5			

1962

Party	Cont	Won	LD	Pct.
CONG	7	4	0	42.7
RRP	3	1	1	11.3
JS	2	0	0	6.3
PSP	2	0	1	5.1
CPI	1	0	0	2.3
Swat	1	0	1	0.7
IND	(19) 7	2	16	31.6
	(35) 7	7	19	
Part:	48.9			

1967

Party	Cont	Won	LD	Pct.
CONG	8	6	0	48.6
Swat	5	0	0	22.5
JS	3	1	0	18.2
PSP	2	0	2	1.2
CPI	1	0	1	0.4
CPM	1	0	1	0.2
SSP	1	0	1	0.1
IND	(14) 6	1	12	8.8
	(35) 8	8	17	
Part:	56.8			

NAGAUR DISTRICT

Population: 934,948
Urban: 12.9 Rural: 87.1
Hindu: 89.0 Muslim: 9.1 Jain: 1.7 Christian: 0.1

1952				
Party	Cont	Won	LD	Pct.
CONG	8	4	0	43.7
RRP	7	4	0	42.9
JS	3	0	3	3.0
KJSP	3	0	3	1.3
KLP	2	0	2	0.6
IND (11)	4	0	10	8.5
(34)	8	8	18	

Part: 53.9

1957				
Party	Cont	Won	LD	Pct.
CONG	8	8	0	51.4
RRP	4	0	0	12.6
JS	2	0	0	8.8
PSP	1	0	1	0.6
IND (15)	7	0	10	26.6
(30)	8	8	11	

Part: 47.6

1962				
Party	Cont	Won	LD	Pct.
CONG	8	6	0	46.5
Swat	5	1	2	13.5
RRP	2	0	1	3.9
JS	3	0	2	3.9
IND (17)	7	1	11	32.2
(35)	8	8	16	

Part: 51.4

1967				
Party	Cont	Won	LD	Pct.
CONG	9	3	0	41.6
Swat	7	5	0	33.7
JS	2	0	0	8.1
CPI	2	0	2	0.5
IND (13)	7	1	9	16.1
(33)	9	9	11	

Part: 64.4

STATE SUMMARY

Population: 33,686,953
Urban: 26.7 Rural: 73.3
Hindu: 89.9 Christian: 5.2 Muslim: 4.2 Other: 0.3

1952

Party	Cont	Won	LD	Pct.
CONG	198	97*	7	37.9
TNTP	34	19	5	8.1
CPI	52	14	10	7.9
SP	93	5	66	5.8
KMPP	54	7	38	4.0
Cmwl	13	6	1	2.1
SCF	23	1	16	1.7
TTNC	10	7	0	1.4
FB(M)	5	3	1	1.3
Justice	9	1	4	0.8
Repub	6	0	2	0.5
TC	10	0	6	0.4
HMS	6	0	6	0.2
FB(R)	5	0	4	0.1
ML	2	0	2	0.1
TPF	2	0	2	#
RSP	1	0	1	#
IND (415)	175	42	296	27.7
(938)	202	202	467	

Part: 53.1
*Uncontested: CONG (1)

1954

Party	Cont	Won	LD	Pct.
TTNC	9	8	0	51.9
CONG	9	0	3	22.5
CPI	3	0	1	8.3
PSP	1	1	0	6.3
IND (4)	4	1	1	11.0
(26)	10	10	5	

Part: 67.1

1957

Party	Cont	Won	LD	Pct.
CONG	205	151*	0	45.4
CPI	54	4	18	7.3
PSP	22	2	8	2.6
INDC	@	22	@	@
DMK	@	15	@	@
SP	@	2	@	@
IND (509)	200	9	298	44.7
(790)	205	205	324	

Part: 48.5
*Uncontested: CONG (3)

1962

Party	Cont	Won	LD	Pct.
CONG	206	139	0	46.1
DMK	143	50	11	27.1
Swat	94	6	59	7.8
CPI	68	2	26	7.7
FB	6	3	0	1.4
PSP	21	0	15	1.3
WT	16	0	11	0.9
ML	6	0	1	0.7
RPI	4	0	1	0.5
SP	7	1	6	0.4
TNP	9	0	8	0.3
SLP	7	0	5	0.3
JS	4	0	4	0.1
IND (207)	128	5	188	5.4
(798)	206	206	335	

Part: 67.9

1967

Party	Cont	Won	LD	Pct.
CONG	234	50	0	41.4
DMK	173	138	0	40.6
Swat	27	20	2	5.3
CPM	22	11	2	4.1
CPI	32	2	24	1.8
PSP	4	4	0	0.9
SSP	3	2	1	0.5
FB	1	1	0	0.3
RPI	13	0	13	0.2
JS	24	0	24	0.1
ML	@	3	@	@
IND (245)	144	3	226	4.8
(778)	234	234	292	

Part: 73.6

MADRAS DISTRICT

Population: 1,729,141
Urban: 100.0 Rural: 0.0
Hindu: 85.0 Muslim: 7.5 Christian: 6.9

1952				
Party	Cont	Won	LD	Pct.
CONG	7	4	0	31.6
SP	5	2	3	11.8
CPI	4	1	1	7.1
Justice	4	0	3	6.0
KMPP	6	0	6	3.6
ML	2	0	2	2.3
SCF	2	0	2	1.3
FB(R)	4	0	4	1.1
TNTP	1	0	1	0.5
IND (53)	8	1	50	34.7
(88)	8	8	72	

Part: 50.1

1957				
Party	Cont	Won	LD	Pct.
CONG	10	6	0	43.0
PSP	2	0	0	4.8
CPI	3	0	2	3.5
DMK	@	3	@	@
SP	@	1	@	@
IND (21)	10	0	9	48.7
(36)	10	10	11	

Part: 38.0

1962				
Party	Cont	Won	LD	Pct.
CONG	10	6	0	41.6
DMK	9	4	0	38.7
Swat	8	0	8	6.7
SLP	1	0	0	2.8
PSP	1	0	1	1.5
CPI	1	0	1	1.5
TNP	2	0	2	1.4
JS	2	0	2	0.5
IND (9)	7	0	8	5.3
(43)	10	10	22	

Part: 70.3

1967				
Party	Cont	Won	LD	Pct.
DMK	10	10	0	48.8
CONG	12	0	0	41.8
Swat	1	1	0	3.6
JS	6	0	6	0.5
CPI	1	0	1	0.4
ML	@	1	@	@
IND (13)	8	1	12	4.9
(43)	12	12	19	

Part: 72.7

CHINGLEPUT DISTRICT

Population: 2,196,412
Urban: 20.7 Rural: 79.3
Hindu: 95.0 Christian: 2.6 Muslim: 2.2

Party	Cont	Won	LD	Pct.
	1952			
CONG	15	8	0	33.1
KMPP	14	6	4	28.4
SP	7	0	5	6.8
Repub	5	0	1	6.3
SCF	4	0	3	2.8
FB(R)	1	0	0	1.5
CPI	1	0	1	0.5
Cmwl	1	0	1	0.3
IND	(25) 13	1	19	20.3
	(73) 15	15	34	
Part: 47.0				

Party	Cont	Won	LD	Pct.
	1957			
CONG	13	10	0	46.3
CPI	2	0	2	2.2
INDC	@	2	@	@
DMK	@	1	@	@
IND	(38) 13	0	21	51.5
	(53) 13	13	23	
Part: 40.5				

Party	Cont	Won	LD	Pct.
	1962			
CONG	14	10	0	47.9
DMK	8	2	0	27.1
Swat	5	1	2	6.7
RPI	1	0	0	2.4
WT	2	0	1	1.3
CPI	1	0	0	1.1
SLP	3	0	3	0.9
SP	1	0	1	0.7
IND	(19) 9	1	17	11.9
	(54) 14	14	24	
Part: 66.9				

Party	Cont	Won	LD	Pct.
	1967			
DMK	14	13	0	56.1
CONG	15	1	0	37.1
Swat	1	1	0	3.6
JS	2	0	2	0.1
IND	(12) 9	0	11	3.1
	(44) 15	15	13	
Part: 75.1				

NORTH ARCOT DISTRICT

Population: 3,146,326
Urban: 20.1 Rural: 79.9
Hindu: 91.2 Muslim: 6.3 Christian: 2.2

1952

Party	Cont	Won	LD	Pct.
CONG	19	8	0	36.2
Cmwl	12	6	0	23.2
SCF	5	1	2	6.4
CPI	4	0	1	4.2
KMPP	7	0	6	3.4
Justice	2	0	0	2.1
SP	5	0	4	1.4
HMS	3	0	3	1.1
IND	(30) 14	4	23	22.0
	(87) 19	19	39	

Part: 49.1

1957

Party	Cont	Won	LD	Pct.
CONG	20	13	0	43.2
CPI	2	1	0	4.4
DMK	@	4	@	@
INDC	@	1	@	@
IND	(50) 20	1	26	52.4
	(72) 20	20	26	

Part: 46.4

1962

Party	Cont	Won	LD	Pct.
CONG	20	9	0	42.3
DMK	18	11	0	41.6
RPI	3	0	1	3.4
CPI	3	0	0	3.2
Swat	7	0	7	2.6
WT	2	0	2	1.1
TNP	1	0	1	0.5
PSP	1	0	1	0.1
IND	(30) 12	0	29	5.2
	(85) 20	20	41	

Part: 66.2

1967

Party	Cont	Won	LD	Pct.
DMK	20	16	0	48.2
CONG	22	4	0	39.4
CPM	1	1	0	2.8
RPI	8	0	8	1.5
CPI	1	0	1	0.2
JS	2	0	2	0.1
ML	@	1	@	@
IND	(26) 14	0	22	7.8
	(80) 22	22	33	

Part: 73.5

SOUTH ARCOT DISTRICT

Population: 3,047,973
Urban: 12.9 Rural: 87.1
Hindu: 93.5 Muslim: 3.2 Christian: 3.0

1952

Party	Cont	Won	LD	Pct.
TNTP	19	13	0	47.8
CONG	19	5	0	40.0
SP	5	0	4	1.6
SCF	1	0	1	0.8
CPI	1	0	1	0.2
IND	(19) 11	1	16	9.6
	(64) 19	19	22	

Part: 52.2

1957

Party	Cont	Won	LD	Pct.
CONG	19	9	0	41.2
CPI	2	0	2	1.1
DMK	@	4	@	@
INDC	@	5	@	@
IND	(45) 19	1	21	57.7
	(66) 19	19	23	

Part: 47.6

1962

Party	Cont	Won	LD	Pct.
CONG	19	11	0	47.2
DMK	16	7	0	38.7
Swat	9	1	6	9.1
CPI	4	0	4	1.6
TNP	1	0	1	0.1
IND	(13) 10	0	12	3.3
	(62) 19	19	23	

Part: 62.8

1967

Party	Cont	Won	LD	Pct.
DMK	20	14	0	50.0
CONG	21	6	0	43.8
CPM	1	1	0	2.1
IND	(34) 16	0	33	4.1
	(76) 21	21	33	

Part: 73.2

DHARMAPURI DISTRICT

Population data included in Salem District.

1952

Party	Cont	Won	LD	Pct.
CONG	6	2	0	32.8
SCF	1	0	0	6.1
KMPP	3	0	2	3.5
TNTP	1	1	0	3.3
CPI	1	0	0	3.3
SP	1	0	1	0.8
IND	(15) 7	4	5	50.2
	(28) 7	7	8	

Part: 39.9

1957

Party	Cont	Won	LD	Pct.
CONG	7	5	0	43.3
CPI	1	0	0	4.2
INDC	@	2	@	@
IND	(23) 7	0	13	52.5
	(31) 7	7	13	

Part: 31.5

1962

Party	Cont	Won	LD	Pct.
DMK	5	4	0	38.5
CONG	7	1	0	36.4
Swat	3	1	1	7.4
WT	2	0	1	3.2
CPI	1	0	0	2.9
IND	(8) 5	1	6	11.6
	(26) 7	7	8	

Part: 56.6

1967

Party	Cont	Won	LD	Pct.
CONG	9	6	0	47.1
DMK	7	1	0	39.5
Swat	2	2	0	10.1
RPI	1	0	1	0.5
CPI	1	0	1	0.5
JS	2	0	2	0.1
IND	(7) 4	0	7	2.2
	(29) 9	9	11	

Part: 66.3

SALEM DISTRICT

Population: 3,804,108 (including Dharmapuri District)
Urban: 16.2 Rural: 83.8
Hindu: 96.2 Muslim: 2.7 Christian: 1.0

1952

Party	Cont	Won	LD	Pct.
CONG	14	7	0	38.1
CPI	3	2	0	11.5
TNTP	2	0	0	3.9
SP	4	0	2	3.0
SCF	2	0	2	1.3
KMPP	3	0	3	1.0
IND	(34) 13	5	22	41.2
	(62) 14	14	29	

Part: 49.6

1957

Party	Cont	Won	LD	Pct.
CONG	16	14	0	48.0
CPI	6	0	5	6.0
PSP	3	0	2	2.9
DMK	@	2	@	@
IND	(40) 16	0	25	43.1
	(65) 16	16	32	

Part: 53.6

1962

Party	Cont	Won	LD	Pct.
CONG	16	11	0	46.0
DMK	15	5	1	41.1
CPI	2	0	1	3.2
Swat	4	0	2	2.8
TNP	3	0	2	2.5
PSP	1	0	0	2.0
WT	4	0	4	0.6
JS	1	0	1	0.3
IND	(12) 8	0	12	1.5
	(58) 16	16	23	

Part: 64.7

1967

Party	Cont	Won	LD	Pct.
DMK	15	15	0	50.6
CONG	17	1	0	40.9
PSP	1	1	0	2.8
CPM	1	0	0	2.8
CPI	2	0	2	0.5
JS	4	0	4	0.3
IND	(18) 10	0	18	2.1
	(58) 17	17	24	

Part: 69.7

NILGIRIS DISTRICT

Population: 409,308
Urban: 43.9 Rural: 56.1
Hindu: 80.9 Christian: 10.7 Muslim: 8.2

1952

Party	Cont	Won	LD	Pct.
CONG	2	1	0	39.1
SCF	1	0	1	5.4
IND	(3) 2	1	1	55.5
	(6) 2	2	2	

Part: 54.1

1957

Party	Cont	Won	LD	Pct.
CONG	2	2	0	49.9
IND	(6) 2	0	4	50.1
	(8) 2	2	4	

Part: 52.3

1962

Party	Cont	Won	LD	Pct.
CONG	2	2	0	50.6
Swat	2	0	1	24.1
CPI	2	0	2	13.3
DMK	1	0	0	11.0
IND	(3) 2	0	3	1.0
	(10) 2	2	6	

Part: 67.6

1967

Party	Cont	Won	LD	Pct.
CONG	3	1	0	40.1
Swat	2	1	0	38.0
DMK	1	1	0	21.0
IND	(1) 1	0	1	0.9
	(7) 3	3	1	

Part: 68.8

COIMBATORE DISTRICT

Population: 3,557,471
Urban: 29.0 Rural: 71.0
Hindu: 94.6 Muslim: 2.8 Christian: 2.6

1952

Party	Cont	Won	LD	Pct.
CONG	19	14*	0	43.2
CPI	9	1	1	13.7
SP	14	1	6	12.5
TNTP	3	0	2	3.1
SCF	2	0	1	1.8
KMPP	1	0	1	0.7
Repub	1	0	1	0.1
IND (32)	18	3	23	24.9
(81)	19	19	35	

Part: 57.6
*Uncontested: CONG (1)

1957

Party	Cont	Won	LD	Pct.
CONG	21	16*	0	48.1
CPI	8	2	0	14.3
PSP	6	1	1	10.9
SP	@	1	@	@
IND (34)	18	1	20	26.7
(69)	21	21	21	

Part: 55.0
*Uncontested: CONG (1)

1962

Party	Cont	Won	LD	Pct.
CONG	21	20	0	48.5
DMK	17	0	7	18.0
CPI	14	0	5	15.4
PSP	8	0	5	5.2
Swat	8	0	6	4.7
SP	5	1	4	3.0
WT	1	0	0	1.8
IND (19)	12	0	18	3.4
(93)	21	21	45	

Part: 70.6

1967

Party	Cont	Won	LD	Pct.
CONG	25	3	0	38.0
DMK	16	14	0	36.9
CPM	3	2	0	6.1
SSP	3	2	1	5.1
PSP	2	2	0	4.3
Swat	2	2	0	3.9
CPI	6	0	4	3.4
RPI	4	0	4	0.5
IND (15)	13	0	14	1.8
(76)	25	25	23	

Part: 72.3

MADURAI DISTRICT

Population: 3,211,227
Urban: 31.6 Rural: 68.4
Hindu: 91.4 Christian: 4.3 Muslim: 4.2

1952

Party	Cont	Won	LD	Pct.
CONG	18	12	0	43.7
SP	10	0	5	10.2
CPI	8	2	4	10.0
FB(M)	2	1	0	6.2
KMPP	10	0	9	5.2
Justice	2	1	1	3.0
SCF	1	0	0	1.4
TNTP	1	0	1	0.3
IND	(28) 16	2	22	20.0
	(80) 18	18	42	

Part: 53.5

1957

Party	Cont	Won	LD	Pct.
CONG	20	17	0	46.8
CPI	4	0	0	6.9
PSP	5	0	4	3.5
INDC	@	3	@	@
IND	(39) 20	0	18	42.8
	(68) 20	20	22	

Part: 49.0

1962

Party	Cont	Won	LD	Pct.
CONG	20	15	0	45.6
DMK	11	3	1	20.1
CPI	9	0	3	12.3
FB	3	1	0	6.2
Swat	8	0	5	5.2
PSP	3	0	3	1.1
SLP	2	0	1	1.1
JS	1	0	1	0.4
IND	(20) 14	1	16	8.0
	(77) 20	20	30	

Part: 70.2

1967

Party	Cont	Won	LD	Pct.
CONG	22	3	0	39.6
DMK	13	12	0	35.3
CPM	5	4	0	12.2
Swat	3	2	0	6.2
FB	1	1	0	3.0
CPI	1	0	1	0.6
JS	3	0	3	0.6
IND	(20) 11	0	19	2.5
	(68) 22	22	23	

Part: 73.9

TIRUCHIRAPALLI DISTRICT

Population: 3,190,078
Urban: 21.3 Rural: 78.7
Hindu: 90.3 Christian: 5.4 Muslim: 4.0

Party	Cont	Won	LD	Pct.
1952				
CONG	18	5	0	34.1
TNTP	6	4	1	17.9
CPI	2	2	0	5.4
KMPP	1	0	0	3.3
SP	7	0	7	2.9
SCF	1	0	1	0.5
HMS	1	0	1	0.1
IND	(48) 16	7	31	35.8
	(84) 18	18	41	
Part: 55.6				

Party	Cont	Won	LD	Pct.
1957				
CONG	20	17	0	43.7
CPI	5	1	3	5.4
PSP	2	0	1	1.7
DMK	@	1	@	@
IND	(68) 20	1	47	49.2
	(95) 20	20	51	
Part: 51.4				

Party	Cont	Won	LD	Pct.
1962				
CONG	20	10	0	45.3
DMK	17	9	0	39.3
Swat	8	0	5	5.9
CPI	3	1	1	4.9
ML	1	0	1	0.7
TNP	2	0	2	0.4
SP	1	0	1	0.1
PSP	1	0	1	0.1
IND	(20) 12	0	19	3.3
	(73) 20	20	30	
Part: 69.1				

Party	Cont	Won	LD	Pct.
1967				
DMK	20	15	0	44.3
CONG	22	6	0	43.6
Swat	1	1	0	3.1
CPI	5	0	4	2.3
CPM	1	0	0	1.9
JS	2	0	2	0.1
IND	(28) 15	0	27	4.7
	(79) 22	22	33	
Part: 75.5				

THANJAVUR DISTRICT

Population: 3,245,927
Urban: 20.4 Rural: 79.6
Hindu: 89.6 Muslim: 6.3 Christian: 3.7

1952

Party	Cont	Won	LD	Pct.
CONG	20	9	0	39.7
CPI	12	6	0	25.4
SP	7	0	6	3.6
TNTP	1	1	0	1.8
SCF	2	0	2	1.1
Justice	1	0	0	1.0
HMS	2	0	2	0.3
IND (38)	16	4	26	27.1
(83)	20	20	36	

Part: 58.0

1957

Party	Cont	Won	LD	Pct.
CONG	20	18	0	48.2
CPI	13	0	2	19.1
PSP	1	1	0	2.0
INDC	@	1	@	@
IND (53)	20	0	38	30.7
(87)	20	20	40	

Part: 52.5

1962

Party	Cont	Won	LD	Pct.
CONG	20	15	0	45.4
DMK	14	4	0	26.8
CPI	13	1	4	15.9
Swat	7	0	6	3.5
PSP	3	0	2	2.4
ML	2	0	0	2.1
SLP	1	0	1	0.3
WT	1	0	1	0.2
IND (12)	10	0	10	3.4
(73)	20	20	24	

Part: 74.1

1967

Party	Cont	Won	LD	Pct.
CONG	23	8	0	43.7
DMK	15	9	0	33.3
CPM	5	3	0	8.7
CPI	8	1	4	6.1
PSP	1	1	0	2.3
JS	1	0	1	#
IND (19)	14	1	17	5.9
(72)	23	23	22	

Part: 80.3

RAMANATHAPURAM DISTRICT

Population: 2,421,788
Urban: 24.8 Rural: 75.2
Hindu: 88.1 Muslim: 6.5 Christian: 5.4

1952

Party	Cont	Won	LD	Pct.
CONG	14	9	0	39.6
FB(M)	3	2	1	10.3
CPI	4	0	0	4.5
SP	8	0	8	4.4
KMPP	4	0	3	2.7
SCF	1	0	1	0.5
IND	(30) 14	4	18	38.0
	(64) 15	15	31	

Part: 55.5

1957

Party	Cont	Won	LD	Pct.
CONG	14	7	0	38.7
CPI	3	0	1	4.6
INDC	@	5	@	@
IND	(37) 14	2	19	56.7
	(54) 14	14	20	

Part: 52.2

1962

Party	Cont	Won	LD	Pct.
CONG	14	8	0	48.7
Swat	9	3	2	22.9
FB	3	2	0	9.9
DMK	3	1	0	7.7
CPI	4	0	2	5.2
ML	1	0	0	1.9
PSP	1	0	1	0.2
WT	1	0	1	0.2
IND	(13) 11	0	13	3.3
	(49) 14	14	19	

Part: 68.7

1967

Party	Cont	Won	LD	Pct.
CONG	17	0	0	39.8
DMK	8	8	0	26.7
Swat	8	8	0	24.9
CPI	4	0	4	1.8
CPM	1	0	1	0.7
JS	1	0	1	0.1
IND	(19) 10	1	18	6.0
	(58) 17	17	24	

Part: 75.3

TIRUNELVELI DISTRICT

Population: 2,730,279
Urban: 31.1 Rural: 68.9
Hindu: 81.4 Christian: 11.9 Muslim: 6.7

1952

Party	Cont	Won	LD	Pct.
CONG	17	13	0	42.3
SP	11	0	9	8.4
KMPP	5	1	4	4.6
CPI	3	0	1	3.8
IND (45)	18	4	28	40.9
(81)	18	18	42	
Part: 53.0				

1954

Party	Cont	Won	LD	Pct.
CONG	1	0	0	44.2
IND (1)	1	1	0	55.8
(2)	1	1	0	
Part: 72.9				

1957

Party	Cont	Won	LD	Pct.
CONG	17	12	0	48.5
CPI	4	0	1	5.3
PSP	3	0	0	4.3
INDC	@	2	@	@
IND (45)	17	3	30	41.9
(69)	17	17	31	
Part: 46.4				

1962

Party	Cont	Won	LD	Pct.
CONG	17	17	0	48.9
Swat	16	0	8	19.6
CPI	8	0	3	10.3
DMK	8	0	2	9.7
WT	3	0	1	4.6
ML	2	0	0	3.3
PSP	1	0	1	0.1
IND (20)	11	0	19	3.5
(75)	17	17	34	
Part: 68.0				

1967

Party	Cont	Won	LD	Pct.
CONG	19	5	0	42.3
DMK	13	9	0	36.5
Swat	2	2	0	5.0
CPI	3	1	2	3.8
CPM	2	0	1	2.4
JS	1	0	1	0.1
ML	@	1	@	@
IND (24)	13	1	20	9.9
(64)	19	19	24	
Part: 71.9				

KANYAKUMARI DISTRICT

Population: 996,915
Urban: 15.1 Rural: 84.9
Hindu: 58.9 Christian: 36.9 Muslim: 4.2

1952

Party	Cont	Won	LD	Pct.
TTNC	10	7	0	42.2
SP	9	2	6	16.2
CONG	10	0	7	14.3
TC	10	0	6	13.8
TPF	2	0	2	1.2
RSP	1	0	1	0.3
IND	(15) 9	1	12	12.0
	(57) 10	10	34	

Part: 64.6

1954

Party	Cont	Won	LD	Pct.
TTNC	9	8	0	57.4
CONG	8	0	3	20.1
CPI	3	0	1	9.2
PSP	1	1	0	7.0
IND	(3) 3	0	1	6.3
	(24) 9	9	5	

Part: 66.5

1957

Party	Cont	Won	LD	Pct.
CONG	6	5*	0	56.5
CPI	1	0	0	10.8
INDC	@	1	@	@
IND	(10) 4	0	7	32.7
	(17) 6	6	7	

Part: 61.6
*Uncontested: CONG (2)

1962

Party	Cont	Won	LD	Pct.
CONG	6	4	0	52.8
CPI	3	0	0	14.0
DMK	1	0	0	5.2
PSP	1	0	0	2.9
IND	(9) 5	2	6	25.1
	(20) 6	6	6	

Part: 65.8

1967

Party	Cont	Won	LD	Pct.
CONG	7	6	0	49.9
Swat	5	0	2	20.6
CPM	2	0	0	9.7
DMK	1	1	0	9.1
IND	(9) 6	0	7	10.7
	(24) 7	7	9	

Part: 71.6

STATE SUMMARY

Population: 73,746,401
Urban: 12.9 Rural: 87.1
Hindu: 84.7 Muslim: 14.6 Sikh: 0.4 Jain: 0.2 Christian: 0.1

1952

Party	Cont	Won	LD	Pct.
CONG	429	390	2	47.9
SP	349	19	231	12.0
JS	211	2	152	6.5
KMPP	266	1	233	5.7
UPPP	58	2	41	1.9
RRP	94	0	80	1.7
SCF	32	0	20	1.5
HMS	62	1	53	1.4
CPI	44	0	40	0.9
RSP	33	0	32	0.4
UPRSP	18	1	15	0.4
FB(R)	1	0	1	#
IND	(1007)392	14	865	19.7
	(2604)430	430	1765	

Part: 37.9

1957

Party	Cont	Won	LD	Pct.
CONG	430	286*	5	42.4
PSP	261	44	96	14.5
JS	236	17	137	9.8
CPI	90	9	50	3.8
RRP	34	0	28	0.8
SP	@	25	@	@
IND	(660)363	49	381	28.7
	(1711)430	430	697	

Part: 44.9
*Uncontested: CONG (5)

1962

Party	Cont	Won	LD	Pct.
CONG	429	249	15	36.3
JS	377	49	192	16.5
PSP	289	38	163	11.5
SP	273	24	202	8.2
CPI	147	14	101	5.1
Swat	167	15	123	4.6
RPI	122	8	96	3.7
HMS	73	2	69	1.1
RRP	42	0	41	0.3
IND	(702)314	31	609	12.7
	(2621)430	430	1611	

Part: 48.6

1967

Party	Cont	Won	LD	Pct.
CONG	425	199	29	32.2
JS	402	98	154	21.7
SSP	255	44	143	10.0
Swat	207	12	178	4.7
RPI	168	10	139	4.1
PSP	166	11	131	4.1
CPI	96	13	65	3.2
CPM	56	1	46	1.3
IND	(1238)369	37	1116	18.7
	(3013)425	425	2001	

Part: 51.0

STATE SUMMARY (Continued)

	1969			
Party	Cont	Won	LD	Pct.
CONG	424	211	14	33.7
BKD	394	99	163	21.1
JS	397	49	177	17.9
SSP	258	33	171	7.8
RPI	181	2	153	3.5
CPI	109	4	80	3.1
PSP	88	2	77	1.7
Swat	71	5	60	1.2
MP	92	0	91	0.5
CPM	21	1	16	0.5
KMP	21	1	17	0.5
SC	26	0	26	0.3
HMS	19	1	17	0.3
RPI-A	23	0	21	0.2
PBI	47	0	47	0.1
FB	4	0	4	0.1
BS	6	0	6	#
RRP	1	0	1	#
IND (689)	306	17	648	7.5
(2871)	425	425	1789	

Part: 54.4

UTTARKHAND AND KUMAUN DIVISIONS

Population: 2,677,342
Urban: 6.6 Rural: 93.4
Hindu: 94.7 Muslim: 3.2 Sikh: 1.8 Christian: 0.2 Buddhist: 0.1

1952 Party	Cont	Won	LD	Pct.
CONG	16	10	0	45.0
SP	12	3	5	15.7
KMPP	3	0	3	1.6
JS	2	0	2	1.0
CPI	1	0	1	0.4
HMS	1	0	1	0.4
IND	(27) 14	3	15	35.9
	(62) 16	16	27	
Part: 26.9				

1957 Party	Cont	Won	LD	Pct.
CONG	17	13*	0	47.8
PSP	8	2	0	22.2
JS	5	1	3	7.4
CPI	2	0	2	2.3
IND	(12) 9	1	4	20.3
	(44) 17	17	9	
Part: 30.2				
*Uncontested: CONG (3)				

1962 Party	Cont	Won	LD	Pct.
CONG	17	15	0	51.4
PSP	13	1	7	17.4
JS	13	0	11	9.2
CPI	6	0	4	4.0
SP	6	0	6	1.3
Swat	1	0	1	1.2
HMS	1	0	1	0.6
IND	(19) 13	1	14	14.9
	(76) 17	17	44	
Part: 32.4				

1967 Party	Cont	Won	LD	Pct.
CONG	17	11	1	38.5
JS	15	1	8	15.2
PSP	4	2	1	8.5
CPI	5	0	3	5.7
Swat	3	1	2	4.4
SSP	5	0	4	1.9
CPM	2	0	2	1.3
RPI	4	0	4	0.8
IND	(37) 12	2	28	23.7
	(92) 17	17	53	
Part: 34.4				

1969 Party	Cont	Won	LD	Pct.
CONG	17	12	0	40.9
JS	15	1	7	19.1
BKD	13	1	7	12.7
CPI	7	1	5	5.5
PSP	4	0	3	3.7
SSP	10	0	10	2.1
RPI-A	1	0	0	1.4
MP	5	0	5	1.3
RPI	6	0	6	0.9
FB	2	0	2	0.7
Swat	1	0	1	0.3
CPM	1	0	1	0.3
KMP	2	0	2	0.1
PBI	1	0	1	0.1
IND	(22) 12	2	18	10.9
	(107) 17	17	68	
Part: 38.5				

UTTAR KASHI DISTRICT

Population: 122,836
Urban: 2.2 Rural: 97.8
Hindu: 99.5 Buddhist: 0.2 Muslim: 0.2 Christian: #

Party	1952 Cont	Won	LD	Pct.
CONG	1	0	0	36.6
IND (1)	1	1	0	63.4
(2)	1	1	0	
Part: 33.0				

Party	1957 Cont	Won	LD	Pct.
CONG	1	1*	0	---
(1)	1	1	0	
Part: n/a				
*Uncontested: CONG (1)				

Party	1962 Cont	Won	LD	Pct.
CONG	1	1	0	71.9
JS	1	0	1	13.8
IND (1)	1	0	1	14.3
(3)	1	1	2	
Part: 25.1				

Party	1967 Cont	Won	LD	Pct.
CONG	1	1	0	55.2
CPI	1	0	0	28.3
JS	1	0	1	16.5
(3)	1	1	1	
Part: 29.2				

Party	1969 Cont	Won	LD	Pct.
CONG	1	1	0	52.2
CPI	1	0	0	37.0
JS	1	0	1	10.8
(3)	1	1	1	
Part: 31.6				

TEHRI GARHWAL DISTRICT

Population: 347,736
Urban: 2.2 Rural: 97.8
Hindu: 99.3 Muslim: 0.6 Christian: #

1952

Party	Cont	Won	LD	Pct.
CONG	2	0	0	30.9
SP	1	0	1	1.4
IND	(5) 2	2	3	67.7
	(8) 2	2	4	

Part: 35.0

1957

Party	Cont	Won	LD	Pct.
CONG	2	2*	0	---
	(2) 2	2	0	

Part: n/a
*Uncontested: CONG (2)

1962

Party	Cont	Won	LD	Pct.
CONG	2	2	0	60.2
CPI	1	0	0	9.6
PSP	2	0	2	9.5
JS	2	0	2	6.7
IND	(2) 1	0	1	14.0
	(9) 2	2	5	

Part: 24.3

1967

Party	Cont	Won	LD	Pct.
CONG	2	1	1	33.9
CPI	1	0	0	22.1
JS	2	0	2	8.5
SSP	1	0	1	1.6
IND	(4) 1	1	2	33.9
	(10) 2	2	6	

Part: 33.0

1969

Party	Cont	Won	LD	Pct.
CONG	2	1	0	42.8
CPI	2	1	1	27.2
BKD	1	0	0	8.4
JS	1	0	1	5.1
SSP	1	0	1	1.2
IND	(1) 1	0	0	15.3
	(8) 2	2	3	

Part: 32.2

GARHWAL DISTRICT

Population: 482,327
Urban: 5.7 Rural: 94.3
Hindu: 98.6 Muslim: 1.0 Christian: 0.2 Sikh: 0.1

1952				
Party	Cont	Won	LD	Pct.
CONG	4	4	0	50.0
SP	2	0	1	5.9
CPI	1	0	1	1.8
IND	(8) 3	0	5	42.3
	(15) 4	4	7	

Part: 21.0

1957				
Party	Cont	Won	LD	Pct.
CONG	3	3	0	53.2
JS	1	0	0	7.4
IND	(4) 3	0	1	39.4
	(8) 3	3	1	

Part: 30.3

1962				
Party	Cont	Won	LD	Pct.
CONG	3	2	0	49.7
PSP	1	0	1	2.6
JS	1	0	1	2.4
IND	(5) 3	1	3	45.3
	(10) 3	3	5	

Part: 33.5

1967				
Party	Cont	Won	LD	Pct.
CONG	3	1	0	31.5
Swat	3	1	2	24.8
JS	2	0	2	5.4
CPM	1	0	1	2.4
IND	(9) 3	1	6	35.9
	(18) 3	3	11	

Part: 37.0

1969				
Party	Cont	Won	LD	Pct.
CONG	3	1	0	35.4
JS	3	0	2	20.7
RPI	2	0	2	2.3
Swat	1	0	1	2.0
MP	1	0	1	1.6
BKD	3	0	3	1.2
SSP	2	0	2	0.7
CPI	1	0	1	0.6
PBI	1	0	1	0.6
IND	(9) 3	2	7	34.8
	(26) 3	3	20	

Part: 41.3

CHAMOLI DISTRICT

Population: 253,137
Urban: 0.0 Rural: 100.0
Hindu: 99.6 Muslim: 0.4 Christian: #

1952

Party	Cont	Won	LD	Pct.
SP	1	1	0	40.3
CONG	1	0	0	36.7
HMS	1	0	1	7.7
IND	(2) 1	0	2	15.3
	(5) 1	1	3	
Part:	25.5			

1957

Party	Cont	Won	LD	Pct.
CONG	2	1	0	41.9
IND	(2) 2	1	0	58.1
	(4) 2	2	0	
Part:	33.7			

1962

Party	Cont	Won	LD	Pct.
CONG	2	1	0	46.8
PSP	1	1	0	22.8
JS	1	0	1	6.1
IND	(4) 2	0	3	24.3
	(8) 2	2	4	
Part:	28.9			

1967

Party	Cont	Won	LD	Pct.
CONG	2	2	0	39.0
JS	2	0	1	23.1
CPI	2	0	2	2.9
IND	(7) 2	0	6	35.0
	(13) 2	2	9	
Part:	27.9			

1969

Party	Cont	Won	LD	Pct.
CONG	2	0	0	29.1
JS	2	1	1	27.0
BKD	2	1	1	21.5
MP	2	0	2	6.2
CPI	1	0	1	1.5
RPI	1	0	1	0.5
IND	(3) 2	0	2	14.2
	(13) 2	2	8	
Part:	39.5			

PITHORAGARH DISTRICT

Population: 263,579
Urban: 0.0 Rural: 100.0
Hindu: 99.0 Buddhist: 0.5 Muslim: 0.3 Christian: 0.2

		1952		
Party	Cont	Won	LD	Pct.
CONG	2	2	0	53.3
SP	2	0	1	17.8
KMPP	1	0	1	4.1
IND	(3) 2	0	1	24.8
	(8) 2	2	3	
Part:	21.3			

		1957		
Party	Cont	Won	LD	Pct.
CONG	2	2	0	60.1
PSP	2	0	0	39.9
	(4) 2	2	0	
Part:	14.5			

		1962		
Party	Cont	Won	LD	Pct.
CONG	1	1	0	46.8
PSP	1	0	0	34.9
IND	(1) 1	0	0	18.3
	(3) 1	1	0	
Part:	24.2			

		1967		
Party	Cont	Won	LD	Pct.
CONG	2	2	0	43.4
JS	2	0	0	26.8
PSP	2	0	1	16.2
SSP	1	0	0	7.9
IND	(3) 1	0	3	5.7
	(10) 2	2	4	
Part:	25.3			

		1969		
Party	Cont	Won	LD	Pct.
CONG	2	2	0	41.3
JS	2	0	0	35.3
FB	1	0	1	7.0
BKD	2	0	2	6.2
SSP	2	0	2	2.7
MP	1	0	1	1.9
RPI	1	0	1	0.8
IND	(3) 2	0	3	4.8
	(14) 2	2	10	
Part:	29.9			

ALMORA DISTRICT

Population: 633,407
Urban: 4.3 Rural: 95.7
Hindu: 99.3 Muslim: 0.4 Christian: 0.2

1952

Party	Cont	Won	LD	Pct.
CONG	4	3	0	45.0
SP	4	1	2	25.1
KMPP	1	0	1	3.1
IND	(6) 3	0	3	26.8
	(15) 4	4	6	

Part: 30.2

1957

Party	Cont	Won	LD	Pct.
CONG	4	3	0	46.9
PSP	3	0	0	23.8
JS	2	1	1	16.2
IND	(4) 2	0	2	13.1
	(13) 4	4	3	

Part: 30.7

1962

Party	Cont	Won	LD	Pct.
CONG	5	5	0	59.3
JS	5	0	3	19.3
PSP	5	0	4	9.6
CPI	2	0	1	4.9
SP	4	0	4	3.3
IND	(4) 4	0	4	3.6
	(25) 5	5	16	

Part: 27.4

1967

Party	Cont	Won	LD	Pct.
CONG	4	3	0	42.9
JS	3	1	0	25.4
SSP	2	0	2	3.3
RPI	2	0	2	2.1
CPI	1	0	1	1.4
IND	(6) 2	0	4	24.9
	(18) 4	4	9	

Part: 30.7

1969

Party	Cont	Won	LD	Pct.
CONG	4	4	0	43.8
JS	3	0	0	25.3
BKD	2	0	0	19.4
SSP	2	0	2	5.5
PSP	1	0	1	2.8
RPI	1	0	1	1.1
MP	1	0	1	0.7
IND	(2) 2	0	2	1.4
	(16) 4	4	7	

Part: 34.5

NAINI TAL DISTRICT

Population: 574,320
Urban: 19.5 Rural: 80.5
Hindu: 78.5 Muslim: 12.8 Sikh: 8.1 Christian: 0.5

1952						1957				
Party	Cont	Won	LD	Pct.		Party	Cont	Won	LD	Pct.
CONG	2	1	0	48.2		CONG	3	1	0	42.6
SP	2	1	0	27.4		PSP	3	2	0	36.7
JS	2	0	2	7.1		CPI	2	0	2	7.5
KMPP	1	0	1	2.3		JS	2	0	2	6.0
IND (2)	2	0	1	15.0		IND (2)	2	0	1	7.2
(9)	2	2	4			(12)	3	3	5	
Part: 39.2						Part: 48.6				

1962						1967				
Party	Cont	Won	LD	Pct.		Party	Cont	Won	LD	Pct.
CONG	3	3	0	41.5		CONG	3	1	0	36.2
PSP	3	0	0	33.5		PSP	2	2	0	29.3
JS	3	0	3	7.1		JS	2	0	1	9.5
CPI	3	0	3	6.0		CPM	1	0	1	3.6
Swat	1	0	1	4.1		CPI	1	0	1	3.1
HMS	1	0	1	2.0		RPI	2	0	2	1.3
SP	2	0	2	1.4		SSP	1	0	1	1.1
IND (2)	1	0	2	4.4		IND (8)	3	0	7	15.9
(18)	3	3	12			(20)	3	3	13	
Part: 51.9						Part: 51.2				

1969				
Party	Cont	Won	LD	Pct.
CONG	3	3	0	43.3
BKD	3	0	1	17.7
PSP	3	0	2	12.4
JS	3	0	2	11.4
RPI-A	1	0	0	5.6
SSP	3	0	3	1.5
CPM	1	0	1	1.4
CPI	2	0	2	1.1
RPI	1	0	1	0.7
KMP	2	0	2	0.5
FB	1	0	1	0.3
IND (4)	2	0	4	4.1
(27)	3	3	19	
Part: 53.6				

ROHILKHAND DIVISION

Population: 8,502,682
Urban: 17.3 Rural: 82.7
Hindu: 69.6 Muslim: 29.1 Sikh: 0.9 Christian: 0.3

Party	Cont	Won	LD	Pct.
1952				
CONG	50	47	0	44.4
SP	49	3	32	13.6
JS	26	1	12	9.1
KMPP	24	0	16	5.0
HMS	12	0	10	3.0
UPPP	4	0	2	1.1
SCF	4	0	4	0.9
UPRSP	4	0	4	0.3
RRP	1	0	1	#
IND	(140) 49	0	120	22.6
	(314) 51	51	201	
Part:	39.7			

Party	Cont	Won	LD	Pct.
1957				
CONG	50	28*	3	38.9
PSP	35	5	12	17.6
JS	28	0	14	10.6
CPI	10	0	9	2.5
RRP	1	0	1	0.4
SP	@	5	@	@
IND	(85) 41	12	51	30.0
	(209) 50	50	90	
Part:	46.1			
*Uncontested: CONG (1)				

Party	Cont	Won	LD	Pct.
1962				
CONG	50	29	4	31.9
JS	47	6	19	19.2
PSP	38	4	22	11.2
RPI	22	3	19	6.2
SP	24	0	19	4.1
Swat	12	0	7	3.2
CPI	12	1	9	3.0
HMS	20	0	20	1.6
RRP	3	0	3	0.2
IND	(106) 42	7	83	19.4
	(334) 50	50	205	
Part:	50.3			

Party	Cont	Won	LD	Pct.
1967				
CONG	49	22	9	27.6
JS	46	13	14	24.6
Swat	39	5	32	10.8
RPI	22	1	18	4.6
PSP	18	2	11	4.4
SSP	22	0	21	2.8
CPM	4	1	3	1.4
CPI	6	0	5	1.0
IND	(202) 45	5	187	22.8
	(408) 49	49	300	
Part:	55.4			

Party	Cont	Won	LD	Pct.
1969				
CONG	49	18	3	32.2
BKD	41	21	8	26.7
JS	48	6	23	18.1
SSP	20	0	17	3.1
PSP	7	0	6	2.8
Swat	12	1	10	2.2
CPI	11	0	10	1.4
RPI	11	1	7	0.9
CPM	4	0	3	0.7

Party	Cont	Won	LD	Pct.
1969 (continued)				
MP	16	0	16	0.7
HMS	4	0	4	0.2
FB	1	0	1	0.1
PBI	1	0	1	#
KMP	1	0	1	#
RPI-A	1	0	1	#
IND	(114) 45	2	107	10.8
	(341) 49	49	218	
Part:	57.0			

BIJNOR DISTRICT

Population: 1,190,987
Urban: 16.4 Rural: 83.6
Hindu: 62.3 Muslim: 36.5 Sikh: 0.9 Christian: 0.1 Jain: 0.1
Buddhist: 0.1

1952 Party	Cont	Won	LD	Pct.
CONG	7	7	0	50.1
SP	7	0	4	14.0
JS	3	0	2	5.2
KMPP	3	0	2	4.0
SCF	1	0	1	1.5
IND (19)	7	0	14	25.2
(40)	7	7	23	
Part: 49.0				

1957 Party	Cont	Won	LD	Pct.
CONG	7	5	0	45.7
JS	5	0	1	20.9
CPI	3	0	2	8.6
PSP	2	0	2	3.5
IND (10)	5	2	8	21.3
(27)	7	7	13	
Part: 59.5				

1962 Party	Cont	Won	LD	Pct.
CONG	7	4	0	38.6
JS	7	2	3	23.1
Swat	3	0	1	5.7
SP	2	0	1	4.3
CPI	1	0	0	3.2
RPI	2	0	2	2.5
HMS	3	0	3	1.2
PSP	1	0	1	0.4
IND (26)	7	1	24	21.0
(52)	7	7	35	
Part: 60.3				

1967 Party	Cont	Won	LD	Pct.
CONG	7	5	0	38.6
JS	7	0	2	21.4
Swat	7	0	6	6.6
RPI	3	0	2	4.7
SSP	4	0	4	2.4
CPM	2	0	2	2.1
CPI	1	0	1	0.5
IND (27)	7	2	24	23.7
(58)	7	7	41	
Part: 60.5				

1969 Party	Cont	Won	LD	Pct.
BKD	6	5	0	40.5
CONG	7	2	0	37.2
JS	7	0	6	7.4
CPI	2	0	1	2.3
CPM	2	0	2	0.7
SSP	1	0	1	0.5
MP	2	0	2	0.3
Swat	1	0	1	0.2
IND (17)	7	0	16	10.9
(45)	7	7	29	
Part: 63.7				

MORADABAD DISTRICT

Population: 1,973,530
Urban: 22.2 Rural: 77.8
Hindu: 61.9 Muslim: 37.3 Christian: 0.4 Sikh: 0.4

1952				
Party	Cont	Won	LD	Pct.
CONG	11	11	0	48.2
SP	11	0	6	14.8
KMPP	7	0	5	6.8
JS	5	0	4	4.8
HMS	4	0	4	4.2
IND	(31) 11	0	27	21.2
	(69) 11	11	46	

Part: 40.6

1957				
Party	Cont	Won	LD	Pct.
CONG	11	6*	0	37.0
PSP	8	1	2	19.1
JS	6	0	2	10.6
RRP	1	0	1	1.8
CPI	1	0	1	0.1
IND	(12) 7	4	4	31.4
	(39) 11	11	10	

Part: 46.0
*Uncontested: CONG (1)

1962				
Party	Cont	Won	LD	Pct.
CONG	11	4	2	25.3
JS	11	0	4	20.6
PSP	11	3	8	12.5
RPI	6	2	4	10.6
Swat	6	0	3	8.1
SP	6	0	4	5.1
CPI	4	1	3	5.0
HMS	4	0	4	1.4
RRP	2	0	2	0.5
IND	(14) 8	1	11	10.9
	(75) 11	11	45	

Part: 53.5

1967				
Party	Cont	Won	LD	Pct.
CONG	11	6	1	26.4
JS	10	1	6	19.1
Swat	11	1	9	12.0
PSP	8	0	6	6.8
RPI	5	0	4	4.7
CPM	1	1	0	4.3
SSP	2	0	2	2.0
CPI	3	0	3	0.9
IND	(44) 11	2	41	23.8
	(95) 11	11	72	

Part: 55.9

1969				
Party	Cont	Won	LD	Pct.
BKD	10	7	1	32.2
CONG	11	1	1	26.4
JS	10	0	7	11.3
Swat	7	1	5	6.4
SSP	4	0	3	4.9
PSP	4	1	3	3.5
CPI	2	0	2	2.2
CPM	1	0	0	1.9
RPI	1	0	1	0.2
IND	(24) 10	1	22	11.0
	(74) 11	11	45	

Part: 60.1

RAMPUR DISTRICT

Population: 701,537
Urban: 20.8 Rural: 79.2
Hindu: 50.8 Muslim: 45.0 Sikh: 3.6 Christian: 0.5

Party	Cont	Won	LD	Pct.
\multicolumn{5}{c}{1952}
CONG	4	4	0	52.7
JS	2	0	0	16.6
HMS	3	0	2	13.2
SP	4	0	3	9.6
KMPP	1	0	1	0.8
IND	(6) 4	0	6	7.1
	(20) 4	4	12	
Part:	49.7			

Party	Cont	Won	LD	Pct.
\multicolumn{5}{c}{1957}
CONG	4	3	0	50.7
PSP	3	0	1	23.3
JS	2	0	2	3.5
IND	(3) 3	1	0	22.5
	(12) 4	4	3	
Part:	43.2			

Party	Cont	Won	LD	Pct.
\multicolumn{5}{c}{1962}
CONG	4	4	0	46.3
JS	3	0	0	20.3
PSP	3	0	1	15.1
HMS	1	0	1	2.4
IND	(8) 3	0	7	15.9
	(19) 4	4	9	
Part:	44.3			

Party	Cont	Won	LD	Pct.
\multicolumn{5}{c}{1967}
Swat	4	4	0	59.4
JS	3	0	0	18.0
CONG	4	0	4	10.0
PSP	1	0	0	8.4
SSP	1	0	1	0.3
IND	(4) 2	0	4	3.9
	(17) 4	4	9	
Part:	63.0			

Party	Cont	Won	LD	Pct.
\multicolumn{5}{c}{1969}
CONG	4	2	0	35.6
BKD	3	1	1	18.7
JS	4	1	2	16.5
PSP	1	0	0	8.6
CPI	1	0	1	0.5
RPI-A	1	0	1	0.1
IND	(8) 4	0	7	20.0
	(22) 4	4	12	
Part:	57.8			

BUDAUN DISTRICT

Population: 1,411,657
Urban: 8.4 Rural: 91.6
Hindu: 82.3 Muslim: 17.4 Christian: 0.3

1952

Party	Cont	Won	LD	Pct.
CONG	8	7	0	37.2
JS	7	1	2	19.3
SP	7	1	6	7.7
UPPP	3	0	1	6.4
UPRSP	4	0	4	2.0
HMS	2	0	2	1.6
IND	(23) 8	0	19	25.8
	(54) 9	9	34	

Part: 37.6

1957

Party	Cont	Won	LD	Pct.
CONG	9	5	1	41.8
PSP	5	1	0	19.2
JS	3	0	0	7.5
CPI	3	0	3	2.8
SP	@	1	@	@
IND	(18) 9	2	12	28.7
	(38) 9	9	16	

Part: 46.6

1962

Party	Cont	Won	LD	Pct.
CONG	9	4	1	33.0
JS	8	2	1	20.9
PSP	6	1	3	11.6
RPI	4	1	3	10.5
SP	5	0	4	4.2
Swat	3	0	3	2.1
HMS	3	0	3	1.5
CPI	2	0	2	1.1
IND	(13) 7	1	11	15.1
	(53) 9	9	31	

Part: 49.4

1967

Party	Cont	Won	LD	Pct.
JS	7	4	0	32.2
CONG	8	2	1	29.3
RPI	5	1	3	9.5
SSP	5	0	4	4.4
CPI	1	0	1	1.2
Swat	2	0	2	0.8
IND	(33) 7	1	31	22.6
	(61) 8	8	42	

Part: 56.2

1969

Party	Cont	Won	LD	Pct.
CONG	8	3	1	33.6
JS	8	2	1	30.0
BKD	6	2	1	20.1
SSP	5	0	5	2.4
MP	2	0	2	0.5
CPI	1	0	1	0.5
IND	(19) 7	1	17	12.9
	(49) 8	8	28	

Part: 59.2

BAREILLY DISTRICT

Population: 1,478,490
Urban: 22.1 Rural: 77.9
Hindu: 69.0 Muslim: 29.9 Sikh: 0.7 Christian: 0.4

Party	Cont	Won	LD	Pct.
		1952		
CONG	9	9	0	48.1
SP	9	0	6	13.9
KMPP	9	0	6	13.1
JS	5	0	2	11.8
SCF	2	0	2	2.3
UPPP	1	0	1	0.5
HMS	1	0	1	0.3
IND	(15) 8	0	14	10.0
	(51) 9	9	32	
Part:	35.8			

Party	Cont	Won	LD	Pct.
		1957		
CONG	9	8	0	43.5
PSP	9	1	3	28.6
JS	6	0	4	10.4
CPI	2	0	2	2.0
IND	(12) 7	0	11	15.5
	(38) 9	9	20	
Part:	42.7			

Party	Cont	Won	LD	Pct.
		1962		
CONG	9	6	0	31.7
JS	9	2	5	16.9
PSP	9	0	5	14.7
RPI	4	0	4	5.3
CPI	3	0	3	2.1
SP	5	0	5	1.7
RRP	1	0	1	0.5
HMS	2	0	2	0.4
IND	(19) 8	1	11	26.7
	(61) 9	9	36	
Part:	51.6			

Party	Cont	Won	LD	Pct.
		1967		
JS	9	5	1	34.8
CONG	9	4	0	33.6
RPI	3	0	3	2.3
Swat	6	0	6	1.9
PSP	3	0	3	1.1
CPM	1	0	1	0.7
SSP	2	0	2	0.5
IND	(42) 8	0	37	25.1
	(75) 9	9	53	
Part:	55.8			

Party	Cont	Won	LD	Pct.
		1969		
CONG	9	4	1	34.9
BKD	8	4	1	30.7
JS	9	1	5	18.5
RPI	2	0	1	2.8
PSP	2	0	2	2.3
Swat	1	0	1	1.7
MP	5	0	5	1.0
CPM	1	0	1	1.0
FB	1	0	1	0.9
HMS	2	0	2	0.5
SSP	4	0	4	0.4
CPI	2	0	2	0.3
KMP	1	0	1	0.1
IND	(17) 7	0	17	4.9
	(64) 9	9	44	
Part:	56.1			

PILIBHIT DISTRICT

Population: 616,225
Urban: 13.7 Rural: 86.3
Hindu: 75.9 Muslim: 21.1 Sikh: 2.7 Christian: 0.2

1952

Party	Cont	Won	LD	Pct.
CONG	4	2	0	36.5
SP	4	2	2	23.6
KMPP	3	0	1	9.4
JS	3	0	2	9.2
HMS	1	0	1	3.6
IND (12)	4	0	12	17.7
(27)	4	4	18	

Part: 40.8

1957

Party	Cont	Won	LD	Pct.
PSP	3	2	0	38.1
CONG	3	1	0	27.1
JS	3	0	2	13.6
CPI	1	0	1	2.7
IND (5)	3	0	4	18.5
(15)	3	3	7	

Part: 38.8

1962

Party	Cont	Won	LD	Pct.
CONG	3	3	0	28.2
PSP	3	0	0	22.7
JS	3	0	1	22.0
CPI	2	0	1	12.5
RPI	1	0	1	0.9
HMS	1	0	1	0.4
IND (6)	2	0	5	13.3
(19)	3	3	9	

Part: 44.6

1967

Party	Cont	Won	LD	Pct.
JS	4	2	1	22.9
CONG	4	1	2	20.0
PSP	4	1	1	17.8
CPI	1	0	0	6.9
Swat	3	0	3	3.0
SSP	2	0	2	1.0
IND (17)	4	0	15	28.4
(35)	4	4	24	

Part: 53.9

1969

Party	Cont	Won	LD	Pct.
CONG	4	1	0	26.6
BKD	3	2	0	24.9
JS	4	1	1	23.5
PSP	3	0	2	7.5
CPI	3	0	3	5.0
MP	4	0	4	3.3
IND (8)	4	0	8	9.2
(29)	4	4	18	

Part: 50.2

SHAHJAHANPUR DISTRICT

Population: 1,130,256
Urban: 13.9 Rural: 86.1
Hindu: 83.9 Muslim: 15.3 Sikh: 0.6 Christian: 0.2

1952

Party	Cont	Won	LD	Pct.
CONG	7	7	0	31.4
SP	7	0	5	16.3
HMS	1	0	0	3.8
SCF	1	0	1	2.1
JS	1	0	0	1.3
RRP	1	0	1	0.4
KMPP	1	0	1	0.1
IND	(34) 7	0	28	44.6
	(53) 7	7	36	

Part: 31.5

1957

Party	Cont	Won	LD	Pct.
CONG	7	0	2	22.0
PSP	5	0	4	5.2
JS	3	0	3	4.1
SP	@	4	@	@
IND	(25) 7	3	12	68.7
	(40) 7	7	21	

Part: 42.9

1962

Party	Cont	Won	LD	Pct.
CONG	7	4	1	26.9
SP	6	0	5	10.2
JS	6	0	5	9.7
PSP	5	0	4	9.6
HMS	6	0	6	4.3
RPI	5	0	5	3.9
IND	(20) 7	3	14	35.4
	(55) 7	7	40	

Part: 41.2

1967

Party	Cont	Won	LD	Pct.
CONG	6	4	1	21.9
JS	6	1	4	17.4
SSP	6	0	6	10.1
Swat	6	0	6	8.7
RPI	6	0	6	7.6
PSP	2	1	1	5.2
IND	(35) 6	0	35	29.1
	(67) 6	6	59	

Part: 43.7

1969

Party	Cont	Won	LD	Pct.
CONG	6	5	0	32.4
JS	6	1	1	26.0
SSP	6	0	4	13.6
BKD	5	0	4	6.3
RPI	4	0	4	3.2
Swat	3	0	3	3.2
PSP	1	0	0	3.1
MP	3	0	3	1.1
HMS	2	0	2	1.0
PBI	1	0	1	0.2
IND	(21) 6	0	20	9.9
	(58) 6	6	42	

Part: 46.7

LUCKNOW DIVISION

Population: 8,320,415
Urban: 12.5 Rural: 87.5
Hindu: 85.8 Muslim: 13.7 Sikh: 0.3 Christian: 0.1

1952

Party	Cont	Won	LD	Pct.
CONG	47	46	0	48.3
JS	30	0	18	9.7
SP	41	0	36	9.3
KMPP	34	0	33	5.6
UPPP	19	0	16	4.5
SCF	9	0	8	2.4
RRP	13	0	13	1.2
CPI	6	0	6	1.0
HMS	6	0	6	0.6
IND (102)	46	1	89	17.4
(307)	47	47	225	

Part: 34.6

1957

Party	Cont	Won	LD	Pct.
CONG	48	22	0	39.2
PSP	35	12	9	21.3
JS	33	5	10	16.9
CPI	11	3	5	5.6
SP	@	2	5	@
IND (51)	34	4	33	17.0
(178)	48	48	57	

Part: 42.3

1962

Party	Cont	Won	LD	Pct.
CONG	48	27	2	37.0
JS	47	14	11	28.0
PSP	30	0	21	9.1
SP	27	4	21	7.7
CPI	21	1	17	4.7
Swat	19	0	19	1.8
RPI	9	0	9	1.3
HMS	9	0	9	0.6
RRP	1	0	1	0.1
IND (76)	37	2	72	9.7
(287)	48	48	182	

Part: 45.0

1967

Party	Cont	Won	LD	Pct.
CONG	48	23	4	31.7
JS	47	18	10	27.3
SSP	25	1	16	7.0
PSP	21	2	14	6.6
Swat	24	0	23	3.6
CPI	14	1	11	2.7
RPI	24	0	24	2.7
CPM	5	0	4	0.9
IND (153)	42	3	144	17.5
(361)	48	48	250	

Part: 47.9

1969

Party	Cont	Won	LD	Pct.
CONG	48	36	0	40.6
JS	44	1	12	23.1
BKD	45	7	26	15.9
SSP	21	2	12	6.6
CPI	10	1	7	2.6
PSP	14	0	11	2.5
RPI	15	0	15	1.5
MP	10	0	9	1.3

1969 (continued)

Party	Cont	Won	LD	Pct.
CPM	2	0	2	0.3
KMP	3	0	3	0.2
Swat	2	0	2	0.1
PBI	3	0	3	0.1
RPI-A	2	0	2	0.1
IND (65)	34	1	61	5.1
(284)	48	48	165	

Part: 46.3

KHERI DISTRICT

Population: 1,258,433
Urban: 5.5 Rural: 94.5
Hindu: 82.1 Muslim: 16.8 Sikh: 1.0 Christian: 0.1

1952

Party	Cont	Won	LD	Pct.
CONG	6	6	0	46.8
JS	5	0	3	11.0
UPPP	3	0	2	7.8
SP	4	0	4	5.9
SCF	1	0	1	2.8
KMPP	1	0	1	2.4
IND	(8) 5	0	5	23.3
	(28) 6	6	16	

Part: 29.7

1957

Party	Cont	Won	LD	Pct.
CONG	7	0	0	36.6
JS	7	2	3	30.0
PSP	5	5	0	24.6
IND	(8) 5	0	8	8.8
	(27) 7	7	11	

Part: 41.1

1962

Party	Cont	Won	LD	Pct.
CONG	7	5	0	42.5
JS	7	2	3	26.6
PSP	7	0	3	21.5
Swat	5	0	5	3.1
CPI	5	0	5	3.0
IND	(6) 5	0	6	3.3
	(37) 7	7	22	

Part: 42.7

1967

Party	Cont	Won	LD	Pct.
JS	7	4	1	34.6
CONG	7	2	1	33.1
PSP	6	1	1	20.8
Swat	1	0	1	1.8
RPI	1	0	1	1.0
CPI	1	0	1	0.3
IND	(11) 4	0	11	8.4
	(34) 7	7	17	

Part: 46.5

1969

Party	Cont	Won	LD	Pct.
CONG	7	7	0	42.2
JS	6	0	0	24.9
BKD	7	0	4	16.3
PSP	6	0	4	10.0
RPI	3	0	3	3.5
CPI	3	0	3	1.2
MP	2	0	2	0.5
IND	(4) 3	0	4	1.4
	(38) 7	7	20	

Part: 41.7

SITAPUR DISTRICT

Population: 1,608,057
Urban: 7.6 Rural: 92.4
Hindu: 83.6 Muslim: 16.3 Christian: #

1952

Party	Cont	Won	LD	Pct.
CONG	9	8	0	45.8
JS	8	0	6	13.1
SP	9	0	7	11.2
KMPP	8	0	7	6.8
UPPP	5	0	5	2.6
RRP	4	0	4	2.1
IND	(18) 9	1	15	18.4
	(61) 9	9	44	

Part: 34.5

1957

Party	Cont	Won	LD	Pct.
CONG	9	5	0	39.4
PSP	9	0	4	19.2
JS	7	1	4	13.9
CPI	3	0	2	4.4
SP	@	2	@	@
IND	(7) 5	1	2	23.1
	(35) 9	9	12	

Part: 41.5

1962

Party	Cont	Won	LD	Pct.
JS	9	5	0	38.1
CONG	9	3	1	31.3
SP	6	1	4	10.5
PSP	4	0	3	4.2
RPI	2	0	2	1.9
Swat	3	0	3	1.5
CPI	2	0	2	1.2
HMS	2	0	2	0.6
IND	(14) 7	0	12	10.7
	(51) 9	9	29	

Part: 44.1

1967

Party	Cont	Won	LD	Pct.
JS	9	6	0	33.4
CONG	9	2	2	26.8
SSP	8	1	4	13.8
Swat	7	0	6	8.9
RPI	5	0	5	3.1
PSP	3	0	3	2.6
CPI	1	0	0	1.8
IND	(18) 9	0	17	9.6
	(60) 9	9	37	

Part: 48.6

1969

Party	Cont	Won	LD	Pct.
CONG	9	8	0	43.8
JS	9	0	1	26.9
SSP	6	1	3	12.6
BKD	8	0	8	6.9
PSP	2	0	1	2.4
RPI	3	0	3	1.3
CPI	1	0	1	1.3
PBI	1	0	1	0.3
MP	2	0	2	0.3
IND	(6) 5	0	5	4.2
	(47) 9	9	25	

Part: 49.0

HARDOI DISTRICT

Population: 1,573,171
Urban: 7.3 Rural: 92.7
Hindu: 88.9 Muslim: 11.0 Christian: #

1952

Party	Cont	Won	LD	Pct.
CONG	9	9	0	46.2
JS	7	0	4	12.6
SP	8	0	7	10.1
SCF	3	0	2	5.7
KMPP	7	0	7	3.4
RRP	2	0	2	0.8
CPI	1	0	1	0.4
UPPP	1	0	1	0.4
IND (21)	9	0	17	20.4
(59)	9	9	41	

Part: 34.4

1957

Party	Cont	Won	LD	Pct.
CONG	9	6	1	44.4
JS	7	1	0	22.6
PSP	5	2	1	20.9
CPI	2	0	1	4.2
IND (6)	5	0	5	7.9
(29)	9	9	7	

Part: 48.8

1962

Party	Cont	Won	LD	Pct.
CONG	9	4	0	36.1
JS	9	4	0	34.8
CPI	7	0	6	7.3
PSP	6	0	6	4.8
RPI	5	0	5	3.4
SP	5	0	5	2.5
HMS	5	0	5	1.7
Swat	3	0	3	1.6
IND (9)	7	1	8	7.8
(58)	9	9	38	

Part: 43.2

1967

Party	Cont	Won	LD	Pct.
CONG	9	4	1	27.7
JS	9	3	1	26.7
RPI	8	0	8	4.9
CPM	1	0	0	2.5
Swat	4	0	4	2.1
SSP	3	0	3	1.6
CPI	2	0	2	0.6
PSP	1	0	1	0.2
IND (44)	9	2	40	33.7
(81)	9	9	60	

Part: 47.3

1969

Party	Cont	Won	LD	Pct.
CONG	9	7	0	38.5
JS	8	0	3	25.6
BKD	9	1	5	14.8
RPI	9	0	9	4.2
SSP	2	0	1	3.0
PSP	2	0	2	1.1
CPM	1	0	1	0.4
RPI-A	2	0	2	0.3
KMP	1	0	1	0.3
Swat	1	0	1	0.2
IND (20)	9	1	18	11.6
(64)	9	9	43	

Part: 49.9

UNNAO DISTRICT

Population: 1,226,923
Urban: 2.4 Rural: 97.6
Hindu: 91.5 Muslim: 8.4 Christian: #

1952

Party	Cont	Won	LD	Pct.
CONG	7	7	0	51.6
SP	6	0	4	10.5
UPPP	4	0	2	10.2
JS	2	0	1	4.6
CPI	2	0	2	3.9
KMPP	4	0	4	3.2
SCF	1	0	1	1.4
IND (10)	7	0	8	14.6
(36)	7	7	22	

Part: 34.7

1957

Party	Cont	Won	LD	Pct.
CONG	7	0	0	32.2
CPI	3	3	0	21.9
PSP	5	2	1	19.5
JS	2	0	1	5.0
IND (9)	5	2	7	21.4
(26)	7	7	9	

Part: 38.0

1962

Party	Cont	Won	LD	Pct.
CONG	7	6	0	32.0
JS	7	0	3	14.8
CPI	4	1	2	12.6
PSP	4	0	2	12.5
SP	3	0	3	2.4
Swat	2	0	2	1.5
RRP	1	0	1	0.8
IND (28)	6	0	28	23.4
(56)	7	7	41	

Part: 40.2

1967

Party	Cont	Won	LD	Pct.
CONG	7	3	0	27.7
JS	7	2	2	22.5
PSP	5	1	3	14.8
CPI	4	1	2	10.3
RPI	5	0	5	4.1
Swat	6	0	6	2.7
SSP	2	0	2	1.2
CPM	2	0	2	1.1
IND (23)	7	0	23	15.6
(61)	7	7	45	

Part: 44.3

1969

Party	Cont	Won	LD	Pct.
CONG	7	4	0	39.0
JS	7	0	3	19.8
BKD	6	2	2	19.4
CPI	3	1	0	12.4
PSP	3	0	3	2.6
Swat	1	0	1	0.6
SSP	3	0	3	0.5
IND (13)	6	0	13	5.7
(43)	7	7	25	

Part: 46.1

LUCKNOW DISTRICT

Population: 1,338,882
Urban: 49.5 Rural: 50.5
Hindu: 78.5 Muslim: 19.9 Sikh: 0.9 Christian: 0.6

Party	Cont	1952 Won	LD	Pct.
CONG	8	8	0	49.5
KMPP	8	0	8	11.9
SP	7	0	7	9.4
JS	4	0	1	8.2
UPPP	4	0	4	7.5
SCF	3	0	3	3.5
RRP	6	0	6	2.6
CPI	2	0	2	1.3
HMS	2	0	2	0.1
IND	(24) 8	0	24	6.0
	(68) 8	8	57	
Part: 38.3				

Party	Cont	1957 Won	LD	Pct.
CONG	8	5	0	39.0
PSP	7	3	2	28.0
JS	4	0	0	11.8
CPI	3	0	2	6.1
IND	(9) 7	0	6	15.1
	(31) 8	8	10	
Part: 40.9				

Party	Cont	1962 Won	LD	Pct.
CONG	8	7	0	45.2
JS	8	1	2	28.7
PSP	7	0	6	12.4
CPI	3	0	2	5.9
SP	5	0	5	2.7
RPI	2	0	2	1.5
Swat	4	0	4	1.1
IND	(9) 5	0	9	2.5
	(46) 8	8	30	
Part: 53.2				

Party	Cont	1967 Won	LD	Pct.
CONG	8	4	0	30.0
JS	7	3	1	26.4
PSP	3	0	3	4.6
Swat	5	0	5	3.8
SSP	4	0	3	3.4
CPI	3	0	3	3.4
RPI	4	0	4	1.9
CPM	2	0	2	1.6
IND	(42) 8	1	39	24.9
	(78) 8	8	60	
Part: 52.1				

Party	Cont	1969 Won	LD	Pct.
CONG	8	4	0	33.2
BKD	7	4	1	27.7
JS	8	0	2	21.8
MP	5	0	4	6.3
SSP	5	0	4	5.0
CPI	3	0	3	2.1
CPM	1	0	1	1.1
KMP	2	0	2	0.8
PBI	2	0	2	0.3
IND	(15) 6	0	15	1.7
	(56) 8	8	34	
Part: 43.7				

RAE BARELI DISTRICT

Population: 1,314,949
Urban: 3.0 Rural: 97.0
Hindu: 90.7 Muslim: 9.2 Christian: #

1952

Party	Cont	Won	LD	Pct.
CONG	8	8	0	51.7
SP	7	0	7	7.2
JS	4	0	3	6.8
KMPP	6	0	6	4.4
HMS	4	0	4	3.9
UPPP	2	0	2	1.4
SCF	1	0	1	1.0
RRP	1	0	1	0.9
CPI	1	0	1	0.7
IND (21)	8	0	20	22.0
(55)	8	8	45	

Part: 35.9

1957

Party	Cont	Won	LD	Pct.
CONG	8	6	0	39.5
PSP	4	0	1	17.5
JS	6	1	2	15.3
IND (12)	7	1	5	27.7
(30)	8	8	8	

Part: 41.3

1962

Party	Cont	Won	LD	Pct.
CONG	8	2	1	35.0
SP	8	3	4	26.4
JS	7	2	3	19.5
PSP	2	0	1	3.2
Swat	2	0	2	2.2
HMS	2	0	2	0.8
IND (10)	7	1	9	12.9
(39)	8	8	22	

Part: 46.7

1967

Party	Cont	Won	LD	Pct.
CONG	8	8	0	46.5
SSP	8	0	4	19.9
JS	8	0	5	19.0
PSP	3	0	3	1.5
CPI	3	0	3	1.3
Swat	1	0	1	0.9
RPI	1	0	1	0.5
IND (15)	5	0	14	10.4
(47)	8	8	31	

Part: 48.3

1969

Party	Cont	Won	LD	Pct.
CONG	8	6	0	46.9
JS	6	1	3	17.9
SSP	5	1	1	16.7
BKD	8	0	6	12.6
PSP	1	0	1	0.7
MP	1	0	1	0.5
IND (7)	5	0	6	4.7
(36)	8	8	18	

Part: 46.1

FAIZABAD DIVISION

Population: 9,286,252
Urban: 4.7 Rural: 95.3
Hindu: 82.9 Muslim: 17.0 Christian: #

1952

Party	Cont	Won	LD	Pct.
CONG	56	48	1	45.6
SP	41	2	31	9.5
JS	27	1	19	7.8
KMPP	38	0	34	6.5
RRP	16	0	9	5.4
HMS	16	1	11	4.2
UPPP	15	1	10	3.4
CPI	5	0	5	1.1
SCF	2	0	2	0.4
RSP	3	0	3	0.4
UPRSP	3	0	3	0.1
IND (92)	42	3	76	15.6
(314)	56	56	204	

Part: 33.7

1957

Party	Cont	Won	LD	Pct.
CONG	57	33	1	41.0
JS	23	5	8	10.2
PSP	19	1	7	6.4
CPI	15	0	10	4.3
RRP	8	0	5	2.5
SP	@	7	@	@
IND (84)	51	11	36	35.6
(206)	57	57	67	

Part: 39.5

1962

Party	Cont	Won	LD	Pct.
CONG	57	30	0	37.3
JS	48	11	15	21.7
Swat	33	7	17	10.6
SP	34	5	22	10.2
PSP	29	0	23	5.7
CPI	12	0	9	2.5
RRP	6	0	6	0.5
HMS	5	0	5	0.3
RPI	2	0	2	0.2
IND (71)	37	4	62	11.0
(297)	57	57	161	

Part: 45.6

1967

Party	Cont	Won	LD	Pct.
CONG	54	24	4	36.0
JS	50	18	18	25.1
SSP	33	6	18	12.6
Swat	24	1	18	5.5
PSP	19	0	18	2.5
CPM	5	0	3	1.5
CPI	8	1	7	1.5
RPI	7	0	6	1.0
IND (100)	46	4	88	14.3
(300)	54	54	180	

Part: 45.9

1969

Party	Cont	Won	LD	Pct.
CONG	54	26	1	36.1
JS	50	13	17	24.2
BKD	50	4	30	13.6
SSP	34	8	20	11.4
CPI	14	1	11	2.3
Swat	9	1	6	2.1
CPM	5	0	3	1.4
MP	11	0	11	0.7

1969 (continued)

Party	Cont	Won	LD	Pct.
RPI	7	0	6	0.7
PSP	8	0	8	0.6
SC	4	0	4	0.3
KMP	2	0	2	0.1
FB	1	0	1	0.1
IND (46)	28	1	42	6.4
(295)	54	54	162	

Part: 46.0

PRATAPGARH DISTRICT

Population: 1,252,196
Urban: 1.7 Rural: 98.3
Hindu: 88.7 Muslim: 11.2 Christian: #

Party	Cont	Won	LD	Pct.
1952				
CONG	8	8	0	61.7
SP	6	0	3	11.5
RRP	3	0	1	5.4
JS	2	0	2	2.1
KMPP	4	0	4	2.0
IND (17)	7	0	15	17.3
(40)	8	8	25	

Part: 31.7

Party	Cont	Won	LD	Pct.
1957				
CONG	8	6	0	47.3
PSP	4	0	3	5.3
RRP	2	0	1	5.3
JS	1	0	0	3.0
SP	@	2	@	@
IND (8)	7	0	0	39.1
(23)	8	8	4	

Part: 38.3

Party	Cont	Won	LD	Pct.
1962				
CONG	8	4	0	38.0
JS	7	3	2	31.1
SP	8	1	5	21.5
RRP	3	0	3	2.4
PSP	4	0	4	1.1
Swat	2	0	2	0.7
IND (9)	4	0	9	5.2
(41)	8	8	25	

Part: 47.8

Party	Cont	Won	LD	Pct.
1967				
CONG	7	6	0	46.4
SSP	7	1	1	31.5
JS	7	0	6	11.6
CPI	1	0	1	0.7
PSP	2	0	2	0.6
IND (15)	7	0	14	9.2
(39)	7	7	24	

Part: 41.9

Party	Cont	Won	LD	Pct.
1969				
SSP	6	5	0	34.6
CONG	7	1	0	31.0
BKD	6	1	4	12.3
JS	5	0	3	11.3
CPI	2	0	2	0.9
PSP	1	0	1	0.4
CPM	1	0	1	0.3
IND (11)	5	0	11	9.2
(39)	7	7	22	

Part: 40.5

SULTANPUR DISTRICT

Population: 1,412,984
Urban: 1.8 Rural: 98.2
Hindu: 87.7 Muslim: 12.2 Christian: #

1952

Party	Cont	Won	LD	Pct.
CONG	9	8	0	44.5
JS	5	0	4	8.5
SP	5	0	4	7.0
KMPP	9	0	9	6.9
UPPP	5	0	4	6.4
CPI	3	0	3	6.0
HMS	5	0	5	4.4
RSP	1	0	1	0.4
IND	(9) 5	1	6	15.9
	(51) 9	9	36	

Part: 29.0

1957

Party	Cont	Won	LD	Pct.
CONG	9	7	0	45.1
PSP	4	0	0	12.7
JS	4	1	2	8.1
CPI	2	0	1	6.4
IND	(10) 7	1	5	27.7
	(29) 9	9	8	

Part: 33.9

1962

Party	Cont	Won	LD	Pct.
CONG	9	8	0	43.4
JS	9	0	2	22.5
PSP	8	0	8	6.0
CPI	3	0	2	4.3
Swat	5	0	4	4.1
SP	3	0	3	1.9
IND	(20) 8	1	18	17.8
	(57) 9	9	37	

Part: 39.4

1967

Party	Cont	Won	LD	Pct.
CONG	8	4	0	40.0
JS	8	3	1	34.2
SSP	4	0	4	3.9
PSP	5	0	5	3.9
CPM	2	0	2	3.0
Swat	2	0	2	1.9
CPI	1	0	1	0.4
IND	(11) 6	1	10	12.7
	(41) 8	8	25	

Part: 37.9

1969

Party	Cont	Won	LD	Pct.
CONG	8	3	0	35.1
JS	7	4	1	33.3
BKD	7	1	4	17.2
SSP	5	0	5	5.6
CPM	1	0	1	2.0
PSP	3	0	3	2.0
MP	1	0	1	0.9
CPI	1	0	1	0.8
RPI	2	0	2	0.8
IND	(8) 5	0	8	2.3
	(43) 8	8	25	

Part: 40.8

FAIZABAD DISTRICT

Population: 1,633,359
Urban: 8.7 Rural: 91.3
Hindu: 88.7 Muslim: 11.2 Christian: #

1952

Party	Cont	Won	LD	Pct.
CONG	11	9	1	39.4
SP	9	1	6	15.0
KMPP	5	0	3	8.9
RRP	5	0	3	8.1
JS	5	0	4	4.6
UPPP	2	0	1	1.9
SCF	1	0	1	1.0
IND	(25) 11	1	18	21.1
	(63) 11	11	37	
Part:	37.5			

1957

Party	Cont	Won	LD	Pct.
CONG	10	7	0	37.2
JS	7	0	4	12.4
PSP	5	0	2	10.5
CPI	8	0	5	10.1
RRP	4	0	4	3.6
SP	@	1	@	@
IND	(16) 8	2	10	26.2
	(50) 10	10	25	
Part:	39.0			

1962

Party	Cont	Won	LD	Pct.
CONG	10	6	0	37.7
JS	8	2	3	18.2
SP	7	0	6	7.4
CPI	3	0	1	6.9
PSP	4	0	2	5.4
RPI	1	0	1	0.6
Swat	2	0	2	0.6
RRP	1	0	1	0.2
IND	(17) 9	2	13	23.0
	(53) 10	10	29	
Part:	47.0			

1967

Party	Cont	Won	LD	Pct.
CONG	10	6	0	36.1
JS	10	1	5	18.8
SSP	5	1	4	6.3
CPI	2	1	1	5.3
CPM	2	0	0	5.3
RPI	3	0	3	2.0
Swat	1	0	1	0.5
IND	(14) 9	1	8	25.7
	(47) 10	10	22	
Part:	51.9			

1969

Party	Cont	Won	LD	Pct.
CONG	10	5	0	32.7
BKD	10	2	0	24.6
JS	10	2	6	15.6
CPI	5	1	2	8.2
CPM	3	0	2	5.4
SSP	6	0	5	3.0
RPI	2	0	1	2.4
PSP	3	0	3	1.1
FB	1	0	1	0.4
MP	2	0	2	0.4
SC	1	0	1	0.1
IND	(7) 6	0	7	6.1
	(60) 10	10	30	
Part:	52.9			

BARA BANKI DISTRICT

Population: 1,414,547
Urban: 5.0 Rural: 95.0
Hindu: 81.1 Muslim: 18.7 Christian: #

1952

Party	Cont	Won	LD	Pct.
CONG	7	6	0	50.0
SP	6	1	3	16.0
UPPP	6	0	4	12.6
KMPP	4	0	4	6.8
JS	3	0	2	4.7
RRP	1	0	1	2.6
SCF	1	0	1	1.0
IND	(5) 3	0	5	6.3
	(33) 7	7	20	
Part:	33.5			

1957

Party	Cont	Won	LD	Pct.
CONG	8	3	0	40.9
JS	3	1	1	7.4
CPI	3	0	2	6.9
PSP	1	0	0	2.3
SP	@	4	@	@
IND	(12) 8	0	5	42.5
	(27) 8	8	8	
Part:	46.7			

1962

Party	Cont	Won	LD	Pct.
CONG	8	2	0	33.7
SP	8	3	2	26.6
JS	8	2	5	20.0
CPI	4	0	4	3.2
PSP	5	0	5	2.8
Swat	5	0	5	2.2
IND	(9) 5	1	7	11.5
	(47) 8	8	28	
Part:	51.4			

1967

Party	Cont	Won	LD	Pct.
CONG	8	3	0	34.7
SSP	8	4	2	31.1
JS	8	0	5	12.0
Swat	5	0	4	4.7
RPI	3	0	3	1.7
PSP	3	0	3	0.9
IND	(21) 7	1	19	14.9
	(56) 8	8	36	
Part:	48.3			

1969

Party	Cont	Won	LD	Pct.
CONG	8	5	0	33.5
SSP	8	2	3	24.7
BKD	8	0	6	13.9
JS	7	0	5	8.0
Swat	1	0	0	4.4
MP	5	0	5	2.3
CPI	2	0	2	0.5
PSP	1	0	1	0.3
IND	(6) 4	1	3	12.4
	(46) 8	8	25	
Part:	49.5			

BAHRAICH DISTRICT

Population: 1,499,929
Urban: 5.3 Rural: 94.7
Hindu: 74.3 Muslim: 25.6 Christian: #

1952

Party	Cont	Won	LD	Pct.
CONG	10	8	0	43.4
RRP	6	0	3	15.4
KMPP	7	0	5	9.5
JS	5	0	5	5.7
SP	6	0	6	3.1
UPPP	2	1	1	2.5
HMS	3	0	3	2.2
CPI	2	0	2	1.5
UPRSP	3	0	3	0.9
RSP	1	0	1	0.8
IND	(14) 8	1	12	15.0
	(59) 10	10	41	

Part: 30.9

1957

Party	Cont	Won	LD	Pct.
CONG	9	5	0	45.2
RRP	2	0	0	8.1
PSP	2	1	0	6.2
CPI	2	0	2	1.6
IND	(12) 8	3	4	38.9
	(27) 9	9	6	

Part: 33.9

1962

Party	Cont	Won	LD	Pct.
CONG	9	4	0	35.4
Swat	6	5	0	24.7
PSP	6	0	2	21.3
JS	4	0	1	6.4
SP	1	0	1	2.1
CPI	2	0	2	0.9
RPI	1	0	1	0.5
IND	(9) 5	0	8	8.7
	(38) 9	9	15	

Part: 42.4

1967

Party	Cont	Won	LD	Pct.
JS	9	9	0	44.5
CONG	9	0	4	21.2
Swat	9	0	6	13.0
PSP	6	0	5	8.9
CPI	3	0	3	1.3
SSP	1	0	1	1.2
CPM	1	0	1	0.2
IND	(21) 8	0	21	9.7
	(59) 9	9	41	

Part: 44.3

1969

Party	Cont	Won	LD	Pct.
CONG	9	6	0	43.1
JS	9	3	0	41.1
BKD	8	0	8	5.4
Swat	4	0	4	2.6
SSP	3	0	3	2.1
CPI	3	0	3	1.6
RPI	3	0	3	1.0
SC	2	0	2	0.7
KMP	1	0	1	0.1
IND	(5) 2	0	5	2.3
	(47) 9	9	29	

Part: 41.4

GONDA DISTRICT

Population: 2,073,237
Urban: 4.9 Rural: 95.1
Hindu: 79.0 Muslim: 20.9 Christian: #

Party	Cont	Won	LD	Pct.
1952				
CONG	11	9	0	41.3
JS	7	1	2	18.1
HMS	8	1	3	15.4
SP	9	0	9	5.9
KMPP	9	0	9	4.0
RSP	1	0	1	0.9
RRP	1	0	1	0.2
IND (22)	8	0	20	14.2
(68)	11	11	45	
Part: 37.6				

Party	Cont	Won	LD	Pct.
1957				
CONG	13	5	1	35.7
JS	8	3	1	22.0
PSP	3	0	2	4.1
IND (26)	13	5	12	38.2
(50)	13	13	16	
Part: 43.2				

Party	Cont	Won	LD	Pct.
1962				
CONG	13	6	0	37.0
JS	12	4	2	28.9
Swat	13	2	4	24.2
SP	7	1	5	4.2
HMS	5	0	5	1.3
PSP	2	0	2	0.9
RRP	2	0	2	0.4
IND (7)	6	0	7	3.1
(61)	13	13	27	
Part: 45.8				

Party	Cont	Won	LD	Pct.
1967				
CONG	12	5	0	39.2
JS	8	5	1	28.6
Swat	7	1	5	9.9
SSP	8	0	6	7.6
PSP	3	0	3	1.8
RPI	1	0	0	1.5
CPI	1	0	1	0.3
IND (18)	9	1	16	11.1
(58)	12	12	32	
Part: 48.8				

Party	Cont	Won	LD	Pct.
1969				
CONG	12	6	1	40.3
JS	12	4	2	34.1
BKD	11	0	8	7.2
SSP	6	1	4	6.1
Swat	4	1	2	4.4
MP	3	0	3	0.7
SC	1	0	1	0.7
CPI	1	0	1	0.4
KMP	1	0	1	0.3
IND (9)	6	0	8	5.8
(60)	12	12	31	
Part: 45.3				

GORAKHPUR DIVISION

Population: 9,975,370
Urban: 4.0 Rural: 96.0
Hindu: 86.6 Muslim: 13.3 Christian: #

1952

Party	Cont	Won	LD	Pct.
CONG	63	55	0	49.6
SP	53	6	34	13.7
KMPP	46	0	39	7.0
JS	30	0	26	5.1
HMS	16	0	14	2.7
UPPP	10	0	6	2.7
RRP	23	0	22	2.5
CPI	9	0	9	1.5
RSP	15	0	15	1.1
UPRSP	2	1	1	0.7
IND (117)	56	1	109	13.4
(384)	63	63	275	

Part: 34.7

1957

Party	Cont	Won	LD	Pct.
CONG	59	43*	1	42.6
PSP	41	6	21	13.0
JS	30	0	24	6.1
CPI	21	2	14	5.3
RRP	6	0	6	0.6
SP	@	1	@	@
IND (102)	55	7	65	32.4
(259)	59	59	131	

Part: 42.5
*Uncontested: CONG (1)

1962

Party	Cont	Won	LD	Pct.
CONG	59	29	0	36.7
JS	48	4	27	15.4
PSP	45	12	21	14.8
SP	54	5	40	12.0
Swat	29	3	20	7.1
CPI	27	5	20	6.3
HMS	16	1	14	3.3
RPI	8	0	8	0.6
RRP	6	0	6	0.3
IND (42)	29	0	40	3.5
(334)	59	59	196	

Part: 46.5

1967

Party	Cont	Won	LD	Pct.
CONG	57	28	3	32.3
JS	55	11	21	22.2
SSP	44	10	19	15.1
Swat	31	2	27	5.0
PSP	28	1	24	5.0
CPI	17	2	14	3.2
RPI	22	0	21	2.1
CPM	12	0	10	2.1
IND (97)	48	3	82	13.0
(363)	57	57	221	

Part: 49.8

1969

Party	Cont	Won	LD	Pct.
CONG	57	29	3	31.8
BKD	55	11	27	17.7
JS	55	3	25	17.3
SSP	44	9	24	12.7
RPI	31	0	27	4.1
CPI	17	0	13	3.1
PSP	13	2	10	2.6
Swat	11	1	8	2.0
HMS	12	1	10	1.9

1969 (continued)

Party	Cont	Won	LD	Pct.
SC	16	0	16	1.6
CPM	2	1	1	0.7
MP	8	0	8	0.4
PBI	7	0	7	0.1
RPI-A	1	0	1	0.1
IND (49)	34	0	46	3.9
(378)	57	57	226	

Part: 48.8

BASTI DISTRICT

Population: 2,627,061
Urban: 1.5 Rural: 98.5
Hindu: 81.3 Muslim: 18.7 Christian: #

1952

Party	Cont	Won	LD	Pct.
CONG	18	18	0	63.7
UPPP	10	0	6	8.6
HMS	7	0	5	5.6
SP	10	0	10	4.6
RRP	8	0	7	3.2
JS	4	0	3	2.2
RSP	8	0	8	2.0
KMPP	6	0	6	1.3
CPI	1	0	1	0.7
UPRSP	1	0	1	0.1
IND	(26) 16	0	25	8.0
	(99) 18	18	72	

Part: 36.2

1957

Party	Cont	Won	LD	Pct.
CONG	16	15	0	51.8
JS	6	0	3	4.9
CPI	4	0	3	2.1
PSP	3	0	2	1.6
RRP	1	0	1	0.5
IND	(26) 15	1	12	39.1
	(56) 16	16	21	

Part: 48.2

1962

Party	Cont	Won	LD	Pct.
CONG	16	9	0	39.9
JS	13	4	4	26.0
Swat	16	3	9	19.7
PSP	4	0	2	3.7
SP	12	0	12	3.6
CPI	5	0	5	2.3
HMS	5	0	5	1.6
RRP	1	0	1	0.4
RPI	1	0	1	0.3
IND	(10) 8	0	10	2.5
	(83) 16	16	49	

Part: 48.6

1967

Party	Cont	Won	LD	Pct.
CONG	15	6	0	35.8
JS	15	7	1	34.8
Swat	15	2	11	15.3
PSP	2	0	1	1.6
SSP	5	0	5	1.5
RPI	5	0	5	0.9
CPI	2	0	2	0.4
CPM	2	0	2	0.2
IND	(26) 12	0	24	9.5
	(87) 15	15	51	

Part: 52.1

1969

Party	Cont	Won	LD	Pct.
CONG	15	10	0	38.7
JS	15	2	3	29.3
BKD	15	1	10	12.4
Swat	6	1	3	6.5
SSP	8	0	8	2.9
CPI	5	0	5	2.5
PSP	2	1	1	2.3
RPI	4	0	4	1.0
MP	3	0	3	0.8
PBI	5	0	5	0.3
IND	(14) 9	0	14	3.3
	(92) 15	15	56	

Part: 49.0

GORAKHPUR DISTRICT

Population: 2,565,162
Urban: 7.3 Rural: 92.7
Hindu: 89.7 Muslim: 10.0 Christian: 0.1 Sikh: 0.1

		1952		
Party	Cont	Won	LD	Pct.
CONG	16	16	0	57.0
KMPP	16	0	14	9.6
JS	8	0	5	7.3
SP	14	0	12	6.6
HMS	5	0	5	2.5
RRP	3	0	3	1.1
RSP	4	0	4	1.0
IND	(41) 16	0	40	14.9
	(107) 16	16	83	
Part:	32.6			

		1957		
Party	Cont	Won	LD	Pct.
CONG	15	11	0	45.3
PSP	11	0	10	8.2
JS	9	0	9	4.2
CPI	5	0	5	3.0
RRP	2	0	2	0.8
IND	(31) 15	0	21	38.5
	(73) 15	15	47	
Part:	38.2			

		1962		
Party	Cont	Won	LD	Pct.
CONG	15	11	0	39.1
SP	15	2	7	21.9
HMS	11	1	9	12.2
PSP	13	1	11	8.3
JS	11	0	10	7.8
CPI	5	0	4	3.2
RRP	4	0	4	0.7
IND	(14) 9	0	12	6.8
	(88) 15	15	57	
Part:	43.2			

		1967		
Party	Cont	Won	LD	Pct.
CONG	15	6	2	29.2
SSP	12	4	6	18.1
JS	13	2	8	14.7
PSP	10	1	8	8.8
CPI	4	0	3	3.7
CPM	3	0	3	2.2
Swat	9	0	9	1.2
RPI	5	0	5	1.1
IND	(33) 13	2	26	21.0
	(104) 15	15	68	
Part:	49.2			

		1969		
Party	Cont	Won	LD	Pct.
CONG	15	8	0	32.5
BKD	15	3	8	19.7
JS	14	0	7	13.6
SSP	13	2	9	11.6
HMS	9	1	7	7.3
PSP	4	1	2	5.1
RPI	7	0	7	2.2
SC	5	0	5	1.8
CPI	2	0	1	1.5
Swat	4	0	4	0.5
CPM	1	0	1	0.5
MP	2	0	2	0.1
IND	(10) 8	0	9	3.6
	(101) 15	15	62	
Part:	47.1			

DEORIA DISTRICT

Population: 2,375,075
Urban: 2.4 Rural: 97.6
Hindu: 88.5 Muslim: 11.5 Christian: #

1952

Party	Cont	Won	LD	Pct.
CONG	15	11	0	41.7
SP	15	4	5	29.1
JS	10	0	10	6.6
KMPP	12	0	12	4.5
RRP	5	0	5	2.3
HMS	4	0	4	2.1
CPI	4	0	4	1.4
RSP	3	0	3	1.1
IND	(19) 11	0	17	11.2
	(87) 15	15	60	

Part: 32.1

1957

Party	Cont	Won	LD	Pct.
CONG	14	10*	0	43.9
PSP	13	3	5	22.7
JS	7	0	6	7.3
CPI	5	0	4	4.0
RRP	1	0	1	0.3
SP	@	1	@	@
IND	(17) 12	0	12	21.8
	(57) 14	14	28	

Part: 37.6
*Uncontested: CONG (1)

1962

Party	Cont	Won	LD	Pct.
CONG	14	6	0	39.6
PSP	14	5	5	23.0
SP	14	3	9	16.7
JS	10	0	4	13.5
CPI	8	0	8	3.1
Swat	4	0	4	1.3
IND	(9) 6	0	9	2.8
	(73) 14	14	39	

Part: 45.7

1967

Party	Cont	Won	LD	Pct.
CONG	13	10	0	38.0
SSP	13	2	4	21.7
JS	13	0	6	18.5
PSP	7	0	7	3.6
RPI	4	0	4	1.5
CPI	1	0	1	0.4
IND	(22) 12	1	17	16.3
	(73) 13	13	39	

Part: 48.1

1969

Party	Cont	Won	LD	Pct.
CONG	13	6	2	29.5
BKD	13	4	3	26.0
SSP	12	3	6	16.6
JS	13	0	9	12.6
SC	8	0	8	3.6
RPI	8	0	8	3.2
PSP	5	0	5	1.9
CPI	4	0	4	0.8
MP	2	0	2	0.5
HMS	2	0	2	0.4
PBI	2	0	2	0.2
IND	(12) 8	0	11	4.7
	(94) 13	13	62	

Part: 48.1

AZAMGARH DISTRICT

Population: 2,408,052
Urban: 4.8 Rural: 95.2
Hindu: 87.3 Muslim: 12.6 Christian: #

1952

Party	Cont	Won	LD	Pct.
CONG	14	10	0	31.9
SP	14	2	7	18.9
KMPP	12	0	7	13.7
JS	8	0	8	5.6
CPI	4	0	4	3.8
RRP	7	0	7	3.0
UPRSP	1	1	0	2.8
IND	(31) 13	1	27	20.3
	(91) 14	14	60	
Part: 37.1

1957

Party	Cont	Won	LD	Pct.
CONG	14	7	1	28.5
PSP	14	3	4	24.0
CPI	7	2	2	12.0
JS	8	0	6	8.6
RRP	2	0	2	1.0
IND	(28) 13	2	20	25.9
	(73) 14	14	35	
Part: 44.6

1962

Party	Cont	Won	LD	Pct.
CONG	14	3	0	27.8
PSP	14	6	3	25.1
CPI	9	5	3	16.3
JS	14	0	9	13.1
SP	13	0	12	7.5
Swat	9	0	7	5.7
RPI	7	0	7	2.2
RRP	1	0	1	0.2
IND	(9) 6	0	9	2.1
	(90) 14	14	51	
Part: 48.4

1967

Party	Cont	Won	LD	Pct.
CONG	14	6	1	26.4
SSP	14	4	4	21.1
JS	14	2	6	19.0
CPI	10	2	8	8.4
PSP	9	0	8	6.1
CPM	7	0	5	6.1
RPI	8	0	7	5.1
Swat	7	0	7	1.8
IND	(16) 11	0	15	6.0
	(99) 14	14	61	
Part: 49.4

1969

Party	Cont	Won	LD	Pct.
CONG	14	5	1	26.5
SSP	11	4	1	19.8
BKD	12	3	6	13.7
JS	13	1	6	13.1
RPI	12	0	8	9.8
CPI	6	0	3	7.2
CPM	1	1	0	2.1
PSP	2	0	2	1.3
SC	3	0	3	1.3
Swat	1	0	1	0.8
RPI-A	1	0	1	0.4
HMS	1	0	1	0.1
MP	1	0	1	0.1
IND	(13) 9	0	12	3.8
	(91) 14	14	46	
Part: 51.0

VARANASI DIVISION

Population: 7,996,537
Urban: 11.1 Rural: 88.9
Hindu: 91.9 Muslim: 8.0 Christian: #

1952

Party	Cont	Won	LD	Pct.
CONG	47	41	0	41.5
SP	44	4	26	15.3
JS	25	0	20	6.5
KMPP	24	0	23	3.5
UPRSP	8	0	6	2.4
RRP	16	0	14	2.2
CPI	7	0	5	1.6
RSP	5	0	5	0.9
HMS	3	0	3	0.2
FB(R)	1	0	1	#
IND (119)	45	2	104	25.9
(299)	47	47	207	

Part: 37.8

1957

Party	Cont	Won	LD	Pct.
CONG	46	35	0	42.5
PSP	29	2	12	13.0
JS	28	3	17	11.5
CPI	15	4	2	9.2
RRP	4	0	4	0.6
SP	@	1	@	@
IND (71)	40	1	48	23.2
(193)	46	46	83	

Part: 48.6

1962

Party	Cont	Won	LD	Pct.
CONG	46	29	1	39.5
JS	39	5	19	16.8
CPI	29	5	15	12.9
SP	34	4	22	11.8
PSP	26	3	20	7.9
RRP	7	0	7	0.3
HMS	4	0	4	0.3
Swat	5	0	5	0.2
RPI	1	0	1	0.1
IND (53)	32	0	45	10.2
(244)	46	46	139	

Part: 52.9

1967

Party	Cont	Won	LD	Pct.
CONG	46	24	1	34.7
JS	46	8	18	23.1
SSP	30	6	14	12.3
CPI	21	5	11	9.1
PSP	23	0	21	3.4
CPM	14	0	11	3.1
Swat	18	0	17	2.8
RPI	10	1	9	1.5
IND (90)	36	2	83	10.0
(298)	46	46	185	

Part: 52.4

1969

Party	Cont	Won	LD	Pct.
CONG	46	24	1	34.9
JS	45	10	22	19.0
BKD	43	6	21	17.5
SSP	31	3	20	8.7
CPI	17	0	6	7.8
RPI	18	0	18	1.7
PSP	16	0	16	1.1
CPM	5	0	5	0.6
SC	5	0	5	0.5

1969 (continued)

Party	Cont	Won	LD	Pct.
MP	11	0	11	0.3
Swat	6	0	6	0.2
PBI	1	0	1	#
RRP	1	0	1	#
KMP	1	0	1	#
IND (66)	33	3	62	7.5
(312)	46	46	196	

Part: 55.8

BALLIA DISTRICT

Population: 1,335,863
Urban: 3.8 Rural: 96.2
Hindu: 94.2 Muslim: 5.7 Christian: #

1952

Party	Cont	Won	LD	Pct.
CONG	8	7	0	32.3
SP	8	0	3	19.1
KMPP	7	0	7	8.6
CPI	3	0	2	6.7
UPRSP	2	0	1	5.8
JS	4	0	4	4.4
RRP	1	0	1	0.4
HMS	1	0	1	0.3
IND	(18) 8	1	16	22.4
	(52) 8	8	35	

Part: 30.7

1957

Party	Cont	Won	LD	Pct.
CONG	8	7	0	34.8
PSP	8	1	3	20.7
CPI	5	0	0	20.2
JS	4	0	3	6.2
IND	(14) 7	0	12	18.1
	(39) 8	8	18	

Part: 47.0

1962

Party	Cont	Won	LD	Pct.
CONG	8	5	0	39.5
PSP	6	1	2	20.2
CPI	6	1	3	15.3
SP	5	1	3	10.4
JS	5	0	5	2.9
Swat	1	0	1	0.3
IND	(7) 5	0	5	11.4
	(38) 8	8	19	

Part: 49.3

1967

Party	Cont	Won	LD	Pct.
CONG	8	3	1	27.6
SSP	7	1	3	14.8
JS	8	2	5	13.8
CPI	5	1	3	10.0
Swat	5	0	5	3.8
PSP	7	0	7	3.4
CPM	5	0	5	3.1
IND	(24) 8	1	20	23.5
	(69) 8	8	49	

Part: 51.0

1969

Party	Cont	Won	LD	Pct.
CONG	8	3	1	32.9
SSP	5	2	2	13.8
CPI	3	0	0	10.4
BKD	7	0	6	7.5
JS	7	0	6	6.4
RPI	1	0	1	1.5
PSP	2	0	2	1.4
CPM	1	0	1	1.1
Swat	1	0	1	0.9
MP	1	0	1	0.3
KMP	1	0	1	0.1
IND	(10) 6	3	6	23.7
	(47) 8	8	28	

Part: 53.4

GHAZIPUR DISTRICT

Population: 1,321,578
Urban: 3.4 Rural: 96.6
Hindu: 91.8 Muslim: 8.2 Christian: #

		1952		
Party	Cont	Won	LD	Pct.
CONG	8	4	0	31.3
SP	8	3	2	25.4
KMPP	6	0	5	6.9
UPRSP	5	0	5	6.7
RSP	4	0	4	4.9
RRP	2	0	2	0.7
JS	1	0	1	0.7
CPI	1	0	1	0.5
IND (18)	6	1	17	22.9
(53)	8	8	37	
Part: 39.5				

		1957		
Party	Cont	Won	LD	Pct.
CONG	8	4	0	30.9
PSP	7	1	1	19.5
CPI	3	3	0	16.2
JS	4	0	4	3.9
RRP	1	0	1	0.8
IND (17)	8	0	11	28.7
(40)	8	8	17	
Part: 46.7				

		1962		
Party	Cont	Won	LD	Pct.
CONG	8	4	1	31.4
CPI	7	3	2	23.5
PSP	8	1	7	10.4
SP	5	0	3	7.6
JS	8	0	7	6.7
RRP	1	0	1	0.1
IND (18)	6	0	15	20.3
(55)	8	8	36	
Part: 52.9				

		1967		
Party	Cont	Won	LD	Pct.
CONG	8	5	0	28.3
CPI	7	2	2	20.4
JS	8	0	7	11.2
Swat	8	0	7	10.0
RPI	3	1	2	6.9
SSP	5	0	3	6.4
PSP	2	0	1	3.2
CPM	4	0	4	3.1
IND (14)	8	0	13	10.5
(59)	8	8	39	
Part: 50.3				

		1969		
Party	Cont	Won	LD	Pct.
CONG	8	7	0	32.2
CPI	6	0	1	18.3
BKD	6	1	3	14.5
JS	8	0	6	14.0
SSP	3	0	1	9.3
RPI	4	0	4	2.3
SC	2	0	2	1.0
MP	3	0	3	0.6
PSP	3	0	3	0.5
Swat	1	0	1	0.1
IND (14)	6	0	14	7.2
(58)	8	8	38	
Part: 54.5				

VARANASI DISTRICT

Population: 2,362,179
Urban: 23.4 Rural: 76.6
Hindu: 89.5 Muslim: 10.3 Sikh: 0.1 Christian: 0.1

1952				
Party	Cont	Won	LD	Pct.
CONG	13	12	0	37.9
SP	13	1	8	18.1
JS	7	0	6	7.1
RRP	9	0	8	4.9
KMPP	6	0	6	1.8
CPI	1	0	0	1.5
UPRSP	1	0	0	1.5
HMS	2	0	2	0.5
FB(R)	1	0	1	0.1
IND	(35) 13	0	29	26.6
	(88) 13	13	60	
Part: 40.9				

1957				
Party	Cont	Won	LD	Pct.
CONG	13	11	0	47.6
CPI	4	1	0	8.6
JS	7	0	4	7.7
PSP	4	0	3	4.6
RRP	2	0	2	0.8
SP	@	1	@	@
IND	(24) 13	0	16	30.7
	(54) 13	13	25	
Part: 55.3				

1962				
Party	Cont	Won	LD	Pct.
CONG	13	8	0	37.3
SP	13	3	5	23.1
CPI	12	1	8	16.5
JS	11	1	6	13.6
PSP	7	0	7	3.9
HMS	4	0	4	0.9
RRP	3	0	3	0.6
Swat	3	0	3	0.4
IND	(9) 8	0	9	3.7
	(75) 13	13	45	
Part: 56.5				

1967				
Party	Cont	Won	LD	Pct.
CONG	13	4	0	32.0
JS	13	3	5	20.4
SSP	7	4	0	19.2
CPI	3	2	0	10.3
PSP	7	0	6	5.6
CPM	3	0	0	5.6
RPI	3	0	3	0.6
Swat	1	0	1	0.3
IND	(30) 10	0	30	6.0
	(80) 13	13	45	
Part: 55.3				

1969				
Party	Cont	Won	LD	Pct.
CONG	13	8	0	35.1
BKD	13	3	4	22.2
JS	13	2	8	16.6
SSP	11	0	8	8.8
CPI	4	0	1	8.4
RPI	9	0	9	2.2
PSP	5	0	5	1.5
CPM	3	0	3	1.0

1969 (continued)				
Party	Cont	Won	LD	Pct.
SC	1	0	1	0.5
MP	5	0	5	0.4
Swat	4	0	4	0.2
PBI	1	0	1	0.1
RRP	1	0	1	0.1
IND	(21) 9	0	21	2.9
	(104) 13	13	71	
Part: 59.6				

JAUNPUR DISTRICT

Population: 1,727,264
Urban: 5.3 Rural: 94.7
Hindu: 91.6 Muslim: 8.3 Christian: #

1952				
Party	Cont	Won	LD	Pct.
CONG	11	11	0	54.4
JS	10	0	7	11.7
SP	9	0	8	7.3
KMPP	5	0	5	2.7
RRP	2	0	2	0.9
CPI	1	0	1	0.5
IND	(25) 11	0	21	22.5
	(63) 11	11	44	
Part:	40.2			

1957				
Party	Cont	Won	LD	Pct.
CONG	10	8	0	47.3
JS	8	1	5	15.5
PSP	8	0	5	11.8
CPI	3	0	2	2.8
RRP	1	0	1	0.9
IND	(13) 9	1	9	21.7
	(43) 10	10	22	
Part:	48.0			

1962				
Party	Cont	Won	LD	Pct.
CONG	10	6	0	45.1
JS	8	3	0	30.0
PSP	3	1	2	5.9
CPI	2	0	0	5.6
SP	6	0	6	2.2
RPI	1	0	1	0.5
RRP	2	0	2	0.3
IND	(10) 7	0	8	10.4
	(42) 10	10	19	
Part:	55.8			

1967				
Party	Cont	Won	LD	Pct.
CONG	10	8	0	47.3
JS	10	1	1	32.4
CPI	5	0	5	4.1
PSP	5	0	5	2.2
SSP	4	0	4	2.1
CPM	2	0	2	1.6
Swat	3	0	3	1.3
RPI	3	0	3	0.7
IND	(14) 6	1	12	8.3
	(56) 10	10	35	
Part:	53.7			

1969				
Party	Cont	Won	LD	Pct.
CONG	10	4	0	40.5
JS	10	5	2	30.0
BKD	10	1	4	20.9
CPI	4	0	4	1.4
SSP	6	0	6	1.1
SC	1	0	1	0.6
CPM	1	0	1	0.5
MP	2	0	2	0.2
PSP	1	0	1	0.1
IND	(15) 8	0	15	4.7
	(60) 10	10	36	
Part:	55.1			

MIRZAPUR DISTRICT

Population: 1,249,653
Urban: 11.5 Rural: 88.5
Hindu: 94.4 Muslim: 5.3 Sikh: 0.1 Christian: 0.1

1952

Party		Cont	Won	LD	Pct.
CONG		7	7	0	47.0
SP		6	0	5	8.5
JS		3	0	2	5.7
RRP		2	0	1	2.6
RSP		1	0	1	0.3
CPI		1	0	1	0.2
IND	(23)	7	0	21	35.7
	(43)	7	7	31	

Part: 35.2

1957

Party		Cont	Won	LD	Pct.
CONG		7	5	0	46.8
JS		5	2	1	27.7
PSP		2	0	0	15.9
IND	(3)	3	0	0	9.6
	(17)	7	7	1	

Part: 42.7

1962

Party		Cont	Won	LD	Pct.
CONG		7	6	0	45.5
JS		7	1	1	31.8
SP		5	0	5	9.4
PSP		2	0	2	1.6
CPI		2	0	2	0.9
Swat		1	0	1	0.5
RRP		1	0	1	0.2
IND	(9)	6	0	8	10.1
	(34)	7	7	20	

Part: 46.1

1967

Party		Cont	Won	LD	Pct.
JS		7	2	0	39.6
CONG		7	4	0	36.3
SSP		7	1	4	18.5
Swat		1	0	1	0.9
PSP		2	0	2	0.5
RPI		1	0	1	0.3
CPI		1	0	1	0.1
IND	(8)	4	0	8	3.8
	(34)	7	7	17	

Part: 49.3

1969

Party		Cont	Won	LD	Pct.
CONG		7	2	0	32.0
JS		7	3	0	29.2
BKD		7	1	4	17.5
SSP		6	1	5	13.3
RPI		4	0	4	2.8
PSP		5	0	5	2.2
SC		1	0	1	0.1
IND	(6)	4	0	6	2.9
	(43)	7	7	23	

Part: 54.1

ALLAHABAD DIVISION

Population: 8,369,942
Urban: 20.5 Rural: 79.5
Hindu: 88.4 Muslim: 10.9 Sikh: 0.4 Christian: 0.2 Jain: 0.1

1952

Party	Cont	Won	LD	Pct.
CONG	45	44	0	50.2
SP	37	1	21	13.9
KMPP	36	0	30	8.7
SCF	6	0	3	2.7
JS	13	0	10	2.4
RRP	13	0	12	1.5
CPI	7	0	5	1.5
HMS	5	0	5	0.9
UPPP	2	0	1	0.7
RSP	2	0	2	0.2
UPRSP	1	0	1	#
IND (122)	41	0	107	17.3
(289)	45	45	197	

Part: 37.6

1957

Party	Cont	Won	LD	Pct.
CONG	47	35	0	43.8
PSP	43	6	15	23.0
JS	30	1	26	7.7
CPI	5	0	4	1.3
RRP	5	0	4	0.7
SP	@	5	@	@
IND (75)	36	0	46	23.5
(205)	47	47	95	

Part: 43.6

1962

Party	Cont	Won	LD	Pct.
CONG	47	24	1	35.4
PSP	42	14	18	20.9
JS	42	3	32	11.2
SP	35	1	23	9.6
RPI	32	0	31	5.3
CPI	11	1	9	3.0
Swat	18	0	17	2.5
RRP	3	0	3	0.1
HMS	3	0	3	0.1
IND (92)	38	4	80	11.9
(325)	47	47	217	

Part: 48.5

1967

Party	Cont	Won	LD	Pct.
CONG	48	23	2	32.1
SSP	44	14	17	20.4
JS	48	6	25	17.6
PSP	27	1	23	4.1
RPI	15	1	13	3.4
Swat	19	0	19	2.2
CPI	7	0	5	1.4
CPM	4	0	4	0.2
IND (165)	41	3	151	18.6
(377)	48	48	259	

Part: 49.4

1969

Party	Cont	Won	LD	Pct.
CONG	48	26	1	31.8
BKD	47	9	18	21.2
JS	46	3	22	15.5
SSP	40	7	20	14.3
RPI	27	0	24	4.2
CPI	7	0	6	1.3
RPI-A	8	0	7	1.1
PSP	12	0	12	0.9
MP	17	0	17	0.8

1969 (continued)

Party	Cont	Won	LD	Pct.
Swat	2	0	2	0.3
PBI	4	0	4	0.1
SC	1	0	1	0.1
HMS	1	0	1	0.1
CPM	1	0	1	#
IND (83)	32	3	77	8.3
(344)	48	48	213	

Part: 51.3

ALLAHABAD DISTRICT

Population: 2,438,376
Urban: 18.2 Rural: 81.8
Hindu: 87.7 Muslim: 11.8 Christian: 0.3 Sikh: 0.2

1952 Party	Cont	Won	LD	Pct.
CONG	14	14	0	54.6
KMPP	12	0	8	15.0
SP	9	0	8	4.5
RRP	6	0	5	3.5
CPI	1	0	0	1.6
JS	3	0	3	0.5
IND	(41) 14	0	39	20.3
	(86) 14	14	63	

Part: 38.7

1957 Party	Cont	Won	LD	Pct.
CONG	14	13	0	58.0
PSP	13	1	4	27.7
JS	9	0	8	6.8
IND	(7) 6	0	3	7.5
	(43) 14	14	15	

Part: 42.7

1962 Party	Cont	Won	LD	Pct.
CONG	14	6	0	42.3
PSP	13	6	5	28.9
JS	12	1	10	8.4
SP	6	0	4	5.8
RPI	5	0	5	2.2
CPI	1	0	1	0.3
IND	(23) 11	1	20	12.1
	(74) 14	14	45	

Part: 45.6

1967 Party	Cont	Won	LD	Pct.
CONG	14	8	0	36.1
SSP	14	3	4	24.9
JS	14	1	9	12.1
PSP	8	0	7	2.5
Swat	2	0	2	0.6
CPI	1	0	1	0.1
IND	(42) 12	2	36	23.7
	(95) 14	14	59	

Part: 43.6

1969 Party	Cont	Won	LD	Pct.
CONG	14	5	1	26.2
SSP	13	5	4	21.3
BKD	14	1	9	16.3
JS	14	2	8	14.4
RPI	7	0	7	3.6
RPI-A	3	0	2	3.4
PSP	3	0	3	0.5
MP	2	0	2	0.4
SC	1	0	1	0.3
HMS	1	0	1	0.3
CPI	1	0	1	0.1
IND	(28) 11	1	25	13.2
	(101) 14	14	64	

Part: 46.6

FATEHPUR DISTRICT

Population: 1,072,940
Urban: 4.0 Rural: 96.0
Hindu: 89.8 Muslim: 10.2 Christian: #

Party	Cont	Won	LD	Pct.
1952				
CONG	5	5	0	39.0
KMPP	5	0	3	14.9
SP	5	0	3	8.9
JS	2	0	0	3.8
CPI	1	0	1	1.7
SCF	1	0	1	1.0
IND	(15) 5	0	11	30.7
	(34) 5	5	19	
Part: 28.0				

Party	Cont	Won	LD	Pct.
1957				
CONG	6	6	0	44.5
PSP	6	0	1	19.7
JS	5	0	5	8.2
RRP	2	0	1	4.0
CPI	1	0	1	1.8
IND	(6) 5	0	2	21.8
	(26) 6	6	10	
Part: 33.5				

Party	Cont	Won	LD	Pct.
1962				
CONG	6	2	0	32.4
JS	5	1	4	13.4
RPI	4	0	3	7.7
PSP	2	0	2	2.5
SP	3	0	3	2.4
CPI	1	0	1	1.5
IND	(14) 5	3	7	40.1
	(35) 6	6	20	
Part: 39.2				

Party	Cont	Won	LD	Pct.
1967				
CONG	6	5	0	32.2
JS	6	0	4	14.4
RPI	2	1	1	10.3
SSP	5	0	5	7.1
PSP	1	0	1	0.7
CPI	1	0	1	0.4
IND	(27) 5	0	23	34.9
	(48) 6	6	35	
Part: 45.6				

Party	Cont	Won	LD	Pct.
1969				
CONG	6	3	0	34.7
BKD	6	2	1	33.7
JS	6	1	3	14.6
SSP	6	0	5	5.7
PSP	2	0	2	0.7
MP	2	0	2	0.4
IND	(10) 5	0	9	10.2
	(38) 6	6	22	
Part: 42.6				

KANPUR DISTRICT

Population: 2,381,353
Urban: 41.0 Rural: 59.0
Hindu: 86.5 Muslim: 12.0 Sikh: 1.0 Christian: 0.3 Jain: 0.1

	1952			
Party	Cont	Won	LD	Pct.
CONG	13	13	0	52.6
SP	11	0	6	16.5
SCF	4	0	2	7.2
KMPP	11	0	11	3.2
JS	4	0	4	3.2
UPPP	1	0	0	2.4
CPI	3	0	2	1.8
RRP	5	0	5	0.6
HMS	1	0	1	0.1
UPRSP	1	0	1	0.1
IND (44)	10	0	38	12.3
(98)	13	13	70	
Part: 38.6				

	1957			
Party	Cont	Won	LD	Pct.
CONG	13	10	0	39.3
PSP	10	0	5	13.3
JS	4	0	4	2.1
CPI	1	0	0	1.8
SP	@	3	@	@
IND (34)	13	0	22	43.5
(62)	13	13	31	
Part: 44.3				

	1962			
Party	Cont	Won	LD	Pct.
CONG	13	9	0	35.8
PSP	13	2	6	16.0
SP	13	1	6	14.7
JS	12	0	11	8.6
CPI	4	1	2	6.8
Swat	7	0	6	4.5
RPI	10	0	10	4.0
HMS	1	0	1	#
IND (26)	11	0	24	9.6
(99)	13	13	66	
Part: 50.8				

	1967			
Party	Cont	Won	LD	Pct.
CONG	14	7	0	31.7
SSP	11	4	5	17.0
JS	14	1	9	15.7
PSP	12	1	9	9.6
CPI	3	0	2	2.4
RPI	4	0	4	1.5
Swat	7	0	7	1.4
CPM	3	0	3	0.6
IND (72)	13	1	69	20.1
(140)	14	14	108	
Part: 52.3				

	1969			
Party	Cont	Won	LD	Pct.
CONG	14	7	0	33.8
BKD	13	3	4	20.5
JS	14	0	8	13.6
SSP	9	2	4	13.6
RPI	11	0	10	4.7
CPI	2	0	1	2.2
PSP	5	0	5	2.1
RPI-A	2	0	2	0.5
MP	6	0	6	0.3
PBI	1	0	1	#
IND (29)	10	2	27	8.7
(106)	14	14	68	
Part: 54.2				

ETAWAH DISTRICT

Population: 1,182,202
Urban: 9.1 Rural: 90.9
Hindu: 93.7 Muslim: 5.9 Jain: 0.2 Sikh: 0.1 Christian: #

1952				
Party	Cont	Won	LD	Pct.
CONG	6	5	0	48.0
SP	6	1	3	24.0
KMPP	5	0	5	7.9
HMS	4	0	4	4.9
CPI	2	0	2	2.4
RRP	1	0	1	0.3
IND	(6) 5	0	5	12.5
	(30) 6	6	20	
Part: 38.2				

1957				
Party	Cont	Won	LD	Pct.
CONG	7	3	0	29.6
PSP	7	1	4	17.7
JS	6	1	5	10.1
CPI	2	0	2	3.5
RRP	1	0	1	0.3
SP	@	2	@	@
IND	(15) 7	0	6	38.8
	(38) 7	7	18	
Part: 44.1				

1962				
Party	Cont	Won	LD	Pct.
CONG	7	5	1	29.8
PSP	7	2	3	20.9
SP	7	0	4	17.6
JS	7	0	5	12.4
RPI	6	0	6	6.7
Swat	5	0	5	4.1
CPI	2	0	2	1.0
HMS	1	0	1	0.2
IND	(23) 6	0	23	7.3
	(65) 7	7	50	
Part: 52.0				

1967				
Party	Cont	Won	LD	Pct.
SSP	7	6	0	32.7
CONG	7	0	2	22.8
JS	7	1	3	19.5
RPI	6	0	5	7.5
Swat	5	0	5	7.3
PSP	3	0	3	2.0
CPI	1	0	1	1.3
CPM	1	0	1	0.1
IND	(9) 5	0	8	6.8
	(46) 7	7	28	
Part: 55.6				

1969				
Party	Cont	Won	LD	Pct.
CONG	7	5	0	29.7
BKD	7	2	0	23.4
JS	6	0	2	16.5
SSP	6	0	4	14.1
RPI	5	0	4	7.4
Swat	2	0	2	2.2
CPI	2	0	2	2.0
MP	3	0	3	1.2
IND	(4) 3	0	4	3.5
	(42) 7	7	21	
Part: 54.2				

FARRUKHABAD DISTRICT

Population: 1,295,071
Urban: 11.0 Rural: 89.0
Hindu: 87.3 Muslim: 12.4 Christian: 0.1 Sikh: 0.1

1952

Party	Cont	Won	LD	Pct.
CONG	7	7	0	46.0
SP	6	0	1	20.2
JS	4	0	3	6.4
SCF	1	0	0	4.6
KMPP	3	0	3	2.8
RRP	1	0	1	1.2
RSP	2	0	2	1.2
UPPP	1	0	1	0.6
IND (16)	7	0	14	17.0
(41)	7	7	25	

Part: 40.7

1957

Party	Cont	Won	LD	Pct.
CONG	7	3	0	37.5
PSP	7	4	1	35.7
JS	6	0	4	14.9
RRP	2	0	2	1.0
CPI	1	0	1	0.7
IND (13)	5	0	13	10.2
(36)	7	7	21	

Part: 54.0

1962

Party	Cont	Won	LD	Pct.
CONG	7	2	0	30.7
PSP	7	4	2	28.1
JS	6	1	2	17.4
RPI	7	0	7	9.4
SP	6	0	6	4.1
CPI	3	0	3	3.2
Swat	6	0	6	2.8
RRP	3	0	3	0.8
HMS	1	0	1	0.1
IND (6)	5	0	6	3.4
(52)	7	7	36	

Part: 53.7

1967

Party	Cont	Won	LD	Pct.
CONG	7	3	0	35.6
JS	7	3	0	29.8
SSP	7	1	3	18.1
RPI	3	0	3	2.9
Swat	5	0	5	2.8
CPI	1	0	0	2.5
PSP	3	0	3	0.9
IND (15)	6	0	15	7.4
(48)	7	7	29	

Part: 52.3

1969

Party	Cont	Won	LD	Pct.
CONG	7	6	0	36.5
JS	6	0	1	19.9
BKD	7	1	4	19.8
SSP	6	0	3	10.9
RPI	4	0	3	4.0
MP	4	0	4	2.1
CPI	2	0	2	2.1
PBI	3	0	3	0.5
RPI-A	3	0	3	0.4
PSP	2	0	2	0.4
CPM	1	0	1	0.1
IND (12)	3	0	12	3.3
(57)	7	7	38	

Part: 59.1

JHANSI DIVISION

Population: 3,498,827
Urban: 13.5 Rural: 86.5
Hindu: 93.6 Muslim: 5.8 Jain: 0.4 Christian: 0.1

1952

Party	Cont	Won	LD	Pct.
CONG	20	17	0	47.4
SP	9	0	3	9.3
UPPP	7	1	5	8.9
KMPP	11	0	11	4.9
SCF	3	0	0	4.6
RRP	5	0	2	2.6
JS	3	0	2	1.3
CPI	1	0	1	0.6
IND (45)	19	2	40	20.4
(104)	20	20	64	

Part: 33.5

1957

Party	Cont	Won	LD	Pct.
CONG	20	16	0	46.4
PSP	11	2	1	18.4
JS	5	0	1	4.1
RRP	4	0	2	2.8
CPI	1	0	0	0.5
IND (24)	16	2	11	27.8
(65)	20	20	15	

Part: 42.3

1962

Party	Cont	Won	LD	Pct.
CONG	20	15	2	41.1
PSP	16	1	4	21.7
JS	19	1	17	9.1
CPI	9	0	5	6.1
Swat	6	1	5	4.2
SP	10	0	10	2.4
RRP	10	0	9	1.8
HMS	3	0	3	0.6
IND (27)	14	2	23	13.0
(120)	20	20	78	

Part: 45.1

1967

Party	Cont	Won	LD	Pct.
CONG	20	8	1	34.8
JS	19	10	2	32.3
SSP	7	0	4	5.1
CPI	7	1	5	4.7
PSP	7	0	6	2.5
RPI	6	0	6	2.2
CPM	4	0	4	0.5
IND (54)	17	1	51	17.9
(124)	20	20	79	

Part: 52.0

1969

Party	Cont	Won	LD	Pct.
CONG	20	14	0	38.1
JS	17	3	2	21.8
BKD	18	1	10	15.0
CPI	12	1	10	8.7
RPI	8	0	7	2.8
SSP	10	0	10	2.5
PSP	3	0	2	1.8
MP	4	0	4	0.4
PBI	2	0	2	0.1
HMS	1	0	1	0.1
IND (32)	15	1	31	8.7
(127)	20	20	79	

Part: 53.9

BANDA DISTRICT

Population: 953,731
Urban: 6.7 Rural: 93.3
Hindu: 94.7 Muslim: 5.2 Christian: #

1952				
Party	Cont	Won	LD	Pct.
CONG	5	5	0	44.0
RRP	4	0	1	15.6
SCF	1	0	0	4.8
SP	1	0	0	4.7
JS	1	0	0	4.0
KMPP	1	0	1	2.5
IND	(12) 5	0	11	24.4
	(25) 5	5	13	

Part: 20.0

1957				
Party	Cont	Won	LD	Pct.
CONG	5	5	0	47.1
RRP	3	0	1	15.5
PSP	3	0	1	13.5
JS	1	0	0	3.2
CPI	1	0	0	2.9
IND	(5) 4	0	3	17.8
	(18) 5	5	5	

Part: 28.3

1962				
Party	Cont	Won	LD	Pct.
CONG	5	3	1	26.6
CPI	5	0	3	16.1
PSP	5	0	3	14.5
JS	4	1	3	14.0
RRP	3	0	2	4.9
SP	1	0	1	0.4
IND	(8) 5	1	6	23.5
	(31) 5	5	19	

Part: 29.3

1967				
Party	Cont	Won	LD	Pct.
JS	5	3	0	29.1
CONG	5	1	1	26.4
CPI	3	1	1	15.2
PSP	4	0	3	6.9
RPI	3	0	3	6.0
SSP	1	0	0	5.0
CPM	4	0	4	2.2
IND	(14) 4	0	14	9.2
	(39) 5	5	26	

Part: 44.0

1969				
Party	Cont	Won	LD	Pct.
CONG	5	4	0	36.9
CPI	5	1	3	23.5
JS	4	0	1	15.5
BKD	4	0	3	7.4
PSP	2	0	1	6.9
RPI	3	0	3	3.6
SSP	2	0	2	3.5
MP	1	0	1	0.3
IND	(6) 3	0	6	2.4
	(32) 5	5	20	

Part: 47.4

HAMIRPUR DISTRICT

Population: 794,449
Urban: 8.4 Rural: 91.6
Hindu: 93.1 Muslim: 6.7 Christian: 0.1

		1952		
Party	Cont	Won	LD	Pct.
CONG	5	3	0	45.6
SP	4	0	0	22.1
SCF	1	0	0	6.6
RRP	1	0	1	0.7
KMPP	1	0	1	0.5
UPPP	1	0	1	0.3
IND	(14) 4	2	12	24.2
	(27) 5	5	15	
Part:	36.1			

		1957		
Party	Cont	Won	LD	Pct.
CONG	5	5	0	45.8
PSP	5	0	0	35.5
JS	1	0	0	2.8
RRP	1	0	1	1.1
IND	(4) 3	0	3	14.8
	(16) 5	5	4	
Part:	47.1			

		1962		
Party	Cont	Won	LD	Pct.
CONG	5	4	0	48.4
PSP	5	1	0	36.2
JS	5	0	5	5.4
SP	2	0	2	2.7
RRP	3	0	3	1.7
IND	(3) 2	0	2	5.6
	(23) 5	5	12	
Part:	50.8			

		1967		
Party	Cont	Won	LD	Pct.
JS	4	4	0	41.5
CONG	5	0	0	32.3
SSP	2	0	2	2.9
PSP	1	0	1	2.0
IND	(6) 3	1	5	21.3
	(18) 5	5	8	
Part:	52.6			

		1969		
Party	Cont	Won	LD	Pct.
CONG	5	4	0	42.0
JS	5	1	1	21.6
BKD	4	0	2	16.2
CPI	4	0	4	7.6
SSP	3	0	3	1.3
RPI	1	0	1	0.9
PBI	2	0	2	0.3
IND	(11) 4	0	11	10.1
	(35) 5	5	24	
Part:	53.6			

JHANSI DISTRICT

Population: 1,087,479
Urban: 23.8 Rural: 76.2
Hindu: 93.6 Muslim: 4.4 Jain: 1.1 Sikh: 0.5 Christian: 0.4

1952

Party	Cont	Won	LD	Pct.
CONG	6	6	0	59.0
UPPP	4	0	4	10.8
KMPP	5	0	5	7.6
JS	2	0	2	2.1
CPI	1	0	1	2.0
SP	2	0	2	1.1
IND	(13) 6	0	12	17.4
	(33) 6	6	26	

Part: 37.5

1957

Party	Cont	Won	LD	Pct.
CONG	6	5	0	55.7
JS	1	0	0	4.1
IND	(10) 6	1	3	40.2
	(17) 6	6	3	

Part: 40.9

1962

Party	Cont	Won	LD	Pct.
CONG	6	5	0	43.0
JS	6	0	5	12.1
PSP	2	0	0	10.0
CPI	2	0	0	9.0
Swat	3	0	3	4.8
SP	3	0	3	2.7
HMS	3	0	3	1.9
RRP	1	0	1	0.7
IND	(8) 4	1	7	15.8
	(34) 6	6	22	

Part: 46.4

1967

Party	Cont	Won	LD	Pct.
CONG	6	4	0	36.6
JS	6	2	2	26.4
CPI	4	0	4	4.9
SSP	1	0	1	2.2
PSP	2	0	2	1.8
RPI	2	0	2	1.5
IND	(25) 6	0	23	26.6
	(46) 6	6	34	

Part: 50.5

1969

Party	Cont	Won	LD	Pct.
CONG	6	3	0	39.6
JS	6	2	0	31.0
BKD	6	1	3	17.7
CPI	2	0	2	4.4
SSP	3	0	3	2.1
RPI	1	0	1	0.7
MP	2	0	2	0.5
HMS	1	0	1	0.2
IND	(8) 5	0	8	3.8
	(35) 6	6	20	

Part: 55.1

JALAUN DISTRICT

Population: 663,168
Urban: 12.8 Rural: 87.2
Hindu: 92.3 Muslim: 7.6 Christian: #

1952

Party	Cont	Won	LD	Pct.
CONG	4	3	0	36.7
UPPP	2	1	0	20.1
SP	2	0	1	10.0
SCF	1	0	0	8.3
KMPP	4	0	4	7.1
IND	(6) 4	0	5	17.8
	(19) 4	4	10	
Part:	41.6			

1957

Party	Cont	Won	LD	Pct.
CONG	4	1	0	35.2
PSP	3	2	0	27.1
JS	2	0	1	6.2
IND	(5) 3	1	2	31.5
	(14) 4	4	3	
Part:	56.3			

1962

Party	Cont	Won	LD	Pct.
CONG	4	3	1	40.0
PSP	4	0	1	25.5
Swat	3	1	2	11.0
JS	4	0	4	6.0
SP	4	0	4	3.0
CPI	2	0	2	2.5
RRP	3	0	3	1.4
IND	(8) 3	0	8	10.6
	(32) 4	4	25	
Part:	55.8			

1967

Party	Cont	Won	LD	Pct.
CONG	4	3	0	42.4
JS	4	1	0	33.2
SSP	3	0	1	10.8
RPI	1	0	1	2.0
IND	(9) 4	0	9	11.6
	(21) 4	4	11	
Part:	63.9			

1969

Party	Cont	Won	LD	Pct.
CONG	4	3	0	33.1
BKD	4	0	2	17.9
JS	2	0	0	15.8
RPI	3	0	2	7.1
SSP	2	0	2	3.4
PSP	1	0	1	1.0
MP	1	0	1	0.6
CPI	1	0	1	0.4
IND	(7) 3	1	6	20.7
	(25) 4	4	15	
Part:	61.4			

AGRA DIVISION

Population: 7,179,264
Urban: 18.8 Rural: 81.2
Hindu: 90.1 Muslim: 8.9 Jain: 0.4 Sikh: 0.3 Christian: 0.2

1952

Party	Cont	Won	LD	Pct.
CONG	41	38	1	44.2
SP	33	0	24	11.8
JS	31	0	22	8.6
KMPP	26	1	23	5.6
SCF	6	0	2	4.0
RSP	5	0	4	1.0
CPI	5	0	5	0.8
RRP	3	0	3	0.5
UPPP	1	0	1	0.3
IND (115)	38	2	95	23.2
(266)	41	41	180	

Part: 45.6

1957

Party	Cont	Won	LD	Pct.
CONG	41	26	0	38.6
PSP	24	5	14	11.3
JS	23	1	12	9.2
CPI	6	0	4	2.2
RRP	2	0	2	0.1
SP	@	2	@	@
IND (82)	41	7	44	38.6
(178)	41	41	76	

Part: 51.1

1962

Party	Cont	Won	LD	Pct.
CONG	40	16	5	25.8
RPI	34	5	16	15.2
JS	38	4	19	14.0
Swat	29	4	21	8.7
SP	26	5	20	7.1
PSP	24	1	17	6.2
CPI	10	0	8	2.7
HMS	7	1	5	2.1
RRP	5	0	5	0.3
IND (138)	38	5	129	17.9
(351)	41	41	245	

Part: 53.3

1967

Party	Cont	Won	LD	Pct.
CONG	41	16	1	29.5
JS	39	10	14	18.8
RPI	32	2	23	9.4
Swat	29	3	20	7.7
SSP	26	3	20	6.0
CPI	4	1	3	1.6
PSP	6	1	5	1.5
CPM	4	0	4	0.8
IND (198)	39	5	183	24.7
(379)	41	41	273	

Part: 54.4

1969

Party	Cont	Won	LD	Pct.
CONG	41	13	2	30.7
BKD	40	17	12	25.9
JS	40	5	23	15.6
RPI	32	0	23	8.4
SSP	21	2	16	4.8
Swat	15	2	12	3.0
PSP	4	0	3	1.2
CPI	4	0	3	0.8
PBI	13	0	13	0.5

1969 (continued)

Party	Cont	Won	LD	Pct.
RPI-A	9	0	9	0.5
CPM	1	0	0	0.5
KMP	1	0	1	0.3
MP	8	0	8	0.2
BS	6	0	6	0.1
HMS	1	0	1	0.1
IND (104)	35	2	101	7.4
(340)	41	41	233	

Part: 56.9

MAINPURI DISTRICT

Population: 1,180,894
Urban: 7.4 Rural: 92.6
Hindu: 94.7 Muslim: 4.7 Jain: 0.4 Christian: 0.1

1952

Party	Cont	Won	LD	Pct.
CONG	7	5	1	33.6
SP	6	0	4	11.4
JS	5	0	4	7.9
RSP	4	0	3	6.7
KMPP	2	1	1	3.9
UPPP	1	0	1	2.2
IND	(21) 7	1	14	34.3
	(46) 7	7	28	
Part:	42.9			

1957

Party	Cont	Won	LD	Pct.
CONG	7	2	0	28.2
PSP	6	3	2	25.1
JS	3	1	1	6.4
CPI	2	0	2	2.0
IND	(20) 7	1	18	38.3
	(38) 7	7	23	
Part:	51.4			

1962

Party	Cont	Won	LD	Pct.
CONG	7	4	2	23.7
Swat	7	2	4	12.5
PSP	7	0	6	10.9
RPI	6	0	5	10.2
JS	7	0	6	8.1
CPI	5	0	4	5.9
SP	5	0	5	2.5
IND	(35) 7	1	32	26.2
	(79) 7	7	64	
Part:	57.0			

1967

Party	Cont	Won	LD	Pct.
CONG	7	2	1	28.4
Swat	6	2	2	18.1
JS	7	1	4	13.6
RPI	6	0	6	7.3
SSP	5	1	4	5.9
CPI	1	1	0	5.3
CPM	4	0	4	4.6
IND	(23) 5	0	21	16.8
	(59) 7	7	42	
Part:	55.2			

1969

Party	Cont	Won	LD	Pct.
CONG	7	2	2	27.5
BKD	7	3	3	26.5
JS	7	1	3	11.5
Swat	3	1	1	9.7
SSP	3	0	2	4.5
CPI	1	0	0	3.7
CPM	1	0	0	2.8
RPI	3	0	3	2.5
PBI	3	0	3	1.6
IND	(18) 6	0	17	9.7
	(53) 7	7	34	
Part:	56.2			

ETAH DISTRICT

Population: 1,299,674
Urban: 9.6 Rural: 90.4
Hindu: 88.7 Muslim: 10.4 Christian: 0.4 Jain: 0.3 Sikh: 0.2

1952

Party	Cont	Won	LD	Pct.
CONG	8	7	0	36.9
JS	8	0	3	16.9
KMPP	7	0	5	10.7
SP	7	0	6	10.4
SCF	1	0	0	2.2
IND (23)	8	1	20	22.9
(54)	8	8	34	

Part: 46.2

1957

Party	Cont	Won	LD	Pct.
CONG	8	5	0	31.1
PSP	7	1	5	16.6
JS	7	0	4	15.1
IND (18)	8	2	8	37.2
(40)	8	8	17	

Part: 51.2

1962

Party	Cont	Won	LD	Pct.
CONG	8	1	0	21.2
JS	7	4	2	20.0
PSP	8	1	4	14.2
RPI	7	0	4	13.5
HMS	7	1	5	11.6
Swat	5	1	3	11.4
SP	6	0	6	2.9
IND (16)	7	0	16	5.2
(64)	8	8	40	

Part: 51.9

1967

Party	Cont	Won	LD	Pct.
CONG	8	5	0	33.0
JS	8	1	0	26.7
RPI	8	1	4	17.4
Swat	8	1	6	11.6
SSP	4	0	4	1.2
IND (27)	8	0	27	10.1
(63)	8	8	41	

Part: 54.6

1969

Party	Cont	Won	LD	Pct.
CONG	8	1	0	30.5
JS	8	3	2	29.4
BKD	7	4	2	20.4
RPI	8	0	6	11.7
PSP	2	0	2	2.1
Swat	3	0	3	1.3
RPI-A	3	0	3	1.2
PBI	5	0	5	1.1
SSP	1	0	1	0.4
HMS	1	0	1	0.3
MP	1	0	1	0.1
IND (11)	5	0	11	1.5
(58)	8	8	37	

Part: 59.3

AGRA DISTRICT

Population: 1,862,142
Urban: 35.9 Rural: 64.1
Hindu: 89.1 Muslim: 9.0 Jain: 1.0 Sikh: 0.5 Christian: 0.3
Buddhist: 0.1

1952

Party	Cont	Won	LD	Pct.
CONG	10	10	0	44.4
JS	7	0	5	8.3
SP	7	0	7	6.8
KMPP	7	0	7	5.5
SCF	2	0	1	3.9
CPI	2	0	2	2.1
RSP	1	0	1	0.1
IND	(40) 10	0	35	28.9
	(76) 10	10	58	

Part: 42.1

1957

Party	Cont	Won	LD	Pct.
CONG	10	5	0	39.0
JS	4	0	3	6.1
PSP	2	1	1	5.0
CPI	1	0	1	0.8
SP	@	1	@	@
IND	(19) 10	3	7	49.1
	(36) 10	10	12	

Part: 51.8

1962

Party	Cont	Won	LD	Pct.
CONG	10	4	0	29.6
RPI	10	3	0	25.6
JS	10	0	6	10.9
SP	6	2	4	8.5
Swat	6	0	5	5.3
PSP	4	0	3	3.8
CPI	1	0	1	0.3
IND	(39) 9	1	38	16.0
	(86) 10	10	57	

Part: 53.8

1967

Party	Cont	Won	LD	Pct.
CONG	10	3	0	27.4
JS	10	3	5	19.5
RPI	10	1	6	15.2
SSP	7	2	3	11.7
Swat	9	0	7	6.8
CPI	1	0	1	0.3
PSP	1	0	1	0.2
IND	(56) 10	1	54	18.9
	(104) 10	10	77	

Part: 54.1

1969

Party	Cont	Won	LD	Pct.
CONG	10	3	0	32.7
BKD	10	4	5	18.2
JS	9	0	5	14.6
RPI	9	0	5	10.5
SSP	5	1	3	9.4
Swat	5	1	4	3.5
RPI-A	5	0	5	1.0
MP	4	0	4	0.6
BS	6	0	6	0.4
CPI	2	0	2	0.4
PBI	1	0	1	0.1
IND	(23) 8	1	22	8.6
	(89) 10	10	62	

Part: 52.3

MATHURA DISTRICT

Population: 1,071,279
Urban: 16.8 Rural: 83.2
Hindu: 92.6 Muslim: 7.0 Sikh: 0.2 Jain: 0.2 Christian: #

1952

Party	Cont	Won	LD	Pct.
CONG	6	6	0	39.4
SP	6	0	6	9.8
JS	5	0	4	9.3
SCF	1	0	1	3.2
RRP	2	0	2	2.4
KMPP	3	0	3	2.2
CPI	1	0	1	0.4
IND	(17) 5	0	14	33.3
	(41) 6	6	31	

Part: 46.5

1957

Party	Cont	Won	LD	Pct.
CONG	6	5	0	45.7
PSP	5	0	2	15.5
JS	5	0	2	13.9
CPI	1	0	1	1.3
RRP	2	0	2	0.6
SP	@	1	@	@
IND	(8) 6	0	4	23.0
	(27) 6	6	11	

Part: 52.3

1962

Party	Cont	Won	LD	Pct.
CONG	6	4	0	34.3
JS	5	0	1	19.1
SP	6	2	4	15.2
RPI	6	0	6	9.5
Swat	5	0	5	6.5
CPI	1	0	1	2.5
PSP	2	0	2	0.5
RRP	1	0	1	0.2
IND	(15) 6	0	14	12.2
	(47) 6	6	34	

Part: 51.2

1967

Party	Cont	Won	LD	Pct.
CONG	6	3	0	29.5
JS	6	1	3	15.7
SSP	5	0	5	6.7
RPI	6	0	6	2.5
IND	(36) 6	2	31	45.6
	(59) 6	6	45	

Part: 57.5

1969

Party	Cont	Won	LD	Pct.
BKD	6	1	0	35.4
CONG	6	5	0	34.3
JS	6	0	5	11.7
SSP	6	0	5	7.3
RPI	5	0	5	5.2
Swat	2	0	2	0.4
PBI	4	0	4	0.3
MP	1	0	1	0.2
IND	(21) 6	0	21	5.2
	(57) 6	6	43	

Part: 59.1

ALIGARH DISTRICT

Population: 1,765,275
Urban: 16.2 Rural: 83.8
Hindu: 87.7 Muslim: 11.6 Sikh: 0.3 Jain: 0.2 Christian: 0.1
Buddhist: 0.1

1952					
Party	Cont	Won	LD	Pct.
CONG	10	10	0	56.3
SP	7	0	1	18.1
SCF	2	0	0	7.8
KMPP	7	0	7	5.0
JS	6	0	6	3.6
CPI	2	0	2	0.9
RRP	1	0	1	0.6
IND	(14) 8	0	12	7.7
	(49) 10	10	29	
Part:	49.6			

1957					
Party	Cont	Won	LD	Pct.
CONG	10	9	0	45.2
JS	4	0	2	7.4
CPI	2	0	0	5.6
PSP	4	0	4	3.2
IND	(17) 10	1	7	38.6
	(37) 10	10	13	
Part:	49.8			

1962					
Party	Cont	Won	LD	Pct.
CONG	9	3	3	21.9
JS	9	0	4	14.2
RPI	5	2	1	12.8
Swat	6	1	4	8.5
SP	3	1	1	7.1
CPI	3	0	2	4.7
PSP	3	0	2	2.9
RRP	4	0	4	1.3
IND	(33) 9	3	29	26.6
	(75) 10	10	50	
Part:	52.7			

1967					
Party	Cont	Won	LD	Pct.
CONG	10	3	0	29.6
JS	8	4	2	17.5
PSP	5	1	4	5.8
SSP	5	0	4	4.1
RPI	2	0	1	3.3
Swat	6	0	5	3.2
CPI	2	0	2	2.4
IND	(56) 10	2	50	34.1
	(94) 10	10	68	
Part:	52.1			

1969					
Party	Cont	Won	LD	Pct.
BKD	10	5	2	30.5
CONG	10	2	0	28.9
JS	10	1	8	11.0
RPI	7	0	4	9.8
SSP	6	1	5	3.0
PSP	2	0	1	2.9
Swat	2	0	2	1.3
KMP	1	0	1	1.2
CPI	1	0	1	0.3
MP	2	0	2	0.2
RPI-A	1	0	1	0.1
IND	(31) 10	1	30	10.8
	(83) 10	10	57	
Part:	58.5			

MEERUT DIVISION

Population: 7,939,770
Urban: 19.4 Rural: 80.6
Hindu: 75.6 Muslim: 22.6 Sikh: 0.8 Jain: 0.8 Christian: 0.2

1952

Party	Cont	Won	LD	Pct.
CONG	44	44	0	58.0
SP	30	0	19	9.7
JS	24	0	21	5.5
KMPP	24	0	21	4.6
SCF	2	0	1	1.1
RRP	4	0	4	0.4
CPI	3	0	3	0.4
RSP	3	0	3	0.2
HMS	3	0	3	0.2
IND (128)	42	0	110	19.9
(265)	44	44	185	

Part: 49.6

1957

Party	Cont	Won	LD	Pct.
CONG	45	35	0	49.5
JS	31	1	22	9.1
PSP	16	3	5	8.4
CPI	4	0	0	1.6
RRP	4	0	4	0.4
SP	@	2	@	@
IND (74)	40	4	43	31.0
(174)	45	45	74	

Part: 53.7

1962

Party	Cont	Won	LD	Pct.
CONG	45	35	0	41.4
PSP	26	2	10	10.8
JS	36	1	22	10.4
SP	23	0	19	6.2
CPI	10	1	5	5.3
RPI	14	0	10	4.3
Swat	15	0	11	3.0
HMS	5	0	5	0.3
RRP	1	0	1	#
IND (78)	34	6	61	18.3
(253)	45	45	144	

Part: 56.0

1967

Party	Cont	Won	LD	Pct.
CONG	45	20	3	31.5
JS	37	3	24	11.8
RPI	26	5	15	10.0
SSP	19	4	10	7.2
PSP	13	2	8	4.8
CPI	7	2	1	4.3
Swat	20	0	20	2.1
CPM	2	0	1	0.4
IND (142)	43	9	119	27.9
(311)	45	45	201	

Part: 59.1

1969

Party	Cont	Won	LD	Pct.
BKD	42	22	4	33.3
CONG	44	13	3	29.0
JS	37	4	24	10.2
RPI	26	1	20	6.9
SSP	27	2	22	4.4
KMP	11	1	7	3.2
CPI	10	0	9	2.0
PSP	7	0	6	1.4
Swat	13	0	13	0.6
PBI	15	0	15	0.3
RPI-A	1	0	1	#
MP	2	0	2	#
IND (108)	38	2	103	8.6
(343)	45	45	229	

Part: 62.3

BULANDSHAHR DISTRICT

Population: 1,737,397
Urban: 12.7 Rural: 87.3
Hindu: 83.3 Muslim: 16.3 Sikh: 0.3 Christian: #

1952

Party	Cont	Won	LD	Pct.
CONG	10	10	0	57.3
SP	9	0	2	18.5
JS	6	0	4	8.9
KMPP	6	0	5	4.7
SCF	1	0	0	4.2
RRP	1	0	1	0.2
IND	(9) 6	0	7	6.2
	(42) 10	10	19	

Part: 45.9

1957

Party	Cont	Won	LD	Pct.
CONG	10	5	0	41.2
PSP	6	2	0	23.0
JS	7	1	6	9.3
RRP	1	0	1	0.7
SP	@	2	@	@
IND	(18) 9	0	13	25.8
	(42) 10	10	20	

Part: 53.3

1962

Party	Cont	Won	LD	Pct.
CONG	10	8	0	39.0
PSP	10	1	1	26.9
RPI	9	0	5	15.4
JS	9	1	5	12.2
SP	4	0	4	2.5
CPI	1	0	1	1.3
Swat	2	0	2	0.4
IND	(10) 5	0	10	2.3
	(55) 10	10	28	

Part: 54.5

1967

Party	Cont	Won	LD	Pct.
CONG	10	3	0	27.0
PSP	9	2	4	19.4
RPI	10	2	6	16.2
JS	10	2	6	15.8
SSP	5	0	5	2.7
Swat	5	0	5	2.1
IND	(20) 9	1	18	16.8
	(69) 10	10	44	

Part: 55.7

1969

Party	Cont	Won	LD	Pct.
BKD	10	4	0	29.8
CONG	10	2	2	24.0
JS	9	1	4	14.5
RPI	7	1	6	8.5
PSP	5	0	4	5.9
SSP	6	0	5	3.1
KMP	1	1	0	2.6
CPI	3	0	3	1.1
Swat	4	0	4	0.9
RPI-A	1	0	1	0.1
IND	(21) 9	1	20	9.5
	(77) 10	10	49	

Part: 57.2

MEERUT DISTRICT

Population: 2,712,960
Urban: 20.6 Rural: 79.4
Hindu: 76.4 Muslim: 21.0 Jain: 1.6 Sikh: 0.8 Christian: 0.2

1952				
Party	Cont	Won	LD	Pct.
CONG	15	15	0	56.0
SP	10	0	7	10.4
KMPP	10	0	8	7.0
JS	9	0	8	4.7
RRP	1	0	1	0.9
CPI	2	0	2	0.7
IND	(41) 15	0	33	20.3
	(88) 15	15	59	
Part: 50.9				

1957				
Party	Cont	Won	LD	Pct.
CONG	15	14	0	58.0
JS	9	0	5	8.7
CPI	3	0	0	3.5
PSP	3	0	1	2.6
RRP	1	0	1	0.1
IND	(21) 14	1	13	27.1
	(52) 15	15	20	
Part: 55.7				

1962				
Party	Cont	Won	LD	Pct.
CONG	15	12	0	42.7
JS	10	0	7	8.6
SP	10	0	9	8.2
CPI	6	0	3	6.1
PSP	5	0	2	5.6
RPI	5	0	5	2.7
Swat	5	0	4	2.7
HMS	4	0	4	0.9
RRP	1	0	1	0.1
IND	(30) 14	3	24	22.4
	(91) 15	15	59	
Part: 55.9				

1967				
Party	Cont	Won	LD	Pct.
CONG	15	4	3	29.5
RPI	9	3	2	15.1
JS	12	1	8	11.9
SSP	3	2	0	7.7
CPI	3	1	1	5.3
Swat	3	0	3	1.4
CPM	1	0	1	0.2
IND	(63) 14	4	56	28.9
	(109) 15	15	73	
Part: 61.3				

1969				
Party	Cont	Won	LD	Pct.
BKD	15	8	3	35.9
CONG	15	4	0	29.4
RPI	12	0	7	10.9
JS	11	1	8	7.5
SSP	10	2	8	5.6
CPI	2	0	2	1.7
PBI	10	0	10	0.5
KMP	1	0	1	0.4
Swat	3	0	3	0.2
MP	2	0	2	0.1
IND	(41) 13	0	40	7.8
	(122) 15	15	84	
Part: 65.2				

MUZAFFARNAGAR DISTRICT

Population: 1,444,921
Urban: 13.2 Rural: 86.8
Hindu: 71.0 Muslim: 28.0 Jain: 0.7 Sikh: 0.3 Christian: #

		1952		
Party	Cont	Won	LD	Pct.
CONG	8	8	0	54.6
JS	4	0	4	5.6
SP	5	0	4	4.5
KMPP	2	0	2	1.3
IND	(31) 8	0	26	34.0
	(50) 8	8	36	
Part:	52.6			

		1957		
Party	Cont	Won	LD	Pct.
CONG	8	6	0	52.0
PSP	3	1	0	11.6
JS	6	0	5	9.8
CPI	1	0	0	2.3
IND	(6) 5	1	1	24.3
	(24) 8	8	6	
Part:	50.7			

		1962		
Party	Cont	Won	LD	Pct.
CONG	8	5	0	36.9
CPI	2	1	0	15.1
PSP	6	1	3	12.4
JS	6	0	4	8.2
SP	3	0	2	6.4
Swat	4	0	4	2.7
IND	(9) 5	1	6	18.3
	(38) 8	8	19	
Part:	58.7			

		1967		
Party	Cont	Won	LD	Pct.
CONG	8	5	0	31.3
CPI	4	1	0	13.8
SSP	4	1	2	9.5
JS	6	0	5	6.6
RPI	5	0	5	5.5
Swat	6	0	6	3.9
CPM	1	0	0	1.7
IND	(27) 8	1	23	27.7
	(61) 8	8	41	
Part:	58.0			

		1969		
Party	Cont	Won	LD	Pct.
BKD	8	8	0	48.6
CONG	7	0	0	24.3
KMP	5	0	4	6.4
JS	7	0	6	5.8
CPI	4	0	3	4.3
RPI	4	0	4	2.4
SSP	3	0	3	1.4
PBI	3	0	3	0.6
Swat	3	0	3	0.5
IND	(15) 7	0	14	5.7
	(59) 8	8	40	
Part:	64.8			

SAHARANPUR DISTRICT

Population: 1,615,478
Urban: 23.0 Rural: 77.0
Hindu: 67.6 Muslim: 31.1 Sikh: 0.8 Jain: 0.4 Christian: 0.1

1952

Party	Cont	Won	LD	Pct.
CONG	9	9	0	65.9
KMPP	6	0	6	3.7
SP	4	0	4	3.5
JS	4	0	4	3.0
RSP	2	0	2	1.0
HMS	2	0	2	0.7
SCF	1	0	1	0.5
RRP	2	0	2	0.4
CPI	1	0	1	0.4
IND	(35) 11	0	33	20.9
	(66) 9	9	55	

Part: 50.0

1957

Party	Cont	Won	LD	Pct.
CONG	10	9	0	43.7
JS	7	0	5	8.0
PSP	4	0	4	1.3
RRP	2	0	2	1.0
IND	(26) 10	1	15	46.0
	(49) 10	10	26	

Part: 53.3

1962

Party	Cont	Won	LD	Pct.
CONG	10	8	0	45.2
JS	9	0	5	12.8
SP	6	0	4	7.9
Swat	4	0	1	6.9
PSP	3	0	3	0.4
IND	(25) 8	2	18	26.8
	(57) 10	10	31	

Part: 55.8

1967

Party	Cont	Won	LD	Pct.
CONG	10	7	0	38.6
JS	7	0	4	10.2
SSP	6	1	3	10.1
Swat	6	0	6	2.1
RPI	2	0	2	1.5
PSP	4	0	4	1.2
IND	(29) 10	2	21	36.3
	(64) 10	10	40	

Part: 60.5

1969

Party	Cont	Won	LD	Pct.
CONG	10	6	1	36.0
BKD	9	2	1	24.4
JS	8	1	6	11.6
KMP	4	0	2	6.0
SSP	7	0	6	5.6
RPI	2	0	2	3.0
CPI	1	0	1	1.5
Swat	3	0	3	1.0
PSP	1	0	1	0.2
PBI	1	0	1	#
IND	(27) 8	1	26	10.7
	(73) 10	10	50	

Part: 63.2

DEHRA DUN DISTRICT

Population: 429,014
Urban: 46.1 Rural: 53.9
Hindu: 85.9 Muslim: 8.1 Sikh: 4.2 Christian: 1.1 Jain: 0.6

Party	Cont	Won	LD	Pct.
1952				
CONG	2	2	0	50.9
SP	2	0	2	7.2
JS	1	0	1	6.7
HMS	1	0	1	1.6
RSP	1	0	1	0.4
IND	(12) 2	0	11	33.2
	(19) 2	2	16	
Part: 45.2				

Party	Cont	Won	LD	Pct.
1957				
CONG	2	1	0	42.0
JS	2	0	1	16.2
IND	(3) 2	1	1	41.8
	(7) 2	2	2	
Part: 56.0				

Party	Cont	Won	LD	Pct.
1962				
CONG	2	2	0	40.3
PSP	2	0	1	16.9
JS	2	0	1	13.8
CPI	1	0	1	3.0
HMS	1	0	1	0.2
IND	(4) 2	0	3	25.8
	(12) 2	2	7	
Part: 54.1				

Party	Cont	Won	LD	Pct.
1967				
CONG	2	1	0	33.4
JS	2	0	1	23.5
PSP	1	0	0	11.3
IND	(3) 2	1	1	31.8
	(8) 2	2	2	
Part: 55.2				

Party	Cont	Won	LD	Pct.
1969				
CONG	2	1	0	36.6
JS	2	1	0	29.4
SSP	1	0	0	9.9
RPI	1	0	1	4.3
PSP	1	0	1	3.3
PBI	1	0	1	0.2
IND	(4) 1	0	3	16.3
	(12) 2	2	6	
Part: 51.0				

STATE SUMMARY

Population: 34,926,279
Urban: 24.5 Rural: 75.5
Hindu: 78.8 Muslim: 20.0 Christian: 0.6 Buddhist: 0.3
Sikh: 0.1 Other: 0.2

1952				
Party	Cont	Won	LD	Pct.
CONG	248	154	4	38.3
CPI	89	28	19	10.4
KMPP	130	15	82	8.6
JS	86	9	62	5.4
FB(M)	48	11	17	5.0
SP	65	0	53	2.8
HMS	33	4	20	2.3
LKS	10	8	0	1.8
FB(R)	32	2	24	1.4
RSP	16	0	10	0.7
RCPI	11	0	8	0.6
Bolsh	8	0	6	0.3
Janata	3	0	1	0.2
RRP	14	0	14	0.1
Jhkh	1	0	1	#
SUC	@	2	@	@
IND	(637)218	17	535	22.1
	(1431)250	250	856	

Part: 41.1

1957				
Party	Cont	Won	LD	Pct.
CONG	251	152*	0	46.1
CPI	104	46	3	18.3
PSP	66	21	6	9.3
FB(M)	26	8	4	4.1
HMS	37	0	25	2.2
JS	33	0	30	1.0
LSS	@	7	@	@
RSP	@	3	@	@
SUC	@	2	@	@
GL	@	1	@	@
IND	(418)196	12	327	19.0
	(935)252	252	395	

Part: 47.8
*Uncontested: CONG (1)

1962				
Party	Cont	Won	LD	Pct.
CONG	252	157*	1	47.3
CPI	145	50	9	25.0
PSP	87	5	52	5.0
FB	34	13	10	4.6
RSP	17	9	3	2.6
HMS	25	0	20	0.8
SUC	11	0	7	0.7
LSS	11	4	3	0.7
SBP	16	1	14	0.6
Swat	24	0	19	0.6
JS	25	0	24	0.5
GL	4	2	0	0.4
WP	8	0	7	0.3
SP	7	0	7	#
IND	(295)155	11	238	10.9
	(961)252	252	414	

Part: 53.4
*Uncontested: CONG (1)

1967				
Party	Cont	Won	LD	Pct.
CONG	280	127	1	41.1
CPM	134	43	17	18.1
BC	80	34	20	10.2
CPI	62	16	22	6.5
FB	42	13	15	4.4
SSP	26	7	11	2.1
PSP	26	7	13	1.9
JS	58	1	52	1.3
Swat	21	1	15	0.8
RPI	1	0	1	#
IND	(328)174	31	248	13.5
	(1058)280	280	415	

Part: 60.8

STATE SUMMARY (Continued)

Party	Cont	1969 Won	LD	Pct.
CONG	280	55	3	41.3
CPM	97	80	1	20.0
BC	49	33	0	8.2
CPI	36	30	0	7.0
FB	28	21	0	5.0
RSP	17	12	0	2.8
SSP	15	9	2	1.9
PML	39	3	30	1.6
SUC	7	7	0	1.5
PSP	24	5	17	1.3
LD	50	0	44	1.0
JS	50	0	46	0.9
INDF	94	1	92	0.8
LSS	6	4	0	0.7
GL	4	4	0	0.5
RCPI	2	2	0	0.4
WP	2	2	0	0.4
PBI	55	0	55	0.2
FB(M)	1	1	0	0.2
NPB	18	0	18	0.2
HMS	7	0	6	0.1
Jhkh	5	0	5	0.1
RPI	9	0	9	0.1
Swat	4	0	4	0.1
RCPI-T	4	0	4	0.1
IND (116)	94	11	97	3.6
(1019)	280	280	433	

Part: 64.8

COOCH BEHAR DISTRICT

Population: 1,019,806
Urban: 7.0 Rural: 93.0
Hindu: 76.0 Muslim: 23.8 Christian: 0.1

Party	Cont	Won	LD	Pct.
1952				
CONG	6	6	0	60.7
FB(M)	2	0	0	8.3
CPI	2	0	1	7.1
KMPP	2	0	2	2.7
SP	2	0	2	2.2
IND (11)	5	0	9	19.0
(25)	6	6	14	

Part: 36.4

Party	Cont	Won	LD	Pct.
1957				
CONG	7	7	0	53.5
FB(M)	4	0	0	22.7
CPI	2	0	0	9.3
HMS	1	0	1	0.3
IND (8)	7	0	7	14.2
(22)	7	7	8	

Part: 48.8

Party	Cont	Won	LD	Pct.
1962				
CONG	7	1	0	39.8
FB	5	5	0	38.5
CPI	2	1	0	16.8
IND (5)	4	0	4	4.9
(19)	7	7	4	

Part: 46.4

Party	Cont	Won	LD	Pct.
1967				
CONG	8	5	0	42.7
FB	6	2	0	33.9
CPM	4	1	1	14.5
Swat	7	0	6	7.9
CPI	1	0	1	0.7
IND (2)	1	0	2	0.3
(28)	8	8	10	

Part: 63.8

Party	Cont	Won	LD	Pct.
1969				
CONG	8	6	0	53.0
FB	6	2	0	34.3
CPM	2	0	0	11.0
PBI	3	0	3	0.5
LD	2	0	2	0.5
JS	2	0	2	0.2
IND (3)	3	0	3	0.5
(26)	8	8	10	

Part: 66.3

JALPAIGURI DISTRICT

Population: 1,359,292
Urban: 9.1 Rural: 90.9
Hindu: 85.4 Muslim: 9.5 Christian: 3.6 Buddhist: 1.3

Party		Cont	Won	LD	Pct.
CONG		10	10	0	56.2
KMPP		5	0	1	13.4
SP		5	0	2	11.5
CPI		2	0	0	5.1
RSP		1	0	0	3.1
FB(R)		2	0	2	1.8
IND	(6)	4	0	5	8.9
	(31)	10	10	10	

1952

Part: 30.4

Party		Cont	Won	LD	Pct.
CONG		9	7	0	49.2
PSP		5	1	0	19.1
CPI		2	1	0	11.4
IND	(14)	9	0	11	20.3
	(30)	9	9	11	

1957

Part: 46.8

Party		Cont	Won	LD	Pct.
CONG		9	7	0	44.7
CPI		6	0	2	17.2
PSP		8	0	5	14.7
RSP		2	2	0	8.9
IND	(16)	8	0	14	14.5
	(41)	9	9	21	

1962

Part: 49.2

Party		Cont	Won	LD	Pct.
CONG		11	6	0	41.1
SSP		3	2	0	10.2
PSP		3	1	0	8.2
CPM		3	0	0	8.0
BC		4	1	2	6.7
CPI		2	0	0	6.0
FB		1	0	1	0.7
JS		1	0	1	0.1
IND	(15)	8	1	10	19.0
	(43)	11	11	14	

1967

Part: 59.9

Party		Cont	Won	LD	Pct.
CONG		11	7	0	49.8
RSP		3	2	0	11.7
SSP		3	1	0	9.9
CPI		2	1	0	9.2
CPM		2	0	0	6.1
PSP		4	0	3	4.8
BC		1	0	0	1.7
INDF		6	0	6	1.7
LD		2	0	2	0.9
PBI		3	0	3	0.8
JS		2	0	2	0.4
IND	(8)	7	0	8	3.0
	(47)	11	11	24	

1969

Part: 59.9

DARJEELING DISTRICT

Population: 624,640
Urban: 23.2 Rural: 76.8
Hindu: 80.3 Buddhist: 13.1 Christian: 3.3 Muslim: 3.1

1952

Party	Cont	Won	LD	Pct.
CONG	5	1	1	29.2
CPI	4	1	1	22.6
KMPP	1	0	0	6.4
SP	2	0	2	3.0
IND	(6) 4	3	2	38.8
	(18) 5	5	6	

Part: 30.8

1957

Party	Cont	Won	LD	Pct.
CPI	4	2	0	28.7
CONG	4	1	0	26.4
JS	1	0	1	2.0
PSP	1	0	1	1.1
GL	@	1	@	@
IND	(17) 5	1	12	41.8
	(27) 5	5	14	

Part: 37.1

1962

Party	Cont	Won	LD	Pct.
GL	4	2	0	31.3
CONG	5	2	0	31.1
CPI	5	1	1	29.1
PSP	2	0	2	0.5
IND	(7) 4	0	6	8.0
	(23) 5	5	9	

Part: 41.0

1967

Party	Cont	Won	LD	Pct.
CONG	5	3	0	39.2
CPM	3	0	1	14.0
BC	1	0	0	5.0
JS	2	0	2	2.1
CPI	1	0	1	0.9
IND	(7) 5	2	2	38.8
	(19) 5	5	6	

Part: 53.0

1969

Party	Cont	Won	LD	Pct.
GL	4	4	0	43.5
CONG	5	1	0	43.5
CPM	1	0	0	6.8
JS	3	0	3	1.8
PBI	2	0	2	0.6
IND	(3) 2	0	3	3.8
	(18) 5	5	8	

Part: 50.6

WEST DINAJPUR

Population: 1,323,797
Urban: 7.5 Rural: 92.5
Hindu: 59.9 Muslim: 39.4 Christian: 0.6

	1952			
Party	Cont	Won	LD	Pct.
CONG	8	8	0	59.1
FB(R)	4	0	1	12.9
RCPI	2	0	0	6.0
CPI	2	0	1	5.2
RSP	1	0	0	3.9
KMPP	2	0	1	2.3
FB(M)	2	0	2	1.7
JS	1	0	0	1.4
SP	2	0	2	1.0
IND	(8) 5	0	8	6.5
	(32) 8	8	15	

Part: 39.5

	1957			
Party	Cont	Won	LD	Pct.
CONG	10	8*	0	44.0
PSP	4	0	0	12.5
CPI	2	1	0	6.5
RSP	@	1	@	@
IND	(19) 7	0	13	37.0
	(35) 10	10	13	

Part: 43.8
*Uncontested: CONG (1)

	1962			
Party	Cont	Won	LD	Pct.
CONG	10	6	0	42.7
CPI	6	2	0	23.5
PSP	8	1	4	11.8
RSP	2	1	0	10.2
Swat	7	0	5	6.4
FB	2	0	2	1.0
IND	(9) 5	0	9	4.4
	(44) 10	10	20	

Part: 45.5

	1967			
Party	Cont	Won	LD	Pct.
CONG	11	6	1	35.5
CPM	5	0	0	10.6
PSP	4	3	1	10.1
CPI	3	0	1	4.2
BC	3	0	2	3.3
FB	2	0	1	2.8
SSP	2	0	1	2.8
Swat	1	0	1	0.1
IND	(26) 11	2	20	30.6
	(57) 11	11	28	

Part: 55.3

	1969			
Party	Cont	Won	LD	Pct.
CONG	11	3	1	39.7
CPM	4	2	0	14.6
RSP	2	2	0	11.4
CPI	2	0	0	9.6
INDF	10	1	8	7.3
PSP	5	1	4	4.5
BC	1	1	0	4.3
FB	1	1	0	3.4
LD	2	0	2	1.1
JS	2	0	2	1.0
PBI	4	0	4	0.4
SSP	1	0	1	0.3
IND	(7) 3	0	6	2.4
	(52) 11	11	28	

Part: 59.7

MALDA DISTRICT

Population: 1,221,923
Urban: 4.2 Rural: 95.8
Hindu: 53.6 Muslim: 46.2 Christian: 0.2

1952

Party	Cont	Won	LD	Pct.
CONG	9	7	0	49.9
CPI	3	1	0	12.5
KMPP	4	0	3	8.1
RSP	1	0	0	3.5
HMS	1	0	0	3.2
IND	(14) 8	1	11	22.8
	(32) 9	9	14	

Part: 37.9

1957

Party	Cont	Won	LD	Pct.
CONG	9	6	0	45.4
CPI	4	0	0	16.0
PSP	1	0	0	2.7
JS	1	0	1	1.4
IND	(15) 6	3	8	34.5
	(30) 9	9	9	

Part: 42.2

1962

Party	Cont	Won	LD	Pct.
CONG	9	5	0	43.8
CPI	4	2	1	18.4
WP	1	0	0	6.2
Swat	2	0	0	4.8
JS	2	0	2	0.7
IND	(16) 6	2	12	26.1
	(34) 9	9	15	

Part: 50.8

1967

Party	Cont	Won	LD	Pct.
CONG	10	6	0	45.0
Swat	9	1	6	11.9
CPI	4	0	2	9.2
CPM	3	1	0	8.3
BC	4	0	4	3.7
JS	1	0	1	1.4
IND	(12) 7	2	8	20.5
	(43) 10	10	21	

Part: 62.5

1969

Party	Cont	Won	LD	Pct.
CONG	10	5	0	47.2
CPI	3	2	0	14.1
BC	2	0	0	6.2
WP	1	1	0	5.5
CPM	2	0	1	5.0
JS	5	0	5	3.7
INDF	4	0	4	2.9
Swat	3	0	3	1.9
IND	(3) 3	2	0	13.5
	(33) 10	10	13	

Part: 65.9

MURSHIDABAD DISTRICT

Population: 2,290,010
Urban: 8.5 Rural: 91.5
Muslim: 55.9 Hindu: 44.1 Christian: #

	1952			
Party	Cont	Won	LD	Pct.
CONG	16	14	0	41.9
KMPP	6	0	4	7.0
HMS	3	0	2	2.7
SP	2	0	1	2.7
RSP	1	0	0	1.7
CPI	1	0	1	0.5
JS	1	0	1	0.2
FB(R)	1	0	1	0.1
IND (53)	16	2	34	43.2
(84)	16	16	44	

Part: 46.4

	1957			
Party	Cont	Won	LD	Pct.
CONG	16	15	0	49.0
PSP	4	0	2	4.0
CPI	1	0	0	2.1
FB(M)	1	0	1	1.0
HMS	1	0	1	0.1
IND (38)	16	1	22	43.8
(61)	16	16	26	

Part: 53.8

	1962			
Party	Cont	Won	LD	Pct.
CONG	16	8	1	39.5
RSP	5	3	0	16.9
PSP	2	1	1	3.9
CPI	1	1	0	3.7
Swat	1	0	0	1.1
SUC	1	0	1	0.1
IND (40)	13	3	28	34.8
(66)	16	16	31	

Part: 48.9

	1967			
Party	Cont	Won	LD	Pct.
CONG	18	13	0	46.2
CPM	3	1	1	5.3
BC	2	1	0	3.7
SSP	1	0	0	2.0
CPI	1	0	1	1.0
JS	1	0	1	0.6
IND (39)	17	3	24	41.2
(65)	18	18	27	

Part: 57.1

	1969			
Party	Cont	Won	LD	Pct.
CONG	18	5	1	33.3
RSP	8	4	0	20.7
PML	11	2	7	12.0
BC	3	2	0	5.2
JS	10	0	8	3.8
CPI	1	1	0	2.8
CPM	1	0	0	2.6
SSP	1	1	0	1.9
NPB	5	0	5	1.3
LD	3	0	3	1.1
INDF	4	0	4	0.5
Swat	1	0	1	#
PBI	1	0	1	#
IND (9)	9	3	2	14.8
(76)	18	18	32	

Part: 62.8

NADIA DISTRICT

Population: 1,713,324
Urban: 18.4 Rural: 81.6
Hindu: 75.0 Muslim: 24.4 Christian: 0.6

Party	Cont	1952 Won	LD	Pct.	Party	Cont	1957 Won	LD	Pct.
CONG	10	9	0	50.8	CONG	11	10	0	57.8
SP	4	0	3	7.6	CPI	3	0	0	17.4
JS	4	0	3	7.1	PSP	4	1	1	8.2
KMPP	3	1	2	4.9	JS	1	0	1	0.4
CPI	1	0	0	2.9	IND	(18) 9	0	14	16.2
HMS	1	0	1	2.2		(37) 11	11	16	
RCPI	1	0	0	1.7	Part: 55.7				
FB(R)	2	0	2	0.5					
RRP	1	0	1	0.1					
IND	(29) 10	0	24	22.2					
	(56) 10	10	36						
Part: 40.8									

Party	Cont	1962 Won	LD	Pct.	Party	Cont	1967 Won	LD	Pct.
CONG	11	6	0	44.4	CONG	14	4	0	38.7
CPI	7	2	0	24.6	BC	6	5	0	23.6
SBP	4	1	2	7.4	CPM	5	2	0	15.8
PSP	2	1	1	3.8	SSP	2	1	1	5.4
JS	4	0	4	0.9	CPI	2	1	1	4.8
FB	1	0	1	0.4	JS	3	0	3	0.6
HMS	1	0	1	0.3	RPI	1	0	1	0.2
SUC	1	0	1	0.3	IND	(14) 10	1	12	10.9
IND	(16) 9	1	12	17.9		(47) 14	14	18	
	(47) 11	11	22		Part: 68.5				
Part: 52.3									

Party	Cont	1969 Won	LD	Pct.
CONG	14	5	0	43.2
BC	5	3	0	17.3
CPM	5	2	0	16.5
SSP	1	1	0	4.0
CPI	1	1	0	3.8
RCPI	1	1	0	3.1
PML	2	0	1	1.5
RCPI-T	2	0	2	1.1
PBI	8	0	8	0.9
INDF	6	0	6	0.5
IND	(12) 7	1	10	8.1
	(57) 14	14	27	
Part: 69.1				

24 PARGANAS DISTRICT

Population: 6,280,915
Urban: 31.8 Rural: 68.2
Hindu: 75.9 Muslim: 23.4 Christian: 0.5 Sikh: 0.1

1952 Party	Cont	Won	LD	Pct.
CONG	40	23	0	34.0
CPI	19	8	1	14.6
JS	26	1	23	9.0
KMPP	24	4	18	8.1
FB(R)	5	1	3	1.5
RCPI	5	0	5	1.1
RSP	5	0	4	1.0
FB(M)	6	0	5	1.0
Bolsh	4	0	4	0.7
SP	4	0	4	0.4
HMS	1	0	1	0.2
RRP	3	0	3	0.1
SUC	@	2	@	@
IND (137)	39	1	117	28.3
(279)	40	40	188	

Part: 44.8

1957 Party	Cont	Won	LD	Pct.
CONG	42	20	0	42.7
CPI	24	14	0	25.1
PSP	12	4	0	11.0
FB(M)	2	1	0	1.2
JS	7	0	7	0.7
HMS	4	0	4	0.5
SUC	@	2	@	@
RSP	@	1	@	@
IND (94)	38	0	80	18.8
(185)	42	42	91	

Part: 50.6

1962 Party	Cont	Won	LD	Pct.
CONG	42	33*	0	49.1
CPI	30	8	1	31.1
PSP	15	0	14	3.2
SUC	7	0	4	2.9
FB	1	0	0	1.2
RSP	3	0	2	0.9
JS	5	0	4	0.7
Swat	7	0	7	0.4
SBP	2	0	2	0.3
HMS	3	0	3	0.2
WP	2	0	2	0.1
SP	1	0	1	#
IND (55)	30	1	45	9.9
(173)	42	42	85	

Part: 60.1
*Uncontested: CONG (1)

1967 Party	Cont	Won	LD	Pct.
CONG	50	12	0	36.8
CPM	29	18	2	25.0
BC	17	9	2	13.0
CPI	17	3	5	8.1
FB	3	2	1	2.6
JS	14	1	13	1.0
SSP	2	1	1	0.9
PSP	4	0	4	0.2
IND (64)	35	4	51	12.4
(200)	50	50	79	

Part: 69.1

1969 Party	Cont	Won	LD	Pct.
CONG	50	4	0	39.0
CPM	25	24	0	30.1
CPI	7	7	0	6.7
BC	9	5	0	6.5
SUC	4	4	0	4.5
PML	18	1	15	3.0
LD	18	0	12	2.8
FB	2	2	0	1.8
RSP	2	2	0	1.8
SSP	1	1	0	1.0

1969 (continued) Party	Cont	Won	LD	Pct.
INDF	21	0	21	0.6
RPI	8	0	8	0.3
JS	3	0	3	0.2
NPB	5	0	5	0.1
PBI	6	0	6	0.1
PSP	1	0	1	#
RCPI-T	1	0	1	#
IND (23)	19	0	23	1.5
(204)	50	50	95	

Part: 70.8

CALCUTTA DISTRICT

Population: 2,927,289
Urban: 100.0 Rural: 0.0
Hindu: 84.0 Muslim: 12.9 Christian: 1.9 Jain: 0.7
Buddhist: 0.3 Sikh: 0.2

1952

Party	Cont	Won	LD	Pct.
CONG	25	17	0	39.7
CPI	9	4	1	12.1
FB(M)	8	3	1	9.5
KMPP	19	0	16	5.4
JS	11	0	11	3.5
FB(R)	6	0	5	2.7
Bolsh	3	0	1	1.8
SP	11	0	11	1.2
HMS	7	0	7	1.0
RSP	5	0	5	0.9
RRP	6	0	6	0.4
IND (122)	25	2	114	21.8
(232)	26	26	178	

Part: 36.6

1957

Party	Cont	Won	LD	Pct.
CONG	26	8	0	42.6
CPI	12	10	0	26.8
PSP	7	4	0	11.5
FB(M)	3	1	0	5.6
JS	3	0	3	0.7
HMS	1	0	1	0.1
RSP	@	1	@	@
IND (36)	21	2	33	12.7
(88)	26	26	37	

Part: 48.0

1962

Party	Cont	Won	LD	Pct.
CONG	26	14	0	47.3
CPI	18	8	1	32.8
FB	3	1	0	5.1
RSP	2	1	0	3.8
PSP	4	0	2	1.9
JS	6	0	6	0.7
WP	2	0	2	0.3
SP	6	0	6	0.2
HMS	3	0	3	0.2
Swat	3	0	3	0.1
SBP	1	0	1	#
IND (24)	15	2	20	7.6
(98)	26	26	44	

Part: 65.0

1967

Party	Cont	Won	LD	Pct.
CONG	23	11	0	44.0
CPM	15	5	2	25.8
CPI	4	4	0	8.6
JS	9	0	6	5.8
FB	5	0	2	4.4
PSP	2	0	1	1.3
BC	1	0	0	1.0
SSP	1	0	1	0.2
IND (37)	15	3	34	8.9
(97)	23	23	46	

Part: 60.3

1969

Party	Cont	Won	LD	Pct.
CONG	23	5	0	43.7
CPM	9	8	0	23.3
CPI	4	4	0	10.2
FB	4	2	0	8.2
RSP	2	2	0	5.0
JS	5	0	3	2.3
WP	1	1	0	2.1
SSP	1	0	0	0.8

1969 (continued)

Party	Cont	Won	LD	Pct.
INDF	6	0	6	0.4
PBI	4	0	4	0.1
RPI	1	0	1	0.1
PSP	2	0	2	#
LD	1	0	1	#
IND (17)	13	1	15	3.8
(80)	23	23	32	

Part: 61.5

HOWRAH DISTRICT

Population: 2,038,477
Urban: 40.5 Rural: 59.5
Hindu: 83.3 Muslim: 16.4 Christian: 0.2 Sikh: 0.1

1952

Party	Cont	Won	LD	Pct.
CONG	16	8	0	34.5
FB(M)	9	5	0	25.7
CPI	6	2	2	8.3
KMPP	7	0	5	3.9
JS	10	0	10	2.6
RCPI	2	0	2	1.1
SP	5	0	5	0.9
RRP	3	0	3	0.4
FB(R)	1	0	1	0.2
HMS	2	0	2	0.1
IND (67)	16	1	62	22.3
(128)	16	16	92	

Part: 47.6

1957

Party	Cont	Won	LD	Pct.
CONG	15	5	0	40.9
FB(M)	7	5	0	26.5
CPI	6	4	0	20.3
PSP	2	1	0	4.5
JS	1	0	1	0.7
IND (14)	10	0	12	7.1
(45)	15	15	13	

Part: 50.1

1962

Party	Cont	Won	LD	Pct.
CONG	15	9	0	50.3
CPI	7	2	0	21.6
FB	7	3	0	20.0
JS	5	0	5	1.9
PSP	5	0	5	0.8
Swat	3	0	3	0.6
SBP	1	0	1	0.1
IND (8)	6	1	6	4.7
(51)	15	15	20	

Part: 58.7

1967

Party	Cont	Won	LD	Pct.
CONG	16	9	0	42.3
CPM	11	3	0	27.3
FB	10	3	5	14.7
BC	3	1	1	5.2
CPI	2	0	2	1.6
JS	2	0	1	1.2
PSP	1	0	1	0.1
IND (11)	7	0	8	7.6
(56)	16	16	18	

Part: 68.8

1969

Party	Cont	Won	LD	Pct.
CONG	16	1	0	40.8
CPM	9	8	0	32.1
FB	5	5	0	19.5
BC	1	1	0	3.5
RCPI	1	1	0	3.3
PBI	8	0	8	0.6
PSP	1	0	1	0.1
INDF	3	0	3	0.1
NPB	1	0	1	#
(45)	16	16	13	

Part: 69.0

HOOGHLY DISTRICT

Population: 2,231,418
Urban: 26.0 Rural: 74.0
Hindu: 87.1 Muslim: 12.7 Christian: 0.1

	1952			
Party	Cont	Won	LD	Pct.
CONG	14	7	0	37.1
CPI	7	4	1	17.1
FB(M)	7	1	1	12.6
JS	4	0	1	5.3
SP	7	0	7	3.4
KMPP	6	0	4	3.1
HMS	3	0	3	2.8
FB(R)	2	0	2	0.3
RRP	1	0	1	0.1
IND	(29) 13	2	26	18.2
	(80) 14	14	46	
Part:	49.8			

	1957			
Party	Cont	Won	LD	Pct.
CONG	15	11	0	56.0
CPI	6	3	0	18.5
FB(M)	3	0	0	5.9
HMS	5	0	3	4.1
PSP	2	0	0	3.2
IND	(14) 9	1	10	12.3
	(45) 15	15	13	
Part:	54.7			

	1962			
Party	Cont	Won	LD	Pct.
CONG	15	10	0	50.8
CPI	11	4	0	33.0
FB	3	1	1	7.5
PSP	6	0	6	1.2
HMS	2	0	2	0.5
SBP	1	0	1	0.1
IND	(12) 9	0	9	6.9
	(50) 15	15	19	
Part:	61.4			

	1967			
Party	Cont	Won	LD	Pct.
CONG	18	7	0	43.8
CPM	12	4	1	25.5
FB	4	3	0	10.2
CPI	5	0	3	6.4
BC	4	1	3	5.1
SSP	1	1	0	2.1
JS	2	0	2	0.3
IND	(13) 10	2	11	6.6
	(59) 18	18	20	
Part:	69.5			

	1969			
Party	Cont	Won	LD	Pct.
CONG	18	2	0	42.8
CPM	9	9	0	28.7
FB	3	3	0	9.3
CPI	2	1	0	6.3
FB(M)	1	1	0	2.9
BC	1	0	0	2.4
SSP	1	1	0	2.3
INDF	6	0	6	0.3
LD	2	0	2	0.2
JS	3	0	3	0.2
PBI	4	0	4	0.1
PSP	1	0	1	0.1
IND	(7) 6	1	6	4.4
	(58) 18	18	22	
Part:	71.0			

MIDNAPUR DISTRICT

Population: 5,341,855
Urban: 7.7 Rural: 92.3
Hindu: 92.3 Muslim: 7.6 Christian: 0.1

Party	1952 Cont	Won	LD	Pct.	Party	1957 Cont	Won	LD	Pct.
CONG	35	12	0	33.6	CONG	32	22	0	48.5
KMPP	28	7	11	18.6	CPI	18	6	1	22.6
CPI	15	6	3	12.9	PSP	12	4	0	15.2
JS	18	8	6	12.7	JS	13	0	10	4.2
SP	16	0	10	7.3	HMS	6	0	5	2.1
FB(M)	5	0	3	3.1	FB(M)	1	0	0	1.3
HMS	1	0	1	0.3	IND (27)	17	0	26	6.1
IND (30)	23	2	19	11.5	(109)	32	32	42	
(148)	35	35	53		Part: 54.0				
Part: 48.2									

Party	1962 Cont	Won	LD	Pct.	Party	1967 Cont	Won	LD	Pct.
CONG	32	27	0	52.6	CONG	35	12	0	40.2
CPI	19	3	1	23.8	BC	18	10	0	24.5
PSP	20	2	8	13.4	CPI	10	8	0	15.3
HMS	7	0	6	1.2	PSP	4	2	0	6.3
SBP	2	0	2	0.6	CPM	11	1	6	6.1
FB	1	0	1	0.3	SSP	8	1	5	3.9
JS	3	0	3	0.2	JS	4	0	4	0.3
IND (20)	12	0	15	7.9	IND (18)	13	1	17	3.4
(104)	32	32	36		(108)	35	35	32	
Part: 57.9					Part: 54.3				

Party	1969 Cont	Won	LD	Pct.
CONG	35	6	0	43.0
BC	16	11	0	24.1
CPI	11	10	0	17.4
PSP	4	4	0	6.9
CPM	3	3	0	4.8
SSP	2	1	1	1.7
Jhkh	5	0	5	0.8
LD	7	0	7	0.7
HMS	2	0	2	0.1
INDF	2	0	2	0.1
PBI	2	0	2	0.1
JS	1	0	1	#
IND (5)	5	0	5	0.3
(95)	35	35	25	
Part: 71.0				

PURULIA DISTRICT

Population: 1,360,016
Urban: 6.8 Rural: 93.2
Hindu: 93.1 Muslim: 6.0 Christian: 0.3 Other: 0.6

1952

Party	Cont	Won	LD	Pct.
LKS	10	8	0	41.4
CONG	10	1	3	22.6
Janata	3	0	1	5.4
CPI	2	0	2	2.7
Jhkh	1	0	1	1.1
RSP	1	0	0	0.7
FB(M)	1	0	1	0.3
IND (21)	10	1	17	25.8
(49)	10	10	25	

Part: 28.5

1957

Party	Cont	Won	LD	Pct.
CONG	11	4	0	37.3
HMS	1	0	1	1.0
CPI	1	0	1	0.8
LSS	@	7	@	@
IND (35)	11	0	21	60.9
(48)	11	11	23	

Part: 32.0

1962

Party	Cont	Won	LD	Pct.
CONG	11	6	0	40.1
LSS	11	4	3	29.7
CPI	5	0	2	9.2
FB	4	1	3	5.1
SUC	1	0	1	1.1
IND (22)	10	0	20	14.8
(54)	11	11	29	

Part: 34.3

1967

Party	Cont	Won	LD	Pct.
CONG	11	4	0	35.5
FB	2	1	0	7.8
Swat	4	0	2	6.1
JS	11	0	10	6.0
CPI	1	0	0	3.2
BC	1	1	0	2.7
CPM	1	0	0	2.3
IND (29)	9	5	22	36.2
(60)	11	11	34	

Part: 47.9

1969

Party	Cont	Won	LD	Pct.
CONG	11	3	1	36.1
LSS	6	4	0	26.0
FB	2	1	0	10.5
SUC	1	1	0	6.5
CPI	1	1	0	5.1
JS	7	0	7	4.0
BC	1	1	0	3.0
LD	4	0	4	2.5
INDF	5	0	5	2.1
PSP	1	0	0	1.3
NPB	2	0	2	0.3
PBI	1	0	1	0.3
HMS	1	0	1	0.1
IND (6)	6	0	6	2.2
(49)	11	11	27	

Part: 47.8

BANKURA DISTRICT

Population: 1,664,513
Urban: 7.3 Rural: 92.7
Hindu: 93.7 Muslim: 4.4 Christian: 0.1 Other: 1.8

		1952		
Party	Cont	Won	LD	Pct.
CONG	13	10	0	34.1
HMS	6	3	0	14.7
CPI	7	0	2	10.8
KMPP	8	0	7	7.3
FB(R)	6	0	5	4.7
JS	3	0	1	3.8
SP	1	0	0	1.6
IND	(24) 12	1	16	23.0
	(68) 14	14	31	
Part:	39.8			

		1957		
Party	Cont	Won	LD	Pct.
CONG	13	13	0	47.9
HMS	10	0	3	17.9
CPI	7	0	1	16.1
PSP	2	0	1	3.3
IND	(20) 10	0	19	14.8
	(52) 13	13	24	
Part:	40.9			

		1962		
Party	Cont	Won	LD	Pct.
CONG	13	9	0	49.3
CPI	7	4	0	23.7
HMS	7	0	3	13.1
PSP	1	0	0	2.8
IND	(16) 9	0	15	11.1
	(44) 13	13	18	
Part:	42.0			

		1967		
Party	Cont	Won	LD	Pct.
CONG	13	9	0	46.0
BC	8	4	2	20.5
CPM	6	0	2	13.0
CPI	2	0	1	3.5
SSP	3	0	2	3.0
JS	5	0	5	2.6
PSP	1	0	1	0.2
IND	(12) 6	0	9	11.2
	(50) 13	13	22	
Part:	56.5			

		1969		
Party	Cont	Won	LD	Pct.
CONG	13	0	0	38.6
BC	6	6	0	24.1
CPM	4	4	0	17.6
CPI	1	1	0	5.0
SSP	1	1	0	3.0
FB	1	1	0	2.8
HMS	4	0	3	2.8
INDF	10	0	10	1.9
JS	3	0	3	0.9
LD	5	0	5	0.6
PBI	3	0	3	0.4
PSP	1	0	1	0.4
IND	(5) 4	0	5	1.9
	(57) 13	13	30	
Part:	59.2			

BURDWAN DISTRICT

Population: 3,082,846
Urban: 18.2 Rural: 81.8
Hindu: 84.3 Muslim: 15.2 Christian: 0.3 Sikh: 0.2

1952

Party	Cont	Won	LD	Pct.
CONG	20	13	0	41.2
KMPP	9	2	5	12.6
CPI	5	2	1	8.4
JS	8	0	6	4.9
HMS	3	1	2	2.5
FB(M)	4	0	3	2.4
FB(R)	3	1	2	1.4
SP	1	0	1	0.2
Bolsh	1	0	1	0.1
IND (56)	18	1	48	26.3
(110)	20	20	69	

Part: 38.4

1957

Party	Cont	Won	LD	Pct.
CONG	21	10	0	46.4
CPI	9	2	0	19.1
PSP	7	5	0	14.0
FB(M)	3	1	2	3.4
HMS	3	0	2	2.2
JS	5	0	5	0.6
IND (30)	13	3	26	14.3
(78)	21	21	35	

Part: 44.1

1962

Party	Cont	Won	LD	Pct.
CONG	21	10	0	48.5
CPI	14	10	0	32.2
PSP	10	0	4	7.4
FB	4	0	2	3.8
SBP	4	0	4	1.0
WP	3	0	3	0.4
IND (16)	9	1	12	6.7
(72)	21	21	25	

Part: 46.5

1967

Party	Cont	Won	LD	Pct.
CONG	25	14	0	45.8
CPM	19	7	0	34.3
SSP	3	1	0	3.7
BC	5	1	3	3.5
CPI	6	0	4	3.3
PSP	6	1	5	2.6
FB	4	0	4	1.1
JS	3	0	3	0.4
IND (12)	10	1	10	5.3
(83)	25	25	29	

Part: 56.4

1969

Party	Cont	Won	LD	Pct.
CPM	18	17	0	43.0
CONG	25	2	0	41.2
SSP	3	2	0	5.2
BC	2	2	0	4.0
CPI	1	1	0	2.4
INDF	5	0	5	0.6
JS	2	0	2	0.3
LD	3	0	3	0.2
PML	1	0	1	0.2
PSP	2	0	2	0.1
PBI	1	0	1	0.1
RCPI-T	1	0	1	#
NPB	2	0	2	#
IND (3)	3	1	2	2.7
(69)	25	25	19	

Part: 60.0

BIRBHUM DISTRICT

Population: 1,446,158
Urban: 7.0 Rural: 93.0
Hindu: 72.2 Muslim: 27.6 Christian: 0.1

	1952			
Party	Cont	Won	LD	Pct.
CONG	11	8	0	37.0
FB(M)	4	2	1	13.6
HMS	5	0	1	10.0
KMPP	6	1	3	8.8
CPI	4	0	2	8.2
SP	3	0	3	3.1
RCPI	1	0	1	0.8
RSP	1	0	1	0.3
IND (24)	10	0	23	18.2
(59)	11	11	35	

Part: 33.1

	1957			
Party	Cont	Won	LD	Pct.
CONG	10	5	0	37.2
CPI	3	3	0	13.5
PSP	3	1	1	11.7
FB(M)	2	0	1	6.2
HMS	5	0	4	5.1
JS	1	0	1	0.4
IND (19)	8	1	13	25.9
(43)	10	10	20	

Part: 38.9

	1962			
Party	Cont	Won	LD	Pct.
CONG	10	4	0	40.2
FB	3	2	0	13.5
RSP	3	2	1	12.2
CPI	3	2	0	11.1
PSP	4	0	0	7.9
SUC	1	0	0	2.8
HMS	2	0	2	0.8
Swat	1	0	1	0.7
SBP	1	0	1	0.5
IND (13)	6	0	11	10.3
(41)	10	10	16	

Part: 39.7

	1967			
Party	Cont	Won	LD	Pct.
CONG	12	6	0	40.7
FB	5	2	1	12.1
CPM	4	0	1	9.9
BC	3	0	1	5.0
PSP	1	0	0	2.7
CPI	1	0	0	1.5
IND (17)	10	4	8	28.1
(43)	12	12	11	

Part: 49.2

	1969			
Party	Cont	Won	LD	Pct.
CONG	12	0	0	37.5
FB	4	4	0	15.5
CPM	3	3	0	13.2
SUC	2	2	0	11.6
BC	1	1	0	3.7
PML	7	0	6	3.3
NPB	3	0	3	2.3
JS	2	0	2	0.8
INDF	6	0	6	0.5
PBI	5	0	5	0.5
LD	1	0	1	0.3
PSP	2	0	2	0.2
IND (5)	4	2	3	10.6
(53)	12	12	28	

Part: 53.9

STATE SUMMARY

Population data exclude area formerly in Hoshiarpur District, Punjab
Population: 2,546,768
Urban: 6.3 Rural: 93.7
Hindu: 96.9 Muslim: 1.4 Sikh: 0.9 Buddhist: 0.7 Christian: 0.1

1952

Party	Cont	Won	LD	Pct.
CONG	47	34*	1	45.3
JS	19	0	15	6.8
KMPP	22	3	10	5.1
CPI	4	0	1	4.4
DCL	2	0	1	2.1
SCF	9	1	4	1.9
SP	8	0	7	1.6
RSP	1	0	0	0.8
HMS	3	0	3	0.3
FB	1	0	1	0.2
IND	(99) 42	12*	71	31.5
	(215) 50	50	114	

Part: 36.2
*Uncontested: CONG (2)
                IND (1)

1962

Party	Cont	Won	LD	Pct.
CONG	13	9	0	45.9
CPI	4	0	1	8.9
JS	4	0	3	6.5
RPI	2	0	1	1.9
PSP	2	0	1	1.4
Swat	2	0	2	0.4
IND	(35) 13	4	25	35.0
	(62) 13	13	33	

Part: 44.0
Former Punjab Area only

1954

Party	Cont	Won	LD	Pct.
CONG	3	3	0	71.4
IND	(4) 3	0	2	28.6
	(7) 3	3	2	

Part: 75.5
Election to PEPSU Assembly

1957

Party	Cont	Won	LD	Pct.
CONG	12	9	0	47.5
CPI	4	1	1	8.9
JS	5	0	5	2.7
PSP	1	1	0	1.7
IND	(26) 11	1	16	39.2
	(48) 12	12	22	

Part: 43.1
Former Punjab Area only

1967

Party	Cont	Won	LD	Pct.
CONG	60	34	1	42.2
JS	33	7	12	13.9
CPI	11	2	7	2.9
Swat	5	1	1	1.9
RPI	4	0	4	0.5
CPM	6	0	6	0.4
SSP	1	0	1	0.1
PSP	2	0	2	#
IND	(147) 55	16	106	38.1
	(269) 60	60	140	

Part: 48.4

"OLD" HIMACHAL PRADESH

Population: 1,351,144
Urban: 4.7 Rural: 95.3
Hindu: 97.0 Muslim: 1.9 Sikh: 0.6 Buddhist: 0.5 Christian: #

1952				
Party	Cont	Won	LD	Pct.
CONG	35	24*	1	47.4
KMPP	22	3	10	14.7
SCF	9	1	4	5.6
JS	10	0	9	3.5
SP	5	0	4	1.4
HMS	3	0	3	0.9
IND (51)	28	8	32	26.4
(135)	36	36	63	

Part: 25.2
*Uncontested: CONG (2)

1967				
Party	Cont	Won	LD	Pct.
CONG	28	18	1	47.5
JS	10	2	3	9.5
Swat	3	1	0	3.3
CPM	3	0	3	0.4
SSP	1	0	1	0.2
IND (55)	24	7	36	39.1
(100)	28	28	44	

Part: 46.0

FORMER PUNJAB AREA

Population: 1,195,624 (excluding former Hoshiarpur area)
Urban: 8.2 Rural: 91.8
Hindu: 96.8 Sikh: 1.2 Buddhist: 1.0 Muslim: 0.8 Christian: 0.2
For 1954, 1957 and 1962 see STATE SUMMARY

1952				
Party	Cont	Won	LD	Pct.
CONG	12	10	0	44.1
JS	9	0	6	8.6
CPI	4	0	1	6.7
DCL	2	0	1	3.2
SP	3	0	3	1.7
RSP	1	0	0	1.2
FB	1	0	1	0.3
IND (48)	14	4*	39	34.2
(80)	14	14	51	

Part: 47.1
*Uncontested: IND (1)

1967				
Party	Cont	Won	LD	Pct.
CONG	32	16	0	37.8
JS	23	5	9	17.5
CPI	11	2	7	5.3
RPI	4	0	4	0.9
Swat	2	0	1	0.8
CPM	3	0	3	0.4
PSP	2	0	2	0.1
IND (92)	31	9	70	37.2
(169)	32	32	96	

Part: 50.7

MALAPPURAM DISTRICT

The Government of Kerala has announced that it plans to constitute a
new district--Malappuram--from portions of Kozhikode and Palghat Districts. This page and the two following give data for the new district and the residual portion of the two existing districts (population data is not available). The State Summary (page 104-105) and
Malabar (page 106) data are unchanged.

		1952		
Party	Cont	Won	LD	Pct.
CONG	7	1	0	34.3
ML	6	5	0	33.0
CPI	5	1	1	16.3
KMPP	2	0	1	7.1
SP	4	0	4	6.1
IND (4)	2	0	4	3.2
(28)	7	7	10	

Part: 51.3

		1957		
Party	Cont	Won	LD	Pct.
CONG	13	2	0	35.7
CPI	9	3	2	18.8
PSP	1	0	0	2.6
RSP	1	0	1	0.4
ML	@	7	@	@
IND (16)	12	1	1	42.5
(40)	13	13	4	

Part: 53.3

		1960		
Party	Cont	Won	LD	Pct.
ML	11	10	0	47.2
CPI	11	1	0	32.1
CONG	2	2	0	14.8
JS	1	0	1	0.3
IND (2)	2	0	0	5.6
(27)	13	13	1	

Part: 73.6

		1965		
Party	Cont	Won	LD	Pct.
ML	10	6	0	38.4
CONG	11	1	2	27.0
CPM	10	3	1	26.9
CPI	2	0	2	1.3
Swat	2	0	2	0.5
JS	1	0	1	0.4
IND (4)	3	1	3	5.5
(40)	11	11	11	

Part: n/a

		1967		
Party	Cont	Won	LD	Pct.
ML	9	9	0	56.1
CONG	11	0	1	30.2
CPM	2	2	0	10.5
JS	5	0	5	3.0
IND (1)	1	0	1	0.2
(28)	11	11	7	

Part: 65.1

KOZHIKODE DISTRICT (RESIDUAL)

See note on page 376.

<table>
<tr><td colspan="5">1952</td></tr>
<tr><td>Party</td><td>Cont</td><td>Won</td><td>LD</td><td>Pct.</td></tr>
<tr><td>CONG</td><td>8</td><td>3</td><td>0</td><td>36.1</td></tr>
<tr><td>SP</td><td>7</td><td>3</td><td>3</td><td>31.2</td></tr>
<tr><td>KMPP</td><td>3</td><td>2</td><td>0</td><td>13.4</td></tr>
<tr><td>CPI</td><td>2</td><td>0</td><td>0</td><td>8.1</td></tr>
<tr><td>ML</td><td>1</td><td>0</td><td>0</td><td>2.5</td></tr>
<tr><td>IND</td><td>(5) 4</td><td>0</td><td>3</td><td>8.7</td></tr>
<tr><td></td><td>(26) 8</td><td>8</td><td>6</td><td></td></tr>
<tr><td colspan="5">Part: 72.7</td></tr>
</table>

<table>
<tr><td colspan="5">1957</td></tr>
<tr><td>Party</td><td>Cont</td><td>Won</td><td>LD</td><td>Pct.</td></tr>
<tr><td>CONG</td><td>12</td><td>7</td><td>0</td><td>39.8</td></tr>
<tr><td>CPI</td><td>8</td><td>3</td><td>0</td><td>22.3</td></tr>
<tr><td>PSP</td><td>6</td><td>2</td><td>1</td><td>16.0</td></tr>
<tr><td>IND</td><td>(10) 8</td><td>0</td><td>1</td><td>21.9</td></tr>
<tr><td></td><td>(36) 12</td><td>12</td><td>2</td><td></td></tr>
<tr><td colspan="5">Part: 63.0</td></tr>
</table>

<table>
<tr><td colspan="5">1960</td></tr>
<tr><td>Party</td><td>Cont</td><td>Won</td><td>LD</td><td>Pct.</td></tr>
<tr><td>CONG</td><td>7</td><td>6</td><td>0</td><td>39.4</td></tr>
<tr><td>CPI</td><td>7</td><td>1</td><td>0</td><td>23.9</td></tr>
<tr><td>PSP</td><td>4</td><td>4</td><td>0</td><td>17.6</td></tr>
<tr><td>ML</td><td>1</td><td>1</td><td>0</td><td>4.3</td></tr>
<tr><td>JS</td><td>1</td><td>0</td><td>1</td><td>0.2</td></tr>
<tr><td>IND</td><td>(5) 5</td><td>0</td><td>0</td><td>14.6</td></tr>
<tr><td></td><td>(25) 12</td><td>12</td><td>1</td><td></td></tr>
<tr><td colspan="5">Part: 85.9</td></tr>
</table>

<table>
<tr><td colspan="5">1965</td></tr>
<tr><td>Party</td><td>Cont</td><td>Won</td><td>LD</td><td>Pct.</td></tr>
<tr><td>CONG</td><td>12</td><td>0</td><td>0</td><td>33.4</td></tr>
<tr><td>SSP</td><td>5</td><td>5</td><td>0</td><td>24.1</td></tr>
<tr><td>CPM</td><td>5</td><td>5</td><td>0</td><td>20.7</td></tr>
<tr><td>ML</td><td>3</td><td>0</td><td>0</td><td>6.3</td></tr>
<tr><td>JS</td><td>8</td><td>0</td><td>8</td><td>1.9</td></tr>
<tr><td>CPI</td><td>6</td><td>0</td><td>6</td><td>1.6</td></tr>
<tr><td>Swat</td><td>2</td><td>0</td><td>2</td><td>0.2</td></tr>
<tr><td>IND</td><td>(8) 6</td><td>2</td><td>5</td><td>11.8</td></tr>
<tr><td></td><td>(49) 12</td><td>12</td><td>21</td><td></td></tr>
<tr><td colspan="5">Part: n/a</td></tr>
</table>

<table>
<tr><td colspan="5">1967</td></tr>
<tr><td>Party</td><td>Cont</td><td>Won</td><td>LD</td><td>Pct.</td></tr>
<tr><td>CONG</td><td>12</td><td>0</td><td>0</td><td>35.2</td></tr>
<tr><td>CPM</td><td>5</td><td>5</td><td>0</td><td>26.8</td></tr>
<tr><td>SSP</td><td>5</td><td>5</td><td>0</td><td>24.5</td></tr>
<tr><td>ML</td><td>1</td><td>1</td><td>0</td><td>5.4</td></tr>
<tr><td>JS</td><td>8</td><td>0</td><td>8</td><td>3.1</td></tr>
<tr><td>Swat</td><td>1</td><td>0</td><td>1</td><td>0.4</td></tr>
<tr><td>KC</td><td>2</td><td>0</td><td>2</td><td>0.3</td></tr>
<tr><td>IND</td><td>(5) 5</td><td>1</td><td>4</td><td>4.3</td></tr>
<tr><td></td><td>(39) 12</td><td>12</td><td>15</td><td></td></tr>
<tr><td colspan="5">Part: 73.6</td></tr>
</table>

PALGHAT DISTRICT (RESIDUAL)

See note page 376.

1952

Party	Cont	Won	LD	Pct.
CONG	9	2	0	27.7
KMPP	3	3	0	14.3
CPI	2	1	0	12.5
SP	6	1	2	11.5
KSP	2	0	0	2.6
ML	1	0	0	1.8
IND	(12) 6	2	7	29.6
	(35) 9	9	9	

Part: 50.4

1954

Party	Cont	Won	LD	Pct.
CONG	2	1	0	48.5
PSP	2	1	0	44.6
TTNC	1	0	1	2.8
IND	(1) 1	0	1	4.1
	(6) 2	2	2	

Part: 61.8
Former Cochin State area
(see page 109).

1957

Party	Cont	Won	LD	Pct.
CPI	9	7	0	43.7
CONG	10	2	0	38.4
PSP	2	0	0	7.1
IND	(6) 5	1	2	10.8
	(27) 10	10	2	

Part: 53.4

1960

Party	Cont	Won	LD	Pct.
CPI	10	9	0	57.0
CONG	6	1	0	25.9
PSP	4	0	0	16.8
IND	(2) 2	0	2	0.3
	(22) 10	10	2	

Part: 78.6

1965

Party	Cont	Won	LD	Pct.
CPM	8	8	0	37.1
CONG	11	0	0	30.9
CPI	10	1	8	14.1
SSP	2	2	0	11.0
Swat	2	0	2	2.0
KC	2	0	2	1.8
JS	2	0	2	1.5
ML	1	0	1	0.3
IND	(5) 4	0	5	1.3
	(43) 11	11	20	

Part: n/a

1967

Party	Cont	Won	LD	Pct.
CPM	9	9	0	50.1
CONG	11	0	0	34.3
SSP	2	2	0	10.5
JS	3	0	3	2.7
Swat	2	0	2	0.9
IND	(3) 3	0	3	1.5
	(30) 11	11	8	

Part: 57.5